Florence
Venice

FODOR'S TRAVEL PUBLICATIONS

are compiled, researched, and edited by an international team of travel writers, field correspondents, and editors. The series, which now almost covers the globe, was founded by Eugene Fodor in 1936.

OFFICES
New York & London

Fodor's Florence and Venice

Editor: Richard Moore
Deputy Editor: Thomas Cussans
Area Editor: Barbara Walsh Angelillo
Editorial Contributors: Robert Brown, Sheila Brownlee, Kristin Jarrett
Drawings: Lorraine Calaora
Maps: Swanston Graphics
Photographs: International Photobank, Spectrum Colour Library
Cover Photograph: M. Gratton

Cover Design: Vignelli Associates

SPECIAL SALES

Fodor's Travel Publications are available at special discounts for bulk purchases (100 copies or more) for sales promotions or premiums. Special editions, including personalized covers, excerpts of existing guides, and corporate imprints, can be created in large quantities for special needs. For more information, write to Special Marketing, Fodor's Travel Publications, 201 East 50th Street, New York, NY 10022. Enquiries from the United Kingdom should be sent to Merchandise Division, Random House UK Ltd, 30–32 Bedford Square, London WC1B 3SG.

Fodor's

2nd SECOND EDITION

Florence
Venice

FODOR'S TRAVEL PUBLICATIONS, INC.
New York & London

ISBN 0–679–01622–8

CONTENTS

PRACTICAL INFORMATION FOR VENICE

FOREWORD

This guide unites in one book two of Italy's greatest treasure houses of history and art. And not only of Italy. Widely separated as Florence and Venice have been throughout the centuries, they have both in their own ways had a deep and lasting effect on the social and cultural history of the Western world.

Though they are both lively modern cities, it is not for their present that millions of tourists visit them every year, but for their opulent past—for their churches and museums, their art galleries, for the views along their streets and canals, in short for the chance to see in reality those much-hyped cultural treasures that have become an integral part of the cultural baggage of 20th-century consciousness. One has only to look at the Grand-Central-Station throng around Michelangelo's *David*, or the press of people in the aisles of St. Mark's, to understand the power of the icons that these two cities contain.

The result of this massive pilgrimage syndrome has meant that both Florence and Venice suffer severely from over-exposure to tourism. It is a Catch 22 situation that has rapidly become a modern commonplace in many parts of the world. Our advice is to try to schedule your visit at quieter times of the year—winter in both cities has a lot to recommend it—and when there to try to plan your explorations carefully, in order to avoid the worst crowds.

We hope that this Guide will help our readers to enjoy their visits more fully. It contains our usual blend of practical advice—especially on the choice of hotels and restaurants—with historical and artistic background information. There are also large sections to assist with exploring these fascinating destinations.

We would like to express our thanks to our indefatigable Area Editor for Italy, Barbara Walsh Angelillo, who has once again put her considerable expertise on, and deep love for, her adopted country at our disposal . . . as well as her tireless capacity for detail.

While every care has been taken to assure the accuracy of the information in this guide, the passage of time will always bring change, and consequently the publisher cannot accept responsibility for errors that may occur.

All prices and opening times quoted in this guide are based on information available to us at press time. Hours and admission fees may change, however, and the prudent traveler will avoid inconvenience by calling ahead.

Fodor's wants to hear about your travel experiences, both pleasant and unpleasant. When a hotel or restaurant fails to live up to its billing, let us know and we will investigate the complaint and revise our entries where the facts warrant it.

Send your letters to the editors of Fodor's Travel Publications, 201 E. 50th Street, New York, NY 10022, or to Fodor's Travel Publications, 30–32 Bedford Square, London WC1B 3SG, England.

FACTS
AT YOUR
FINGERTIPS

FACTS AT YOUR FINGERTIPS

Planning Your Trip

NATIONAL TOURIST OFFICE. The major source of information for anyone planning a vacation to Italy is the Italian National Tourist Office. They can supply a wealth of information on all aspects of travel to and around Italy, from which type of vacation is best suited to your needs and purse to the most economical ways of getting there. They also have much information on hotels, restaurants, excursions and museums. In short, they produce copious amounts of material, much of it free and all of it useful.

Their addresses are:

In the U.S.: 630 Fifth Ave., New York, NY 10111 (212–245–4822); 500 North Michigan Ave., Chicago, IL 60611 (312–644–0990); 360 Post St., Suite 801, San Francisco, CA 94108 (415–392–6206).

In the U.K.: 1 Princes St., London W1R 8AY (01–408 1254).

TOURS AND TOUR OPERATORS. From the U.S. Florence and Venice are two of Italy's most popular destinations; finding a tour that will introduce you to them is easy. Maupintour offers "Italy's Famous Places," a 12-day tour of Milan, Venice, Florence, and Rome. Highlights include visits to the Medici chapel, the Uffizi Gallery, and the Pitti Palace. "Italy's Great Cities" ranges from $2,959 to $3,189, airfare excluded.

Pan Am, in conjunction with Perillo Tours, offers "The Three Cities," 14 days in Rome, Venice, and Florence, with sidetrips to Pisa and Siena. Sights seen include St. Mark's Square and Basilica, the Doge's Palace, and the Bridge of Sighs (in Venice); and the Duomo, Baptistery, Piazza della Signoria, and Piazzale della Signoria (among others in Florence). Cost is $2,199–$2,999, *including* airfare.

For the budget-minded, Globus-Gateway/Cosmos has "Venice, Florence, and Rome," 8 days through Italy's three most popular cities for $476–$633 (from London) or $309–$416 (from Venice). Similarly, Melia Tours offers "Renaissance Italy," eight days in Rome, Milan, Pisa, Florence, and Venice (four days are set aside for the last two) from about $850.

If you don't like the idea of traveling in a group, and would prefer to explore on your own, but still want assistance making your plans, you have several options. Strata Tours International specializes in putting together personalized itineraries for travel through Italy. And if you really want to go it alone, the Italian National Tourist Office has lists of apartments and houses for rent in Florence and Venice.

Selected U.S. Tour Operators

Alitalia Tours, 666 Fifth Ave., New York, NY 10103 (212–582–8900).

American Express Vacations, Box 5014, Atlanta, GA 30302 (800–241–1700).

Central Holiday, 206 Central Ave., Jersey City, NJ 07307 (800–526–6045; in NJ, 201–798–5777).

Globus-Gateway/Cosmos, 95–25 Queens Blvd., Rego Park, NY 11374 (718–268–7000).

Cultural Heritage Alliance, 107–115 S. Second St., Philadelphia, PA 19106 (215–923–7060).

Donna Franca Tours, 470 Commonwealth Ave., Boston, MA 02215 (617–227–3111).

Maiellano Tours, 441 Lexington Ave., New York, NY 10017 (212 –687–7725).

Maupintour, 1515 St. Andrews Dr., Lawrence, KS 66046 (913–843–1211).

M.I. Travel Inc. (agent for Melia International), 450 Seventh Ave., Room 1803, New York, NY 10123 (212–967–6565).

Pan Am Holidays, Pan Am Bldg., New York, NY 10017 (800–THE TOUR).

Perillo Tours, 577 Chestnut Ridge Rd., Woodcliff Lake, NJ 07675 (914 –735–2000).

Strata Tours International, 240 Prospect Ave., Hackensack, NJ 07601 (201–646–0300).

TWA Getaway, 28 South Sixth St., Philadelphia, PA 19106 (800–438–2929).

From the U.K. There's no shortage of tours to both Florence and Venice from Britain, many taking in both cities and/or Rome. And in some cases a number of other cities are also included. They fall into two broad categories. First, there are those tours that simply get you to Florence or Venice, put you up in an hotel and leave you to get on with it. Second, and generally much more expensive, there are a series of art tours, covering just about every possible permutation of the Florence/Venice equation and normally including expert lectures and guides.

Both Travelscene and Sovereign Holidays offer packages in the first category, with a very wide selection available.

Art tours to Florence and Venice are very much more diverse. Swan Hellenic, for example, offer a 15-day "Renaissance Italy" tour for around £1,890 per person, flights, hotels and most meals included. This covers the ground with a vengeance. Venice, Padua, Ravenna, Urbino, Borgo San Sepolcro, Arezzo, Siena, San Gimignano, Florence, Pisa, Lucca, Florence (again), Bologna, Verona and Milan are all visited (in this order). An expert guide accompanies the party.

Prospect Art Tours offer a very much more discerning series of holidays, though those with little background knowledge of art may find it all a bit overpowering, not to mention exhausting. They warn that not only is a deal of walking done but that evening lectures are normal. Flights, hotels and most meals are included in the prices. They have three Florence trips, all dealing with the Renaissance in one way or another, ranging from four to seven nights—from around £399 to £585—and two trips to Venice, one of eight nights (from £620), and one of eleven nights (from £925). Tours to Tuscany are also available, as is a "Palladio" 5-day tour around the Veneto villas (£479).

Selected U.K. Tour Operators

CIT, Marco Polo House, 3–5 Lansdowne Rd., Croydon, Surrey CR9 1LL (tel. 01–686 5533).

Prospect Art Tours Ltd., 10 Barley Mow Passage, Chiswick, London W.4 (tel. 01–995 2163/4).

Serenissima Travel Ltd., 21 Dorset Square, London N.W.1 (tel. 01–730 9841/723 6556). *Also,* 41 East 42nd St., Suite 2312, New York, NY 10017 (tel. 800–358–3330).

Sovereign Holidays Ltd., P.O. Box 10, London (Heathrow) Airport, Hounslow, Middlesex TW6 2JA (tel. 01–897 4545).

Swan Hellenic Art Treasures Tours, 77 New Oxford St., London WC1 (tel. 01–831 1616).

Travelscene Ltd., Travelscene House, 94 Baker St., London W.1 (tel. 01–935 1025).

WHEN TO GO. Both Florence and Venice have the same big problem: tourists. Christmas, Easter and early-July through August are the worst periods. Moreover, the summer heat can also be a problem, especially in Venice where the canals become ever more malodorous. Florence also suffers from a rash of shop and restaurant closures in August. Spring and fall in both cities, however, can be delightful. The crowds are very much less thick on the ground and the weather is almost perfect, not too hot and not too cold. Winter in Florence can be bitter, though by way of compensation there are few tourists (except at Christmas). There is much to be said for visiting Venice in the winter, when the fog rolls off the lagoon and chill winds and high tides drive you into the warmth of a wineshop. And when it's bathed in cold, brilliant sunshine, Venice is captivating. Carnival time in February interrupts Venice's winter solitude: merrymakers arrive in droves to dance and revel in the *calli,* but merriest of all are the Venetians in their extravagant costumes.

National Holidays 1989. January 1; April 19 and 20 (Easter); April 25 (Liberation Day); May 1 (May Day); June 2 (Liberation Day); August 15 (Assumption, known as *Ferragostà*); November 1 (All Saints' Day); December 8 (Immaculate Conception); December 25 and 26.

WHAT TO PACK. The first principle is to travel light. If you plan to fly across the Atlantic, airline baggage allowances are now based on size rather than weight. Economy class passengers may take free two pieces of baggage, provided that the sum of their dimensions is not over 106 inches and neither one singly is over 62 inches height, width and length. For first class the allowance is two pieces up to 62 inches each, total 124 inches. The penalties for oversize are severe; to Western Europe around $50 per piece.

These restrictions also apply to Alitalia's domestic flights. One piece may be carried as cabin baggage, maximum size $18 \times 14 \times 7$ ins.

Do not take more than you can carry yourself; it's a lifesaver if you go to places where porters are hard to find. It's a good idea to pack the bulk of your things in one large bag and put everything you need for overnight, or for two or three nights, in another. This obviates packing and repacking at every stop. If you plan to be traveling by train, take smallish or medium-sized bags, easier to get on and off trains and into overhead racks.

The weather is considerably milder in Italy than in the north and central United States or Great Britain all the year round. In the summer season, make your clothing as light as possible—but women should have a scarf, light stole or jacket handy to cover bare shoulders and arms when visiting churches, where pants suits are acceptable but shorts are taboo (they can be very strict about this in Italy). It's no longer necessary for women to cover their heads in churches, however. A sweater or woolen stole is a must for the cool of the evening, even during the hot months. In the summer, brief afternoon thunderstorms are common in Rome and inland cities, so carry a featherweight folding raincoat. And if you go into the mountains, you will find the evenings there quite chilly. During the winter, a medium-weight coat will stand you in good stead, while a raincoat is essential. You'll probably need an umbrella, too, but you can pick it up on the spot (or invest in a good folding one).

The deluxe spots are still dressy, but not formal. Men aren't required to wear ties or jackets anywhere, especially in the summer, except in some of the grander hotel dining rooms and top-level restaurants. However, Italian casual wear can be very elegant; "informal" is definitely not a synonym of "sloppy." Formal wear is very definitely the exception rather than the rule at the opera nowadays. For the huge general papal audiences, no rules of dress apply except those of common sense. For other types of audience, the Vatican Information Office will illustrate requirements.

If you wear glasses, take along a spare pair or the prescription and if you have to take some particular medicine regularly, especially if it is made up only on prescription, better bring a supply. Its exact equivalent may be difficult for the average pharmacist to identify, although it undoubtedly exists.

TAKING MONEY ABROAD. Traveler's checks are still the standard and best way to safeguard your travel funds, as most companies will replace them quickly and efficiently if loss occurs. You should always keep a note of the check numbers separate from the checks themselves to help with the replacement process. You will usually get a better exchange rate in Italy for traveler's checks than for cash.

In the U.S. many of the larger banks issue their own traveler's checks, which are almost as well recognized as those of the longer established firms American Express, Thomas Cook and Barclays. Many banks will carry one or other of those brands of check as well as their own.

The best known British checks are Thomas Cook's, Barclays, Lloyds, Midland and National Westminster banks—as well as American Express, of course.

It is always a good idea to have some local currency on arrival for taxis and tips. Some banks provide this service; alternatively contact Deak International, Ltd., 630 Fifth Ave., New York, NY 10111 (212–757–0100— call for other locations).

Britons holding a Uniform Eurocheque card and cheque book can cash cheques for up to £100 a day at banks, and write cheques in restaurants, hotels, etc.

Credit Cards. Credit cards are now an integral part of the Western Financial Way of Life, and, in theory at least, are accepted all over Europe. But, while the use of credit cards can smooth the traveler's path considerably, they should not be thought of as a universal answer to every problem.

Firstly, there is growing resistance in Europe to the use of credit cards, or rather to the percentage which the credit card organizations demand from establishments taking part in their schemes. Not so long ago, 200 restaurants in Paris refused to accept credit cards—and some of them still refuse—simply because they felt that the benefit credit cards bring is all on the side of the customer. There are also many thrifty Italian restaurateurs who are damned if they see why they should turn over any part of their hard-earned money to credit card companies, and stoutly refuse to accept plastic payment. A great many of these are the more atmospheric, regional establishments, most likely the very ones you will want to eat in. So keep an eye open for those little signs in the window; you could easily find yourself in an embarrassing situation otherwise.

Another point that should be watched with those useful pieces of plastic is the problem of the rate at which your purchase may be converted into your home currency. If you want to be certain of the rate at which you will pay, insist on the establishment entering the current rate onto your credit card charge at the time you sign up—this will prevent the management from holding your charge until a more favorable rate (to them) comes along, something which could cost you more dollars than you counted on.

We would advise you, also, to check your monthly statement very carefully indeed against the receipts or carbons you got at the time of your purchase. It has become increasingly common for shops, hotels or restaurants to change the amounts on the original you signed, if they find they have made an error in the original bill. Sometimes, also, unscrupulous employees make this kind of change to their own advantage. The onus is on you to report the change to the credit card firm and insist on sorting the problem out.

We have included in this edition credit card information for as many establishments as we have been able to verify. There are some surprising omissions of hotels or restaurants that you would think would accept credit cards, but don't. The initials we use for this information are AE, DC, MC and V—which stand for American Express, Diner's Club, MasterCard (alias Access, EuroCard, and Cartasì) and Visa (Barclaycard in Britain).

ITALIAN CURRENCY. The Italian monetary unit is the lira (plural, *lire*). There are coins worth 10, 50, 100, 200 and 500 lire; the bills are in 1,000, 2,000, 5,000, 10,000, 50,000 and 100,000 lire denominations. Take your time when counting: the 200 and 500 coins are dangerously similar, and many of the bills have more than one design. Copper telephone tokens cost 200 lire and are widely used in place of money, so don't be afraid to accept them.

PASSPORTS. In the U.S. Apply in person at U.S. Passport Agency Offices, local county courthouses or selected Post Offices. If you have a passport not more than 12 years old you may renew your passport by mail; otherwise you will need:

—proof of citizenship, such as a birth certificate;

—two recent identical photographs two inches square, in either black and white or color, on non-glossy paper;

—$35 for the passport itself plus a $7 processing fee if you are applying in person (no processing fee when renewing your passport by mail) for those 18 years and older, or if you are under 18, $20 for the passport plus a $7 processing fee if you are applying in person (again, no extra fee when applying by mail);

—proof of identity such as a driver's license, previous passport, any governmental ID card, or a copy of an income tax return.

Adult passports are valid for 10 years, others for five years; they are not renewable. Allow four to six weeks for your application to be processed, but in an emergency, Passport Agency offices can have a passport readied within 24–48 hours, and even the postal authorities can indicate "Rush" when necessary.

If you expect to travel extensively, request a 48- or 96-page passport rather than the usual 24-page one. There is no extra charge. When you receive your passport, write down its number, date and place of issue in a separate, secure place. The loss of a valid passport should be reported immediately to the local police and to the Passport Office, Dept. of State, 1425 K St., NW, Washington, DC 20524; if your passport is lost or stolen while abroad, report it immediately to the local authorities and apply for a replacement at the nearest U.S. Embassy or consular office.

Britons. You should apply for passports on special forms obtainable from main post offices or a travel agent. The application should be sent or taken to the Passport Office according to residential area (as indicated on the guidance form) or lodged with them through a travel agent. It is best to apply for the passport 4–5 weeks before it is required, although in some cases it will be issued sooner. The regional Passport Offices are located in London, Liverpool, Peterborough, Glasgow and Newport. The application must be countersigned by your bank manager or by a solicitor, barrister, doctor, clergyman or justice of the peace who knows you personally. You will need two full-face photos. The fee is £15; passport valid for 10 years.

British Visitor's Passport. This simplified form of passport has advantages for the once-in-a-while tourist to most European countries (Yugoslavia and Eastern Europe countries presently excepted). Valid for one year and not renewable, it costs £7.50. Application may be made at main post offices in England, Scotland and Wales, and in Northern Ireland at the Passport Office in Belfast. Birth certificate or medical card for identification and two passport photographs are required—no other formalities.

Canadians. Apply in person to regional passport offices, post offices or by mail to Bureau of Passports, Complex Guy Favreau, 200 Dorchester West, Montreal, Quebec, H2Z 1X4. A $25 fee, two photographs, a guarantor, and evidence of citizenship are required. Canadian passports are valid for five years and are non-renewable.

VISAS. Not required by passport holders of the U.K., Eire, the U.S.A., and Canada for stays of up to three months, but visas are required for citizens of some Commonwealth countries.

HEALTH AND INSURANCE. The different varieties of travel insurance cover everything from health and accident costs, to lost baggage and trip cancellation. Sometimes they can all be obtained with one blanket policy; other times they overlap with existing coverage you might have for health and/or home; still other times it is best to buy policies that are tailored to very specific needs. Insurance is available from many sources, however, and many travelers unwittingly end up with duplicate coverage. Before purchasing separate travel insurance of any kind, be sure to check your regular policies carefully.

Generally, it is best to take care of your insurance needs before embarking on your trip. You'll pay more for less coverage—and have less chance to read the fine print—if you wait until the last minute and make your purchases from, say, an airport vending machine or insurance company counter. If you have a regular insurance agent, he or she is the person to consult first.

Flight insurance, which is often included in the price of the ticket when the fare is paid via American Express, Visa or certain other major credit cards, is also often included in package policies providing accident coverage as well. These policies are available from most tour operators and insurance companies. While it is a good idea to have health and accident insurance when traveling, be careful not to spend money to duplicate coverage you may already have . . . or to neglect some eventuality which could end up costing a small fortune.

For example, basic Blue Cross-Blue Shield policies do cover health costs incurred while traveling. They will not, however, cover the cost of emergency transportation, which can often add up to several thousand dollars. Emergency transportation is covered, in part at least, by many major medical policies such as those underwritten by Prudential and Metropolitan. Again, we can't urge you too strongly that in order to be sure you are getting the coverage you need, check any policy carefully before buying. Another important example: Most insurance issued specifically for travel does not cover pre-existing conditions, such as a heart condition.

Several organizations offer coverage designed to supplement existing health insurance and to help defray costs not covered by many standard policies, such as emergency transportation. Some of the more prominent are:

Travel Assistance International, the American arm of Europ Assistance, offers a comprehensive program providing medical and personal emergency services and offering immediate, on-the-spot medical, personal and financial help. Annual membership is $5 per person and trip protection ranges from $35 for an individual for up to eight days to $220 for an entire family for a year. Full details from travel agents or insurance brokers, or from *Europ Assistance Worldwide Services, Inc.,* 1333 F St., NW, Washington, DC 20004 (800–821–2828). In the U.K., contact Europ Assistance Ltd., 252 High St., Croydon, Surrey (01–680 1234).

Carefree Travel Insurance, c/o ARM Coverage Inc., 120 Mineola Blvd., Box 310, Mineola, NY 11510, underwritten by the Hartford Accident and Indemnity Co., offers a comprehensive benefits package that includes trip cancellation and interruption, medical, and accidental death/dismemberment coverage, as well as medical, legal, and economic assistance. Trip cancellation and interruption insurance can be purchased separately. Call 800–654–2424 for additional information.

International SOS Assistance Inc., Box 11568, Philadelphia, PA 19116 (800–523–8930) has fees from $15 a person for seven days, to $195 for a year.

IAMAT (International Association for Medical Assistance to Travelers), 417 Center St., Lewiston, NY 14092 (716–754–4883) and 188 Nicklin

Road, Guelph, Ontario, N1H 7L5 (519–836–0102) makes available a free list of English-speaking doctors throughout Europe that adhere to the following fee schedule: office calls, $20; hotel calls, $30; night and holiday calls, $40.

The British Insurance Association, Aldermary House, Queen St., London E.C.4 (01–248 4477) will give comprehensive advice on all aspects of vacation travel insurance in the U.K.

Another frequent inconvenience to travelers is the loss of baggage. It is possible, though often complicated, to insure your luggage against loss through theft or negligence. Insurance companies are reluctant to sell such coverage alone, however, since it is often a losing proposition for them. Instead, it is most usually included as part of a package also covering accidents or health. Remuneration is normally determined by weight, regardless of the value of the specific contents of the luggage. Should you lose your luggage or some other personal possession, be sure to report it to the local police immediately. Without documentation of such a report, your insurance company might be very stingy. Also, before buying baggage insurance, check your homeowners policy. Some such policies offer "off-premises theft" coverage, including loss of luggage while traveling.

The last major area of traveler's insurance is trip cancellation coverage. This is especially important to travelers on APEX or charter flights. Should you get sick abroad, or for some other reason be unable to continue your trip, you may be stuck having to buy a new one-way fare home, plus paying for space on the charter you're not using. You can guard against this with trip cancellation insurance, usually available from travel agents. Most of these policies will also cover last minute cancellations.

LANGUAGE. There is no problem for a non-Italian speaker in the main tourist cities; you will always find someone who speaks English. But it would be a pity not to try to acquire at least a useful smattering of Italian, it is a very beautiful and expressive language. A combination of a phrase book and close attention to the Italians' astonishing pantomime of gestures will go a long way. If you happen to be an opera buff you will be amazed what a short compendium of operatic words and phrases can accomplish. You will hear words coming back at you that you thought were the private territory of *Tosca* and *Rigoletto.*

But the best preparation for getting the most out of your trip is to take an evening class in Italian the previous winter. You do not need a lot—just enough to help you in your day to day contact, and to be able to disentangle the signs and labels in some of the world's finest museums. Who knows, you might get a taste for it and embark on Dante.

ITALIAN TIME. Italian summer time operates from the last weekend of March to the last weekend of September, it is then one hour ahead of Britain and six ahead of New York. As the U.S. changes its clocks at a slightly different date, there will be a couple of weeks when the system is out of sync.

Getting to Italy

From the U.S.

BY AIR. Air fares are in a constant state of flux, and our best advice is to consult a travel agent and let him or her make your reservations for you. Agents are familiar with the latest changes in fare structures—ever more confusing despite "deregulation" among U.S. carriers who now allegedly base prices on distance traveled—as well as with the rules governing various discount plans. Among those rules: booking (usually) 21 days in advance, minimum stay requirements, maximum stay allowances, the amount that (sometimes) must be paid in advance for land arrangements. Lowest prices overall will, of course, be during the off-season periods.

Generally, on regularly scheduled flights, you have the option, in descending order of cost, of First Class, Club or Business Class, APEX or Stand-by tickets. APEX is by far the most used and the most useful of these categories. Some charter service is still available; again, an agent will be able to recommend which ones are reliable. Sometimes it is also worth investigating package tours even if you do not wish to use the tours' other services (hotels, meals, etc.); because a packager can block book seats, the price of a package can be less than the cost when air fare is booked separately.

If you have the flexibility, you can sometimes benefit from last-minute sales tour operators have in order to fill a plane. A number of brokers specializing in such discount sales have also sprung up. All charge an annual membership fee, usually about $35–50. Among these: *Stand-Buys Ltd.,* 311 W. Superior, Suite 404, Chicago, IL 60610 (312–943–5737); *Moments Notice,* 40 E. 49th St., New York, NY 10017 (212–486–0503); *Discount Travel Intl.,* 114 Forrest Ave., Narberth, PA 19072 (215–668–2182); and *Worldwide Discount Travel Club,* 1674 Meridian Ave., Miami Beach, FL 33139 (305–534–2082). Sometimes, tour and charter flight operators themselves advertise in Sunday travel supplements, as well. Do try to find out whether the tour operator is reputable and whether you are tied to a precise round trip or whether you will have to wait until the operator has a spare seat in order to return.

Airlines specifically serving Italy from major U.S. cities (usually via New York; Alitalia flies non-stop from Boston, Chicago, and New York to Rome and from Los Angeles to Milan) include:

Alitalia, 666 Fifth Ave., New York, NY 10103 (212–582–8900).

Pan Am, Pan Am Bldg., New York, NY 10017 (212–973–4000).

TWA, 605 Third Ave., New York, NY 10016 (212–290–2121).

From the U.K.

BY AIR. Of the two cities, Florence has the better service. There are two direct flights daily to Florence from London (Heathrow) airport, one by British Airways, the other by Alitalia. Both are conveniently timed morning departures, with a flying time of a little over two hours. However, these flights go to Galileo Galilei airport just outside Pisa which acts as the airport for Florence. From the airport there is a direct train service—

with roughly hourly departures—to Florence. The rail journey takes around an hour. Using an APEX ticket with restricted availability the fare costs around £185 return. The full Eurobudget return fare costs around £300. Alternatively it is possible to fly to Florence itself—landing at Peretola airport—by changing at Milan.

Venice also has two flights daily. These are also operated by British Airways and Alitalia. Each operate one flight daily from London (Heathrow) airport. The flying time in both cases is around two hours. The return fare during the peak summer starts at around £186. The full Eurobudget fare costs around £310. Venice is also served by a large number of charter flights, and seats on these can be bought by independent travelers, often at greatly reduced prices.

BY TRAIN. To Florence. During the summer there is a through train daily from Calais to Florence. The connecting service leaves London (Victoria) in mid-morning for Dover. The main train pulls out of the Gare Maritime in Calais just before 4 P.M. and arrives in Florence at 10:20 the following morning. There are second class couchettes throughout, and first and second class sleepers from Thionville to Florence. On this train the full return fare works out at around £160 in second class, £210 with a berth in a three berth sleeper. For a quicker journey, or at other times of the year, travel to Paris by day. The Hoverspeed Citylink service gives the quickest connection, and takes you to the Gare du Nord in under five hours. Then board the express train, the "Galilei," which leaves the Gare de Lyon at 7.32 P.M. and reaches Florence at 7.56 the following morning. First and second class sleepers, and second class couchettes are available throughout. A light refreshment service is provided from Paris to Dole.

To Venice. Venice also has a through train from Calais from June to September. At other times of the year it is necessary to change trains and stations in Paris. However, during the summer there is the choice of going by the fast and modern trains of the state railways, or choosing the privately-owned and sumptuous "Venice-Simplon Orient Express" as the treat of a lifetime.

For mere mortals, the boat train for Dover and the ferry to Calais leave London Victoria Station at 2.30 P.M. The through train then leaves Calais Gare Maritime at 7.32 and runs overnight via Paris, Lausanne, and Milan. Venice (Santa Lucia) station is reached a little after 3 in the afternoon. First and second class sleeping compartments are available throughout, as are second class couchettes. Out of summer, or for a faster transit, catch the "Galilei" as recommended above. This train has a portion which reaches Venice at 8:45 in the morning. Fares to Venice are almost the same as to Florence. First and second class sleepers are available throughout.

The exclusive "Venice Simplon-Orient-Express" runs once a week to Venice and once a week to Vienna during July and August; in September and October it runs twice weekly to Venice. The first part of the journey from London (Victoria) to Folkestone harbor is made on board magnificently restored British Pullman carriages. The crossing to Boulogne is by British Ferries, with a specially reserved lounge for V.S.O.E. passengers. At the quayside in Boulogne the continental Wagons-Lit train in its imposing blue livery is waiting to convey the traveler through to Venice in style, via Paris, Zurich, Innsbruck and Verona. The train draws in to Santa

Lucia station at 6:50 the following evening. For the ultimate in comfort, little modernities such as air-conditioning have been discreetly added. The train has to be seen to be believed. The one-way fare, including all meals (but not drinks), works out at around £680. Details from Orient-Express, One World Trade Center, Suite 2565, New York, NY 10048 (800–223–1588; 212–938–6830, in New York State); in the U.K. from V.S.O.E. Ltd, Sea Containers House, 20 Upper Ground, London SE1 9PF (01–928 6000). A wide range of inclusive tours centered on the train are available; contact your travel agent for details, or the Italian Tourist Office.

BY BUS. Florence has a daily bus service from London in high summer. This service is run by National Express-Eurolines. The coaches leave London (Victoria Coach Station) at 9 in the evening on Day 1 and reach Florence at the unsocial hour of 5:30 in the morning two days later (Day 3). The Channel crossing is made in the middle of the night, and there are no other overnight stops, so the journey is not particularly restful! The roundtrip fare from London works out at around £115; slight reductions for students.

Venice has one bus a week from London (Victoria Coach Station). The bus leaves London at 9 P.M. on Fridays and reaches Venice at 4 A.M. on Sunday. This service is also run by National Express-Eurolines. The roundtrip fare works out at around £110.

Details from National Express-Eurolines, The Coach Travel Center, 13 Regent St., London, SW1Y 4LR (01–730–0202); or from National Express-Eurolines, 52 Grosvenor Gardens, London, SW1W 0AU (01–730 3433).

Fares do not compare very favorably with either the charter air fares, or with travel by train.

BY CAR. There is a wide choice of Channel crossings and routes suitable for reaching both Florence and Venice. The easiest routes are through France and Switzerland. Though in France the autoroute tolls can mount up, and in Switzerland it is necessary to purchase a motorway tax sticker (valid for a year, 1988 price Sfr. 30) either in advance from the Swiss National Tourist Office, or at the frontier. Alternatively, take one of the longer Channel crossings to Belgium and then drive down using the toll free motorways through West Germany and Austria. Or cut across Switzerland now that the Expressway runs right through from Basel to Chiasso on the Italian frontier. As a guide, the Channel crossing in peak season taking one of the shorter routes from Dover will work out at around £90 one way for a car and one passenger. The distance from the Channel ports to Florence is some 840 miles, and 780 miles to Venice. So at least one, if not two, overnight stops will be required en route. If you are driving to Florence and Venice it is well worth contacting the Italian National Tourist Office for full details of the pack of reduced price petrol and motorway toll vouchers for northern Italy.

If you don't fancy the long drive south there are several Motorail services to Northern Italy. The most useful is the service from Boulogne to Milan. This runs southbound on Saturdays from the end of May until the end of September, and also on Wednesdays from early July. The second class single fare for a car and one passenger, with a two-berth sleeper, works out around £400 including the Channel crossing.

CUSTOMS ON ARRIVAL. There are three levels of duty free allowance for people entering Italy. Entering Italy from outside Europe, you may import duty free: 400 cigarettes or 100 cigars or 200 cigarillos or 500 grams of tobacco; plus, ¼ of a liter of spirits more than 22° proof or two liters of alcohol less than 22° proof; plus, 50 grams of perfume and ¼ of a liter of toilet water; plus, other goods to the value of 15,000 lire; plus, 500 grams of coffee or 200 grams of coffee extract or 40 grams of tea extract. Entering Italy from an EEC country, you may import duty free: 300 cigarettes or 75 cigars or 150 cigarillos or 400 grams of tobacco; plus, 1½ liters of spirits more than 22° proof or three liters of light wine less than 14° proof and three liters of wine or of alcohol less than 22° proof; plus, 75 grams of perfume and 1/3 liter of toilet water; plus, other goods up to the value of 75,000 lire; plus, 750 grams of coffee or 300 grams of coffee extract or 150 grams of tea or 60 grams of tea extract. Entering Italy from a European country not in the EEC, you may import duty free: 200 cigarettes or 50 cigars or 100 cigarillos or 250 grams of tobacco; plus, ¼ of a liter of spirits more than 22° proof or two liters of alcohol less than 22° proof; plus, 50 grams of perfume and ¼ of a liter of toilet water; plus, other goods to the value of 15,000 lire; plus, 500 grams of coffee or 200 grams of coffee extract or 100 grams of tea or 40 grams of tea extract.

Any amount of foreign currency may be imported into Italy provided it is declared on arrival; the balance may also be exported. You may also import up to several hundred thousand lire. Currency regulations are being eased to comply with EEC directives. Inquire at ENIT offices outside Italy. The same amount can also be exported provided you present a V2 form when you leave. This must be collected on arrival.

Staying in Italy

For specific information on staying in Florence and Venice, see the Practical Information *sections for both cities.*

CHANGING MONEY. Banks and exchange office will give you the best rate for your money, but hotels, restaurants and shops will change it, too. Exchange rates fluctuate wildly, so bear this in mind both before and during your trip. Have a look around before you cash your traveler's checks—you'll be surprised at how much rates can vary. And remember that most banks and exchange offices charge a flat fee, so it may be more economical to change all your money at once. Should you lose your money later, however, you will then have no serious chance of getting it back again.

It's a good idea to carry an emergency supply of one-dollar bills. That way, if you find long lines at the railway station or airport, you can pay porters and taxi drivers and change your money later.

TELEPHONES. A phone call costs 200 lire. Pay phones take either 100- or 200-lire coins or a token (*gettone*). If you happen on one of the older pay phones that take only tokens and have a little knob at the token slot, buy a token from the nearest cashier or token vending machine. Insert the token (which doesn't drop right away), dial the number, and wait for an answer, then complete the connection by pushing the knob. The token drops and your party can hear you. If you're dialing long-distance, deposit five or six tokens before dialing and have more on hand. You'll hear them dropping into the machine; just keep feeding them in and retrieve the left-overs afterward.

International Calls. You can call London direct by dialing 0044, the prefix and the number. If you want to use the operator dial 15, but be prepared to wait. To call the USA and Canada, dial 170 and reserve with the operator, who speaks English. You can call parts of the States direct, by dialing 001, the area code and the number. Bear in mind that it's practically impossible to get through on international holidays.

Long-distance rates are lower on weekdays after 7:30; the lowest rates are weekdays after 11 P.M., Saturday after 2:30 P.M., and all day Sundays and holidays.

Telegrams. You can dictate telegrams over the phone, by dialing 186. There is a small fee for this service. Don't worry about spelling; just use the Italians' clever alphabet based on city names. Say Ancona for **a,** Bologna for **b,** and so on:

Ancona	Jolly	Siena
Bologna	Kappa	Torino
Como	Livorno	Udine
Domodossola	Milano	Venezia
Empoli	Napoli	Washington
Firenze	Otranto	**EEKS**
Genova	Pisa	**EE GRECO**
Hotel	**KOO**	**ZETA**
Imola	Roma	

ELECTRICITY. Florence and Venice function on 220 voltage, and your hotel plugs will be marked accordingly. Many Deluxe and Expensive hotels have safety hairdriers in the bathrooms, but you'd be wise to pick up an adaptor plug before you leave for your own hairdrier or travel appliances.

TIPPING. Charges for service are included in all hotel bills and generally appear as a separate item on restaurant checks. However, it is customary to leave an additional 5 percent tip at restaurants. In general, chambermaids should be given 1,000 lire per room per day; or 4–5,000 per week; bellboys about 1–2,000 lire for carrying your bags; tip a minimum of 1,000 lire for room service and valet service. Give a doorman 500 lire for calling a cab. Give the hotel *portiere* about 15 percent of the bill for extra services, or from 5,000 to 10,000 lire depending upon how helpful he has been.

Checkroom attendants expect 500 lire; ushers the same, depending on the cost of your seat. Give washroom attendants about 200 lire. Tip 100 lire for whatever you drink standing up at a cafe, 500 lire or more for table service in a smart cafe, less in neighborhood coffee bars. Give a barber 1,000 lire and up, adding for extra treatments. A women's hairdresser should get from 2–5,000 lire, depending upon what you've had done.

These are average figures. In deluxe hotels and restaurants you should increase the amounts by up to half, in accordance with the service given.

Railway and airport porters charge a fixed rate per bag. Tip an additional 500 lire per person, more if the porter is very helpful. Taxi drivers expect about 5–10 percent. Tip guides 1,000 lire per person for a half-day tour, more if very good.

RESTAURANTS. Basically, there are three kinds of eating place in Italy: *ristorante, trattoria* or *osteria.* These names once distinguished the type of clientele and price, but today they are essentially interchangeable, and the only sure way to tell what's in store is to check the menu that's posted by law either inside or outside the front door. Remember that you must add *pane e coperto* (cover charge) and *servizio* (service charge) to the menu prices; this increases the bill 15 to 20 percent. If you choose the *menu turistico,* taxes and cover are included, but you'll usually have to pay for drinks.

Some items are marked by weight on menus, either SQ (according to the quantity) or by the hg., which is 100 grams (about three and a half ounces). This generally includes fish and Florentine steaks or fillets, so if you're on a budget, stay away from them. The same also goes for *porcini* mushrooms and truffles. When the meal is over, insist on getting a *ricevuta fiscale,* which is an official bill with a tax number. This is Italy's way of making sure restaurants pay their taxes, and you could be fined if police catch you outside without it.

Leaving Italy

CUSTOMS RETURNING HOME. Americans. U.S. residents may bring in $400 worth of foreign merchandise as gifts or for personal use without having to pay duty provided they have been out of the country more than 48 hours and provided they have not claimed a similar exemption within the previous 30 days. Every member of a family is entitled to the same exemption, regardless of age, and the exemptions can be pooled. For the next $1,000 worth of goods a flat 10% rate is assessed.

Included in the $400 allowance for travelers over the age of 21 are one liter of alcohol, 100 non-Cuban cigars and 200 cigarettes. Only one bottle of perfume trademarked in the U.S. may be brought in. However, there is no duty on antiques or art over 100 years old. You may not bring home meats, fruits, plants, soil or other agricultural products.

Gifts valued at under $50 may be mailed to friends or relatives at home, but not more than one per day of receipt to any one addressee. These gifts must not include perfumes costing more than $5, tobacco or liquor.

If you are traveling with such foreign-made articles as cameras, watches or binoculars that were purchased at home or on a previous trip, either carry the receipt or register them with U.S. Customs prior to departure.

Canadians. In addition to personal effects, and over and above the regular exemption of $300 per year, the following may be brought into Canada duty free: a maximum of 50 cigars, 200 cigarettes, 2 pounds of tobacco and 40 ounces of liquor, provided these are declared in writing to customs

on arrival. Canadian customs regulations are strictly enforced; you are recommended to check what your allowances are and to make sure you have
kept receipts for whatever you may have bought abroad. Small gifts can
be mailed and should be marked "Unsolicited gift, (nature of gift), value
under $40 in Canadian funds." For other details, ask for the Canada Cus-
toms brochure *I Declare.*

British Customs. There are two levels of duty free allowance for people entering the U.K.; one, for goods bought outside the EEC or for goods
bought in a duty free shop within the EEC; two, for goods bought in an
EEC country but not in a duty free shop.

In the first category you may import duty free: 200 cigarettes or 100
cigarillos or 50 cigars or 250 grammes of tobacco (*Note* if you live outside
Europe, these allowances are doubled); plus one liter of alcoholic drinks
over 22% vol. (38.8% proof) or two liters of alcoholic drinks not over
22% vol. or fortified or sparkling wine, or two liters of still table wine;
plus two liters of still table wine; plus 50 grammes of perfume; plus nine
fluid ounces of toilet water; plus other goods to the value of £32.

In the second category you may import duty free: 300 cigarettes or 150
cigarillos or 75 cigars or 400 grammes of tobacco; plus 1½ liters of alcoholic drinks over 22% vol. (38.8% proof) or three liters of alcoholic drinks
not over 22% vol. or fortified or sparkling wine, or three liters of still table
wine; plus five liters of still table wine; plus 75 grammes of perfume; plus
13 fluid ounces of toilet water; plus other goods to the value of £250 (*Note*
though it is not classified as an alcoholic drink by EEC countries for Customs' purposes and is thus considered part of the "other goods" allowance,
you may not import more than 50 liters of beer).

In addition, no animals or pets of any kind may be brought into the
U.K. The penalties for doing so are severe and are strictly enforced; there
are *no* exceptions. Similarly, fresh meats, plants and vegetables, controlled
drugs and firearms and ammunition may not be brought into the U.K.
There are no restrictions on the import or export of British and foreign
currencies.

FLORENCE

FLORENTINE HISTORY

A number of legends surround Florence's origins. One says that it was called after Fiorino, a Roman commander who set up camp by the Arno and was murdered by assassins from nearby Fiesole. A less bloodthirsty one maintains it was given the name "Florentia" (later "Fiorenza" and later still "Firenze") because it was built on a flowery meadow. Its founding date, in any case, is 59 B.C.. when a Roman colony was set up here to guard the Arno bridge. It turned into a regular Roman city with baths, temples, a forum and a 15,000-seat amphitheater. Little is known of the city during the Dark Ages. It is not until around A.D. 1000 that Florence begins to feature in historical records.

Popes and Emperors

11th century. During the 11th century Italy becomes a battlefield in the duel between the Holy Roman Emperors and the Popes. The Western Holy Roman Empire (founded by Constantine in the 4th century and now consisting of parts of western and northern Europe) has two rulers: the Emperor, who has absolute administrative power, and the Pope, who is the spiritual and cultural leader. But the Papacy has begun to have ambitions outside its spiritual sphere and in 1059 it decrees, among other things, that the Pope should no longer be nominated (appointed, in other words) by the Emperor. This is the first link in the chain of events that leads to Pope Gregory VII excommunicating Emperor Henry IV, Henry in turn deposing Gregory, and open war in which northern Italy and southern Germany are both split in two over the question of allegiance.

1082. Emperor Henry IV besieges Florence after declaring war on Countess Matilda of Tuscany, an ally of the Pope. (The courtyard of her castle at Canossa had been the scene of Henry's humiliation five years earlier when, following his excommunication, he had stood for three days in the driving snow begging for absolution from Gregory VII who was staying there as Matilda's guest. It was eventually given, after Henry had sworn submission—an oath he was soon to break.) Luckily for Florence, long exposure to the overpowering heat forces Henry to withdraw his troops.

1215. A member of the Buondelmonti family is murdered on the way to his wedding because he had broken off an engagement to one of the Amidei family. This sparks off feuds that last for generations. Indeed, the 13th century is one of perpetual fighting between the two main factions, the Guelphs, who represent the Pope's interests, and the Ghibellines, who are pro-Emperor. (The names Guelph and Ghibelline are Italianized versions of two German names, deriving from the rival German camps of Otto of Bavaria, whose family name was Welf—hence Guelph—and who supported the Pope, and the Hohenstaufens, whose castle was called Wibeling—hence Ghibelline—who supported the Emperor, and indeed were shortly to become the Emperors.) In reality, however, the wider European struggle is little more than an excuse for a bitter internal power struggle in Florence and among her neighbors.

Moreover, whether you become a Guelph or a Ghibelline depends not so much on your view of the Papacy vs. Empire conflict but simply which family you belong to. And to confuse matters further, the Guelphs are themselves divided, again according to family, into the "Black" Guelphs and the "White" Guelphs. Roughly speaking, Guelphs represent the more modern, commercial side of the Florentine way of life, and the Ghibellines the old feudal nobility—aspects that can never be reconciled. In the main, Florence tends to be Guelph and Siena—her "natural enemy"—Ghibelline.

1246. The Ghibelline Uberti family drive out the Guelph Buondelmonti family and the city is in Emperor Frederick II's power until his death in 1250 when the Guelphs set up a democratic government, conquer Siena, Pisa and Pistoia, and capture Arezzo, Volterra and San Gimignano.

1260. Florence is defeated at the battle of Montaperti but the city is spared from destruction by Farinata degli Uberti. His generosity is not appreciated by the Florentines who raze the Uberti part of the city (around Palazzo Vecchio) to the ground.

1265. Dante Alighieri, the famous poet, author of *The Divine Comedy* and a treatise on the Italian language, an early proponent of Italian unity, is born.

1282. An executive council, or Signoria, is set up, consisting of elected members from the professions and the trade guilds, excluding the nobles from any rights of government. Giano della Bella—an ex-aristocrat who takes up the democratic cause—takes measures to widen the electorate by increasing the number of guilds (for innkeepers, bakers, etc.) allowed to vote. He is also the driving force behind the "Ordinances of Justice" (1292–4) whereby any "non-democratic" person, in particular any of the greedy wool merchants or bankers from the most powerful guilds, or arrogant nobles of his class, can be arrested on mere suspicion of "treachery." Individuals are even made responsible for their relatives' crimes. It is a rule of terror (the first time in democratic history that political informers have been granted social status) that later claims Giano himself as its victim. He ends up an exile in France, running a branch of a Florentine bank.

1289. The Guelphs win back Florence at the battle of Campaldino. They entrench themselves firmly in the city, but are torn apart by internal feuding between the Blacks and the Whites. Pope Boniface VIII calls Frenchman Charles of Valois in to make peace and 600 Whites (including Dante) are sent into exile in 1302–3.

Expansion and Consolidation

In spite of this constant warring, the 13th century sees Florence grow both in population and in wealth. Previously held back by the handicap of its inland position, it has established itself as the southern stopping-off point on the major trade route across the Apennines and has developed ties with both the Papacy and with the French Angevin rulers of Naples. The victory of the Guelphs means that a number of aggressive Florentine merchant families are now able to obtain useful economic concessions from their allies in and outside Italy. They take over the Papal banking monopoly from the Sienese and set up branches all over Europe, in North Africa and on the Levant. (The "florin" coin was introduced to England by Florentine bankers.) They exploit the Kingdom of Naples through their monopoly of its grain market. But it is the wool trade that rakes in the highest profits. By a happy chance the Flemish wool trade is on the decline during this period and the Florentines, who have the advantages of an international mercantile network, a plentiful water supply (for dyeing and washing the wool) and a talent for marketing and promotion, jump into the breach.

1296. Plans are made to channel some of this accumulated wealth into public projects such as the Duomo, the Cathedral, which is to be the glory of Florence and outshine other Tuscan cathedrals.

1285–1340. Walls to fortify the city are put up, remaining more or less intact until the 1860s.

1304. Petrarch, the first "modern" poet, is born.

1312. A joint attempt is made by Pope Clement V and Emperor Henry VII to unite Italy, but Florence, which has allied itself with Naples, is saved from destruction by the Emperor fortuitously dying outside the city walls just before he is due to attack.

1313. Giovanni Boccaccio, author of *The Decameron,* is born.

1321. Dante dies in exile.

1333. Devastating floods sweep away Florence's guardian statue (the god Mars).

1342. The Florentines ask the duke of Athens (Walter de Brienne) to take power since they are unsatisfied with their current form of government, attributing to it their recent defeat by Pisa. This is a bad idea because Walter turns out to be even worse. The city revolts against him and drives him out in 1343.

1340 and 1348. Two outbreaks of the Black Death reduce the population by half. Quite apart from the many dead (over 40,000) and the psychological impact it has on the rest of the population, it leads to famine, unemployment and a reversal of the economic growth that Florence has been enjoying over the last three centuries. In 1399 Edward III of England has gone bankrupt, bringing down the Florentine banking houses, the Bardi and the Peruzzi, who had backed him in his wars.

These disasters herald a new phase of civil unrest. The most momentous of these outbreaks of violence, which see much rioting, looting, burning of palaces and the lynching of policemen, is the *Ciompi* (clothmakers') revolt in 1378. As a result of the revolt, the working-class Michele di Lando rises to power but is unable to quell the squabbling between the guilds about how many seats each should have, and this—as so many attempts to govern Florence—falls through in a matter of months, and the guilds come under their employers' jurisdiction again. Michele di Lando is banished in 1382.

The Rise of the Medici

Florence manages through sheer tenacity to maintain (though not increase) its relatively wealthy position, in spite of the crippling blows it receives, one after another, throughout the 14th century. If it *had* gone under, the cultural achievements subsidized by the Medici in the 15th century might never have taken place.

1393–1421. The Albizzi faction rules as a kind of dictatorship, having reversed the reforms brought about by the *Ciompi.*

1406. Pisa falls to Florence.

1421. Florence purchases Livorno. Maso degli Albizzi dies and the first important member of the family, Giovanni (born 1360), takes over as leader of a democratic government—as opposed to the Albizzis' form of oligarchy—until his death in 1429. The Medici are not a noble family. They are—originally—pharmacists (perhaps that is why their coat-of-arms, according to their enemies anyway, has pills on it). To have the "common touch" comes in very useful to the Medici in appealing to the masses.

In the early 1430s Cosimo de' Medici, as the new head of the Medici faction, finds himself at daggers drawn with Rinaldo degli Albizzi, who took power after Giovanni's death.

1444. The Albizzi banish Cosimo to a 10-year exile in Padua, but instead (and this should be a warning to the Albizzi) he is received as an honored guest in Venice. Meanwhile, the Signoria unexpectedly returns pro-Medici and expels the Albizzi from government. Rinaldo degli Albizzi trudges off to banishment in Naples at the same time as Cosimo is returning from Venice. From 1434 to 1492 the Medici are unofficial despots, while maintaining a facade of democracy.

Cosimo shrewdly engineers his rule in such a way that he always has the support of the workers, that the positions of power are allotted to his supporters, that his opponents in the Albizzi faction are all fined and/or exiled, and that crippling taxes should be paid by the rich. A considerable proportion of these taxes are spent upon patronage of the arts, book-collecting and restoration of church buildings.

Meanwhile, in Milan Duke Filippo Maria Visconti is plotting action, goaded on by Rinaldo degli Albizzi and other Florentine exiles, against his old enemy. However, it is Florence that wins, first the battle of Barga in 1437, then the battle of Anghiari in 1440. The Visconti are decisively beaten and Francesco Sforza (who has been supported by Cosimo, his banker) becomes duke of Milan. It is Cosimo's dream to create an alliance with Milan to hold the balance of power against Papal Rome and Republican Venice.

1464. Cosimo dies, leaving as his heir the sickly Piero ("the Gouty") who starts off on the wrong foot by demanding that his father's creditors pay up. A rival faction to the Medici—the Pitti—grows in strength; a plot to assassinate Piero is foiled in 1466; most of the Pitti are banished from Florence; an attempt by the exiles to declare war on Florence is stepped on by the Pope.

1469. Piero dies. His heirs are the 20-year-old Lorenzo and the 16-year-old Giuliano. The enemies of the Medici are secretly jubilant, deciding to take no action but simply wait for the brothers to make a botched job of governing and be ousted in due course. Lorenzo is ugly, short-sighted, has a Roman wife (unpopular with the Florentines), no experience either of fighting or government, and altogether seems a bad bet. But Florence is in for a surprise.

1478. Lorenzo has not only managed to keep his head above water, he has centralized the government to his advantage and has demonstrated his king-like position to the world as well as to his subjects by a dazzling display of magnificence (well earning the title "Lorenzo the Magnificent") on the occasion of the visit of Galeazzo Maria Visconti and his wife to the city. But, as always in Florentine history, there is the brooding enemy within (the Pazzi family) and without (Pope Sixtus IV and Francesco Salviati, the archbishop of Pisa) to contend with. These three plot to assassinate the Medici brothers and seize power. The Pazzi conspiracy matures on Sunday, April 26, while Giuliano and Lorenzo are at Mass in the Duomo. Giuliano is murdered but Lorenzo, though wounded, succeeds in limping to the sacristy and locking himself in. Outside, Salviati's assault on Palazzo della Signoria fails and the people turn on the conspirators and hang them, afterwards cutting their bodies into pieces.

One outcome of the conspiracy is more centralization of power. Lorenzo creates the partisan Council of 70 (which he will cut down to 17 in 1488) of which he is to be a member.

Like his grandfather Cosimo, Lorenzo is a great patron of the arts and sciences. He takes under his protection philosophers, poets, artists, architects and musicians, and organizes all kinds of cultural events, festivals and medieval-style tournaments. They look back to the 14th century, the time of Dante, Petrarch and Boccaccio, as the Golden Age. Even more, they dream nostalgically of classical antiquity as a period in which civilization was at its peak. Mythological paintings and poems are popular, as is ancient Roman-style architecture.

Savonarola and the Republic

1482. Arrival from Ferrara of the Dominican monk Savonarola at the monastery of San Marco in Florence. He becomes a familiar figure in the pulpit but is expelled from Florence in 1487. This is probably because Lorenzo is not at all keen on Savonarola's sermons in which he warns the

people that they will burn in hell if they continue in their pursuit of pagan
pleasure (the Medici way of life).

1489. Savonarola is recalled by Lorenzo, who has had pressure put on
him to do so by his friend, the poet and philosopher Pico della Mirandola,
who has become one of the monk's converts.

1492. Death of Lorenzo. He is succeeded by the 22-year-old Piero, who
has not inherited his father's diplomacy or astuteness. In the threatening
conflict between Ferdinand of Naples and Lodovico il Moro of Milan,
Florence (in the person of Piero) allies itself with Naples. Lodovico, with
his back against the wall, has to resort to asking for help from Charles
VIII of France, heir to the throne of Naples. Savonarola by this time has
turned up the volume of his wrath and is now fulminating about Florence
being "the city of Babylon," about "wicked princes who suck the blood
of their people," about the corruption of the Church, and about a "new
Cyrus" who will conquer, unresisted, the whole of Italy. Terrified, the people sit and wait for this calamity to occur. Rumors have been going round
for some time about Charles VIII's plan . . .

1494. Charles VIII invades Italy. Piero de' Medici goes to meet him
at Sarzana but fails to put his case convincingly and ends up signing away
most of Florence's key fortresses. The people of Florence are furious at
this dishonorable defeat and Piero (plus brothers Giovanni and Giuliano)
have to flee to Bologna. Their houses and possessions are sacked by the
first of the French armies to reach Florence. Lorenzo's changes to the
structure of government are abolished, a "republic" is set up (though actually it is very similar to Cosimo's Signoria) and Savonarola becomes leader
of the people, in spite of the fact that he isn't actually a member of the
government. He activates a moral clean-up operation which the Florentines all take to with fanatical enthusiasm. The famous "Bonfire of Vanities" takes place in Piazza della Signoria: people are encouraged to throw
into the flames their profane books and pictures, jewelry, ornaments, wigs
and make-up.

Charles VIII continues south to Naples but Italy, which at first watched
his progress like a hypnotized rabbit, now forms a league consisting of
Venice, the Pope, Maximilian of Germany, Ferdinand of Aragon and,
later, also of Lodovico il Moro. Charles understandably decides to leave
the same way he came. The League now turn against Florence for having
collaborated so willingly with Charles, and Pope Alexander VI (Borgia)
accuses Savonarola (who had stormed against "corrupt popes") of heresy,
demanding that he should be handed over to him. The case is taken up
by the Franciscans of Santa Croce who challenge him to a trial by fire.
Savonarola accepts, then refuses. On instructions from the Pope, the Signoria then arrests Savonarola, tortures him for a confession, and hangs
him together with two of his followers, afterwards burning their bodies
in the Piazza della Signoria, on the precise spot where he had held his
"Bonfire of Vanities."

1499. Amerigo Vespucci, who is an agent for the Medici bank, reaches
a new continent and it is called after him (America).

1499–1501. Cesare Borgia, Pope Alexander VI's nephew, threatens
Florence, intent on forming his own state in Central Italy, but agrees to

leave it in peace, Machiavelli (author of *The Prince*) acting as diplomatic mediator in the negotiations.

1503. Piero de' Medici drowns.

1508. Florence is persuaded by the kings of France and Spain to join their League of Cambrai against Venice. This carries with it the advantage of easily being able to win back Pisa (lost in 1494) because of the powerful support Florence can now call on.

Decline and Fall

1512. After an unsettled period of internal unrest (Savonarolites versus Mediceans) and warring outside the city, the Republic falls and the Medici brothers Giovanni and Giuliano and their cousin Giulio take over, recreating a Lorenzo-style government again. By now Florence is no longer a European force to be reckoned with. In fact, it is considered as little more than just another Papal state. An exodus of Florentine artistic talent which began in the late 15th century continues to the 1530s, by which time Michelangelo has finally left for good, and only the nutty Jacopo Pontormo is left in Florence.

1527. While Giulio de' Medici is away from Florence, a riot breaks out and a new "republic" is set up. Machiavelli dies. The Sack of Rome takes place a month later and is followed in 1529 by an 11-month siege of Florence (by the troops of Charles V).

1530. Alessandro de' Medici is installed by Pope Clement (allegedly his father) and made duke of the Florentine Republic. He rules as a tyrant and is assassinated by Lorenzino de' Medici ("Lorenzaccio" in the 19th-century play by Alfred de Musset) in 1537. The Florentines have entered into a state of apathy, and do nothing to find a replacement. Lorenzino runs away to Venice. Cosimo delle Bande Nere accepts the post of leader and proceeds to rule as an absolute monarch, although Florence had ceased to exist as a leading power years earlier.

1559. The final nail in the coffin is hammered in when Florence is subjugated by France and Spain at the Peace of Château-Cambrésis. From now on, a series of Grand-dukes rule, all descendants of the Medici, until the last dies heirless in 1737, after which Tuscany is handed over to Austria.

In the late 16th century the physicist Galileo Galilei makes important discoveries in Florence but he is accused of unorthodox beliefs and put on trial when he is already old and sick. He dies later at a villa in Florence, after being forced by the Inquisition to retract his theories.

1799. The French expel the Austrians from Florence.

1800–1808. Napoleon Bonaparte allows Florence to become (nominally) capital of the kingdom of Etruria (ancient name for the region of Tuscany and Umbria), but which is really under Murat's jurisdiction.

1808. Florence is reunited properly with France.

1814. Italy falls to Austria in the now familiar French-Austrian tug-of-war.

1860. Florence demands to be annexed to the new kingdom of Italy.

1864–71. King Vittorio Emmanuele chooses Florence as the capital of Italy.

1882. Publication of the children's book *Pinocchio* by the Florentine Carlo Lorenzini (pseudonym "Collodi").

In the 19th century Florence is "discovered" by the historian Jacob Burkhardt and the artist/art historian John Ruskin. It becomes a mecca for travelers, who generally stay in villas just outside the town and paint watercolors of the charming countryside.

World War II. Florence suffers terrible damage from bombings. Every bridge except the Ponte Vecchio is destroyed. The Allies occupy in 1944.

1966. The Arno once more overflows its banks in one of the worst floods for centuries.

FLORENCE—ART AND ARCHITECTURE

If Florence hadn't existed it's just possible that artists in the Western world might still be painting nothing but sallow Madonnas on gold backgrounds. Only in Florence did artists have the drive, the imagination, the intellectual curiosity, the skill, and the financial backing necessary to ensure the astounding artistic progress they made. They aimed at producing paintings and statues that would amaze the spectator, the figures were so life-like. And this desire for realism is a *leitmotiv* that runs through the best of Florentine art from Giotto to Michelangelo.

THE MIDDLE AGES AND EARLY RENAISSANCE

It all began in the 13th century, the era of St. Francis, who preached a new, humane approach to Christianity. Giotto expressed this new humanity in his art, and was really the first artist to break decisively with the formalized Byzantine style that had dominated Italy for centuries. Even if his sense of perspective was nowhere near correct and his figures still had typically Byzantine slanting eyes, he was painting palpably solid people who stood in their own space (instead of being bunched up together so as to leave no gaps) and who you could tell were subject to real emotions.

By the end of the 14th century the International Gothic style (which had arrived in Italy from France) had made further progress towards realism, but more as far as plants, animals and clothes were concerned than

27

in the human figure. Moreover, as you can see from Gentile da Fabriano's *Adoration of the Magi*, it was still mainly a decorative art, like a Byzantine mosaic: pretty, but nothing that would stop you dead in your tracks.

Architecturally, Florence was no less distinguished in the 13th and 14th centuries. The city developed its own, distinctly individual Romanesque style, more graceful than its northern European counterparts. It's dominated by simple geometrical forms covered with decorative, almost toy-like patterns picked out in multi-colored marble. It is this that makes the Baptistery and San Miniato so unusually striking compared to the duller, stodgier church architecture elsewhere in Italy.

The 13th century was a time of great political and economic growth in Tuscany, and there was a desire to reflect the new wealth and power in its buildings. This is why civic centers such as Palazzo Vecchio (1298) are so big and fortress-like. The Cathedral (Duomo) was built on that colossal scale simply to outdo the Pisans and the Sienese—Florence's rivals. In fact, its design was too ambitious for the masons of the time as the space at the crossing was too vast to bridge using the techniques currently available. The authorities, desperate for a solution, suggested filling the relevant part of the church with earth, building the dome on top of it, then disposing of the earth by mixing coins at intervals and enticing the citizens of Florence to come and take it away in order to get at the money. These buildings are in the Italian version of Gothic, a style which originated in France and found its expression there in tall, soaring, light and airy verticality, intended to elevate the soul. The spiritual aspect of Gothic never really caught on in Italy where the top priority was for a church (as representative of a city) to be grander and more imposingly solid than the neighboring city's church.

Medieval and Early-Renaissance Painters and Sculptors

Cimabue (*c.*1240–1302). The stepping-stone between the rigid Byzantine style and the proto-Renaissance (i.e. naturalistic) painter, Giotto. (Uffizi, Santa Croce).

Giotto (Giotto di Bondone, c.1266–1337). Supposed to have been spotted as a boy drawing a sheep on a stone by Cimabue, and subsequently became his pupil. Generally considered the founder of Renaissance painting for his treatment of space, the solidity of his figures, and the real emotion conveyed by their pose and, importantly, expression. Most famous works are at Assisi and Padua. (Uffizi, Santa Croce). (See also "Medieval Architects" below).

Gentile da Fabriano (*c.*1370–1427). Painter of charming courtly scenes in the International Gothic style. Extensive use of gold, paintings crammed with detail: landscapes, animals, hilltop castles. (Uffizi).

Lorenzo Ghiberti (1378–1455). Famous mainly as the sculptor of Biblical scenes on two of the three bronze doors of the Baptistery (the Gate of Paradise), the commission for which he won in a competition in 1401. The harmonious, flowing style is reminiscent of International Gothic, even if his correct perspective indicates familiarity with early-Renaissance realism. First artist to write an autobiography. (Also Bargello, Duomo, Orsanmichele, San Egidio, Santa Maria Novella, Santa Croce).

Filippo Brunelleschi (1377–1446). Lost the 1401 sculpture competition for the Baptistery doors to Ghiberti but went on to better things as an architect. (See also "Renaissance Architects" below).

Masolino (c. 1383–1447). Not always distinguishable from Masaccio (see below) who was his master for a time (in spite of the disparity in age). Less progressive though than Masaccio since—as far as we know—he always worked in the International Gothic style. (Uffizi, Museo Horne, Carmine).

Medieval Architects

Nicola Pisano (d. c. 1280). Supposed to have built Santa Trinita in the 1250s.

Arnolfo di Cambio (1232–1301). Started out as assistant to Nicola Pisano but by 1296 was master mason on the Duomo with a number of Gothic-inspired decorative buildings and sculptures to his name. May have built Santa Croce, the Badia and Palazzo Vecchio.

Andrea Pisano (c. 1290–1349). Sculptor and architect, responsible for the third bronze door of the Baptistery (Ghiberti was to make the other two).

Giotto (c. 1266–1337). No knowledge of architecture but was made *capomaestro* (architect-in-chief) of the Duomo anyway, during which time he designed the Campanile. (His design was altered after his death.) (See also "Medieval and early-Renaissance Painters and Sculptors" above).

Orcagna (the di Cione family). **Andrea** (c. 1308–68). Primarily a painter, but also sculptor and architect and involved in the construction of the Duomo. His masterpiece is the Tabernacle of Orsanmichele (the most expensive work of art commissioned in Italy at the time), which with its gold backgrounds and delicate pinnacles combines Byzantine and Gothic elements. **Nardo,** architect of the Strozzi Chapel at Santa Maria Novella. **Benci,** joint architect with Simone Martini of the Loggia dei Lanzi, in which a perfect balance is struck between the unusual (for the time) Roman-style round arches and the graceful balustrade above.

Francesco Talenti (c. 1300–69). Became *capomaestro* for the Duomo in 1351 and modified Giotto's overly ambitious plans.

THE RENAISSANCE

The gap between Gentile da Fabriano and his near-contemporary, the sculptor Donatello, is vast. Donatello wants to astound rather than please the spectator by his defiant warts-and-all likenesses with their intense, heroic gaze. In painting, Masaccio's figures have a similarly self-confident air, and again there is no sign of compromise: no reassuring smiles or pretty colors. Art had "grown up" in the early Renaissance—artists had to study classical remains and the new science of perspective. All energies were put into the creation of a noble, moving, realistic and, above all, *serious* art. Even the paintings that today seem wacky in the extreme (such as Uccello's *Battle of San Romano*) were conceived in a spirit of scientific experiment.

Serious realism was not all the Renaissance produced. There was a change of attitude towards the artists themselves: where previously they had been considered mere workmen trained to carry out commissions, now they were giant personalities. It was a time when their creations reached a huge size as if to express their creators' greatness, as witness, for example, Botticelli's *Birth of Venus*. An element of ambiguity crept into art—something about a picture or statue that only the Artist Himself could understand. Why is Mona Lisa smiling her knowing smile? What is actually happening in Uccello's *Deluge?* Who are the half-finished, provocative *Slaves* of Michelangelo's imprisoned in the stone?

In architecture, the Gothic excess of the 13th century was toned down in the 14th, while the 15th century ushered in a completely new approach. Now, Florence didn't need to prove anything to its neighbors any more. Consequently, its architecture reflects the Humanist ideal, chiefly dignity, expressed through classical Roman design. Brunelleschi used Roman columns for the Basilica of San Lorenzo, Roman-style rustication (massive, rough-surfaced blocks on the facades) for the Pitti palace, and Roman round arches—as opposed to pointed Gothic ones—for his Foundling Hospital (Ospedale degli Innocenti), which is generally considered the first truly classical building of the Renaissance. Leon Battista Alberti's treatise on ideal proportion was even more influential as a manifesto of the Renaissance movement. Suddenly architects had become erudite scholars, and architecture correspondingly far more earnest.

Renaissance Painters and Sculptors

Donatello (*c.* 1386–1466). The greatest Florentine sculptor until Michelangelo, yet also enormously influential on 15th-century Florentine painting. Shared with his friend Brunelleschi the same beliefs as to the importance of realism and the dignity of man. This intense belief is reflected in his statues, for example the gaunt, unkempt *Magdalen* (Museo del Duomo) which has an extraordinary inner power. Also carved in the classical manner: his bronze *David* is the first free-standing nude since antiquity. (Orsanmichele, Palazzo Vecchio, Museo del Duomo, Bargello).

Paolo Uccello (Paolo di Dono, 1397–1475). Fascinated by perspective but not particularly interested in realism, he produced frescoes such as the apocalyptic *Deluge* (Santa Maria Novella) which have a vertiginous, dream-like quality about them. Condemned in the past as simply an incompetent theorist (because his perspective is often off the beam, despite his obsessive interest in the subject), he strikes a chord with the modern spectator who will not necessarily be so dismissive of his blue rocking-horses. Specialized in foreshortening (the way an object seems squashed up into the space of a few inches when seen from certain angles). (Uffizi, Duomo, San Martino alla Scala).

Fra Angelico (*c.* 1400–55). A Dominican friar whose best known works are the delicate, translucent frescoes in the monks' cells at San Marco, intended as images for contemplation. (Uffizi).

Masaccio (Tommaso di Ser Giovanni di Mone, 1401–28). Innovated a new, emotionally charged, realistic style which, however, enjoyed relatively little popularity in his short lifetime. Feel the desolation in *The Expulsion from the Garden of Eden* in the Carmine and compare it with the pretty but bland style of the currently fashionable International Gothic artists. (Uffizi, Museo Horne).

Luca della Robbia (1400–82), and nephew **Andrea** (1435–1525). Principally famous for their glazed terracotta works with white figures set against a blue or green background, cute children and sweet-faced Madonnas which verge on the kitsch. (Duomo, Bargello, Campanile, Santa Trinita, Santa Croce, Innocenti, Palazzo di Parte Guelfa, San Miniato).

Fra Filippo Lippi (*c.*1406–69). A monk who led a highly colorful life. Ran away with a nun, had an illegitimate child by her, was taken to court for abduction and also for fraud. His art is surprisingly devotional in feeling (the *Madonna and Child* in the Pitti, for instance). Made important progress in solving the problem of how to render movement. (Uffizi, Palazzo Medici-Riccardi, Museo Horne, San Lorenzo).

Piero della Francesca (1410/20–92). Like Uccello, not appreciated until recently. Most famous frescoes are in Arezzo. In the Uffizi are the strange profile portraits of Battista Sforza and Federico da Montefeltro (with part of his nose missing) with the surreal *Triumphal Allegory,* which shows his mastery of perspective, his characteristically hypnotic stillness, pale coloring and rejection of decorative elements.

Andrea del Castagno (*c.*1421–57). Assumed and discarded several styles in his lifetime, but best known for his intense, sculptural Donatello-inspired style as in *Illustrious Men and Women* in the Uffizi. (Castagno Museum, Santissima Annunziata).

Benozzo Gozzoli (*c.*1421–97). Assistant to Fra Angelico but his own paintings are entirely secular in feeling, as for example the attractive *Procession of the Magi* (Palazzo Medici-Riccardi), which is actually a flattering portrait of the Medici family on the occasion of the Emperor's visit in 1439.

Antonio Pollaiuolo (*c.*1432–98), and brother **Piero** (1443–96). Among the first painters to use oils and to study anatomy. The *Hercules and the Hydra* is a true Renaissance painting: an allegory of heroic man dominating Nature. (Bargello, San Miniato, Uffizi).

Andrea del Verrocchio (1435–88). Painter, goldsmith and sculptor, who worked mostly for the Medici. His light, graceful, carefully-finished statues (the cherub in Palazzo Vecchio, the bronze *David* in the Bargello) contrast markedly with Donatello's raw, tragic approach. (Orsanmichele, Uffizi).

Botticelli (Sandro di Mariano Filipepi, 1447–1508). Popular for his large-scale mythological paintings (such as the *Primavera*) which are actually complicated Christian allegories. The pallidly beautiful, melancholy female figures, the graceful contours, the profusion of pastel-colored flowers, hide neuroses and anxiety caused partly by the religious crisis he seems to have undergone toward the end of his life. (Innocenti, Pitti, Uffizi).

Domenico Ghirlandaio (1449–94). Known chiefly as the young Michelangelo's master. His frescoes (he never attempted oils) are interesting more for the period detail than for the style, which is unadventurous. (Ognissanti, Santa Trinita, Santa Maria Novella, Innocenti).

Leonardo da Vinci (1452–1519). One of the greatest "Renaissance men" with talent for engineering, mathematics, architecture, anatomy, and much else besides painting. He completed relatively few works for his long lifetime. Spent short periods in Florence, during one of which he painted the *Mona Lisa* (now in the Louvre). Famous also for his ability to create atmosphere by means of a *sfumato* (skillful blurring of tone) effect. (Uffizi).

Filippino Lippi (1457/8–1504). Son of Fra Filippo Lippi. Worked for a while with Botticelli and like him his style (full of movement, bright colors, with pieces of antiquity popping up everywhere) went out of fashion during his lifetime. (Badia, Carmine, Accademia, Uffizi, Sant'Ambrogio, Santo Spirito).

Piero di Cosimo (*c.* 1462–1521). An eccentric, interested in freaks of nature. Painted monstrously ugly dragons, but also calmer, obscure mythological scenes. (Uffizi, Pitti, Museo Horne, Innocenti).

Renaissance Architects

Filippo Brunelleschi (1377–1446). Greatest architect of the early Renaissance. Brought back from his stay in Rome a thorough understanding of the principles of classical architecture. Saved Florence from neighboring cities' ridicule by managing to span the gaping hole in the Duomo crossing with a dome that was a tremendous feat of engineering for its time. Famous also for his discovery of linear perspective (enormously influential on Florentine painting). (San Lorenzo, Innocenti, Santo Spirito, Pazzi Chapel in Santa Croce, Bargello).

Michelozzo di Bartolommeo (1396–1472). Assistant initially to Ghiberti, shared a studio with Donatello, succeeded Brunelleschi as *capomaestro* on the Duomo in 1446. Most important works are his Medici residences, including the Villa Medici at Fiesole and Palazzo Medici-Riccardi (the first Renaissance palace), the sacristy, cloisters and library of San Marco, and parts of San Marco and Santissima Annunziata. Elegant, well-proportioned buildings, but less inventive than those of Brunelleschi on whose principles he based his own style.

Leon Battista Alberti (1404–72). Carried Brunelleschi's theories of classical proportion into secular architecture, for example, Palazzo Rucellai. A painter, playwright, scientist, musician and athlete, he is remembered principally as an architect although he designed only half a dozen buildings and had no part in the actual construction of them. His treatise on town planning *(De Re Aedificatoria)* of 1452 influenced generations of Western architects. (Upper half of facade of Santa Maria Novella).

Bernardo Rossellino (1409–64). Chiefly a sculptor but carried out Alberti's designs for the Palazzo Rucellai.

HIGH RENAISSANCE AND MANNERISM

Florence in the late 15th century underwent a traumatic political and religious upheaval which naturally came to be reflected in art. Classical proportion and realism no longer seemed enough. Heroism suddenly looked hollow and out of date. Artists such as Pontormo and Rosso found expression for their unease in discordant colors, elongated forms, tortured looks in staring eyes. Giambologna carved his *Hercules and the Centaur* at the most agonizing moment of their battle, when Hercules bends the Centaur's back to the point where it is about to snap. This is Mannerism—the optimistic self-confidence has gone. What remains is a self-conscious, stylized show of virtuosity, the effect of which is neither to please (like Gothic) nor to impress (like Renaissance art) but to disquiet. Even Bronzino's portraits—though no pain is apparent in his subjects' eyes—are cold and unsmiling, and far removed from the relaxed mood of the Renaissance portrait.

Mannerism found a fairly precise equivalent in architecture. The rebellious younger generation (Michelangelo, Ammanati, Vasari) used the same architectural vocabulary as the Renaissance architects, but distorted it bizarrely and deliberately in a way that would have made Alberti's hair stand on end. Michelangelo's staircase at the Biblioteca Laurenziana, for instance, spreads out like a stone fan, filling almost the entire floorspace of the vestibule. Likewise, the inside walls are treated as if they were facades, though with columns and niches disproportionately large for the size of the room. But Mannerism could also produce a highly elegant effect by using old elements in a new way. Look at the way Buontalenti's Porta delle Suppliche on the Uffizi has a pediment broken into two pieces set back to back: this is more than just an architectural game.

High Renaissance and Mannerist Painters and Sculptors

Michelangelo (Michelangelo Buonarroti, 1475–1564). Another Renaissance giant. Worked alternately for the Medici in Florence and the Pope in Rome, where he lived for the last years of his life, as painter (which he despised as an "unmanly" profession), sculptor and architect. His most famous works in Florence include the intensely moving *Pieta* (Museo del Duomo), and the extremely manly *David* in the Accademia. (Uffizi, San Lorenzo, Palazzo Vecchio). (See also "Mannerist Architects" below).

Andrea del Sarto (1487–1531). The most important painter working in Florence while Raphael and Michelangelo were in Rome. A typically High Renaissance painter, though more interested in color than the average Florentine. Academic but fairly naturalistic. (Santissima Annunziata, Uffizi, Pitti).

Jacopo Pontormo (1494–1556). A deranged agoraphobic, hypochondriac recluse. Co-creator (with Rosso) of Mannerism partly in reaction to Andrea del Sarto, under whom they worked. His is an uncomfortable art, with corpse-like figures staring out at the spectator, and lurid colors: acid orange, poisonous green, candyfloss pink. (Santissima Annunziata, Uffizi, Santa Felicita, Pitti).

Rosso ("Rosso Fiorentino", 1494–1540.) Worked in Florence (where he lived with a baboon) from 1513–1523, then went to Rome and later to Venice and France. Obsessed with anatomy, he was a neurotic like Pontormo and it shows, in his screaming colors, contorted poses, unbalanced compositions and simpering idiot children. (Uffizi, Pitti, Santissima Annunziata, San Lorenzo).

Agnolo Bronzino (1503–72). A pupil of Pontormo and one of the most important Mannerist portrait painters. He compresses the malaise of Mannerism into an icily restrained, emotionless elegance of almost photographic clarity. (Uffizi, San Lorenzo, Santissima Annunziata, Badia, Santa Croce, Santa Felicita).

Benvenuto Cellini (1500–71). Sculptor, goldsmith and writer of a well-known autobiography (packed with adventures, fights, love affairs, and boasting). Graceful, sophisticated work with characteristically Mannerist lack of feeling. (Loggia dei Lanzi, Bargello).

Bartolommeo Ammanati (1511–92). A sculptor influenced by Michelangelo. Best known work is the *Neptune* fountain in Piazza della Signoria, the commission for which he won in a competition with Cellini and Giambologna. (Bargello, Boboli Gardens). (See also "Mannerist Architects" below).

Giorgio Vasari (1511–74). A second-rate painter—though never afraid to work on the largest scale—a better architect and sculptor, but an extremely important (if not always accurate) biographer of contemporary and earlier artists. (Palazzo di Parte Guelfa, Uffizi, Santa Croce). (See also "Mannerist Architects" below).

Giambologna (Jean de Boulogne, 1524–1608). A French sculptor who trained in Flanders and stayed in Rome before settling in Florence. His more-than-lifesize figure groups, such as the *Rape of the Sabine* (Loggia dei Lanzi) are showpieces of virtuosity: notice how the centaur's fingers are sinking into the Sabine woman's flesh. (San Marco, Palazzo Griffoni, Santo Stefano al Ponte, Boboli Gardens grotto).

Mannerist Architects

Giuliano da Sangallo (Giuliano Giamberti, 1445–1516). Sculptor, military engineer and architect, eldest of the Sangallo family of architects. His palaces (Gondi, and possibly Corsi, now the Museo Horne) are similar to earlier ones but with a smoother surface texture. (Palazzo Bartolommeo della Scala, Santo Spirito, Santa Maria Maddalena dei Pazzi).

Benedetto da Maiano (1442–97). Built the massive, factory-like Palazzo Strozzi on the same lines as the Medici and Rucellai palaces in collaboration with Simone del Pollaiuolo, called **Il Cronaca** (1454–1508). Cronaca's most celebrated work is the elegant Guadagni Palace.

Michelangelo (Michelangelo Buonarroti, 1475–1564). Revolutionized architecture away from the Renaissance ideals of classical order and symmetry to designs in which buildings were conceived as living organisms, not just flat surfaces to be covered with ornament. (Few finished in his lifetime.) The Biblioteca Laurenziana is his most famous building in Florence, where the decoration is used as an integral part of the structure. As with the Medici chapel, he takes classical elements (pediments, niches, pilasters) and deliberately misuses them, reversing the rules laid down by earlier architects.

Bartolommeo Ammanati (1511–92). A Mannerist sculptor who designed the graceful Ponte Santa Trinita, extended and altered Pitti Palace (including the overly rusticated garden-side facade), completed Palazzo Grifoni and oversaw the building of Michelangelo's peculiar staircase at the Biblioteca Laurenziana. (Palazzo Pucci).

Giorgio Vasari (1511–74). Best known as the author of *Lives of the Artists,* he also designed the Uffizi (the then government offices), achieving a typically Mannerist dramatic effect by means of its long, narrow tunnel-like courtyards.

Bernardo Buontalenti (c. 1536–1608). Sophisticated Mannerist architect who worked mainly for the Medici family as painter, sculptor and fireworks expert. Succeeded Vasari at the Uffizi in 1574. (Works at Santo Stefano, Santa Maria Maddalena dei Pazzi, Santo Stefano al Ponte, Boboli Gardens, Santa Maria Maggiore, etc.).

EXPLORING FLORENCE

Florence, the city where the Renaissance first assumed the form and spirit that made it the most decisive and influential period in the history of Western thought and art since antiquity, has a surprisingly unpretentious aspect. It is a small, compact city, built of dark rusticated stone, its narrow streets, paved with smooth gray slabs, only occasionally giving way to a spacious, but often largely unplanned, piazza. It is an intimate city and a reassuring place to visit, with the gracious and elegant manner of past centuries.

But though you may never feel overwhelmed by the city itself, you may well be struck almost numb by the sheer quantity and magnificence of its artistic treasures. Cultural overkill is an ever-present danger here. There is so much to see, and for most visitors so little time to see it in, that it's easy to find churches, museums, paintings, sculptures and the great roll call of artists the city spawned dissolving and melting after just a few days into a vast, hazy, muddled dream.

So take it slowly. Let the city come to life. Plan to see just one major museum a day. And don't try to see everything in it. A couple of paintings paused over and savored will tell you far more about this remarkable city and the men it produced than a whole gallery full of paintings and sculptures rushed through at breakneck speed in a desperate attempt to see it all. Break up your sightseeing with less purposeful strolls. Sit in the cafes and soak up the atmosphere. And there are any number of excursions out into the Tuscan hills around the the city that will give you that broader perspective.

As you wander through Florence, observe the Florentines, usually brisk and businesslike, true sons and daughters of the merchant families which

FLORENCE

0 miles ¼

0 km ¼

Points of Interest

1 Badia
2 Baptistery
3 Casa Buonarroti
4 Casa di Dante
5 Casa Guidi
6 Duomo (Cathedral)
7 Forte di Belvedere
8 Galleria dell'Accademia
9 Galleria degli Uffizi
10 Loggia dei Lanzi
11 Mercato Nuova
12 Museo dell'Antica Casa Fiorentina
13 Museo Archaeologico
14 Museo Bardini/Galleria Corsi
15 Museo del Bargello
16 Museo Ebraico (Jewish Museum)
17 Museo dell'Opera del Duomo
18 Museo Storico Topografico: (Historical Florence)
19 Museo Zoologico 'La Specola'
20 Ognissanti
21 Orsanmichele
22 Ospedale degli Innocenti
23 Palazzo Antinori
24 Palazzo Corsini
25 Palazzo Medici-Riccardi
26 Palazzo Nonfinito
27 Palazzo Pitti
28 Palazzo Rucellai
29 Palazzo Spini-Ferroni
30 Palazzo Strozzi
31 Palazzo Vecchio
32 Porta Romana
33 Porta San Miniato
34 San Felice
35 San Jacopo Sopr'Arno
36 San Lorenzo/Medici Chapels/ Biblioteca Laurenziana
37 San Marco
38 San Miniato al Monte
39 Santa Croce
40 Santa Maria del Carmine
41 Santa Maria Maddalena dei Pazzi
42 Santa Maria Novella
43 Santa Trinita
44 Santi Apostoli
45 Santissima Annunziata
46 Santo Spirito

ℹ️ Tourist Information

✉️ Post Office

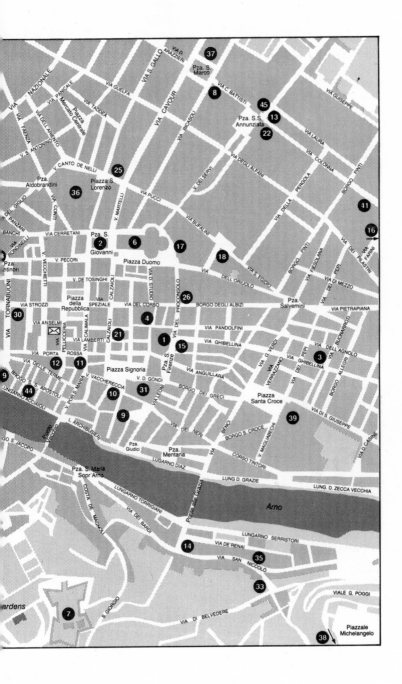

built her great churches and palaces to glorify God and themselves. Watch carefully and you'll see them fall occasionally into languid, graceful poses as they relax in a cafe or window-shop along Via Tornabuoni. And you'll recognize the same intense faces and classical gestures in the sculptures and frescoes in their museums. Listen to their quick sing-song intonations and the aspirated vowels that make their dialect so distinctive and turn Coca Cola into *hola hola.*

Less dependent than the Venetians on tourism for their livelihood—not that you'd know it sometimes, such are the crowds that descend on their noble city—they are in general tolerant of the sunburnt armies that march through their streets to a rendezvous with Michelangelo's *David.* Don't be offended if you find them somewhat sharp and edgy. That's the way they are even among themselves. The Florentines have a reputation for caustic tongues and quick wits.

Like them, though, you may sometimes find yourself wishing all the other tourists would go away and leave you to enjoy the city in peace. But you can get away from the crowds if you can plan your day carefully. Heed our advice on when to visit museums. If you find your destination overrun with tour groups, well, make for a cafe and wait for the crowds to abate. Don't feel obliged to visit only the best known sites. Take off on your own and get the feel of everyday life. Florence is so small and simple in its lay-out that you can't get lost for long. You'll find it an extraordinarily homogeneous city, with a soothing regularity about it that will make you feel at home from your first day.

Around Piazza del Duomo

The historical heart of Florence is Piazza Duomo, the square surrounding the city's majestic cathedral, the Duomo. This was the center of the Roman colony of Florentia, founded by decree of Julius Caesar in 59 B.C. to control trade routes on the river Arno and the Via Cassia, the road to Rome. Today it is dominated by the cathedral, but originally this was the site of the praetorium, the Roman military commander's imposing palace. Later, probably in the 5th or 6th century, the church of Santa Reparata and the octagonal baptistery were built here. Santa Reparata has long since disappeared, replaced by the sumptuous Gothic/Renaissance Duomo, properly known as Santa Maria del Fiore, but the baptistery is still here, though it has been much altered over the centuries.

The steps outside the Duomo are a favorite rendezvous point for young Florentines and foreign students who sit waiting—in the summer months at least—for their friends to show up. Their serried ranks can make the transit from the cathedral to the baptistery (or vice versa) something of an obstacle course for tourists.

Unfortunately it's impossible to get a really good view of the Duomo from the ground as there are buildings close on every side, and to stand in the busy road looking up can be a health hazard.

The Baptistery

Standing foursquare in front of the Duomo in Piazza San Giovanni, the baptistery is one of the supreme monuments of the Italian Romanesque. Its most distinctive features—its curious striped green-and-white marble exterior and unusual white pyramid shaped roof—were probably both added in the 12th century, though some contend the roof may be 13th century. There is no such dispute, however, over its most famous feature, the magnificent sets of bronze doors created for its south, east and north sides. The earliest is that made for the south side. This was created in around 1330 by Andrea Pisano. Originally, it stood on the east side, facing the cathedral, and was moved in 1452. Its 20 upper panels bear reliefs showing scenes from the life of John the Baptist (appropriately enough), while below them are eight figures representing the theological virtues— Faith, Hope and Charity—and the cardinal virtues. The door frames surrounding Pisano's work were added later, in 1452, by Vittorio Ghiberti, son of the sculptor Lorenzo Ghiberti. Their tangle of tiny animals, plant forms, cherubs and birds contrasts with the austere simplicity of Pisano's Gothic creations.

In 1401 the city announced a competition for the design of a new set of doors. Six artists submitted designs, including Filippo Brunelleschi, later architect of the cathedral's ingenious dome. However, the competition was won by Lorenzo Ghiberti. His winning design is generally held to be the first stirring of the Renaissance, that key moment when the formality and artifice of Gothic art began gradually to give way to the new naturalism that more than any other characteristic can be said to be the distinguishing quality of Renaissance art.

Ghiberti's first doors were installed on the north side of the baptistery. They consist of 20 panels, the upper panels showing scenes from the New Testament, the eight lower panels showing the Evangelists and Doctors of the Latin Church. It so pleased his fellow citizens that the Merchant's Guild commissioned a second set—the east doors—unusually allowing Ghiberti a free hand as to subject matter and treatment. The Guild's faith in Ghiberti was more than amply rewarded. So much so in fact, that many years later Michelangelo dubbed these doors the "Gates of Paradise." From top to bottom, left to right, the panels in this east door show: the creation of Adam and Eve; Cain and Abel; Noah; Abraham and Isaac; Esau and Jacob; Joseph; Moses; the Israelites; David and Goliath; King Solomon and the Queen of Sheba. The 24 niches around the main panels hold statues of Prophets and Sybils, interspersed with portrait heads. Among them, Ghiberti inserted his own head. He is the bemused, bald man, third from the bottom on the right frame of the lefthand door.

All three doors were removed for safe keeping in World War II. But they suffered badly in the terrible floods of 1966. Five panels were actually ripped off their doors by the murky waters and lay buried in the mud. Plans are now afoot to remove all the doors—replacing them with copies—to the safety of the Museo dell'Opera del Duomo, the cathedral museum. Many panels have been removed for restoration, and the rest will follow them to safekeeping.

To enter the baptistery, make for the south door. Inside, you'll probably find a milling crowd. For all that, the solemn beauty of the massive circular interior is clear to see. Until 1577 the baptismal font stood in the center of the building. Then it was removed, along with the choir, by architect Buontalenti, under orders to spruce the place up for the baptism of Franceso I's grandson, Filippo. Simple red terracotta tiles mark the spot where the font stood, and where Dante and so many other Florentines were christened. The rest of the pavement is decorated with 13th-century signs of the zodiac in inlaid marble. A grate near the altar reveals the flooring of the original Roman fortress/palace—the praetorium—that once stood on this site. Among the many other objects of interest here is the tomb of Pope John XXIII by Donatello and Michelozzo, standing to the right of the tribune. This pope is not to be confused with the Pope John XXIII who called the Second Vatican Council in 1964. He was, rather, an "Antipope," a rival pope as it were, based in Avignon in France, who died in Florence in 1419.

It's worth getting a crick in your neck looking up at the colorful ceiling mosaic, packed with Biblical scenes, the liveliest of which is the imaginatively depicted Judgment Day (below Christ to His left), with a monstrous Lucifer and smaller, blue demons with pointed ears making life hell for the damned souls.

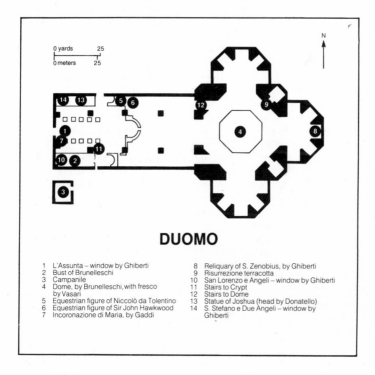

DUOMO

1 L'Assunta – window by Ghiberti
2 Bust of Brunelleschi
3 Campanile
4 Dome, by Brunelleschi, with fresco by Vasari
5 Equestrian figure of Niccolò da Tolentino
6 Equestrian figure of Sir John Hawkwood
7 Incoronazione di Maria, by Gaddi
8 Reliquary of S. Zenobius, by Ghiberti
9 Risurrezione terracotta
10 San Lorenzo e Angeli – window by Ghiberti
11 Stairs to Crypt
12 Stairs to Dome
13 Statue of Joshua (head by Donatello)
14 S. Stefano e Due Angeli – window by Ghiberti

The Duomo

In 1296, Arnolfo di Cambio was commissioned to build "the loftiest, most sumptuous edifice human invention could devise" on the site of the old church of Santa Reparata. The project—like so many of its kind—did not prove straightforward. Di Cambio died in 1310, leaving only half the facade and parts of the walls completed and the bulk of the site still occupied by Santa Reparata and a motley collection of other buildings. Giotto was then appointed architect, but he seems to have expended his energies exclusively on designing the campanile, the bell tower, that stands just to one side of the cathedral. From about 1355 a host of other architects were all employed to work on the great cathedral. By about 1415, their combined efforts had, with two key exceptions, produced the building that stands today. The first of these exceptions was the facade. Though he had left it unfinished, di Cambio's designs for the facade were nonetheless adhered to after his death. By about 1585, however, tastes had changed to such an extent that it was decided to demolish the original facade and replace it with something more appropriately classical. The first part of this decision was carried through, but not the second. In fact it was only in 1870, when of course tastes had changed again, that the present Gothic facade began to go up. This was completed in 1887.

The second exception is the dome of the cathedral. If Ghiberti's baptistery doors can be said to represent the first stirrings of the Renaissance in Florence, the dome of Florence cathedral—begun, by Brunelleschi, in

1419 and completed in 1436—may be said to represent its most triumphant early maturity, an emphatic statement of the new confidence of Renaissance Florence. Technically, the building of the dome was an immense
achievement, silencing for good all those skeptics who claimed Brunelleschi's daring design would crumble into the cathedral. But the full significance of the dome was as much architectural as technical, a decisive rejection of Gothic models in favor of the classical architecture of the ancient
world. In this respect, it is the direct ancestor of many such later domes,
that at St. Peter's in Rome, for example, even that over the Capitol in
Washington.

The dome immediately became a symbol of the city and of Florentine
pride, a monument to the audacity, skill and imagination of her citizens.
It was Michelangelo himself who asked to be buried in the church of Santa
Croce so that he could, when the doors of the church were opened, see
Brunelleschi's dome over the rooftops of the city for all eternity.

Inside the Cathedral

Don't be surprised if you feel overpowered on entering the cathedral.
It is the fourth largest in the world. The austere Gothic atmosphere may
be chilling, but the sparse decorations bear the unmistakable stamp of the
Renaissance. Turn as you go in to see Ghiberti's stained-glass windows
on the rear wall and Uccello's huge clock, with figures of the prophets
at its corners. Over the main door is a lunette containing an early 14th-
century mosaic by Gaddo Gaddi of the *Coronation of the Virgin.* Along
the right hand wall of the nave are some illusionistic frescoes, while on
the left hand wall are two equestrian monuments. The first, and earliest,
painted by Uccello, honors one Giovanni Acuto, as the Florentines know
Sir John Hawkwood, British soldier of fortune who died in their defense
at the end of the 14th century. The adjacent monument, to Niccolò da
Tolentino, another *condottiere,* was painted 20 years later, in 1456, by Andrea del Castagno. Close by is Ciuffagni's rather awkward statue of *Joshua.* The expressive—and entirely ill-matched—head was added by Donatello. Brunelleschi's tomb is also in the cathedral, in the vast crypt. You
can see it here, along with some old frescoes and other remains of the original church of Santa Reparata, all of which have recently been excavated.

Finally, if you can face the steep 463 steps, you can also climb to the
dome. The entrance is in the north aisle. Once up here, you can walk between the two layers of the dome, and also climb up to the lantern sur-
mounting the dome, from where you will be rewarded with a wonderful
view over Florence. Note, however, that because of ongoing structural repairs to the dome and restoration of Vasari's fresco, all or parts of this
stairway may be closed.

The Campanile

The campanile, or bell tower of the cathedral, stands immediately to
the south of the great church. Giotto, as we have seen, began the tower,
working on it from 1334 to his death in 1337, but he built only the first
floor. Thereafter, Andrea Pisano and Francesco Talenti were responsible
for the rest of it, building the second and third floors, and taking the decision also to leave its summit flat, rather than include a steeple as was the

usual practice then. Although Nathaniel Hawthorne was later to quip that it could be taken for a giant toothbrush case, the campanile, with its brilliant marble decoration and delicate Gothic windows, is an excellent example of 14th-century Florentine Gothic, tempering northern European lines with Latin spirit. The climb up it is much less strenuous than that to the top of the cathedral dome. As you make you way up its 414 shallow steps, there are interesting glimpses of the city from the windows. And you'll have a breathtakingly close view of Brunelleschi's dome from the very top.

The Loggia del Baggio and Dante's Stone

To the southwest of the campanile, on the corner of Piazza Giovanni and Via Calzaioli, is the Loggia del Baggio, built in 1358 for the Confraternity of Mercy, the Compagnia della Misericordia. Its exquisite little arcade was used to display lost or abandoned children for adoption or public charity. The Confraternity's main headquarters are still across the street, at # 19. Founded in 1240 by Pietro Borsi, who persuaded his young friends to pay a fine each time they uttered a profanity, the Confraternity was composed entirely of volunteers. Dressed in black robes, they trod the streets barefoot, administering medication, dressing wounds and caring for the sick. All citizens of good standing devoted some time to the Confraternity; even grand dukes could, on occasion, be seen rising from the table at the toll of the bell that called volunteers to duty. In the 19th century, Charles Dickens reports seeing passers-by tip their hats to the brethren when they saw them on the streets. Today, the Confraternity's 3,000 members travel by ambulance. The service is still free, but the brethren now wear shoes.

Just across from the campanile, between # 54r and 55r, a marble plaque marks the site of Dante's stone. Here, the great poet would sit and watch the building of the cathedral. The city's din makes it hard to imagine anyone concentrating on anything here now. But Longfellow, Wordsworth and Tennyson were all inspired by the place where, in the words of Elizabeth Barrett Browning, Dante came to "pour alone the lava of his spirit when it burned."

The Cathedral Museum

The Museo dell'Opera del Duomo, the cathedral museum, lies just to the rear of the cathedral itself, at the eastern end of the Piazza del Duomo. Walking to it from the campanile, there's a good view of the cathedral from the corner of the piazza and Via del Proconsolo. The museum contains works that were all, at one time or another, in the cathedral and have been moved here for their protection. The bronze doors of the baptistery may have joined them by now.

Among the treasures are Arnolfo di Cambio's sculptures from his original facade, notably his austere statue of Pope Boniface VIII and a reclining Madonna of the Nativity. Two smaller rooms hold a wooden model of Brunelleschi's dome and some of the tools used in its construction. On the mezzanine floor is one of Michelangelo's most moving Pietàs, intended for his own tomb. Fellow artist and contemporary chronicler Vasari relates that Michelangelo chiseled his own features on one of its figures, Nicodemus. Old and bad tempered, Michelangelo grew impatient with the work, however, and abandoned it, having tried to smash it. It was repaired, but Christ's left arm still bears the scars.

The Sala delle Cantorie upstairs contains two very different but fascinating *Cantorie,* or "singing galleries," the work of Luca della Robbia and Donatello. The singing putti in della Robbia's delicate masterpiece are particularly beautiful. The same room also contains a further 16 figures by Donatello and his assistants, made originally for niches on the campanile.

The Sala delle Formelle displays relief panels by Andrea Pisano and Luca della Robbia which also originally decorated the campanile. In the Sala dell'Altare is the beautiful silver altar from the baptistery, to which Verrocchio contributed a vivid *Beheading of St. John the Baptist.*

An Exploding Cart

For centuries, the Florentines have gathered in the Piazza Duomo on Easter Sunday. They come here to celebrate the Scoppio del Carro, literally, the "explosion of the cart." This venerable ceremony originated after the First Crusade, in the 11th century, when the Florentine Pazzino de' Pazzi reputedly raised the first Christian flag over the walls of Jerusalem. His reward was to be given three shards from the stone of the Holy Sepulcher. He used these fragments of stone to light a sacred fire on his return to Florence. This was then drawn through the streets on an elaborately decorated cart, and its embers distributed to members of every Florentine family. Today, these same flints are still used to ignite the flame for the ceremony.

SIGHTSEEING DATA. For general information on museum and church opening times and entrance fees, see "Sightseeing Tips" under *Miscellaneous* in the *Practical Information for Florence.*

Campanile. Open daily Apr. to Sept. 9–7:30, Oct. to Mar. 9–5:30. Admission 3,000 lire.

Cathedral Dome and Lantern. Open Mon. to Sat. 8:30–12:30, 2:30–5:30. Admission 3,000 lire.

Museo dell'Opera del Duomo (Cathedral Museum), Piazza del Duomo 9. Open Mon. to Sat. 9–6, Sun. 9–1. Admission 3,000 lire.

West and North of the Duomo

From Piazza del Giovanni and the baptistery, head west down Via Cerretani in the northwest corner of the square. Santa Maria Maggiore, one of Florence's oldest churches, is halfway down on your left. A Roman bust, nicknamed Berta, is cemented onto the adjoining Romanesque bell tower. If you are lucky enough to find the church open, have a look at its rich Baroque interior. The Byzantine Madonna in low relief over the altar is an interesting example of painted wooden sculpture. There is also a lovely little cloister.

A little beyond Santa Maria Maggiore the road splits in three. Take the left fork, Via Rondinelli, and follow it a short distance to little Piazza Antinori. Overlooking the little piazza is the Palazzo Antinori, built in about 1460 and, happily, boasting a little ledge for the tired passer-by to perch. The palace has a charming little courtyard with a small and pretty well. It's not open to the public but peep in nonetheless; one of the secret joys of Florence is its hidden courtyards. Still, though this courtyard may be closed, the atrium is not, and the Antinori, who have lived here since the early 16th century, have converted it into an elegant wine cellar. Light meals are available, or you may prefer simply to taste their magnificent wines, among the very best from the Chianti district. Opposite the palace is the little church of San Gaetano, with a fine 17th-century facade.

Along Via Tornabuoni

Just beyond Palazzo Antinori, the piazza narrows to become Via Tornabuoni. All the top designers have their smart shops here, with, a little lower down, the glamor spilling over into the side streets of Via della Vigna Nuova, Via del Parione and Borgo Santi Apostoli. But Via Tornabuoni is very much more than just a chic shopping street. Lined with palaces large and small, it has been a fashionable address for centuries. It reached its zenith during the 19th century when the great and the good from all over the world were to be found here, blocking the street in their two-wheeled carriages on their way to have their morning *cappuccino* or afternoon tea in the city's most exclusive cafes and elegant drawing rooms. Over the decades, the endless horse-drawn jams may have trapped such luminaries as the Brownings, George Eliot, Mendelssohn—who was only 26 when he came to Florence, and a little scandalized by the ostentation he saw—Queen Victoria, King Victor Emmanuel of Italy, Debussy and Gide. By the time the likes of Ezra Pound, Somerset Maugham and D. H. Lawrence had arrived the horses had given way to cars but the jams were just as thick.

Giuseppe Verdi also lived here for a while, in a pension on the corner of Via della Vigna Nuova. On the night of March 14, 1847, he anxiously waited here to hear the reactions to the debut of his opera *Macbeth,* playing across town at the Teatro della Pergola. Donizetti, Rossini, Meyerbeer, Gounod and George Eliot were all also partial to this pension. The junction of Via della Vigna Nuova and Via Tornabuoni also boasts the Palazzo Strozzi. The best view of it is from Piazza Strozzi. It was built at the end of the 15th century for the Strozzi, one of the city's greatest merchant families. However, they lived in it only from 1504 to 1538. Then, the owner's son, an arch enemy of Grand Duke Cosimo de' Medici, was imprisoned and committed suicide, and the family's properties were confiscated.

Though architecturally distinguished, Palazzo Strozzi nonetheless takes second place to nearby Palazzo Rucellai, located a short distance down Via della Vigna Nuova. It was designed in around 1450 by the versatile architect Leon Battista Alberti, a Renaissance man if ever there was one. His subtle and scholarly application of Roman architectural elements, welded to contemporary needs, proved tremendously influential on later palace designs throughout Italy.

Back on Via Tornabuoni, you pass a further three palaces as you head south towards the Arno. These are Palazzo della Commenda di Castiglione at # 7, attributed to Vasari, and Palazzo Minerbetti, at # 3, and Palazzo Medici Tornaquinci, at # 12, the latter pair dating from the 14th century.

Via Tornabuoni becomes Piazza Santa Trinita at its southern end. The major sight here is the church of Santa Trinita, one of the oldest and most cherished churches in Florence, though it has been much remodeled over the years. There are traces inside of the original 11th-century foundation. Be sure to visit the Sassetti Chapel, decorated by Domenico Ghirlandaio with three tiers of bright frescoes showing scenes from the life of St. Francis and populated by the Medici and other Florentine nobles, including, of course, the chapel's donors, the Sassetti. In the left transept is Luca della Robbia's jewel-like tomb of Bishop Benozzo Federighi.

Opposite the church are two further palaces. The northernmost is Palazzo Bertolini Salimbeni, built at the beginning of the 16th century. Opposite it is the fortress-like bulk of Palazzo Spini, now the British Institute. Built in 1289 it is one of the city's most impressive and best-preserved medieval buildings. Running between the two palaces is the little street of Borgo Santi Apostoli. There's a wonderful little Romanesque church here, just a few steps below street level. Take the Latin inscription which says the church was founded by Charlemagne with a pinch of salt—it's only a legend.

Ponte alla Carraia and Ognissanti

Via Tornabuoni ends at the Arno, at the Ponte Santa Trinita. There's been a bridge here for many hundreds of years, regularly swept away by winter floods until, in 1567, the present bridge was built by Mannerist architect Ammanati. The Germans blew it up in World War II, but it was immediately rebuilt following Ammanati's plans.

Turning right at the bridge up Lungarno Corsini, which runs along the river, you come to Palazzo Mosetti at # 2. It was here, in the 18th century, that the poet Vittorio Alfieri died, after 20 years of bliss with Louise d'Albany, who had deserted her husband, the tragic Bonnie Prince Charlie, to run off with the Italian. Next door at # 4 the Bigordi family sold garlands for young girls. So successful were they, they became known as the Ghirlandai, the garland-makers. However, the most famous member of their family, Domenico Ghirlandaio, achieved eminence as a painter rather than a garland maker. Just up from here is the great bulk of Palazzo Corsini, built in the mid 17th century. It still houses the Corsini picture collection, a good if not exceptional collection of old masters. The entrance to the gallery is at the back of the palace, in Via del Parione.

Continuing past Palazzo Corsini you quickly reach Piazza Goldoni and the Carraia bridge. The original bridge here was probably built in the 13th century, and, like most of the city's bridges, was periodically washed away by flooding. In 1304 it also suffered the ignominious fate of collapsing under the weight of a huge crowd that had gathered on it to watch a representation of hell, complete with flames and demons spiking their pitchforks into naked souls who wailed for mercy—all this set up on a floating stage made of boats. Like Ponte Santa Trinita the present bridge was rebuilt in 1944, following the 16th-century designs of Ammanati, after it had been blown up by the Germans.

From Piazza Goldoni, cut up Borgo Ognissanti, which takes its name from the Ognissanti church half way along it. Number 12 here is called the "upside down house"—have a look a the windows and balcony to discover why! Farther down, at # 20, is the birthplace of Amerigo Vespucci, the man who gave his name to the New World. In Florence Amerigo was much less celebrated than his cousin's beautiful wife, Simonetta, beloved of Giuliano de' Medici as well as being Lorenzo de' Medici's lifelong secret heartthrob. Nicknamed the Renaissance Venus, she was immortalized by countless artists, most famously in Ghirlandaio's fresco in the Ognissanti church of the *Madonna of Mercy*. Here, the Madonna is shown protecting the Vespucci family; the boy to the right of the Madonna is probably Amerigo. When Simonetta died a huge crowd filed down this street to her funeral in the church.

The Ognissanti stands on the site of a 13th-century church, put up by a Benedictine order. It was rebuilt in the 17th century in a contemporary Baroque idiom. It contains a number of interesting tombs, among them Simonetta's, of course, and Botticelli's, marked simply Filipepi, his family name. It's in a little chapel in the south transept. The Refectory of the adjacent convent contains a fine fresco of the *Last Supper* by Ghirlandaio and Botticelli's powerful *St. Augustine*.

Santa Maria Novella

Backtracking a short distance down Borgo Ognissanti you'll find Via della Porcellana on the left, a quiet little street lined with the homes and workshops of furniture restorers. Three-quarters of the way along it, turn right into Via Palazzuolo for a look at San Paolino, a 10th-century church with the Medici, Pandolfini and Pazzi arms on its facade.

Via del Porcellana itself runs into Via della Scala, named after the nearby Santa Maria della Scala Foundling Hospital, where turn-of-the-century British travel writer Augustus Hare tells us that the children were weaned by goats! The faded *graffiti* decorations on the Hotel Aprile here, originally the Palazzo dal Borgo, illustrate scenes from the life of David.

Heading left down Via della Scala you quickly reach the pentagonal Piazza di Santa Maria Novella, overlooked by the great Gothic church of Santa Maria Novella. The piazza itself was originally laid out for St. Peter, or so the story goes, who required a large space for open-air preaching. In 1563 Cosimo de' Medici introduced a yearly chariot race in the piazza. The course was marked by wooden obelisks. These were replaced in 1608 by Ferdinando I de' Medici with the present elaborate marble obelisks wittily supported by bronze tortoises.

A series of famous folk have lived in and around the piazza over the years. In 1874, for example, Henry James lived in the house at the corner of Via della Scala, across the street from the Loggia di San Paolo. Halfway up the square, at the corner of the poetically-named Via delle Belle Donne and Via dei Banchi, is the house where the Brownings stayed in 1847, fresh from the elopement that had so shocked London society. Two centuries earlier, the poet John Milton lived in nearby Via del Giglio. And where the Minerva Hotel now stands there was once a palazzo which played host over the years to so many popes it was nicknamed the Papal Hostel. In 1439, the Byzantine Emperor John VI Palaeologus left this palace to attend the sessions of the Council of Florence, where he agreed to the historic union of the eastern and western churches in the hopes of defeating the Turks. More than 400 years later, Longfellow lived in this same building while working on his translation of Dante's *Inferno.* It's no wonder that this square has been called the Foreigner's Mecca.

The mighty church of Santa Maria Novella itself, ablaze with colored marbles, is one of the most beautiful and important Gothic churches in Italy. Readers of Boccaccio, the rumbustious 14th-century Florentine writer, will remember that the church was the starting point for his earthy and dramatic tales, the *Decameron,* for it was from here that the group of young nobles fled to the hills of Fiesole to escape the great plague of 1348. The church is the second on this site, the first having been put up around 1090. Work on today's church began in about 1245 and was largely complete by the middle of the following century. About 100 years after this, Alberti was called in to remodel the upper part of the facade. He designed the splendid classical pedimented temple front, supported on either side by two majestic scrolls, that sits over the lower part of the facade.

The interior of the church is every bit as imposing. Wide and spacious, it is strikingly decorated with gray banding on the arches and vaulting of the nave. There are a number of important works of art throughout the church. The principal treasure in the nave is Masaccio's superb fresco of the *Trinity, Virgin and St. John,* probably the first example anywhere in Italy of a painter illusionistically extending the real architecture surrounding his picture into the picture itself. His figures have all the monumental and noble massiveness characteristic of his finest work. The other major works here are all at the far end of the church. In the Rucellai chapel in the right transept is Andrea Pisano's splendid marble *Madonna.* Close by, in the Filippo Strozzi chapel, are a series of breathtaking frescoes by Filippino Lippi; put 200 lire in the machine to light them up. Lippi painted these energetic frescoes at the end of the 15th century, with their fantastic architecture and dynamic groups of figures. Behind the main altar—undergoing restoration in 1988—are Ghirlandaio's most famous frescoes, representing a large number of religious subjects, but more than anything vividly portraying Florentine life at the end of the 15th century. It is probable that the young Michelangelo was among the apprentices who worked with Ghirlandaio on these frescoes. To the left of the altar, in the Gondi chapel, is Brunelleschi's *Crucifixion,* his only surviving sculpture. At the far left of this end of the church is the Strozzi chapel—not to be confused with the Filippo Strozzi chapel in the right transept—containing Nardo di Cione's unusual frescoes. They were painted in the mid 14th century. The Baroque sacristy in the left transept is also worth seeing, though you may think it gaudy after the starkness of the nave. The Crucifix painted by Giotto that hung above the door was removed for restoration in 1988.

Be sure to visit both the cloisters and the refectory. The entrance to both is to the left of the main door of the church. The cloisters, or Green Cloister—Chiostro Verde in Italian—were originally decorated with a superb fresco cycle by Paolo Uccello, painted around the middle of the 15th century. Uccello used an unusual olive-green pigment called *terraverde,* or green earth, when working on the frescoes, hence the unusual name of the cloisters, and indeed the greenish hue of the pictures themselves. These have now all been removed from the cloisters to prevent further deterioration (they are in a sadly damaged state) and placed in the refectory. Among them, the best are probably the *Deluge* and the *Sacrifice of Noah,* the former in particular employing a complex and, for the period, immensely accomplished foreshortening, ample proof of Uccello's fascination with perspective. Just to the north of the cloisters is the Spanish chapel, so-called because Cosimo I's wife, Eleonora of Toledo, had it reserved for the use of the city's Spanish community.

Immediately to the east of Santa Maria Novella is Piazza dell'Unita Italiana. An obelisk was placed here in 1882 to commemorate those who had died in the struggle to bring about the unification of Italy. There's a fine view of the church's Romanesque-Gothic bell tower from the piazza. Running northeast out of the square is Via Sant'Antonino, with, over the door of # 11, a bust of Galileo. Continue up Via Sant'Antonino a short way and turn left onto Via Faenza. Here, at # 42, you'll find the Sant'Onofrio Oratory where, in 1845, a fresco of the *Last Supper* was discovered. At the time it was believed to be by Raphael, but has since been recognized as the work of Perugino, Raphael's master. The tranquil Umbrian landscape in the picture is utterly characteristic of the calm and serenity of so much of Perugino's work. Unfortunately, the Oratory has been closed for restoration for many years and may not have been reopened by 1989. But inquire at the tourist office just in case.

The Central Market and San Lorenzo

A short walk along Via Sant' Antonino from Piazza dell'Unita Italiana, will bring you to the mammoth, cast-iron edifice sheltering the large food market at Piazza del Mercato Centrale, just to the north of the massive church of San Lorenzo, site of the Medici chapels. Whether or not you're planning a picnic, take a walk around the stalls with their gleaming vegetables, juicy meats, pungent salamis and sausages, fleshy wild mushrooms and mouthwatering fruit. If you see what look like lumps of dirt in a basket, lean over and take a sniff—they're truffles.

Heading south from the market, down Borgo La Noce, you quickly reach a second market, a sprawling outdoor affair with hundreds of stalls, selling just about anything you can think off, and all at rock bottom prices.

You'll have fun stocking up on inexpensive gifts and souvenirs, and bargaining will get you somewhere. Just remember though that you may also get rock bottom quality if you're not careful.

Borgo La Noce gives on to Canto dei Nelli, overlooked by the lofty domed bulk of the Medici Chapels and the side of San Lorenzo. Wade through the stalls to Piazza San Lorenzo, dominated by the rough brick facade of the church itself and Baccio Bandinelli's huge monument to Giovanni delle Bande Nere, Pope Leo X's legendary soldier of fortune. Father of Medici Grand Duke Cosimo I, Giovanni was famed for his loyalty and bravery. He died in 1527 of complications after his leg was amputated. 19th-century physicians who examined his body were amazed he hadn't expired *during* the operation, but stalwart Giovanni not only waved away the soldiers who wanted to steady him during the ordeal, but insisted on holding the torch to give his doctors light. His death so grieved his troops that they wore black mourning bands ever after, hence his nickname.

The rough, unfinished exterior of San Lorenzo in no way prepares you for its harmonious and elegant interior. The church was largely built by Brunelleschi, between about 1420 and 1445, on the site of a very much earlier church, believed to have been founded in A.D. 393. Almost entirely financed by the Medici, it soon became, in effect, their family church, where almost every member of their family was baptized, married and buried. In the 15th century Michelangelo designed a facade for the church, only the interior wall of which was ever built. The battered brick of the outside of the church has remained untouched to the present.

There are a number of important works of art inside San Lorenzo, the most important of which are two Donatello pulpits, designed in about 1460 and the great Florentine sculptor's last works. They contain a series of vividly realized and slightly gruesome scenes from the Passion and Crucifixion. At the end of the right aisle is a marble tabernacle by Desiderio da Settignano. But the principal attractions here are architectural. First, visit the Old Sacristy, in the left transept. This is the oldest part of the church, built between 1420 and 1430, and, like the rest of San Lorenzo, the work of Brunelleschi. Its contemplative and graceful air mark it out as a key early-Renaissance work. Donatello contributed the four medallions in the spandrels of the vault, the painted terracotta roundels of the Evangelists in the lunettes, and the bronze doors.

The Cloisters and the Laurentian Library

From the Old Sacristy make for the cloisters and the Laurentian library, both of which can also be reached from outside the church (take the door at the extreme left of the facade). The cloisters themselves are elegant if not outstanding. They have the distinction, however, of having once been the city's official home for stray cats. Scraps collected every day from all parts of Florence were brought here and handed out daily at noon to the famished felines. The library, or Biblioteca Laurenziana, is reached up a short three-part flight of stairs—a little masterpiece of design—in the cloister just by the entrance to the church proper.

The library is famous both for its magnificent collections of ancient Greek and Latin manuscripts and for its unusual architecture, the work of Michelangelo. The library was commissioned by Pope Clement VII, a Medici needless to say, in 1524 to house the family's growing collections

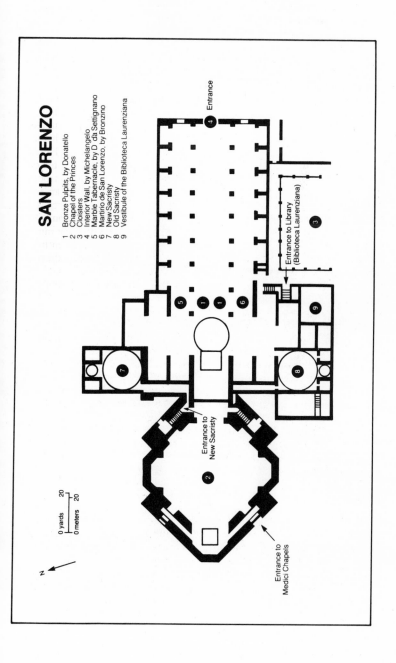

SAN LORENZO

1 Bronze Pulpits, by Donatello
2 Chapel of the Princes
3 Cloisters
4 Interior Wall, by Michelangelo
5 Marble Tabernacle, by D. da Settignano
6 Martirio de San Lorenzo, by Bronzino
7 New Sacristy
8 Old Sacristy
9 Vestibule of the Biblioteca Laurenziana

Entrance

Entrance to Library
(Biblioteca Laurenziana)

Entrance to
New Sacristy

Entrance to
Medici Chapels

0 yards   20
0 meters   20

N

of books and manuscripts. As with so many of his projects, this one was
endlessly delayed, with Michelangelo being frequently called away to
Rome. The vestibule in fact, though designed by Michelangelo, was completed only after his death. As has been pointed out on numerous occasions, Michelangelo's use of contrasting gray stone—*pietra serena*—and
white walls imparts a distinctly sculptural quality to the library. But of
more immediate impact is the curious, slightly cold and almost distorted
quality the great man gave his architecture, chilling in every sense.

The Medici Chapels

From the library you must then leave the church and walk all the way
around it to Piazza Madonna degli Aldobrandini to reach the Medici
Chapels, a remarkable series of buildings containing the tombs of practically every member of the Medici. Entering the chapels, you walk first
through the crypt of the Cappella dei Principi, the Chapel of the Princes,
externally at least the most striking structure of the complex and built at
the beginning of the 17th century. The crypt, smoothly subterranean, contains Cosimo the Elder's simple tomb and, next to it, that of Donatello,
so devoted to his patron that he asked to be buried next to him. The stairs
on the right lead up to the Chapel of the Princes itself. Spacious and airy,
it nonetheless manages to convey a sense of claustrophobia through its
bewildering array of colored marbles and semi-precious stones, the whole
striking a distinctly gaudy note reminiscent of a certain kind of funeral
parlor. Six Medici are buried here, while along the baseboard are inlaid
coats-of-arms of the 16 Tuscan territories ruled by the family.

From here, head into Michelangelo's New Sacristy, the entrance to
which is diagonally opposite that to the Chapel of the Princes. This was
the artist's first architectural work, commissioned in 1520 by Cardinal Giulio de' Medici and Pope Leo X, son of Lorenzo the Magnificent. As with
the Laurentian Library, work on the building proceeded only slowly, with
numerous interruptions, chiefly during the exile of the Medici from Florence between 1527 and 1530 and then after 1534 when Michelangelo left
Florence for good, disillusioned with the political climate in the city. The
architecture was finished in the middle of the century by other hands,
though to Michelangelo's designs. What remained unfinished, however,
were the tombs themselves. The original plan had called for three of these,
but only two were constructed. They remain, however, a stunning pair,
among the artist's most dramatic and moving creations.

The two Medici thus honored are Lorenzo, duke of Urbino and grandson of Lorenzo the Magnificent, and Giuliano, duke of Nemours, and third
son of Lorenzo the Magnificent. Interestingly, for all the splendor of their
tombs, they were no more than minor members of the mighty dynasty.
Each tomb boasts a seated statue of the man it commemorates, Lorenzo
plunged deep in thought, Giuliano seated in his armor, alert and ready
for action. Below both are reclining nude figures: Dawn and Dusk below
Giuliano, Night and Day below Lorenzo. They represent the typical Mi-
chelangelesque obsession with the passage of time and inevitability of
death. Opposite the tombs is the tomb of Lorenzo the Magnificent,
brought here after the building had been completed. It contains only one
work by Michelangelo, a *Madonna and Child,* the artist's last sculpture
of this subject. Lorenzo's brother Giuliano is also buried here, though

again not in a tomb designed by Michelangelo. Architecturally, the New Sacristy is a striking contrast to Brunelleschi's Old Sacristy. Where Brunelleschi strove to achieve balance, harmony and grace in his building, Michelangelo created a characteristically melancholic and obsessional interior, complex and more than a little disturbing with its strangely distorted forms and hidden light sources. As is so often the case in Florence today, however, the crowds that flock here make it difficult to appreciate the place.

Palazzo Medici-Riccardi

Diagonally opposite San Lorenzo is Palazzo Medici-Riccardi, built in the middle of the 15th century for Cosimo the Elder by architect Michelozzo. This was the Medici's principal Florentine residence for almost 100 years, and tremendously influential on the design of many later Florentine palaces. Michelangelo lived here for two years as a youth under the aegis of Lorenzo the Magnificent, and Catherine de' Medici, later queen of France, was born here. In 1659 it was taken over by another powerful Florentine clan, the Riccardi, who extended it. Today it is the city prefecture.

Walk into the elegantly arcaded courtyard. Here there's a small museum, also used for temporary exhibits, containing Lorenzo the Magnificent's death mask; the tunic worn by his brother Giuliano at his death has the rents of the Pazzi daggers still clearly visible; and a *Madonna and Child* by Filippo Lippi. The major point of interest in the palazzo is the chapel, however, reached by a little staircase by the courtyard. Designed by Michelozzo with coffered ceiling and beautiful marble floor, the chapel is famous chiefly for the brilliantly colored and detailed fresco of the *Journey of the Magi* that covers almost the entire wall space. Painted by Benozzo Gozzoli at more or less the same time as the palace was being built, it is a veritable explosion of color, like a brilliant tapestry. But its real interest is not so much its decorative quality, striking though this is, as its marvelously detailed portrayal of Florentine courtly life in the mid 15th century. Despite his ostensible subject matter, Gozzoli has really produced an out and out portrait of the family of his patron, snaking in a gorgeous procession through the Florentine hills. To the left of the door, the handsome youth on a fiery charger is probably the assassinated Giuliano de' Medici. The three girls behind the king on the wall opposite the altar are the daughters of Piero the Gouty and Lucrezia Tornabuoni. Lorenzo the Magnificent, their brother, parades across the adjacent wall on his glorious steed. Gozzoli included a portrait of himself; he is in the crowd behind Lorenzo, the words *opus Benotti* written in gold across his cap. His teacher, Fra Angelico, stands behind him.

If you're lucky, you may find this jewel-like little room mercifully almost empty. It is not on many of the main tour routes. The gallery on the same floor of the palace was decorated in the mid 17th century by Neapolitan painter Luca Giordano, and contains a series of sumptuous frescoes glorifying the Medici.

You emerge from the palace on to Via Cavour, named after the hero of Italian unification (until 1860 and the fall of the dukes of Lorraine, this, then the largest street in Florence, was called the Via Larga). The house at #13 was built in the 18th century over the remains of several older

Medici residences. After Duke Cosimo I moved the Medici family home to the Palazzo Vecchio in around 1540, these original buildings were turned over to the widows, children and members of the cadet line of the family. One of them was Lorenzino, who subsequently murdered Alessandro de' Medici. After Lorenzino had been duly declared a traitor, his house was torn down and the site abandoned for two centuries until, in the 18th century, the existing building was put up. A plaque testifies that the composer Rossini also lived here for a time.

SIGHTSEEING DATA. For general information on museum and church opening times and entrance fees, see "Sightseeing Tips" under *Miscellaneous* in the *Practical Information for Florence*.

Biblioteca Laurenziana (Laurentian Library), Church of San Lorenzo, Piazza San Lorenzo 9. Open Mon. to Sat. 8–2. Closed Sun. and Aug. Admission free.

Cappelle Medicee (Medici Chapels), Piazza Madonna degli Aldobrandini. Open Tues. to Sat. 9–2, Sun. 9–1. Admission 4,350 lire.

Cenacolo del Ghirlandaio (The Last Supper), Borgognissanti 42. Open 9–12, 4–6.

Chiostri Monumentali (Cloisters of Santa Maria Novella), Piazza Santa Maria Novella. Open Mon. to Thurs., Sat. 9–2, Sun. 9–1. Closed Wed. Admission 3,000 lire.

Palazzo Medici-Riccardi, Via Cavour 1. Open Thurs. to Sat., Mon. and Tues. 9–12, 3–5, Sun. 9–noon. Closed Wed. Admission free.

San Marco, the Accademia and Santi Annunziata

This chapter takes in the major sites in the north of the city, all of them easily reached from the center up Via Cavour. Make first for the attractive little Piazza San Marco, overlooked by the graceful Baroque facade of the church of San Marco. From here, head west down Via degli Arazzieri, which, after one block, becomes Via 27 Aprile. Here, at # 1 is the entrance to the Convent of Sant'Apollonia, the refectory of which houses Andrea del Castagno's dramatic *Last Supper,* painted in 1450. The nuns here lived in such strict seclusion that the frescoes remained almost completely unknown until the convent was closed in 1860. Above the *Last Supper* are three further frescoes by Castagno: the *Crucifixion, Deposition* and the *Resurrection,* less famous perhaps than the celebrated *Last Supper* but none the less remarkable.

Outside, head north up Via San Gallo where, at # 74, you'll find Palazzo Pandolfini. It was designed by Raphael but is unfortunately not open to the public, though you may be able to peep through the main gate. From the palace, turn right into Via Salvestrini and then right again back into Via Cavour. Within just a few yards you'll come to the entrance to the elegant little Chiostro dello Scalzo, a cloister built for the Confraternity of St. John the Baptist. Andrea del Sarto's 16 frescoes here depicting the life of the saint are among his greatest works. Executed over a 12-year period beginning in 1514, the pictures were painted, rather unusually, in a sort of monochrome and employ a delicate and skillful *chiaroscuro,* or variations in light and shade.

San Marco

Founded in 1299, the church and monastery of San Marco were handed over to the Dominicans in about 1440 when, with Cosimo the Elder footing the bill, the complex was extensively remodeled by Michelozzo. The church itself was added to again in about 1580 and largely rebuilt in 1678, while in 1780 a new facade was added. Among the Dominicans who lived and worshipped here in the Renaissance were: Sant'Antonino, who became archbishop of Florence in 1446; Savonarola, banished from the city in 1487 before being recalled in 1489 to become prior of San Marco and to rivet all Florence with his terrifying denunciations of moral corruption and Renaissance hedonism and, in 1494, briefly to become effective ruler of the city before being burnt at the stake; and Fra Angelico, the painter-monk, Beato Angelico as the Italians call him. It is the work of Fra Angelico that now constitutes the principal attraction at San Marco.

During his many years as a friar here Fra Angelico, aided by a variety of assistants, decorated much of the monastery with frescoes of religious subjects, chiefly with the object of providing the other friars with images

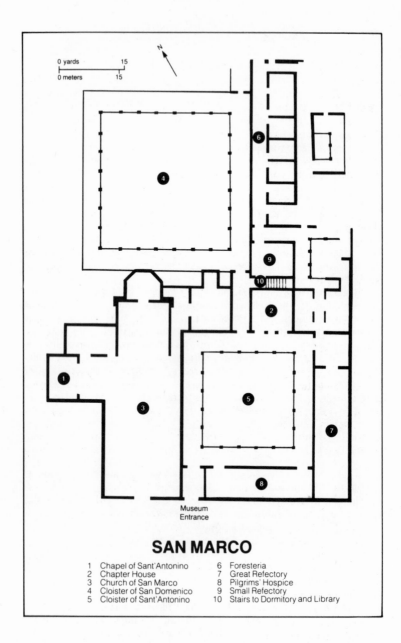

0 yards 15
0 meters 15

N

SAN MARCO

1 Chapel of Sant'Antonino
2 Chapter House
3 Church of San Marco
4 Cloister of San Domenico
5 Cloister of Sant'Antonino

6 Foresteria
7 Great Refectory
8 Pilgrims' Hospice
9 Small Refectory
10 Stairs to Dormitory and Library

Museum
Entrance

of contemplation and inspiration. The presence of so many of the humble monk's works has lead to the establishment at San Marco of a permanent museum—the Museo dell'Angelico—devoted to Fra Angelico. Many of his works from other churches in Florence have been brought here to augment the already rich collections.

Before heading into the monastery buildings, however, look around the church itself. Michelozzo gave it a richly-gilded coffered ceiling, but the original 14th-century polychrome wooden ceiling may still be seen: ask at the Sacristy and you'll be shown the space formed between the two ceilings. There are a good many works of art in the church, though none of outstanding importance.

The entrance to the monastery and museum is just to the right of the church. It leads into an elegant little cloister, designed by Michelozzo. Immediately to your right is the entrance to the Pilgrim's Hospice, full of masterpieces by Fra Angelico, most originally painted for other churches. Of particular interest is the *Deposition,* a marvelously colored and delicate work. The figure in blue with the black hood is a portrait of Michelozzo. The *Last Judgement* is also here. True to form, the man who couldn't bring himself to paint evil has barely sketched in the figures representing Hell, whereas Paradise is depicted with loving care. Opposite the Hospice, on the other side of the cloister, is the Chapter House, the Sala Capitolare, site of Fra Angelico's large *Crucifixion.*

Just behind the Chapter House are the small refectory—housing Ghirlandaio's *Last Supper*—and the stairs leading up to the dormitory, a series of little cells arranged around three sides of the cloister and all decorated by Fra Angelico and his assistants. To the rear of the cells is the library, outside which Savonarola—who was one of San Marco's most famous monks—was arrested in the 1490s. The library itself, also designed by Michelozzo, breathes the grace and calm of the best early-Renaissance architecture, and always has a large exhibition of manuscript books on view.

The Accademia

The large building on the eastern side of Piazza San Marco, now part of Florence's university, was originally the stables of the grand duke. Being the Medici, mere horses were not good enough to be kept here. Cosimo I, for example, kept lions as well, an appropriate symbol of the city's potency, and of course that of the Medici, too.

Directly down from the university building, located on Via Ricasoli, is the Galleria dell'Accademia. In peak tourist seasons what seems an endless line snakes along the street here, as visitors wait for their chance to see Michelangelo's *David* and the gallery's other treasures.

Beyond the entrance hall, the first large room contains early 16th-century Florentine paintings, including Fra Bartolomeo's *Job,* Filippino Lippi's *St. John the Baptist* and *Mary Magdalene,* a touching *Deposition* begun by Perugino but completed by Filippino Lippi, and Perugino's serene *Assumption with Saints.* Arranged in a corridor leading off this first room are a series of magnificent Michelangelo statues, the "Slaves," many of them intended for the monumental tomb of megalomaniac Pope Julius II that the artist labored over for so many years. Fascinatingly, like the tomb, a great many of these works are unfinished. The powerful, rough-hewn effect created by them is quite remarkable and a striking contrast to the highly finished and exquisitely carved earlier work of the brooding Florentine genius.

The best, or at any rate the most famous, example of this earlier technique is found in the small apse-like room at the end of this corridor. Here stands the original of Michelangelo's *David,* a massive work and the perennial symbol of the Florentine Republic's determination to remain free. The statue is not only a tour de force of magnificent—if somewhat distorted—anatomical detail with its almost tangible sense of physical power, but a technical tour de force too. Michelangelo was obliged to make do with a marble block that was considerably thinner than he had wanted—as the side view makes clear—for it had previously been botched by an earlier sculptor. Today, its major problem—or, to be more accurate, the major problem facing anyone intent on giving it more than a five-second glance for the dubious privilege of being able to boast of having actually seen it—is the shuffling throng of visitors that clusters permanently around it, putting to shame even those crowds of supplicants found paying homage to the *Mona Lisa* in Paris. Go early in the day if you want a relatively leisurely look.

The picture galleries at the Accademia have works by a series of late-Gothic and Renaissance Tuscan painters. In Room III, stop to see the *Visitation,* attributed to Ghirlandaio or Perugino, and Botticelli's *Madonna and Child with St. John and Angels.* The same artist's delicate *Madonna of the Sea* is in the next room. One of the great 14th-century masterpieces, Giovanni da Milano's poignant *Pietà,* is in Room VII.

The Foundling Hospital, Santissima Annunziata, and the Archeological Museum

Outside, take a deep breath and head right along Via Cesare Battisti to Piazza Santissima Annunziata. This charming square is not only among the most beautiful in Florence, it is also the site of perhaps the single most important early-Renaissance building in the city. This is the Ospedale degli Innocenti, the Hospital of the Innocents, the oldest foundling hospital in the world. It was built between 1421 and 1445, but it is its colonnade, a row of simple arches topped by small pedimented windows, that is its great joy and which is generally taken as the first truly classical structure in Florence. It seems almost superfluous to add that it was built by Brunelleschi. The spaces between the arches contain a series of very pretty roundels, each depicting a baby in swaddling clothes, designed in about 1485 by Andrea della Robbia. At one end of the arcade a small window with a grate marks the spot where unwanted babies were deposited on a large turntable which would then be gently rotated inwards by unseen hands. Upstairs is a collection of detached frescoes and a gallery containing 14th-to 18th-century paintings, sculptures, illuminated books and furnishings. Notable are Ghirlandaio's *Adoration of the Magi,* Neri di Bicci's *Coronation of the Virgin* and Botticelli's affectionate *Madonna and Child with an Angel.*

At the northern end of the square is the sumptuous church of the Santissima Annunziata, reconstructed by Michelozzo over four decades in the 15th century, but founded originally in 1250. Through the middle door, surmounted by Ghirlandaio's beautiful *Annunciation* mosaic, you'll enter the tiny votive cloister. Among the many superb frescoes is Andrea del

Sarto's *Birth of the Virgin,* in the far righthand corner. Signed and dated on the chimney, this detailed portrayal of a wealthy Florentine's bedroom is one of the best-known works by this artist who reputedly "could make no mistakes." Legend has it that the woman in the middle is Lucrezia, the matron he married after a courtship that scandalized all Florence. For a self-portrait of the artist, see his *Arrival of the Magi,* on the adjacent wall, in which he is the figure wearing an orange robe. Incidentally, if you're wondering why the Virgin in the fresco to the right of the nativity scene has no face, it's because the artist, Franciabigio, scraped off her features in a fit of rage after learning that the monks had peeped before it was completed!

From the cloister, you then enter the church itself. It is one of the most opulent in Florence, with its heavily gilded ceiling and hundreds of ex-votos in the little marble tabernacle by Michelozzo on the left of the entrance. Legend has it that the image of the Virgin above the altar was painted by a 13th-century monk who stopped short of the head, unable to depict it satisfactorily—an angel generously finished it off while the poor brother slept. Florentine brides always visit this altar and leave their wedding bouquets in homage. Be sure to have a look at Andrea del Castagno's fiercely realistic *Trinity* and haunting *Vision of St. Julian* in the second chapel on the left. Through a door to the left of the church, you can enter the Chiostro dei Morti (Cloister of the Dead) to see Andrea del Sarto's fresco, the *Madonna del Sacco,* or Virgin with a Bag. It's above a doorway.

In the center of the piazza is a grand equestrian statue, cast around 1608 by the sculptor Giambologna. It is in fact his last work. The statue is of Grand Duke Ferdinand I, Medici ruler of Florence. On its pedestal is a bronze queen bee, surrounded by her disciplined swarm. They represent the material opulence the later Medici like to think they brought to Florence, achieved, moreover, without the use of force. Florentines believe you'll have good luck if you can count all the bees without touching them.

On the northeast corner of the piazza, reached from Via Colonna, is the Museo Archeologico, the Archeological Museum. The museum has been greatly reorganized in recent years, chiefly as a result of serious damage in the 1966 floods. The ground floors especially have been modernized, and contrast sharply with the dusty exhibits on the upper floors. The principal treasures of the museum are the Etruscan collections: a magnificent series of vases, sculptures and bronzes that will take your breath away, especially if you haven't had other chances to admire this early Italian civilization's serene art. There is also a rich Egyptian section, put together mostly by Napoleon during his plundering in Egypt.

Santa Maria dei Pazzi and the Synagogue

Finally, you might like to walk east a few blocks down Via Colonna to the convent attached to the church of Santa Maria Maddalena dei Pazzi. The great treasure here is a superb fresco of the *Crucifixion* by Perugino, typically restrained and tranquil.

From here, walk on one block further to Via Farini and turn right. One of the most uncharacteristic buildings in the city is here, the 19th-century synagogue, built in a lavish Moorish style. A small museum charts the history of Florence's Jewish community.

Outlying Places to Visit

Three interesting places that lie beyond the route described above are well worth your attention. The first is the Museo Stibbert, a private home that has become one of the most bizarre museums you are likely to see. It was the collection of Frederick Stibbert, a 19th-century artist and traveler, that he presented to the city of Florence. It has rich leather wall coverings, a world-famous collection of armor that features an entire cavalry battalion on its way to a 15th-century war, and some fine paintings. It is a gorgeous Victorian grab-bag. To get there—it's a long walk—take bus 1 from the Duomo or the station.

The English Cemetery lies to the northeast, on the wide ring avenue that circles the city. It stands on a high knoll, in the middle of Piazza Donatello, and is planted with funereal cypresses. As its name suggests it is fully occupied by English—or English-speaking—tenants. Walter Savage Landor's inscription was written by Swinburne; Elizabeth Barrett Browning, Arthur Clough, Frances Trollope, and Theodore Parker, a celebrated preacher from Lexington Mass., are all here, as well as many unknowns. The tombstones are frequently fine pieces of period art.

Southeast of the cemetery, east of Piazza Beccaria—take the 20 bus from Piazza San Marco—is the Cenacolo di San Salvi, which houses a magnificent *Last Supper* by Andrea del Sarto. It is, in fact, a kind of mini del Sarto collection, with several other works by him as well as copies.

SIGHTSEEING DATA. For general information on museum and church opening times and entrance fees, see "Sightseeing Tips" under *Miscellaneous* in the *Practical Information for Florence*.

Cenacolo di San Salvi, Via di San Salvi 16. Open Tues. to Sun. 9–2. Closed Mon. Admission 2,000 lire.

Cenacolo di Sant'Apollonia, Via XXVII Aprile 25. Open Tues. to Sat. 9–2, Sun. 9–1. Closed Mon. Admission free.

Chiostro dello Scalzo, Via Cavour 69. Open Tues. to Sat. 9–2, Sun. 9–1. Closed Mon. Admission 2,000 lire.

English Cemetery, Piazza Donatello. Ring the bell at the entrance. Open Mon. to Sat. Apr. to Sept. 9–12, Oct. to Mar. 9–12, 3–5; Sun. 9–12.

Galleria dell'Accademia (Academy Gallery), Via Ricasoli 60. Open Tues. to Sat. 9–2, Sun. 9–1. Closed Mon. Admission 4,000 lire.

Museo dell'Angelico, Piazza San Marco 1. Open Tues. to Sat. 9–2, Sun. 9–1. Closed Mon. Admission 3,000 lire.

Museo Archeologico (Archeological Museum), Via della Colonna (Palazzo della Crocetta). Open Tues. to Sat. 9–2, Sun. 9–1. Closed Mon. Admission 3,000 lire.

Museo Ebraico (Jewish Synagogue and Museum), Via Farini. Open May to Sept. Sun., Mon., Wed. 9–6, Tues., Thurs. 9–1, Oct. to Apr. Sun. and Thurs. 9–1. Admission free.

Museo Stibbert, Via Stibbert 26. Open Mon. to Wed., Fri. and Sat. 9–2, Sun. 9–12:30. Closed Thurs. Admission 2,000 lire.

Opificio delle Pietre Dure (Hardstone Workshop), Via Alfani 78. Open Mon. to Sat. 9–1. Closed Sun. Admission 2,000 lire.

Ospedale degli Innocenti (Innocenti Hospital Gallery), Piazza Santissima Annunziata 12. Open Thurs. to Sat., Mon. and Tues. 9–2, Sun. 9–1. Closed Wed. Admission 2,000 lire.

Perugino's Crucifixion, Borgo Pinti 58. Open daily 9–12, 5–7. Admission free.

A Historical Circuit

This section describes a wide swing round the areas encircling the Piazza della Signoria and the Uffizi—which appear in the next chapter. It takes in the church of Orsanmichele, the straw market, Santa Croce, Michelangelo's house, Dante territory, the Badia, and the Bargello. Any part, of course, can be done separately, but it will provide an interesting series of impressions if taken as a whole.

Orsanmichele

A short walk from the Piazza della Signoria in the direction of the Duomo will take you to Via dei Calzaioli (Street of the Stocking-Makers)—many streets in this area are named after the guilds of merchants and craftsmen which dominated Florentine life from medieval times. The Medici themselves were a merchant family above all, and throughout the golden age of the Renaissance, the rich merchant families and guilds made patronizing the arts a most honorable activity. Orsanmichele (as the church of San Michele in Orto is called) is the crowning glory of this philosophy.

You'll find it on the left, two blocks from the Signoria, but don't be surprised if you have trouble recognizing it. Few people would take this building for a church. The original loggia, built in 1290 by Arnolfo di Cambio (who designed the cathedral) for grain storage was burned down in 1304. It was replaced in 1337 by a larger loggia which doubled as a market. The arches were walled up in 1380 so that the building could be used for religious services. Most of the funds were supplied by the Confraternity of San Michele which had received a huge fortune in donations during the disastrous plague of 1348. While the brethren were building their church, in 1404 the guilds added two upper floors for their grain. Business is business!

Before entering the church, circle the building for a look at the statues in the niches, each of which was commissioned by a guild. In Via dei Calzaioli (left to right): for the Judges and Notaries, Giambologna's *St. Luke;* in Donatello and Michelozzo's niche for the Merchants' Tribune, Verrocchio's magnificent bronze *St. Thomas* (due for restoration in 1988–89); Ghiberti's *St. John the Baptist* for the Merchants' Guild, appropriately swathed in lots of fabric. On Via Lamberti (left to right): for the Silk-Weavers and Goldsmiths, *St. John the Evangelist* with a medallion by Andrea della Robbia; for the Physicians and Chemists, the *Madonna of the Roses* with a medallion by Luca della Robbia; for the Furriers, Lamberti's *St. James;* for the Flax-Dressers, young Donatello's *St. Mark.* On

Via Arte della Lana—named for the Clothworkers, one of the richest guilds whose headquarters, now a posh menswear emporium, are joined to the church by an overpass—Nanni di Banco's *St. Eligius* for the Farriers; Ghiberti's *St. Stephen* for the Clothworkers, and the same artist's *St. Matthew,* an appropriate choice for the Bankers.

According to local legend, the Gothic image of *St. Mary of the Trumpet* on the corner of Palazzo dell'Arte della Lana is said to have been successfully invoked to halt a disastrous fire. The side of the church on Via Orsanmichele bears a copy of the greatest sculpture to have adorned it, Donatello's *St. George,* executed for the Armorers. The original is in the Bargello. There are also Nanni di Banco's *Four Crowned Saints* for the Builders, Blacksmiths and Carvers; the same artist's *St. Philip,* commissioned by the Tanners, and a marble *St. Peter* by Donatello for the Butchers.

The entrance to Orsanmichele is on Via Calzaioli. Inside, the pillars and vault are decorated with frescoes commissioned by the guilds which couldn't find space on the exterior for their artistic contributions. Over one altar is Francesco da Sangallo's marble *St. Anne,* commissioned after the city was freed of the hated duke of Athens on the saint's day in 1343. In the right nave is Andrea Orcagna's wonderful tabernacle of inlaid marble.

Across the road from Orsanmichele is the church of San Carlo dei Lombardi with one of the oldest facades in the city. Continue up Via Calzaioli and turn left into Via degli Speziali (Street of the Chemists) which leads to Piazza della Repubblica, an open wound for most Florentines. Originally this was the old market, one of Italy's most picturesque squares, with turreted palaces, tiny churches, loggias and stalls (you'll see lots of pictures in the Florence-As-It-Was Museum). After the unification of Italy the new Savoy monarchy chose Florence as its capital in 1865, and set about making it a modern metropolis. However, the government was soon moved to Rome, but not before it tore down Arnolfo di Cambio's 13th-century city walls (second only to Rome's for size and beauty) and razed the lovely old market to create this unlovely Piazza. However, you can have a pleasant hour here at one of the large outdoor cafes, the most famous being Le Giubbe Rosse, patronized over the years by Henry James, Aldous Huxley, Apollinaire, Maxim Gorky, André Gide, Dylan Thomas, Picasso, Lenin, and dozens more.

Bygone Florence and the Straw Market

On the southeast corner of the square, Via Calimala gets its name from the Greek *kallos malos,* meaning beautiful fleece, for this was the street of the wool merchants. Via Pellicceria is on the next corner; take it to Via Porta Rossa, where a few steps to the right you'll find the austere Palazzo Davanzati (# 9) on your left, site of the Museo della Casa Fiorentina Antica (Museum of the Old Florentine Home). This offers a unique opportunity to see how people lived in centuries gone by. These authentic rooms are quite fascinating, arranged as if the medieval merchant family has just stepped out for an afternoon stroll, with the details correct right down to the antique pasta machine in the kitchen—an interesting room in its own right, at the top of the house where they were sited in those far-off days, presumably to stop the smell of cooking permeating the whole building.

In the nearby square is the Casa Torre Foresi, a medieval town house topped with a good sample of the forest of towers that fringed the Florentine skyline in the 13th century. In those days, keeping up with the Joneses meant building a taller tower. By 1250 things were getting so out of hand that the city limited the height of all constructions to 25 meters (82 ft.).

Take Via Porta Rossa back across Via Pellicceria one block down on your right to Piazza del Mercato Nuovo for the straw market. Once a meeting place for silk and gold merchants, it is now the best place to buy such local crafts as bags, gloves, scarves, lace, straw products and Florence's distinctive gilded wooden items. A disc in the middle of the square marks the place where the *Carroccio* was kept in the Middle Ages, but you'll have trouble finding it under the stalls. The Carroccio was a war-chariot covered with standards and banners, symbolizing the freedom of an Italian city, jealously guarded in times of war. On the Arno side of the market is the *Porcellino,* the bronze boar Pietro Tacca modeled in 1612 after the classical marble one in the Uffizi. Hans Christian Andersen wrote a story about a little boy who rides the pig through the streets of the city one night in his dreams. You can rub its shiny snout for good luck and, if you want to be sure to return to Florence, throw a coin into the fountain at its feet.

Running south from the straw market, Via Por Santa Maria is a lively shopping street. Until it was almost entirely destroyed by bombs during World War II, it was one of the most picturesque medieval streets in the city. If you've been wanting a good snap of the Piazza della Signoria, stop at the corner of Via Vacchereccia for it. Then continue two blocks down Via Por Santa Maria where the delightful little church of Santo Stefano al Ponte, with its Romanesque facade, stands in a tiny square off to the left. Severely damaged during the war, the church was completely restored, only to be menaced again by the 1966 flood. For the last few yards Via Por Santa Maria has miraculously conserved some of its wonderful old palazzi. To the right is Lungarno Acciaioli where Longfellow and Dickens stayed at the Arno Hotel, another victim of wartime devastation.

A left turn at the end of the Ponte Vecchio here, and a short walk along the river bank, brings you to the next bridge, Ponte alle Grazie. This area was a favorite with the British. It was here Oscar Wilde wrote *Near the Arno* and D.H. Lawrence had his first Florentine residence. A few yards away from the bridge, at Via de' Benci #6, is the small 15th-century Palazzo Corsi (Museo Horne) that British art critic Herbert Percy Horne bequeathed to the city on his death in 1916 along with paintings by Filippo Lippi, Dosso Dossi, Masaccio and others, clay models by Giambologna and Bernini, and Giotto's splendid *St. Stephen.* Horne's collection also includes an admirable series of drawings by some of the greatest Renaissance artists, as well as some by Gainsborough and Constable. Via de' Benci is named after the family into which the sister of Lorenzo the Magnificent married; she is immortalized in Leonardo's *La Dama del Ginepro.*

Santa Croce

Borgo Santa Croce—second on the right—is worth a short detour. Peek in at the courtyard of # 6, a real 15th-century gem of serenity. Giorgio Vasari, the biographer of Renaissance artists and an artist himself, was born at # 8, and Palazzo Spinelli, at # 10, has another delightful court-

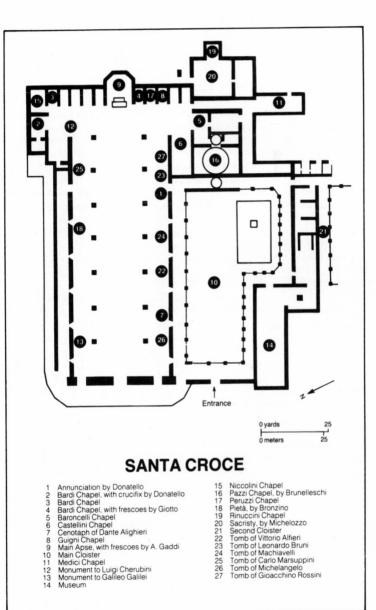

Entrance

0 yards   25
0 meters   25

SANTA CROCE

1 Annunciation by Donatello
2 Bardi Chapel, with crucifix by Donatello
3 Bardi Chapel
4 Bardi Chapel, with frescoes by Giotto
5 Baroncelli Chapel
6 Castellini Chapel
7 Cenotaph of Dante Alighieri
8 Guigni Chapel
9 Main Apse, with frescoes by A. Gaddi
10 Main Cloister
11 Medici Chapel
12 Monument to Luigi Cherubini
13 Monument to Galileo Galilei
14 Museum
15 Niccolini Chapel
16 Pazzi Chapel, by Brunelleschi
17 Peruzzi Chapel
18 Pietà, by Bronzino
19 Rinuccini Chapel
20 Sacristy, by Michelozzo
21 Second Cloister
22 Tomb of Vittorio Alfieri
23 Tomb of Leonardo Bruni
24 Tomb of Machiavelli
25 Tomb of Carlo Marsuppini
26 Tomb of Michelangelo
27 Tomb of Gioacchino Rossini

yard with Corinthian columns and floral decorations. Retrace your steps and continue a little way up Via de' Benci, turning left into Piazza dei Peruzzi. Lined with 14th-century houses and towers, this piazza has retained the curved form of the Roman amphitheater over which it was built. Follow the curve round, along Via Bentaccord and into Via Anguillera. A plaque at the corner marks the house where Michelangelo spent his adolescence.

The street comes out opposite Piazza Santa Croce, site of the city's first popular government in 1250, and later used for jousting tournaments. Later still, popular soccer games were held here, the most famous being one played during Charles V's siege of 1529. This was the plucky Florentines' way of showing their enemies that they weren't done for yet. A marble disc on the facade of # 21 (with delightful decorations executed in 20 days by 12 artists) marks the median line for ball games which are still played today in June after a colorful parade of horsemen, bandoliers and infantry in 16th-century costume. The final game is played at 5.30 P.M. on June 24th, in honor of St. John. The teams, representing the San Giovanni, Santa Croce, Santa Maria Novella and Santo Spirito neighborhoods, play rough and sometimes so do the spectators. After some major historical landmarks suffered damage in the melee, the games were moved to more suitable venues and the winning team no longer gets a calf to roast. Buy your tickets at the Chiosco degli Sportivi, Via degli Anselmi, near Piazza della Repubblica.

Despite its rather unsuccessful mock Gothic facade, sponsored by Englishman Francis Sloan in 1863, the church of Santa Croce is perhaps the loveliest Gothic church in Italy. Its unusual interior is based on the shape of an Egyptian (tau) cross. So many luminaries are buried here that it has been dubbed Italy's Westminster Abbey. Note the ceiling's wooden beams and the 279 tombstones on the floor; until recently the walls were literally encrusted with more of the same. Michelangelo's tomb is on the right wall—he chose this spot so that he could see Brunelleschi's dome when the doors were open. It is a large and somewhat melodramatic monument executed by Vasari, in which the weeping figures of Painting, Sculpture, and Architecture remember the night the artist died, when the whole city flocked in tears to see his battered face one last time.

The next monument is Florence's tribute to the banished Dante, exiled even in death. The next—by the internationally famous neo-classical sculptor, Canova—celebrates Italy's great poet, Vittorio Alfieri. It was commissioned by Louise d'Albany, who left her husband Bonnie Prince Charlie to spend 20 years of extramarital bliss with Alfieri. Her own monument, in the Castellani chapel in the right transept, was the last in Europe to bear the lion and unicorn of the Stuart arms. Next to Alfieri's, Machiavelli's unimpressive monument carries a Latin inscription which reads "For such greatness no eulogy can suffice." Beyond, Donatello's magnificent *Annunciation* is made of gilded stone, even though it looks carved from wood. Next to it is Rossellino's trend-setting tomb of Leonardo Bruni, dated 1444. Opposite it, in the left aisle, stands Desiderio da Settignano's delicately sculpted tomb of Carlo Marsuppini.

The Baroncelli chapel at the end of the right transept was decorated by Giotto's disciple, Taddeo Gaddi, with a fresco of the *Life of the Virgin.* Then comes the entrance to a corridor leading to Michelozzo's austere sacristy. Across the sacristy lies the Rinuccini chapel, with some outstanding 14th-century frescoes. Back along the corridor is the Medici chapel, designed for Cosimo the Elder by Michelozzo; note here Andrea della Robbia's unusual *Madonna and Saints.*

Returning to the body of the church, the chapels flanking the principal altar hold some exceptional works of art. Two Bonapartes are buried in the third chapel from the right facing the altar, the Giugni. Next is the Peruzzi chapel, with frescoes of scenes from the life of St. John by the elderly Giotto. These paintings have deteriorated badly, partly because they were originally done on dry walls, but also because they were covered with whitewash in the 18th century (as were countless other precious frescoes in the city) then badly restored during the 19th. Giotto painted every inch of the Bardi chapel, next along, with scenes from the life of St. Francis of Assisi, and here the frescoes are in better condition.

Agnolo Gaddi's frescoes in the main apse date from 1380. The massive wooden crucifix and altarpiece, by 15th-century artists, gleam with gold. In another Bardi chapel, fifth left from the main altar, an interesting fresco shows St. Silvester closing the dragon's mouth and resuscitating two wizards killed by the beast's breath; the scene is set in the Roman forum. Next door in the Niccolini chapel, one of the first pre-Baroque structures to be decorated with polychrome marble, is a copy of Michelangelo's *Moses.* Yet another Bardi chapel is at the end of the left transept; behind the great wrought iron screen is Donatello's poignant wooden crucifix which Brunelleschi scornfully called a "peasant on the cross." Just before turning the corner you'll see the monument to the composer Luigi Cherubini, a local parishioner. Galileo Galilei's memorial is the last on this side of the nave. He was buried in this spot in 1642 but not granted a Christian burial until 1737, when a monument was set up to him, located a few feet inside the west door. This is not to be confused with the tomb of one of his doctor ancestors with the same name, just a few feet away in the center of the nave.

For the museum and the Pazzi chapel, go through the cloister at # 16, on your left as you leave the church. A plaque here once commemorated Florence Nightingale, born in this city and named after it. This plaque and hundreds of others were lost during the 1966 flood—the waters reached 15 feet here. The museum contains many Florentine masterpieces, notably Cimabue's *Crucifixion,* the flood's most illustrious victim, but you can still make out the sinuous lines of Christ's body and the lifelike expression on his face. The museum also boasts Donatello's *St. Louis of Toulouse,* one of his earliest works, and Bronzino's *Christ in Limbo,* strangely sensual for an altar painting.

At the far end of the airy main cloister stands the Pazzi chapel, Brunelleschi's exquisite exercise in proportion. From the gray stone accents on the white walls to the terracotta medallions by Luca della Robbia—the only elements of color in the chapel—nothing is out of place. Both the cloisters are atmospheric works of art in their own right, and lovely places to relax in.

Stop off for a well-deserved *gelato* (superb fruit ice cream, such as wild strawberry) at popular Vivoli, in Via Isola delle Stinche, before proceeding to Via Giovanni da Verrazzano—of Narrows fame—on the right of the square (looking from the church); a plaque marking the explorer's home was placed at #20 in 1909, the "year the United States celebrated the British continuers of this Florentine's work."

Returning to Piazza Santa Croce, turn left down Via di San Giuseppe until you come to the tiny church of Santa Maria della Croce al Tempio, founded in 1428 for the comfort of prisoners awaiting execution. After this the street is called Via de' Malcontenti in memory of the many unfortunates who trudged along it to meet their fate. Retrace your steps a bit (three blocks) and take Borgo Allegri on your right, where the house at #78 was the birthplace of Lorenzo Ghiberti of the Baptistery doors.

Turn left onto Via Ghibellina. The house one block up, at the corner of Via Buonarroti, purchased by Michelangelo for his nephew, is now the Buonarroti museum. Here you will see several portraits of the master, along with some of his personal belongings. The museum also has the plans for the fortification of Florence during the 1530 siege, and dozens of drawings, sketches, and clay models of Michelangelo's work on display. Among the many fascinating pieces to be seen are two amazingly assured early works, created when the master was still in his teens, the marble *Madonna of the Steps,* and *The Battle of the Centaurs.*

Dante Territory

To make the historical jump from Michelangelo land to Dante territory, turn west along Via Ghibellina to Via Giuseppi Verdi, then turn right and walk along to Piazza Salvemini. From here you will plunge into a maze of little streets and alleyways between the Duomo and Piazza della Signoria.

Head down Borgo degli Albizi to the tiny little Piazza San Pier Maggiore. What looks like an old city gate here was in fact the church of San Pier Maggiore. You've entered the territory of the Donati family, one of the most powerful medieval clans in Florence. The tower on the left was one of their residences, as was the palazzo with adjoining medieval tower at # 11. Borgo degli Albizi has a series of wonderful courtyards. Those at # 14 and 15 are particularly fine. Heading west, the Pazzi coat of arms appears over the arched vault of an alleyway, Volta dei Ciechi. Note the faded but charming 14th-century shrine on the corner of Via de' Giraldi, and peep into the old paper warehouse at # 86r.

Where Via Proconsolo meets Borgo degli Albizi you'll find two palaces. To the north is Palazzo Nonfinito, now the Museo Nazionale di Antropologia ed Etnologia (the Museum of Anthropology and Ethnology); to the south is Palazzo Pazzi-Quartes. Palazzo Nonfinito, built from the end of the 16th century but never entirely finished, as its name makes clear, boasts a splendid courtyard, rigorously classical. The museum houses collections of tools, artefacts and craftwork from every corner of the world. Palazzo Pazzi-Quartes, built in the middle of the 15th century, was the family home of the Pazzi. It was here that Jacopo Pazzi fled in 1478 having fatally stabbed Giuliano de' Medici in the Duomo, and from here that he was dragged to be hanged from Palazzo Vecchio.

At this point Borgo degli Albizi becomes Via del Corso. This signals your entrance into Dante land. At # 6 is the lovely 16th-century Palazzo Salviati, built on the site of the Portinari family home where Dante first saw his beloved Beatrice. He was only nine at the time, but old enough to know he'd fallen in love for life. The two youngsters often met at the tiny church of Santa Margherita, just a step away. But marriages for love were practically unheard of in Dante's day, and his father, a man of modest means with an eye on the social ladder, wasn't about to miss the chance to betroth his son to Gemma, ugly daughter of the powerful Donati family. It was either in Santa Margherita or at the nearby church of San Martino that the two were married. While you're here, pay a visit to Dante's probable birthplace at Via Santa Margherita # 1, now the Casa di Dante.

The Badia and the Bargello

A block or two down from Palazzo Nonfinito and Palazzo Pazzi-Quartes on Via Proconsolo is the Badia, originally a Benedictine church, built in around 980, but reconstructed in the prevailing Baroque manner in the 1620s. The entrance is just on Piazza San Firenze, through a richly ornamented doorway that gives onto a Renaissance arcade. Off to the right is the gracious hexagonal bell tower, with two rows of Romanesque windows surmounted by two more rows of Gothic ones. Inside the church, notice the carved wood ceiling and Filippino Lippi's exquisite *Madonna Appearing to St. Bernard.* The cloisters have more frescoes of the saint's life. On your way out, have a look at the second chapel on the right side of the arcade, the former location of the church of Santo Stefano Protomartire. Here, 50 years after Dante had died in exile, the Florentine Republic asked Boccaccio to give the first public reading of Dante's *Divine Comedy.*

Across the street from the Badia is the grim bulk of the Bargello, archetypically Florentine and central to the city's history. Built in the 13th and 14th centuries, it was originally the residence of the Podestà, the leading civil magistrate. Then it served as a prison from the 16th century to the middle of the 19th century.

The oldest part of the building is the bell tower, which dates back to 1250. For half a century, until it was melted down and recast, the bell would toll every evening to signal the curfew. Anyone found abroad after this hour would be punished by the amputation of a hand. This extraordinary cruelty was by no means confined to curfew violators. Those found guilty of other crimes were exhibited in iron cages for the citizens of Florence to jeer and poke at them. Criminals who were lucky enough to escape the long arm of the law were struck by the wicked arm of art. Their effigies were painted upside down on the tower walls. Andrea del Castagno painted so many Medici enemies he came to be known as Andrea degli Impiccati, "of the hanged." Botticelli portrayed the main wrong-doers in the notorious Pazzi Conspiracy.

Today, the Bargello has long since put behind it this grisly past and is the Museo Nazionale, Italy's leading Renaissance sculpture gallery. Cool and spacious, with the exhibits placed at a reasonable distance from each other, the museum is far more conducive to sensitive appreciation than the crowded Uffizi. Room I, just off the elegantly massive courtyard, contains a superb series of 16th-century works, dominated by Michelangelo. His tipsy, anti-classical *Bacchus* is here, as is his celebrated *Pitti Tondo,* a charming circular relief of the Madonna and Child. Most interesting is his *Brutus,* a late work and generally believed to be the only bust Michelangelo made. It was carved, in a burst of Republican zeal, in 1540, three years after the death of the despotic Alessandro de' Medici, murdered by his idealistic cousin Lorenzino.

Cellini is the other star of this room. Though known today almost as much for his autobiography, a magnificently bombastic piece of work, as for his work, Cellini was in fact a superb craftsman and sculptor, inventive and daring. Among his works here are the model for his exquisite statue of *Perseus,* languidly holding aloft the severed head of Andromeda, in the Loggia dei Signoria, and his virtuoso bust of Cosimo I.

Cross the courtyard, with its cannon and coats of arms, and head up to the loggia on the second floor. Here you'll find Giambologna's extraordinarily life-like bronze animals and his masterpiece, the winged *Mercury,* today, unfortunately for Giambologna, better known as a deliverer of flowers world-wide rather than of divine messages. Just off to the right is a room devoted to Donatello. His glorious *St. George,* shown slaying the dragon, was commissioned for the Armorer and Swordmakers' Guild for the church of Orsanmichele. Among the other treasures by Donatello are the Martelli *St. John,* consumed with the fires of mysticism, and his magnificent bronze *David,* the first free-standing Renaissance nude.

Seven other rooms hold an admirable collection of goldwork, ivories, enamelwork, ceramics and other minor arts. Room IV, decorated with frescoes once attributed to Giotto, was the chapel where the condemned awaited execution. Dante is supposedly shown on these walls, but the poet would never have seen his likeness; it was painted after his exile. Upstairs again are more rooms containing fine works by the Della Robbias and Verrocchio, Leonardo's master. Verrocchio's stunning bronze *David* in Room III is yet another masterful interpretation of a favorite Renaissance subject.

From the Bargello head left into Piazza San Firenze. From the steps of the vast Baroque church of San Firenze—now in the law courts—there's a lovely view of Brunelleschi's dome over the cathedral and of the infamous Bargello bell. Opposite is Palazzo Gondi, built toward the end of the 14th century by Sangallo. Leonardo da Vinci lived at # 2 Via dei Gondi. From here, you are but a step away from Piazza della Signoria, epicenter of the Florentine Republic.

SIGHTSEEING DATA. For general information on museum and church opening times and entrance fees, see "Sightseeing Tips" under *Miscellaneous* in the *Practical Information for Florence.*

Casa Buonarroti (Michelangelo's House), Via Ghibellina 70. Open Wed. to Mon. 9–1. Closed Tues. Admission 4,000 lire.

Casa di Dante (Dante's House), Via Santa Margherita 1. Open Thurs. to Sat., Mon. and Tues. 9:30–12:30, 3:30–6:30. Closed Wed. Admission free.

Museo del Bargello, Via del Proconsolo 4. Open Tues. to Sat. 9–2, Sun. 9–1. Closed Mon. Admission 3,000 lire.

Museo dell'Antica Casa Fiorentina (Museum of the Historical Florentine Home), Via Porta Rossa 13. Open Tues. to Sat. 9–1:30, Sun. 9–12:30. Closed Mon. Admission 2,000 lire.

Museo dell'Opera di Santa Croce (Santa Croce Museum), Piazza Santa Croce 16. Open Thurs. to Tues., 9–12:30, 3–6:30. Closes at 5 in winter. Closed Wed. Admission 2,000 lire.

Museo di Storia della Scienza (History of Science Museum), Piazza dei Giudici 1. Open Mon., Wed. and Fri. 9:30–1, 2–5. Admission 5,000 lire.

Museo Horne, Via dei Benci 6. Open Mon. to Sat. 9–1. Closed Sun. Admission 1,500 lire.

Museo Storico Topografico: Firenze Com'era (Florence As It Was Museum), Via dell'Oriuolo 24. Open Fri., Sat. and Mon. to Wed. 9–2, Sun. 9–1. Closed Thurs. Admission 1,000 lire.

Santa Croce, Open 7–12:30, 3–6:30.

Palazzo Vecchio and the Uffizi

If ever proof were needed of the self-confidence and daring that buoyed up Florence toward the end of the Middle Ages and swept it along until it exploded into the Renaissance, it is supplied in plenty by Piazza della Signoria. This splendid open space, vast in comparison to the cramped and twisting streets that surround it, was laid out originally in about 1300, at more or less the same time that the heavy bulk of Palazzo Vecchio was built. It was expanded greatly toward the end of the century until, by 1385, it had reached more or less its present dimensions. At about the same time, the lofty and spacious Loggia dei Lanzi, originally known as the Loggia della Signoria, was also put up. The grandeur of these buildings and their setting are the clearest possible evidence of the powerful sense of civic pride and wealth the Florentines enjoyed, and of their tremendous confidence in themselves and their city. It was only natural that, in 1504, the Republic should have chosen to display here Michelangelo's giant *David,* enduring symbol of freedom and the triumph of Republicanism.

This was the *real* heart of Florence—the seat of power in Palazzo Vecchio and, outside, an ideal arena for any public event from riots to festivals. Florentines hope that by the end of 1989 their great piazza will be presentable again—that the restoration of Palazzo Vecchio and the Loggia dei Lanzi will have been completed so that they will be entirely visible again, and that the controversial question of repaving the piazza and covering up the archeological remains found there will have been settled. Since some very interesting chunks of ancient Roman and early medieval Florence have been uncovered under Piazza della Signoria, archeologists want to keep digging, at least in patches. Florentines hold this detrimental to the dignity of their beloved square and want the 18th-century gray paving stones put back in place.

Around Piazza della Signoria

The dominant building by far in the piazza is Palazzo Vecchio, the Old Palace, so called because it was from here that Cosimo I moved to the Pitti Palace at the middle of the 16th century. Built from 1299 as the seat of the city's government—the Signoria—it is still Florence's city hall. While the interior of the palace (see below) has undergone numerous restorations and renovations, externally its aspect has remained much as it was when first put up, a great medieval stronghold topped by its distinctive and seemingly top-heavy tower, set off to one side. Running under the arches that form the base of the battlements are the coats of arms of the city's nine districts, solitary splashes of color among the rough, sandy stone.

A number of statues stand in front of it. From left to right as you face the palace they are: the Neptune Fountain, a graceful mid-16th-century fountain by Ammanati, in the center of which stands a vast marble Neptune, considerably criticized for its lack of vigor but impressive nonetheless, if only by virtue of its giant scale; copies of Donatello's heraldic lion of Florence and of his *Judith and Holofernes* (the original has been restored and can be seen inside); a copy of Michelangelo's *David* (the original was moved to the Accademia in 1874); and *Hercules and Cacus,* probably the most mocked work of art in the city, its unhappy reputation stemming from its sculptor, Bandinelli, rashly comparing it to *David* next to which it was set up in about 1540 and against which it pales alarmingly. Adding insult to injury, the block from which it was carved, and which had already been refused by Michelangelo, fell into the Arno before Bandinelli had set to work on it, with the inevitable result that the Florentines claimed that it had tried to commit suicide rather than submit to Bandinelli's chisel. Standing on its own to the left of the palace is Giambologna's bronze equestrian statue of Cosimo I, cast in 1595.

Just a few yards in front of Ammanati's fountain a granite disc marks the spot where Savonarola was executed on May 23, 1498. Thousands crowded into the square to witness the gruesome spectacle, while city notables kept a watchful eye from stands erected especially for the event. Great pains had been taken to keep the gallows from resembling a cross for fear of touching off a popular revolt. By one of those quirks of poetic justice that makes history such a delight, the firebrand priest—an early version of the Ayatollah Khomeni—was put to death on the very spot where he had fanatically caused huge Bonfires of Human Vanities to be lit, burning pictures, books, musical instruments, cosmetics, masks, and many other profane objects.

At #5, above the bank, is a collection of modern art—the Raccolta Alberto della Ragione—a private donation which would certainly have been fuel for Savonarola's bonfire.

The Loggia dei Lanzi

To the right of Palazzo Vecchio is the Loggia dei Lanzi, today a veritable open-air display case of fine sculptures (at presstime still undergoing structural repairs, with some statues slated for restoration when the main job is finished). The Loggia was built as a grandoise setting for the public ceremonies of the Signoria, the city government. As has been remarked by many, its three giant roundheaded arches, very different from the pointed Gothic arches of the period, look forward to the revival of classical architecture that the Renaissance so decisively introduced. But it should still be seen as a Gothic structure, and as such a marvelous example of the central Italians' free way with Gothic models.

The two most important sculptures in the loggia are Cellini's *Perseus,* the model for which is in the Bargello, and, at the far right hand side of the loggia, Giambologna's *Rape of the Sabines.* Between them, on either side of the small flight of steps, are two lions, that on the left a 15th-century copy of the original ancient Greek lion on the right. A series of generally less important Roman sculptures lines the rear of the loggia, while three further creations—the one on the far left, *Hercules and the Centaur,* is also by Giambologna—stand along the center line.

But the *Perseus* is the finest work here. It was cast by Cellini in 1545 and, in a typical display of bravado, carries the name of the sculptor on the sash draped over Perseus' torso. It is, however, a superb piece of crafts-manship, alive with wonderful details, from the gorgeous winged cap perched on the languid youth's curly mop to the four charming figures that decorate the base (these are copies; the originals are also in the Bargel-lo). Like Michelangelo's *David,* the work also had important political over-tones. But whereas the *David* celebrates the triumph *of* Republicanism, *Perseus,* commissioned by Cosimo I, is a paean to the grand duke's despot-ic triumph *over* Republicanism. Such was the volatility of 16th-century Florentine political life. Giambologna's complex and muscular *Rape of the Sabines* dates from 1579–83. Like Cellini, Giambologna was concerned here as much as anything to display his own virtuosity, specifically to create a completely three-dimensional group that could be seen from any angle. Giambologna has frequently suffered from comparisons with Mi-chelangelo, but this powerful and assured work, the sculptor's last, makes clear that such comparisons are not always fair.

Inside Palazzo Vecchio

The interior of Palazzo Vecchio, a magnificent array of Renaissance and Mannerist decoration, Medicean vainglory and priceless furnishings, pres-ents a striking contrast to its rough-hewn exterior. As it is still the seat of the city's government, significant sections of the palace are not open to the public, but almost all the state rooms and more interesting private apartments can be seen.

The palace provides an accurate reflection of the changing political cli-mate of 15th- and 16th-century Florence. From its foundation in 1300 to the establishment of the Florentine Republic in 1494, the palace was known as the Palazzo del Popolo. A considerable quantity of painting and decoration, modest in comparison to what came later but of interest none-theless, was carried out during this period, especially around the middle of the 15th century. During the short-lived Republic (1494–1512) its name was changed to Palazzo della Signoria after the elected officers, the Sig-noria, that made up the government. It's a name that is still sometimes used. This period also saw the construction of the most imposing room in the palace, the Salone dei Cinquecento or Hall of the Five Hundred, so-called because it was here that the 500 members of the Republican gov-ernment met. A number of ambitious decorative schemes celebrating the Republic were put in hand during this period, few of which, unfortunately, materialized. But the key moment in the history of the palace, as least as far as its appearance is concerned, came in 1540. It was then that Cosimo I de' Medici, by now grand duke of Florence and hereditary ruler of the city, decided that he should live here. The palace accordingly had its name changed again, becoming the Palazzo Ducale, was extended to the rear, and Vasari was called in to take charge of the massive redecoration, all trumpeting the Medici in one way or another.

Entering through the main door on Piazza della Signoria, the contrast between medieval exterior and Renaissance interior is immediately appar-ent. You walk into a graceful little courtyard, built by Michelozzo in 1453

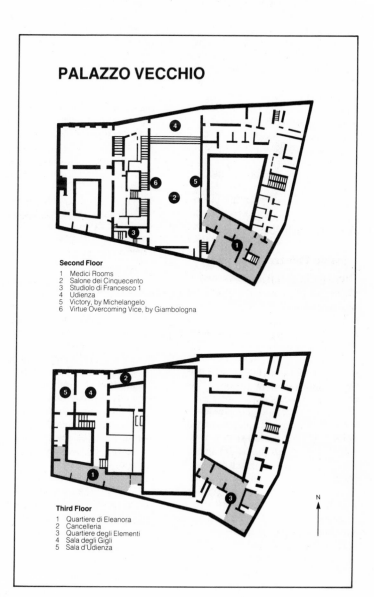

PALAZZO VECCHIO

Second Floor

1 Medici Rooms
2 Salone dei Cinquecento
3 Studiolo di Francesco 1
4 Udienza
5 Victory, by Michelangelo
6 Virtue Overcoming Vice, by Giambologna

Third Floor

1 Quartiere di Eleanora
2 Cancelleria
3 Quartiere degli Elementi
4 Sala degli Gigli
5 Sala d'Udienza

N

but redecorated by Vasari and his assistants in 1565 in celebration of the marriage of Francesco, son of Cosimo I, to Joan of Austria. The "grotesque" decorations here—grotesque only in an art historical sense: this is a technical term used to describe the many little ornamental details painted all over the courtyard walls, the form of which were loosely taken from antique models—is absolutely typical of Mannerist decoration. There's a pretty little fountain in the middle of the courtyard with a copy of Verrocchio's bronze *Boy with a Dolphin* on top of it.

A handsome staircase, built by Vasari, leads from the courtyard to the second floor and the Salone dei Cinquecento. The room is, without doubt, Vasari's masterwork (if not his masterpiece), containing a series of vast frescoes proclaiming the virtues of Medici Florence and the Medici themselves, chiefly victories of Florence over neighboring cities. The richly gilded coffered ceiling panels also contain a series of allegorical works, all underlining further the splendor and magnificence of the Medici, particularly Cosimo I. Around the walls are arranged a series of statues, most by a somewhat obscure Florentine sculptor called Vincenzo di Rossi, of the labors of Hercules. They present a rather comical contrast to the best works here: Giambologna's *Virtue Overcoming Vice* and, directly opposite it, Michelangelo's *Victory* group, intended for Pope Julius II's tomb but placed here in 1565. At one end of the room is the Udienza, a raised dais decorated with a further series of heroic statues.

Interestingly, this enormous room is almost as famous for two monumental frescoes that were never actually painted as it is for its great Cosimo inspired decorations. Just as Cosimo wished his deeds and person to be celebrated in paint, so the Republic, in 1503, commissioned the two foremost artists of the day, Leonardo and Michelangelo, to paint two vast scenes of Florentine victories to celebrate the virtues of the city (as opposed to her rulers, as was the case with Cosimo). Neither man got very far. Leonardo began first, but, through a combination of his habitual procrastination and, with hindsight, rash experimentation with untried techniques, what little he did produce before disappearing off to Milan in 1506 either decayed almost immediately or was shortly thereafter destroyed by Cosimo. However, his preparatory drawings survived for long enough for copies to be made—most famously by Rubens—with the result that at least the broad outlines of his intentions are known. Michelangelo didn't even get that far. He did, it is true, like Leonardo, make a fairly detailed preparatory sketch, copies of which also survive, but he never actually painted so much as a single brushstroke before being summoned to Rome by Pope Julius II. An American attempt in the early '80s to prove that Leonardo's fresco, or parts of it anyway, survive behind Vasari's frescoes sadly came to nothing.

At one end of the great room, to the right of the entrance as you come in, is an extraordinary little room, decorated throughout by Vasari and Bronzino in 1570. This is the Studiolo, or study, of Francesco I, son of Cosimo. The room is an almost perfect marriage of tastes and interests between patron and painter. Francesco had a profoundly melancholy disposition and was much given to philosophizing on the world and its mysteries, especially alchemy. The complex and highly ornate allegories with which Vasari set about decorating the room are a perfect pictorial expression of this gilded obsession of the grand duke. From here, a tiny staircase climbs to Cosimo's study, where in the carved walnut cupboards the wily duke is thought to have kept his greatest treasures. Opposite the entrance to the Studiolo is a set of rooms again decorated by Vasari for Cosimo I with a further series of history pictures charting the glorious attributes of the Medici.

Five ramps of stairs, or the elevator, take you to the third floor and the Sala dei Gigli, the Room of the Lilies, so called because of the lilies that decorate it. This is one of the most appealing rooms in the entire palace, decorated mainly by Ghirlandaio toward the end of the 15th century. Leading off it is the office, or Cancelleria, used by Machiavelli when secretary of the Republic. Verrocchio's original bronze *Boy with a Dolphin,* a copy of which is on the fountain in the courtyard downstairs, is here. On the opposite side of the Sala dei Gigli is the Sala d'Udienza, again richly decorated. But the major treasure here is Donatello's bronze *Judith and Holofernes,* one of the earliest Renaissance sculptures intended to be seen in the round. It originally stood in the garden of the Medici palace. In 1495, following the expulsion of the Medici from Florence, it was placed in front of the Palazzo Vecchio by the Republican government. The work shows Judith, sword raised, about to decapitate the sleeping Holofernes. Never at a loss in ascribing a moral to a good story, the Republic had an inscription placed on the base of the statue as a warning to would-be despots. Surprisingly, Cosimo allowed the statue to stay in front of Palazzo Vecchio, inscription and all, following his rise to power in 1529. It was moved here in 1980.

Backtracking past the stairs you come to Eleonora of Toledo's apartments, decorated with a series of Mannerist frescoes. The most attractive room here is the chapel, frescoed by Bronzino. From here, a narrow corridor leads to the balcony overlooking the Salone dei Cinquecento. A mid-15th-century copy of Leonardo's *Battle of Anghiari*—his doomed fresco in the Salone itself—is here. Just beyond is a further set of apartments, the Quartiere degli Elementi, literally the Rooms of the Elements. These contain a detailed and scholarly set of allegorical frescoes, again by Vasari, charting the Elements. But even those with a more than averagely developed taste for Mannerist allegory will probably have had their fill by now of these highly refined and artificial, in the original sense, works. You may prefer instead to make for the stairs by the Sala dei Gigli and—if it is open (not always the case)—climb the tower to the Little Hostel, the grim cell where Savonarola and, before him, Cosimo the Elder were incarcerated. There's a superb view over the city.

Finally, you can also visit the Loeser Collection, a representative assembly of mainly 15th- and 16th-century Italian works given to the city in 1928 by American art critic Charles Loeser.

The exit from the Palazzo Vecchio is onto Via dei Leoni, at the rear of the building. To get back to Piazza della Signoria, turn right and then right again onto Via della Ninna, passing under the little walkway built in 1565 and linking Palazzo Vecchio with the Uffizi. Incorporated into the wall on your left are some terracotta columns from the ancient church of San Piero Scheraggio which stood on the site now occupied by the Uffizi.

The Uffizi

Running between Piazza della Signoria and the river Arno is the Galleria degli Uffizi, generally known simply as the Uffizi, the foremost art collection in Florence and one of the world's great galleries. It was built by Vasari for Cosimo I between 1560 and 1575 as offices, or *uffizi*, of the city administration, handily positioned next to Palazzo Vecchio for Cosimo to keep an eye on his officials and indeed linked to it by a short aerial walkway (see above). Later, Cosimo also got Vasari to build an enclosed corridor—the famous Corridoio—running the entire way from Palazzo Vecchio, through the Uffizi, over the Arno and thence to Palazzo Pitti, to which Cosimo had then moved, in order to enable the grand duke to get from home to headquarters and vice versa without having to mingle with the common herd. Vasari, ever with an eye on the main chance, lost no opportunity in boasting that the corridor had been built in only five months.

The Uffizi itself occupies rather an awkward site, long and thin and narrower at the river end than at the Palazzo Vecchio end. It also has a road running through it—Piazza degli Uffizi—the end result being that the building itself is U shaped, the arms of the U forming long corridors. It is along these corridors that the great collections are displayed.

Before heading into it, take a look at what remains of Palazzo della Zecca, where for many years the city's famous gold florins were minted. It's on the right, on the ground floor, as you look down Piazza degli Uffizi. In the last century 28 statues of famous Tuscans were set into niches on the ground floor of the Uffizi. They include (counting from the far right corner of the Zecca): 1 Cellini; 9 Galileo; 14 (closest to the Arno on the left) Amerigo Vespucci; 16 Machiavelli; 17 Boccaccio; 18 Petrarch; 19 Dante; 20 Michelangelo; 21 Leonardo; 23 Donatello; 24 Giotto; 26 Andrea Orcagna (gazing toward the Loggia dei Lanzi, which he is thought to have designed).

The Uffizi draws hordes of visitors. In the summer, when frankly it's hell, you may have to wait in line to get in, and then push through the crowds to get a peek at the most famous paintings. The best time to visit is right at opening time or towards closing time. As you make your way through the gallery, try to keep away from the tour groups, who are both noisy and distracting. The ideal time to come here is, of course, the winter, when you can best appreciate the gallery's architectural beauty, lively fresco decorations and chronological arrangement of its paintings, which illustrate clearly the development of Florentine Renaissance painting. It's easy to advise making two or more visits, but possibly very much harder to put into practice. But if you can afford the time, repeat visits are amply repaid. For one thing, you can frequently get to see things second or third time around that were crowded out on earlier visits.

Around the Uffizi

The collections are on the third floor, but pause as you go in to see what's left of the church of San Piero Scheraggio, just beyond the foyer, demolished by Vasari to make room for the Uffizi. You can look down from a walkway at its heavy stone foundations, unearthed in 1971 during restorations occasioned by the 1966 flood. Here, too, are Andrea del Castagno's frescoes of *Illustrious Men and Women,* originally painted for the Villa Pandolfini in Legnaia. In an adjacent room is Botticelli's elegant *Annunciation* fresco. From here, take the elevator or climb the 126 steps of Vasari's staircase to the main galleries. Almost everything is worth seeing, and the following is no more than a brief rundown of the many high-lights.

Room II contains three key pre-Renaissance works by Cimabue, Duccio and Giotto. Their subject is the same, the *Maestà,* the Virgin and Child in majesty. Each shows a new awareness of the naturalistic representation of space and the human form, the Giotto in particular. These are nonethe-less still clearly medieval works, but they look forward confidently to what was to come. In Room III you will find Simone Martini's exquisite *Annun-ciation,* dated 1333. Here the example of Giotto especially is very clear. There is movement in the angel's draperies and in the sinuous figure of Mary, who seems to shrink from the angel's portentous words. Room IV contains Gentile da Fabriano's *Adoration of the Magi,* a work that almost certainly influenced Benozzo Gozzoli's gorgeous treatment of the same subject in Palazzo Medici-Riccardi.

Room VII takes you firmly into the early Renaissance. Here, the *Ma-donna with St. Anne,* painted in 1424 by Masolino and his pupil Masaccio, introduces a new monumentality and weightiness to the figures and the beginnings of a convincingly realistic treatment of space. Paolo Uccello's spectacular *Battle of San Romano,* painted just a few years later, under-lines not only the astonishingly rapid development of the realistic handling of space and the human form in early-Renaissance Florentine painting, but also Uccello's near obsessional interest in perspective, and indeed his love of the dramatic. Room VIII is home to Filippo Lippi's *Madonna and Child with Angels,* the Madonna's devotion contrasting with the saucy glee of the angels. There are several other works by Filippo Lippi in this room.

You're bound to find a traffic jam in Rooms X to XIV, now knocked together, as they are devoted to the works of Sandro Botticelli, among other mid-Renaissance painters. Start with his most famous masterpiece, the *Primavera,* or Spring, an enigmatic celebration of classical myths, with all kinds of fascinating and delicate detailing now revealed. Here too is his *Birth of Venus,* a supremely graceful work. The *Adoration of the Magi* is practically a Medici family portrait, with Cosimo the Elder kneeling before the Christ Child, Piero the Gouty seen from the back and Giovanni kneeling by his side. Behind him stands Giuliano. The figure in yellow at the far right is probably Botticelli himself. Botticelli's later works spurned the Medicean *joie de vivre* of his early days and possess some of the grim terror inspired in the painter by Savonarola. The *Madonna of the Magnificat* and *Madonna of the Pomegranate* both show clearly the more tortured, positively mystical quality the firebrand priest aroused in him. Also here, and striking a distinctively different note from its Floren-tine contemporaries, is Hugo van der Goes' *Portinari Altarpiece,* or Adora-tion of the Shepherds. Though his work lacks nothing in terms of grace and elegance, Flemish artist Hugo van der Goes imbued this wonderful painting with a wealth of exact detail and a certain earthy naturalism quite different from the idealized beauty that so distinguishes Italian Renais-sance work. Ghirlandaio's *Madonna with Saints* and Filippino Lippi's *Ad-oration of the Magi* are among the many other treasures in this huge room.

In Room XV stop to admire Leonardo's unfinished *Adoration of the Magi.* Despite its incomplete state, the poetic and deeply atmospheric quality of Leonardo is absolutely unmistakable. Equally striking is the dreamlike landscape in the background.

Room XVIII, the Tribuna, octagonal in shape, was designed in about 1580 by Buontalenti as the centerpiece of the gallery where all the most important works were displayed. Occupying center stage here is the Medici *Venus,* a Roman copy of an ancient Greek statue that aroused enormous interest when discovered in the 15th century. Modern taste, however, seems distinctly unimpressed by this type of antique wonder, and the powerful series of portraits by Bronzino here generally excite much more interest. His *Eleonora of Toledo* and *Lucrezia Panciatichi* are both typical of the elongated beauty Bronzino excelled at.

Room XX provides a glimpse of the Northern Renaissance in the shape of Cranach and Dürer. But Room XXV brings you back to the Italian High Renaissance with a vengeance. The highlight here, and indeed one of the highlights of the entire collection, is Michelangelo's *Doni Tondo,* a circular portrait of the Holy Family, painted on the occasion of Maddalena Strozzi's marriage to Agnolo Doni in 1504, and one of only a handful of oil paintings by Michelangelo. The work has a taut, almost muscular quality, and is painted in brilliant, cold colors, more glorious than ever after a recent cleaning. Next door, in Room XXVI, are two of Raphael's finest works: the portrait of *Leo X* and the *Madonna of the Goldfinch,* the latter painted when Raphael was only 23. Andrea del Sarto liked to paint himself into his compositions; he is St. John the Evangelist in his *Madonna of the Harpies.* You'll meet two old friends in Room XXVIII: Titian's *Flora* and his resplendent *Venus of Urbino.*

Just here is the entrance to Vasari's Corridor (*Corridoio*), leading to Palazzo Pitti. We describe it in more detail below. Continuing round the galleries, however, now make for Room XLI, where two magnificent Rubens can be found. These are *Henry IV at the Battle of Ivry* and the *Triumphant Entry of Henry IV into Paris,* commissioned by Marie de' Medici, the French king's wife. Rooms XLIII and XLIV harbor works by Caravaggio and Rembrandt. The former's *Medusa* is painted on leather, unusual even for this unusual painter. Caravaggio's *Bacchus* was painted when he was only 18, but already the earthy sensuality and naturalism that exerted so decisive an influence on 17th-century painting and which have helped make him so popular today are much in evidence.

Following these rooms, at the end of the corridor, there is a very handy bar and cafe, with a terrace that gives stunning close-up views of Palazzo Vecchio and the rooftops. From here you can return to explore the famous Corridor (*Corridoio*), if you have made an appointment. It's lined with a series of self-portraits by Raphael, Andrea del Sarto, Titian, Bernini, Rubens, Rembrandt, Velásquez, David, Ingres and Delacroix among others, a more than slightly astounding collection. If you get a chance to make this trip, there are marvelous views from the windows as you wind your way over the Arno and bend toward the Pitti Palace. The exit leaves you in the Boboli Gardens.

SIGHTSEEING DATA. For general information on museum and church opening times and entrance fees, see "Sightseeing Tips" under *Miscellaneous* in the *Practical Information for Florence.*

Galleria degli Uffizi (Uffizi Gallery), Piazzale degli Uffizi 6. Open Tues. to Sat. 9–7, Sun. 9–1. Closed Mon. Admission 5,000 lire. **Vasari Corridor,**

Piazzale degli Uffizi 6. Admission by appointment only, on Tues. and Sat. at 9:30 A.M.

Palazzo Vecchio, Piazza Signoria. Open Mon. to Fri. 9–7, Sun. 8–1. Closed Sat. Admission 4,000 lire, Sun. free.

Raccolta Alberto della Ragione (Della Ragione Modern Art Collection), Piazza Signoria 5. Open Mon. and Wed. to Sat. 9–2, Sun. 8–1. Closed Tues. Admission 2,000 lire.

Across the Arno

Ponte Vecchio, one of the world's most famous bridges, was spared by the German mines, apparently because Hitler admired its unique design. He might have been less merciful if he'd known a telephone line ran along it, linking the Liberation Committee with the British Army Command.

There was probably a bridge here even in Roman times, part of the ancient Via Cassia. The present structure, by Neri di Fioravante, dates back to 1345. At the time of the Medici's triumphant return to Florence, it was lined mainly with butchers' shops, but Cosimo I considered this undignified and, in the mid 16th century the butchers were replaced by the goldsmiths who have been there ever since. Later he had Vasari build the corridor which starts at the Uffizi, follows the Lungarno and runs across the bridge above the shops on the left, for a total of one kilometer. While Cosimo was inspecting the work he met and fell in love with Carmela Martelli whose father had a jewelry shop on the bridge. She became his mistress and—when Eleonora of Toledo died—he made her his wife. But Eleonora's children didn't accept this upstart, as they saw her, and when their father died they had her locked up. She died many years later in a convent, quite mad.

Take a look inside the charming little shops whose wares range from the reasonable to the extravagant. Those on the right were heavily damaged by the 1966 flood but have been restored. Photos show the jewelers patiently sifting through tons of mud looking for gold and gems. The man many consider the greatest goldsmith of all time, Benvenuto Cellini, is remembered in a bust above the fountain halfway across the bridge.

Till Death Do Us Part

Borgo San Jacopo begins on the right at the far end of the bridge where a 16th-century *Bacchus* tops a fountain made from an ancient Roman sarcophagus. This street is a charming combination of medieval towers, trendy boutiques and unusual antique shops. A plaque on the left shows the level reached by the Arno during the flood—more than six feet above street level! A few steps down the street on your right is the 12th-century Romanesque church of San Jacopo sopr'Arno. Here the city nobles assembled in 1293, pledging to take up arms against the decree that had just excluded them from municipal government.

The street ends at Piazza Frescobaldi, with the palazzo of the same name at #2r. Here, in 1301, Pope Boniface VIII played host to Charles of Valois, brother of the king of France. As a result of that visit Dante—along with 600 other members of the anti-papal White faction—was expelled from Florence. The palace is still the home of the Frescobaldi family, prestigious winemakers and promoters of Florence.

To your left is Via Maggio, lined with fine 14th- to 17th-century palaces. Grand Duke Francesco I commissioned the gifted architect Buontalenti to remodel the house at #26 for his favorite, the lovely Venetian Bianca Cappello (Allori's portrait of her in the Uffizi shows what a true Titianesque beauty she was). The young Medici scion had seen her one day at a window and fallen hopelessly in love. Bianca was already married but her husband was quickly persuaded to look the other way in exchange for this palazzo and an appointment at court. The love affair lasted for the rest of their lives, even during Francesco's politically important marriage to Joan of Austria. After Joan's death the two married and spent their remaining nine years of legitimate happiness mostly at the magnificent Medici villa in Poggio a Caiano. After 24 years of devotion they died within a few hours of each other, a fitting end to one of Florence's favorite love stories.

Via Maggio ends at Piazza San Felice with its jewel-like church. Built over an early Christian graveyard, the medieval structure has an unusual doorway and a fine facade by Michelozzo. Across the street at # 8 is Casa Guidi, immortalized by Elizabeth Barrett Browning in her poem of the same name. A plaque tells that she died here in 1861, but it doesn't say that during her stay she startled Florentines by holding the most passionately pro-unification (of Italy) salon in this divided city. The Brownings lived here for 14 years and the house is open to the public on some afternoons.

Off to your left is Piazza Pitti, where Dostoevski lived at #22 while finishing *The Idiot*. #18 was the home of Paolo dal Pozzo Toscanelli, the cartographer and astronomer, who put forward the theory in the 1470s that it was possible to reach the east by traveling west. The map he drew to this effect helped persuade Christopher Columbus to undertake his momentous sea-voyage west, though Toscanelli was dead by the time news of the unexpected outcome of his idea—the discovery of the New World—was brought back to Europe.

Palazzo Pitti

The massive brown-brick building you can see across the square is not a World War I munitions factory but the Pitti Palace, Florence's most monumental palazzo. The building was commissioned in 1457 by Luca Pitti, friend-turned-foe of the Medici, who went bankrupt trying to keep up with his rivals. Not about to admit his defeat, the plucky nobleman is said to have seated his numerous house-warming guests on cushions filled with gold florins. The inevitable occurred about 80 years later when the Medici, in the person of Eleonora of Toledo, bought and enlarged the building. It remained the residence of the rulers of Florence (whether Medici, Austrian or French) more or less uninterruptedly until 1865 when Florence became the capital of Italy and King Victor Emmanuel II held court here for six years.

Today the palace houses an extraordinary collection of 15th- to 19th-century art. Because the rooms have been left the way the owners arranged them, the Pitti offers a unique opportunity to see the very regal home of some very prodigal patrons. The walls are crowded with paintings hung frame-to-frame or are covered with frescoes—a clear case of artistic over-kill. Try to visit on a bright day, as there's precious little artificial light, many of the paintings are in shadowy corners, and many are glazed, turn-ing them into highly effective mirrors.

The Galleria Palatina is on the first floor; rooms I to V were decorated by Pietro de Cortona and include: in Room I, Titian's *Concert;* his *Portrait of Pietro Aretino,* one of his most famous portraits, and the renowned *La Bella.* Room II is a treasure trove with works by Rubens, Guido Reni, Del Sarto and Guercino in addition to Titian's celebrated *Portrait of a Gentleman,* and the much admired *Mary Magdalene.* Room III is domi-nated by Ruben's vast *Consequences of War,* a heartfelt allegory in which Venus (Love) tries to restrain Mars (War) who escapes her grasp to follow Discord as Plague and Famine hover overhead; behind Venus, Europe im-plores Mars to desist but, unheeding, he tramples the Arts, Charity and Study. Rubens portrayed himself at the far left of the *Four Philosophers.*

Room IV has Raphael's famed portrait of *La Velata* or *La Fornarina* whom Vasari identified as the artist's great love. Next door, Room V, are Raphael's renowned *Madonna della Seggiola,* his portrait of *Maddalena Doni,* and the *Madonna del Granduca,* which was such a favorite of Ferdi-nand III (the "grand duke") that he took it with him wherever he went.

The subsequent labyrinth of rooms is of patchy interest for the general visitor. Some contain undoubted masterpieces, and among these are Room VI with fine paintings by Velásquez, Veronese, two by Andrea del Sarto (one an especially fine *Assumption*), Titian (a portrait of Philip II), and a Raphael portrait of a pregnant woman. Some of the later rooms are more interesting for their Empire decorations and furnishings than for the pic-tures they contain. Room XV, for instance, was the bathroom of Napo-leon's wife, the Empress Maria Louisa. The last of the sequence, Room XXVI, the Sala della Stufa, is decorated with wonderful frescoes, especial-ly those of Pietro da Cortona, the *Four Ages of Man,* and has an attractive 17th-century tiled floor.

The Pitti also houses the sumptuous Appartamenti Monumentali (State Apartments); the Museo degli Argenti (Silver Museum, one of the world's most valuable collections of what can only be called glorious bric à brac); and the Galleria d'Arte Moderna (Modern Art Gallery), whose exhibits range from massive 19th-century battle pieces, to J. S. Sargent, Böcklin and De Chirico—a gathering of mainly minor pictures, but with much of interest among them.

The Boboli Gardens

Through the archway at the far left of the building, you enter the Boboli gardens, created for Eleonora of Toledo, Cosimo I's wife, in the 1540s. Maria de' Medici, queen of France, took this gracious park as a model when she commissioned the Luxembourg Gardens in Paris. With its shady avenues of dark cypresses, deep fountains and grassy slopes it's one of the freshest places to spend a few hours in Florence, away from the crowded, dusty streets of the town center. You'll probably start your visit in the area directly behind Palazzo Pitti, passing the startlingly grotesque but lifelike *Bacchino* (little Bacchus) fountain, a naked pot-bellied figure, mod-eled on Cosimo I's court dwarf, sitting astride a turtle. Opposite the en-trance is Buontalenti's grotto, a series of interlinking artificial caves encrusted with fake stalactites and each containing a statue or fresco: Michelangelo's *Slaves* used to stand here before they were moved to the Accademia. Above the majestic terrace with its "Artichoke" Fountain, you'll see the 18th-century amphitheater where elaborate spectacles have been staged since Roman times. It is actually based on ancient models, and the fountain in the middle is a tub from Rome's Baths of Caracalla, surmounted by a 3,500-year-old obelisk from Luxor.

Farther up the stairs is Neptune's Basin. Off to the left is the Forte Belvedere, part of the fortifications Michelangelo designed to defend Florence during the siege of 1529–30, and which sometimes now houses art exhibitions. Climb to the top of the gardens for a fabulous view, a look at the delightful Monkey Fountain and the Porcelain Museum which contains the vast Medici and Lorraine tableware collections. The coffee house off to the left is a good place for a late morning or afternoon drink, but don't make the mistake of planning to lunch on the dismal sandwiches.

Right at the other end of the gardens, towards the Porta Romana, is the charming Piazzale dell'Isolotto—a water garden enclosed by a thick ilex hedge, with a statue of the Ocean in the center, surrounded by figures of the young Nile, the adult Ganges, and the old Euphrates.

Santo Spirito and Santa Maria del Carmine

Returning to Piazza San Felice, take Via Mazzetta. The second block down on your right is huge Palazzo Guadagni, one of the finest aristocratic homes of the Renaissance and residence of James Jarves from 1852 to 1882. He was an American art critic and collector, who acquired a considerable amount of Italian art works which he exhibited in the United States and eventually bequeathed to the Yale and Cleveland museums.

Just past the Palazzo Guadagni, Piazza Santo Spirito is like no other in Florence. It has plenty of atmosphere, with its generous shade trees, the huge carp that glide and glint in the depths of its murky fountain, the vendors who sell a random selection of fruit and vegetables, socks, and frying pans in its tiny open market. This square is the heart of the Florentine's Florence.

At the far end of the square is the church of Santo Spirito. Don't be misled by its simple facade, this is one of the purest architectural creations of the Renaissance. Brunelleschi's nave, with its 31 pillars, its arches and vaults, is as harmonious as any you will ever see. Sunlight filters in through the stained-glass windows, which include a representation of the *Descent of the Holy Spirit,* designed by Perugino. The *Pietà* on the right is a copy of Michelangelo's original at St. Peter's in Rome. Directly across the nave is a copy of his *Resurrection.* The elaborate main altar looks completely out of place in this serene setting, but it is a fine example of Baroque style. Walk around to the back to see the wooden crucifix which has been attributed to the 20-year-old Michelangelo. The side chapels—a few with coin-operated lights—have plenty of interesting pictures, some by famous artists, others by virtual unknowns. In one to the right of the altar is Filippino Lippi's *Madonna and Child with Saints,* a lovely work. Below the organ, a door leads to the vestibule with its richly decorated vaulted ceiling. From here, you can enter Giuliano da Sangallo's octagonal sacristy and the frescoed cloister.

To the left of the church, at no. 29, is the Cenacolo di Santo Spirito (Refectory) which contains Andrea Orcagna's *Last Supper* (in poor shape), surmounted by his eerily unreal *Crucifixion*. The room, which was originally a refectory, has other fine frescoes and some interesting sculpture.

Returning to the far end of the square, turn right up Via Sant'Agostino to Via dei Serragli. This is another place where the lions that symbolized Florence's ferocious independence were once kept in a menagerie. Nathanial Hawthorne lived on this street while writing *The Marble Faun*.

Cross Via dei Serragli into Via Santa Monaca, past the tiny church of the same name, at the intersection with Via dell'Ardiglione, on which Filippo Lippi was born. A few steps more will bring you to Piazza del Carmine, now a gigantic parking lot. It's hard to believe that earthy, everyday Piazza Santo Spirito is only three blocks away from this huge square.

The Carmine church contains the celebrated fresco cycle by Masaccio in the gloomy Brancacci chapel, at last on view again after a delicate 4-year restoration. During cleaning and consolidation of the frescoes, restorers removed the 17th-century postiche foliage added to cover what was then considered the indecent nudity of Adam and Eve. These stunningly innovative frescoes illustrate scenes from the *Life of St. Peter*, the *Temptation of Adam and Eve* and the *Banishment of Adam and Eve from Paradise*. Begun by Masolino in 1425, they were continued by Masaccio, his pupil, from 1426 to 1428 and completed 50 years later by Filippino Lippi.

Masaccio's frescoes in the Branacci chapel represented a turning point in Renaissance art. Every painter in Florence came to study his profoundly human conception, his realistic use of light and perspective, his creation of space and depth. The chapel was a classroom for the artists of the time from Fra Angelico to Filippo Lippi, Andrea del Castagno, Verrocchio, Botticelli, Ghirlandaio, Perugino, Leonardo, Michelangelo and Raphael. Observing the way the young artist combined deep psychological understanding, brazen inventiveness and mighty skill, you may well wonder what he might have accomplished had he not died when only 27.

At the far end of the square from the church, turn left onto Borgo San Frediano. The strange, squat bell tower on your right belongs to San Frediano in Cestello, which you enter around the corner in Piazza Cestello. This ornate 18th-century Baroque church looks strange after the plain Carmine and Santo Spirito! In the third chapel on the left there is a lovely early painted-wooden *Madonna*. Outside, you're likely to see a crowd of young men on motorcycles in front of the large building across the square. Today it is the office of the draft board, but when it was built in 1695 it was Grand Duke Cosimo III's granary. Join the draftees for the best view of San Frediano's elegant dome. From Lungarno Soderini (off the Piazza) you can see the small Santa Rosa tower and part of the old walls, which lead to Porta San Frediano, built in 1332 by Andrea Pisano. Across the river is the Ognissanti church.

Returning left along Borgo San Frediano, lined with offbeat antique and junk shops, you will come to Piazza Nazario Sauro. Around the corner to your right, Lungarno Guicciardini was once the site of the Pensione Schneider, a favorite with artists and musicians. A weary Sir Walter Scott came here late in life, and Mendelssohn, Goethe, and Lord Byron all stayed here. Farther up, near the Ponte Santa Trinita, is the Pensione Bartolini where E. M. Forster set many of the scenes in his famous novel *A Room with a View.*

San Miniato and San Salvatore al Monte

From Piazza Nazario Sauro at the end of Ponte alla Carraia, take bus 11, 36 or 37 along the river to Porta Romana, the only part of the third medieval wall (built in the late 13th century) still standing. From here take bus 13 up the hill and ask the driver to let you off at San Miniato. On the way you'll pass some magnificent homes including Villa Cora, now a five star hotel but formerly the residence of the Empress Eugenia, mother of Napoleon III. Another tenant was Nadejda von Meck, Tchaikovsky's patroness. Although he was living only a few blocks away working on his *Third Suite for Orchestra,* the two never met and continued to communicate by letter as they had in Russia! Von Meck entertained many musicians at the villa, including a French trio. One of the three players was 18-year-old Claude Debussy, who asked the countess for her daughter's hand and was politely refused.

When you get off the bus, walk about 100 yards more and take the driveway that veers off to the right. At the top of the monumental stairway is the church of San Miniato al Monte, begun in the 11th century, finished in the 13th, and a rare example of Florentine Romanesque. Michelangelo converted the bell tower into a redoubt during the siege of Florence in 1529–30, protecting it with mattresses and bales of wool (the south side still bears signs of the imperial cannon). Much later Oscar Wilde composed his sonnet to the *Queen of the Heavens* here.

The church's attractive facade in patterned green and white marble carries a striking 12th-century mosaic which gleams gold in the sun and is topped by a gilded bronze eagle, emblem of San Miniato's sponsors, the Calimala (Wool Merchants' Guild). Inside you'll find a delightful mix of colors and stylized designs, all contained in an approachably small setting, that make a welcome antidote to the massive plainness of Renaissance churches. A floor plate in front of the right door commemorates the early Christian cemetery that was on this site. Walk between the pews to see the splendid 13th-century inlaid marble floor with signs of the zodiac, animals and birds. Michelozzo's elegant little chapel, in the form of a tabernacle, is in front of the crypt.

Spinello Aretino's clear-cut frescoes in the sacristy are considered his masterpiece. If the tiny cloister is open, go in to see Paolo Uccello's frescoes on the upper loggia. Climb the steps to the presbytery with its delicately-carved marble screen and magnificent elevated pulpit, both from the early 1200s. The mosaic in the apse dates from 1297, and portrays Christ between Mary and St. Miniato. Down the stairs from the presbytery, the Portuguese cardinal's chapel is one of the richest Renaissance works in Florence, with its glorious glazed terracotta medallions by Luca della Robbia, and its frescoes by Pollaiuolo. Preserved in the 11th-century crypt are the bones of St. Miniato, a hermit who lived for years in a nearby cave. Supposedly, when lions refused to harm the holy man, the Emperor Decius had him beheaded, but he merely placed his head back on his shoulders and returned to this spot to die in his cave—a saintly case of the walking wounded.

A small shop (closed Wed.) in the square sells herbal liqueurs and medicines made by the monks. Walk through the archway to the bell tower, cemetery (where a stone marks the grave of Carlo Collodi, author of *Pinocchio*) and the massive fortifications improvised by Michelangelo at the time of the 1530 siege. Go back down the stairs and continue along the driveway to the church of San Salvatore al Monte. Begun in 1499 to a design by Cronaca it, too, was sponsored by the Wool Merchants. The inner facade consists of an arcade surmounted by windows, an innovative departure for the time. The most striking part of this simple, peaceful church is the original wooden ceiling. Note also the wooden beams in the cloister.

Piazzale Michelangelo

Farther down the hill you'll come to the monumental Piazzale Michelangelo with its copy of the artist's *David,* a pleasant restaurant, outdoor cafes and an unbeatable view over Florence, especially at night. The best place to stand is at the outer left corner of the square, which is also the most popular spot for the ubiquitous street vendors—lots of overpriced jewelry and leather goods here. The Piazzale is *the* romantic place for young couples, and consequently even fuller (of Italians anyway) at night than during the day.

A few steps back up Viale Galileo, take the long staircase that leads down the hill, this side of the cafe. Still much the same as when Dante mentioned it in his *Purgatory,* it leads down to the charming 14th-century Porta San Miniato. On the other side of the gate is the tiny church of San Niccolò sopr'Arno, where Florentines assembled in 1529, swearing to defend their city against the pope and the imperial forces. The story goes that later, when the courageous Florentines had to surrender, a merciful sexton hid Michelangelo in the belfry until Clement VII promised to forgive him for building the fortifications.

Take Via San Niccolò to the left and you'll be entering the area Augustus Hare called "the shady part of town." Try to schedule this walk for the early evening hours, when you will encounter few passersby to break the spell cast by this purely medieval neighborhood. Countless foreign artists have been enchanted by this area, including Rainer Maria Rilke who wrote his *Florentine Diary* here, in Prince Nicholas Demidoff of Russia's palace at # 56. Pope Gregory X stayed in the gigantic Palazzo dei Mozzi at #121–2 when the peace was finally established between the Guelphs and Ghibellines in 1273. Over six hundred years later D.H. Lawrence wrote his poems *Birds, Beasts,* and *Flowers* here, inspired by the owls that lived in the tower. George Eliot claimed to have spoken with 14th-century ghosts on this street, where she wrote *Romola.* Elizabeth Barrett Browning actually participated in seances here, much to her adoring husband's fury.

At the end of the street on the right is the Bardini Museum and Corsi Gallery, with a sizeable collection of sculpture, paintings, furnishings, ceramics, tapestries and weapons ranging from the 12th to the 19th centuries. Around the corner in Piazza de' Mozzi, the imposing Palazzo Torrigiani (#5) bears the family's coat of arms, a tower.

Nearby, on the bank of the Arno is the foot of the Ponte alle Grazie, named after an image of the Virgin in a chapel that once stood on the right bank. Built in 1237, the bridge was strong enough to withstand 700 years of floods, but not the German mines. Like its sisters, it was entirely rebuilt after the war but to a modern design. Originally the houses here were hermitages inhabited by nuns who had been shocked by the rampant immorality in their convents. They lived here in absolute retreat, inspired by the view of San Miniato on the hillside above.

After the intersection by the Bardini Museum, Via S. Niccolò becomes Via dei Bardi, who were one of Florence's greatest families, and the protagonists of yet another famous love story. Dianora de' Bardi was secretly married to Ippolito Buondelmonti whose family were the Bardi's hereditary enemies. Seized when climbing into her room one night, the young husband was condemned to death as a thief. As he was being led to his execution he begged to be allowed to pass her home. She saw him, ran downstairs and proclaimed the truth. His heroism and her devotion so impressed the Florentines that he was pardoned and peace reigned throughout the town, but only for one season! In the long run, the Bardi brought such economic disaster to Florence that the enraged population burned 22 of the Bardi buildings on this street.

As if human destruction weren't enough, the hillside gave way so often here that tiny Santa Lucia church was dubbed "Lucy in the ruins." Beyond Piazza Santa Maria Sopr'arno, where the street meets Lungarno Torrigiani, Via dei Bardi suddenly takes on a depressingly modern look, again as a result of German mines set to render Ponte Vecchio inaccessible.

SIGHTSEEING DATA. For general information on museum and church opening times and entrance fees, see "Sightseeing Tips" under *Miscellaneous* in the *Practical Information for Florence*.

Cenacolo di Santo Spirito, Piazza Santo Spirito 29. Open Tues. to Sat. 9–2, Sun. 8–1. Closed Mon. Admission 1,000 lire, Sun. free.

Museo Bardini (Bardini Museum and Corsi Gallery), Piazza de' Mozzi 1. Open Thurs. to Sat., Mon. and Tues. 9–2, Sun. 8–1. Closed Wed. Admission 2,000 lire.

Museo delle Porcellane (Porcelain Museum), Casino del Cavaliere, Boboli Gardens. Open Tues., Thurs. and Sat. 9–2. Admission free.

Palazzo Pitti (Pitti Palace). Mostly open Tues. to Sat. 9–2, Sun. 9–1. Closed Mon. Admission 4,000 lire. **Carriage Museum** is closed for restoration.

"La Specola" Zoological Museum, Via Romana 17. **Zoology Section:** Open Tues. 9–12:30, Sun. 9–12. **Wax Models:** Open Sat., summer 2–5, winter 3–6. Admission free.

Excursions from Florence

Tuscany has provided nourishment for artists, writers, mystics, greedy invading armies, and avid culture-vultures for centuries. Its unique fusion of scenery and human achievement has created a very special experience, which has had a lasting effect on Western civilization.

For today's visitor, Florence can provide a perfect base from which to explore this fascinating region. Fairytale hill towns like San Gimignano, its skyline bristling with medieval towers; rolling fields dotted with cypress trees, looking like the background for a painting by Leonardo or Botticelli; once-great and powerful cities like Pisa, with its miraculous leaning tower and cathedral; the extravagant Renaissance villas of Poggio a Caiano, Castello and Petraia, set in lavishly formal gardens; the costumed pageantry of Siena's Palio or Lucca's medieval crossbow competition; narrow, winding streets flanked by such Pisan-style monuments as Pistoia's San Giovanni Fuorcivitas, with its tiers of intricately carved marble loggias; Prato's 11th-century Swabian castle—all these unique facets of Tuscany's rich heritage can be easily visited from Florence. These side trips can be tailored to the time you have available, from a few hours for Fiesole, its heart still pulsing to an Etruscan beat, to a couple of days to take in Siena or Pisa. In this section we cover just Fiesole and the Medici villas, close in to Florence. The lack of space forbids us to roam farther afield, though most of the places you may wish to add to your stay in Florence are covered in our main *Guide to Italy.*

FIESOLE

Only a 20-minute bus ride from Santa Maria Novella rail station, this tiny hill town, poised high above Florence, is light years removed from the noisy, jostling sidewalks of the city. The ride, though short, is a very pretty one, with ever-widening views as the bus climbs a road lined with cypresses and wealthy villas. This is a highly prized residential area for both rich Italians and well-heeled foreigners. As Fiesole is only four miles away, it would be possible to walk—or rather climb—up, though most people might prefer to ride one way and walk back down.

Try to plan your visit to Fiesole for the early morning or late afternoon, when the heat is more bearable, and the brilliant sun does not wash out the views, which are a main reason for the trip. You'll also need to wear shoes that can cope with roughish terrain.

There was an Etruscan settlement where Fiesole now stands as early as 700 B.C., the fortress that protected the vital trade route which crossed the Arno at this point. Captured by the Romans, its name was changed

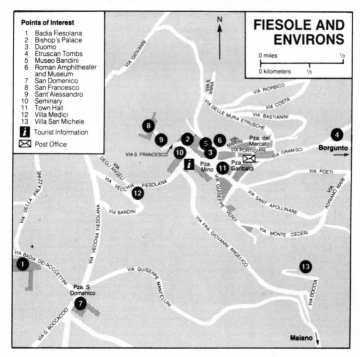

Points of Interest

1. Badia Fiesolana
2. Bishop's Palace
3. Duomo
4. Etruscan Tombs
5. Museo Bandini
6. Roman Amphitheater and Museum
7. San Domenico
8. San Francesco
9. Sant'Alessandro
10. Seminary
11. Town Hall
12. Villa Medici
13. Villa San Michele

ℹ️ Tourist Information

✉️ Post Office

FIESOLE AND ENVIRONS

to Faesulae in 80 B.C., when it became the principal town of the region, with a forum, capitol buildings, a temple, theater, and baths. But it was temptingly poised in the path of barbarian marauders, whose depredations hastened its decline. As it decayed Florence rose, and after a battle in 1125, Fiesole finally gave in to its neighbor's domination.

Your visit to the town begins in the main square, laid out over the original Roman forum and named after the sculptor Mino da Fiesole. On your left as you enter is the large seminary, dating back to the end of the 17th century. Next to it is the bishop's palace, with a stretch of the Etruscan wall at the far end of the garden, part of the remaining outer perimeter of the original settlement. These vestiges of the massive Etruscan bulwarks can be seen at several points round the town.

Next on the piazza is the Duomo, with its skinny, castle-like belfry built in 1213, visible for miles around. The cathedral's facade is a bland late 19th-century titivation, but inside is a wonderful, if severe, Romanesque basilica with a fine wooden roof. In the raised presbytery the Salutati chapel has colorful frescos by Roselli, and a surprising portrait bust of Bishop Salutati by Mino da Fiesole, whose work in the 15th century put the town on the artistic map. After you've viewed the many 14th- and 15th-century works in the cathedral, go down into the crypt, part of the original 11th-century structure, with some ancient stonework.

Via San Francesco scales the hill between the bishop's palace and the seminary, a steep climb but worth the effort. It leads first to a belvedere, surrounded by silvery olive trees, with superb views of the town and beyond. Here you are standing below the original acropolis. A little higher is the church of Sant'Alessandro, built on a site which saw first an Etruscan temple, then a Roman one consecrated to Bacchus. The present church dates back to the 7th century, with many later changes. Up the hill again and to the left are the tiny Santa Cecilia and the larger church of San Francesco, which replaced a medieval castle destroyed in 1125 during the battle with Florence. If the church is open, go in to see the 15th-century paintings, but even more to take a peek at the peaceful cloisters, which have associations with St. Bernadino of Siena. There is also a fusty little missionary museum, with a few priceless artifacts from China and some sizeable chunks of the Etruscan citadel.

Back at the foot of the hill, the Roman amphitheater lies behind the cathedral. It was discovered in 1809, but not properly excavated for another 70 years, when the baths (right) and the temple (left) also came to light. The serried rows of seats have been restored to allow drama to be presented again. Plays are held mainly during July and August, when the Estate Fiesolana takes place, a summer festival that fills the town's monuments with plays, concerts, ballet, and movies. Towards the baths' side of the area is a fair amount of Etruscan wall which, though restored, still gives a good idea of the impressive skill of those early masons.

Near the entrance to the site are two museums. One—on the right as you go in—is the archeological museum attached to the excavations, with finds from the immediate vicinity and from the region in general. It has a lot of exhibits that will interest anyone keen on the Etruscans. Across the way, on the other side of the site entrance, is the Bandini Museum, with a large collection of 14th- and 15th-century paintings and sculpture, bequeathed to the town in the last century by Angiolo Maria Bandini, a librarian of the Laurentian Library in Florence. A few yards of Roman road are incorporated into Via Duprè here. You can see them as you go down hill.

A detour here—or the first part of your walk if you are legging it back to Florence. From Piazza Mino, as the locals call it, take the steep little street that plummets down the hill beyond the seminary (Strada Vecchia Fiesolana). During this pleasant 15-minute walk, you'll see the remains of an Etruscan gate and, on your left, the Medici villa where the Pazzis had originally planned to carry out their conspiracy. It is not open to the public. After the bench that Queen Victoria had installed so that she could enjoy her favorite view in comfort, you'll pass several beautiful old villas and emerge in Piazzale San Domenico di Fiesole, with its 15th-century church. Inside, a sparklingly restored *Madonna and Child with Angels and Saints* is the only one left of the many works painted for this church by Fra Angelico who lived here for the first five years of his priesthood. But there is a wonderful gilded tabernacle over the altar and the adjacent monastery has two Fra Angelico frescoes, one of them a *Crucifixion*.

Before returning to Florence, take tiny Via di Badia dei Roccettini, across the street from San Domenico, to the 11th-century Badia, Fiesole's first cathedral. It was remodeled in the 15th century to Brunelleschi's designs on the orders of Cosimo the Elder who often stayed in the abbey. The old Romanesque facade is actually incorporated into the new one; the interior is a surprising gem of Renaissance purity. The original abbey buildings at one side now house the European University Institute, and you can get another magnificent view of Florence, spread out below, from the vantage point in front of the church.

PRACTICAL INFORMATION FOR FIESOLE

GETTING THERE. By Bus. City bus #7 from the station, cathedral or San Marco to the end of the line (about 20 minutes). You can pick up the same bus at San Domenico on the way back.

By Car. From Porta San Gallo take the Via Fiesolana (about 10 minutes' drive).

LUNCH SPOTS. Villa San Michele (E), Via Doccia 4 (tel. 055–59.451). One of the great hotels of Italy, indeed of Europe. Magnificent food, though costly. Lovely buildings and fabulous views. AE, DC, MC, V.

Aurora (M), Piazza Mino da Fiesole 39A (tel. 055–59.166). Tables outside under a cool arbor in summer. Closed Mon. and Nov. or Feb. AE, DC, MC, V.

Reggia degli Etruschi (M), Via San Francesco. Has reopened after modernization, and is a good bet for hearty food and a great view.

At **Maiano,** 3 km. away, **Trattoria Le Cave** (M), tel. 055–59.133. For the car-borne, this one has highly recommended authentic local cuisine, pleasant service, and outdoor tables in summer. Not well marked, but once you are on the road to Maiano there are faded signs pointing the way. Closed Sun. evening, Thurs. and Aug. AE, DC.

SIGHTSEEING DATA. Archeological Area (Roman Amphitheater) and Museum. Open daily 9–7 in summer; winter 10–2, closed Mon. Admission 2,500 lire.

Bandini Museum. Open 10–12 all year; summer 3–7; winter 2:30–5. Closed Sun. Admission 2,000 lire.

Missionary Museum. Open summer 10–12, 3–6; winter 10–12, 3–7.

Summer Festival. For schedules and tickets for the Estate Fiesolana (usually July and August) check with the E.P.T. office in Piazza Mino da Fiesole 45 (tel. 055–598.720), or at Globus, Piazza Santa Trinita 2 in Florence.

Tourist Office. E.P.T., Piazza Mino da Fiesole 45 (tel. 055–598.720).

THE MEDICI VILLAS

As the Medici ruled Florence for upward of three centuries, they naturally established country homes outside the city where they could relax, entertain guests, plot against their enemies, and generally behave like modern tycoons hidden in the Hamptons. Some of their houses were more modest than others, some have fallen into disrepair. Of the many that have passed into State ownership some have met odd fates—lovely Careggi, for instance, is now the local outpatient clinic of the government health service. All of them are well off the beaten tourist track, and so have a lonely charm all their own. Enough of them are open to warrant planning a visit, and here we will concentrate on three of the best: Poggio a Caiano, Castello, and Petraia. Be sure to wear comfortable shoes that can stand up to pebbly garden paths!

Poggio a Caiano

When Lorenzo the Magnificent decided to build a country villa worthy of his sobriquet, he had Giuliano da Sangallo transform an existing villa that belonged to the Strozzi family, 11 miles northwest of Florence. The result, Poggio a Caiano, is considered the most splendid of all the Medici villas.

Here Lorenzo, one of the world's most eminent and creative patrons, surrounded himself with men of arts and letters. A hundred years later, the villa became the love nest of Bianca Cappello and Francesco de' Medici, the legendary couple who died in 1587 within a few hours of each other, the crowning touch to a lifetime of thwarted love and a few years of secluded bliss. When Italy was united, Victor Emmanuel II used Poggio a Caiano as his residence while Florence was the capital of the fledgling State.

As in many of the grander Medici villas, the furnishings you see today are all a legacy of Victor Emmanuel's residence, but, if you have seen Palazzo Medici-Riccardi you can imagine what it looked like in Lorenzo's day. Most of the frescoes, many by Pontormo, are original, as is the cavernous kitchen. The stables are next door, and there's a gigantic park behind the villa to wander in, complete with grottoes, statues, and fountains. From the rooftop terrace you'll have a refreshing view over Florence and the hills separating the city from Prato and Pistoia. In summer excellent concerts are held in the villa, a delightful way of spending a relaxed evening.

Castello and Petraia

In the 14th century, Villa di Castello—just three miles to the north of the city—was called Il Vivaio (the Greenhouse). The Medici bought it in 1480, but when Piero the Gouty was banished from Florence, it was sacked and destroyed. The indomitable Cosimo I had Vasari restore it, and today its facade is a gem of Renaissance simplicity.

Italy's ancient and prestigious Accademia della Crusca—the Italian version of France's Académie, whose purpose is to monitor the language—has been established here since 1966, so you won't be able to see inside. But the wonderful gardens designed by Tribolo are open to the public, called "the richest, most magnificent, and ornate in all Europe" by Vasari. The amazing fountains, decorated with animals, were designed by Giambologna's pupils. For the best view of the gardens, climb the hill to the terrace.

If you continue along a sleepy little road from the entrance to Villa di Castello's gardens, lined with the modest homes Italians call *villette,* you will come to the 17th-century Villa Rinieri, which looks positively Rococo after the stark Medici facades. It was here that Robert Dudley, duke of Northumberland and designer of Livorno's "new" port, died in 1669.

Turn left and climb the hill to Villa di Petraia, originally a medieval castle belonging to the Brunelleschi family, who successfully defended it against John Hawkwood (the English mercenary portrayed by Paolo Uccello in Florence cathedral). The building passed to the Bardi, Strozzi and

Salutati families and finally, in 1575, to Ferdinand I de' Medici, who hired Buontalenti to remodel it. The splendid villa still incorporates the original tower.

One of Buontalenti's great innovations was the graceful inner courtyard, decorated by Cosimo Daddi with frescoed scenes of Medici family glory. In 1636, Volterrano added the allegorical frescoes under the side porticoes, which deal with the Medici at their zenith and portray Catherine de' Medici, Lorenzo and Giuliano de' Medici, Maria de' Medici, and the Medici pope Clement VII in the act of crowning the Hapsburg emperor Charles V. Unfortunately, Victor Emmanuel decided to "improve" the courtyard by covering it in with a glass roof, and hanging a gaudy chandelier. However, he did rescue the frescoes from the heavy coat of whitewash with which they were covered in Napoleonic times.

The royal apartments on the ground floor are mainly legacies of the Savoy era, but the New Chapel has luminous 17th-century frescoes by Pier Dandini, while upstairs the Old Chapel still has Daddi's original frescoes.

The house looks out on magnificent Italian gardens, which are especially spectacular in May when hundreds of roses are in bloom. Designed by Tribolo, who also created the Boboli gardens for Duke Cosimo I, they include an ornamental garden to one side of the main building. Behind stretches a fine park, thick with pines and cypresses, with views off into the distance, but it is extremely unlikely that if the Medici were still around they would have allowed anyone to spoil their panorama with the high-tension wires and anonymous apartment blocks that ruin this lovely corner of Tuscany today.

PRACTICAL INFORMATION FOR THE MEDICI VILLAS

GETTING THERE. By Bus. For Poggio a Caiano, take the Co.Pi.T. bus marked "Quarrata" from Piazza Santa Maria Novella. After a ride of about 30 minutes, it stops directly in front of the villa.

For Castello and Petraia, take the city bus #28 from the station and ask to get off at Villa di Castello; walk down the long driveway to the villa.

By Car. Take the Statale 66 from Porta al Prato to the town of Poggio a Caiano; the villa is on the right after about 30 minutes.

For Castello and Petraia, from Ponte alle Mosse follow the signs to Sesto Fiorentino; in the town of Castello, the villa is on the right at the end of a long driveway. About 20 minutes' drive.

LUNCH SPOTS. Sadly, the area around these lovely villas is full of a dreary commuter sprawl, with few—if any—good restaurants. The best idea is to pack a picnic and enjoy it in one of the gardens or parks of the villas themselves.

SIGHTSEEING DATA. All the villas have the same opening hours: 9–6:30 from May to Aug.; 9–5:30 in March, April, Sept., and Oct; 9–4:30 from Nov. to Feb. The house at Petraia is open 9–2, and until 1 on holidays. The house at Poggio a Caiano is open for guided visits Tues. to Sat. 9–1:30, Sun. 9–12:30. All are closed on Mon.

Poggio a Caiano Concerts. For schedules and tickets contact Arno Agency, Piazza Ottaviani 7, Florence (tel. 055–295.251). A free round-trip bus service is provided, leaving Santa Maria Novella at 8:45 P.M.

PRACTICAL INFORMATION FOR FLORENCE

Arriving in Florence

SECURITY. Where Venice is happily free from petty crime, Florence—Firenze to the Italians—sadly is not. Really, the best way to protect your valuables is to leave them at home. Ask yourself if you really need expensive jewelry or favorite heirlooms on your trip. If you do without them for a few weeks, you'll have the rest of your life to enjoy them.

Even if you have nothing of great value, you should still be cautious. Where there's a crowd there's a purse-snatcher, so be on the lookout at all times. Have an inconspicuous little shoulder bag and wear it bandolier-style. If you must carry a large or hand-grip bag, hold it firmly and carry it on the side away from the curb. Keep your ears open for motorbikes approaching from behind. It might be an innocent kid out for a ride, or two hoods aiming for your bag.

Never rest your purse or camera on a table or chair at a sidewalk cafe or restaurant.

Pickpockets are especially fond of crowded buses, so be careful of billfolds and purses. Trains are also risky, especially during those hectic moments of arrival and departure. *Never* leave your baggage unattended. And be careful when you're on trains, too. Thieves have been known to use sleeping gas on overnight trains, so if you really must travel with valuable jewelry or cash, devise a clever hiding place for it before you drop off to sleep. When flying, keep valuables in your hand luggage.

Even an empty shopping bag might tempt someone to break your car window, so don't leave anything in your car. If you must stop briefly, lock everything in the trunk out of sight. But *don't* leave cameras or valuables even there. Park at guarded parking spots or in garages; the small fee is well worth it. There are reports of smashed windows and windscreens, even while passengers are waiting for a traffic light, so keep cameras and purses out of sight, *not* on the rear seat.

Unaccompanied females should be very careful anywhere in Florence. Groups of youths, often on motorbikes or screaming out of cars, are a permanent nuisance and occasionally an actual threat. Even the most crowded areas suffer from these pestilential gangs, regardless of time of day. Whether sitting down for a moment to rest your feet or doing the rounds of the cultural hotspots, there's a near certainty of being bothered by them. It's unlikely that you will come to serious harm—their bark is very much worse than their bite, though nonetheless unpleasant for all that—but it's only sense to avoid the more deserted areas of the city, *especially* at night, and to stay clear of parts of the Boboli Gardens.

GETTING IN FROM THE AIRPORT. The local airport at Peretola is expanding services and is now regularly connected with Rome and Milan and with other cities in Italy and southern Europe. But it's more likely that, if you fly here, you'll be landing at Pisa's Galileo Galilei airport, some

85 km. (53 miles) from town. Moreover, though international flights do land at Pisa, it is still a fairly small airport. Added to which, for some inexplicable reason, the excellent bus service that used to link it to Florence has been suspended, so unless you want to spend upwards of 200,000 lire for a taxi, you'll be taking the "Capanone Express" train into Florence's main Santa Maria Novella station. The fare is about 6,000 lire, and the trip takes about 60 minutes. Trains start running at 8:52 A.M. and leave roughly every hour, 15 minutes before the hour, until 10:45 P.M. Trains leave Florence for Pisa every hour from 6:25 A.M. to 8 P.M. But allow yourself ample time in case of delays, or you may well miss your flight. And any time you fly out of any Italian airport, call first to make sure no strikes have been announced. For flight information, call 296.102; 214.721 for international flights.

If you decide to take a cab into town, head for the taxi stand in front of the terminal. Use only authorized cabs, which are white with a yellow stripe or box on the sides. Strictly avoid the pirate cab drivers who will harass you; their fares are guaranteed to be even higher than a city cab's.

TOURIST OFFICES. Before you start sightseeing, stop in at the *EPT (Ente Provinciale di Turismo)* office at Via Manzoni 16 (open Mon. to Fri. 8:30–1:30, 4–6:30, Sat. 8:30–1:30), at the Azienda Autonoma di Turismo, Via Tornabuoni 15 (open 9 A.M.–1 P.M.) or at the ITA information stand in the station. Their free brochures will give you information on museum locations and closing times, what's going on that week, how to get around town and how to book any special activities you might have in mind. Ask for *Welcome to Florence,* a monthly English-language newspaper with local entertainment listings and suggestions about what to see and do. The bi-monthly brochure, *Florence Today,* is available free at tourist offices or for 100 lire at newsstands.

For details of accommodations offices and services, see "Hotels" below.

CHANGING MONEY. Exchange offices observe regular shop hours.
American Service Bank, Via della Vigna Nuova 2r (tel. 218.141). Open Mon. to Sat., 8:30–4:30.
Banca Nazionale delle Comunicazioni, inside the railway station. Open Mon. to Sat., 8:20–7.
Cambival, Via Guicciardini 10r (tel. 219.028), and Borgo San Lorenzo 33r (tel. 210.816). Open Mon. to Sat., 9–7.
Cassa di Risparmio di Firenze, at the Firenze Nord service station of the Autostrada del Sole. Open Mon. to Sat. 9–1, 2–4. Useful if you're arriving by car.
CIT, Via Cavour 57–59 (tel. 294.306), and Piazza della Stazione 51 (across from station), (tel. 284.145).
Intertravel, Via Lamberti 39–41r (tel. 217.936).
Lazzi Express, Piazza della Stazione 47r (tel. 294.178).
Melia, Via Cavour 63r (tel. 219.190).
Roller Tour, Piazza della Stazione 23r (tel. 298.158).
Wagons Lits Turismo, Via del Giglio 27r (tel. 218.851).
Universalturismo, Via degli Speziali 7r (tel. 217.241). American Express agent in Florence, but does not accept wired money.

Banks. Bank hours are generally Mon. through Fri., 8:20–1:20. A few banks are open one hour in the afternoon, usually 3–4.

Getting Around Florence

ORIENTATION. Florence has an unusual street-number system. All commercial addresses are followed by a red "r" and residential addresses are written in blue. So don't expect no. 87r to be next door to 87 blue; it might be up to a block away. And don't panic if you get "locked" into a building. If the front door doesn't have a spring lock, you'll find a button on the wall somewhere near the door; press it and the door will open.

BY BUS. Florence is well-served by its public bus system. Most lines run from 5:10 A.M. to 1 A.M., and those that stop earlier in the evening often double up with another line. Check the signs at the bus stand. If your bus number is followed by an asterisk, a note at the bottom of the sign will tell you what alternative bus to take, and when it will come by. Some lines are suspended in July and August; a notice will tell you this. *Fermata a richiesta* atop any bus sign means the driver is not required to stop unless you signal him. The bus company used to issue route maps, but lately they have been somewhat lax. Ask at the tourist offices. You will find a bus map in the *TuttoCittà* insert of the telephone directory.

Except during the morning rush hour (7:30–8:30) buses are rarely overcrowded, so respect the rules. Get on through the door marked *salita,* usually at the back. Exit at the middle door; monthly pass holders use the front door to get on. Buy your *biglietto d'autobus* (ticket) before you board; they are available singly or in booklets of five at many tobacconists or newsstands. Single fares cost 600 lire; a ticket good for 70 minutes (*biglietto orario*) on an unlimited number of buses costs 700 lire; a ticket good for an entire day (*biglietto giornaliero*) costs 2,500 lire; one for eight rides with no time limit costs 4,200 lire. Whichever ticket you buy, stamp it as soon as you get on the bus; time-length tickets need only the first stamp, whereas multiple-ride tickets must be stamped each time.

BY CAR. Even if you drive to Florence, there's very little point in using your car while you're here. Most of the historic center is off-limits to vehicles, and the streets that do take traffic are exasperatingly narrow. Your best bet is to garage the car until you leave town, so don't forget to include garage fees in your budget. You are strongly advised not to leave the car parked on the street, unless it is directly in front of your hotel doorman. If you are staying at a hotel in the center, the doorman will give you a receipt to attach to your windshield; this will allow you to drive as far as the garage after unloading your bags.

If you simply can't resist driving around town, you'll find large blue signs marked with a white "P" to indicate the areas where parking is allowed. Many of Florence's beautiful squares have been turned into guarded parking lots; you can distinguish these spots because the parking sign has a list of hours (usually 8 A.M. to 8 P.M.) and fares under the big "P." During these posted hours, your car will be watched by authorized attendants who will give you a ticket when you arrive and collect the fare when you leave. If you suspect your car has been towed away by traffic police, call 351.562.

If you use your car for day trips, have your hotel give you detailed instructions for getting out of town. The EPT has a helpful brochure on the province of Florence, which includes a map of major access roads to the city.

Don't let yourself run out of gas in the center of town, where there are no gas stations. Fill up on the avenues that run along both sides of the old city walls. In Italy, you don't usually get a discount if you serve yourself, although the practice is starting to catch on. Those "self-serve" signs you'll see refer only to the machines that are switched on after closing hours. Note that service stations close for the lunch break and are usually open 7:30–12:30 and 3–7:30. There are all-night stations at Via Antonio del Pollaiuolo, Viale Guidoni, Via Rocca Tebalda, Via Senese and Viale Europa.

Car Hire. Several companies have cars for hire in Florence. Apart from Hertz and Avis, you might try Maggiore and Europcar, both international firms. Of course you can reserve through your local travel agent or any Italian travel agent. Be sure not to hire a station wagon; you won't be able to conceal your luggage in it.

Avis is at Borgognissanti 128r (tel. 213.629) and Galileo Galilei airport (tel. 050–42.028) in Pisa.

Eurodrive is at Via della Scala 48ar (tel. 298.639) and at Galileo Galilei airport (tel. 050–500.192).

Europcar is at Borgognissanti 120r (tel. 294.130) and at Galileo Galilei airport (tel. 050–41.017).

Hertz is at Via Maso Finiguerra 33r (tel. 282.260) and Galileo Galilei airport (tel. 050–44.426).

Inter-rent is at Via Il Prato 1 (tel. 218.665) and at Galileo Galilei airport (tel. 050–462.09).

Italy by Car is at Borgognissanti 113r (tel. 293.021) and at Galileo Galilei airport (tel. 050–45490).

Maggiore is at Via Maso Finiguerra 11r (tel. 294.578) and at Galileo Galilei airport (tel. 050–42.574).

BY TAXI. Generally speaking, cabs do not cruise in Florence. You'll find them at stands in all the strategic points of the city. Remember that cabs are white, with a yellow stripe or box on the driver's door. You can call a cab (call 47.98 or 43.90), in which case the driver will start his meter when he receives the call. The meter starts at 2,000 lire; there is a 1,500 lire supplement after 9 P.M., an additional 1,200 lire supplement for Sundays and holidays, and you'll pay 400 lire for each piece of luggage.

BY BICYCLE. A few years ago, Florence's city council decided to tempt its citizens away from their cars by offering two free bikes for two hours to those who park in authorized areas. Look for the Bici-Città booths at Fortezza da Basso parking lot or call SCAF (tel. 296.335), if you're interested in biking around town. Otherwise, Ciao & Basta has bikes for rent at Via Alamanni (across from the station) (tel. 293.357) and Via Costa dei Magnoli 24 (tel. 263.985), not far from Ponte Vecchio. It's always a good idea to reserve a day ahead, if you can. If you're interested in **mopeds** or **motorbikes,** contact Program, at Borgognissanti 96 (tel. 282.916); again, reserve ahead.

ON FOOT. This can be harrowing, in fact a duel to the death, but it's the only way to see Florence. Keep in mind that Italian drivers are entirely unpredictable at all times, so don't expect them to stop for you on the zebra stripes, obey traffic lights or stay out of pedestrian islands. Just think of yourself as Mr. or Ms. Pacman, and go to it!

Wear comfortable shoes, with spongy soles to absorb the impact with the pavement. Skinny heels only get stuck between the cobblestones. Heed our warning on security.

BY HORSE-DRAWN CARRIAGE. Florence has even fewer of these than some other European cities, but they offer a pleasant way to see part of the old city. There are always three or four carriages between the Cathedral and the Baptistery and others in Piazza della Signoria. Going rates are about 20,000 lire for 20 minutes, 40,000 for half an hour, or 70,000 for an hour. But this is one chance for you to unleash all your bargaining skills and hope to come out on top.

GUIDED TOURS. You may want to take a bus tour around the city for initial orientation. CIT, Via Cerretani 57–9r (tel. 294.306) and Globus, at Piazza Santa Trinita 2r offer half-day tours. Your hotel concierge can help you book, too.

"The Florence Experience" is a pleasant way to get oriented. This 45-minute multi-vision (movies and slides) program is shown every hour on the hour from 9 A.M. to 10 P.M. (to 3 P.M. in winter) at the Edison Cinema (tel. 213.110) in the Piazza Repubblica arcade.

The Cooperative Giotto, at Viale Gramsci 9a (tel. 247.8188) has licensed guides who can take you on half-day tours; they are also the only authorized museum guides. For up to 17 people, you'll pay about 60,000 lire for a half-day.

Agriturist, in Piazza San Firenze 3 (tel. 287.838) organizes interesting day trips to the gardens of the great Florentine villas, including Sir Harold Acton's breathtaking La Pietra and Bernard Berenson's I Tatti (April to June); and to the farms around Florence (September to October). You'll stop for afternoon tea along the way.

Tuscany by Air. Splurge on a really different sightseeing tour. Delta Air Taxi (tel. 372.250) offers sightseeing flights over Florence and/or the Chianti vineyard region for up to three passengers. Or you can plan your own itinerary; phone for rates and other information.

Where to Stay

HOTELS. For a city of its size, Florence has an extraordinary number of hotels, many of which have been receiving guests for over a century. All accommodations are officially classified according to a star system: five-star hotels are deluxe, four stars stand for first class, and so on. Look for the stars on brochures and outside the main entrance. Florence used to be famed for its little pensions, but some of these have grown so luxurious over the years that it was decided to abolish the category; now they are included in the hotel category, even though most of them still call themselves *pensioni.* They are generally smaller than hotels, family-run and more informal. With their cosy, old-world atmosphere, they can be charming places to stay. Pensioni and one- or two-star hotels are required by law to offer some rooms without bath, which allow considerable savings on costs. But if you like room service or valet parking, you'd be better off in a four- or five-star hotel. Most of the latter are positively palatial and offer impeccable service.

Whatever the category, you'll find a fairly broad price range within each, so check first. Often the more expensive hotels have some rooms that cost much less than others. But if you opt for this way of saving, be prepared to discover the reason for the discount. Check the notice attached to the inside of your door (or inside the closet). This will tell you exactly what you're paying for the room and any additionals you are required to pay. Some hotels charge extra for airconditioning or parking; one- or two-star places may charge a fee for each shower or bath you take.

Generally speaking, the hotel's room rate should include V.A.T. and sojourn tax, but it's a good idea to check that it's *tutto compreso* (all-inclusive). If the answer is no, be prepared to add 14 percent V.A.T. in five-star hotels, 9 percent in all others; the sojourn tax comes to a few hundred lire per day.

In high season you'll have trouble finding a hotel that doesn't require you to take breakfast, so be sure to ask if the charge is included. If it's extra, Continental breakfast—coffee or tea, rolls, butter and jam—can cost anywhere from a minimum of 5,000 to 25,000 lire in a deluxe hotel. An American-style breakfast will cost much more, though then again few places provide it. If your hotel gives you the option, you might prefer to have a real Italian breakfast at a nearby coffee bar, where *cappuccino* and *brioches,* or perhaps a *spremuta di arancia* or *pompelmo* (freshly squeezed orange or grapefruit juice) will cost much less.

In recent years, Florence has become a trade-fair town, which puts rooms at a premium for most of the year. Make it a rule to book well in advance. If you do arrive with no booking, there are several offices that will help you out. The *ITA* (Hotel Association) booths at the rail station are open from 8 A.M. to 9:30 P.M. every day of the year, except Christmas. Or try member associations: COOPAL, Viale Il Prato 2r (tel. 219.525); or Florence Promhotels, Via Volta 72 (tel. 570.481), which charges no fee for its services. Call these places first to make sure they are open. If you're arriving by car, ITA has two offices on the Autostrada, one at the "Peretola" service station on route All (tel. 440.790, open year-round); the other at the "Chianti Est" station on route Al (tel. 621.349, open Apr. to Nov.). If you use these services you'll be expected to pay for the first night when you book; you'll be given a receipt to prove you've paid.

Our hotel listings give details of which of the major credit cards are accepted by each hotel we list. These appear as AE for American Express, DC for Diners Club, MC for MasterCard (incorporating Access, Cartasi, and EuroCard), and V for Visa.

Hotel Prices. We have divided all the hotels in our listings according to price. Two people in a double room in a Florentine hotel can expect to pay, in lire:

Deluxe	325,000 and up
Expensive	200,000–275,000
Moderate	125,000–150,000
Inexpensive	70,000–90,000
Rock Bottom	35,000–55,000

Deluxe

Excelsior Italie, Piazza Ognissanti 3 (tel. 264.201). 207 rooms. A Ciga Hotel. Florence's premier hotel, in former residence of the Boccaccio family and Caroline Bonaparte, now beloved of stars and magnates. Lavishly appointmented, and boasting famous *Il Cestello* restaurant, as well as roof garden, grill room and piano bar, not to mention beauty salon and garage. Private Cessna airplane available for guest rental. AE, DC, MC, V.

Grand Hotel Villa Cora, Viale Machiavelli 18 (tel. 229.8451). 56 rooms. Royal service in a restored 19th-century villa just below Piazzale Michelangelo. Fabulous period detailing and furnishings. Heated outdoor pool with restaurant; large garden; limousine service to Ponte Vecchio. Solarium has Florence's best view. A favorite with privacy-loving glitterati. AE, DC, MC, V.

Regency Umbria, Piazza Massimo d'Azeglio 3 (tel. 245.247). 27 rooms. A 19th-century town house converted into a small, select hotel, decorated in flamboyantly rich fabrics and period pieces. Just outside the historic center, it has a garden and the excellent *Jardin* restaurant. AE, DC, MC, V.

Savoy, Piazza della Repubblica 7 (tel. 283.313). 101 rooms. Extravagantly appointed rooms with all comforts. Most centrally located deluxe hotel, in the heart of the shopping and museum district. Valet service, elegant restaurant, grill room and piano bar. AE, DC, MC, V.

Villa Medici, Via Il Prato 42 (tel. 261.331). 107 rooms. Famous for its large rooms and huge baths, idyllic garden swimming pool and regal furnishings. Easily reached by car. Private terraces have breathtaking views. *Lorenzaccio* restaurant; piano bar. AE, DC, MC.

Villa San Michele, Via di Doccia, Fiesole (tel. 055–59.451). 26 rooms, 2 suites. Small and excessively select, this is one of the most desirable and expensive hotels in Italy. It's about 15 minutes out of town, in Fiesole, set on a hillside with a fabulous view over Florence. The building itself—now a national monument—was originally a monastery, parts of which were built by Michelangelo. A heated pool, fine restaurant, terrace piano bar and large shady park number among the many facilities. AE, DC, MC, V.

Expensive

Anglo-American Hotel Regina, Via Garibaldi 9 (tel. 282.114). 118 rooms. A bit out of the way in quiet residential district, but a charming 19th-century building with modern rooms; some balconies. Saunas, beauty salon; peaceful courtyard bar; restaurant. AE, MC, V.

Astoria Pullman, Via del Giglio 9 (tel. 298.095). 90 rooms. Centrally located in 17th-century palace near the Medici Chapels. Restaurant and terrace cocktail bar. The Baroque convention center, with frescoes by Luca Giordano, is a favorite for high-fashion shows. Garage service. AE, DC, MC, V.

Augustus, Vicolo dell'Oro 5 (tel. 283.054). 67 rooms. Some rooms with balconies. Breakfast only. Comfortable, modern establishment on the river next to Ponte Vecchio. AE, DC, MC, V.

Bernini Palace, Piazza San Firenze 29 (tel. 278.621). 86 rooms. Very conveniently located behind Palazzo Vecchio, it opened in 1987 on historic premises. Furnished with austere but luxurious simplicity in pastel fabrics and custom-made mahogany pieces. Airconditioning, soundproofing; no restaurant. AE, DC, MC, V.

Croce di Malta, Via della Scala 7 (tel. 282.600). 100 rooms. Many rooms are duplexes. Ask for a room overlooking the garden. A rather bizarre blend of post-modern and 16th-century decor, this Best Western hotel has a swimming pool in a quiet flowery garden. Piano bar, restaurant. AE, MC, V.

Grand Hotel Baglioni, Piazza dell' Unità Italiana 6 (tel. 218.441). 195 rooms. Well-appointed rooms decorated in antique Florentine style. Redecorated rooms on 4th floor are attractive, with atmosphere. Spacious, elegant in the tradition of European grand hotels. Charming roof terrace with superb view of cathedral dome and good restaurant. AE, DC, MC, V.

Grand Hotel Majestic, Via del Melarancio 1 (tel. 264.021). 104 rooms. Most double rooms have two baths. Big splashy modern establishment near the station. Piano bar, excellent restaurant. Own garage. AE, DC, MC, V.

Grand Hotel Minerva, Piazza Santa Maria Novella 16 (tel. 284.555). 112 rooms. Half- or full-pension rates available. Just around the corner from the station, this all-modern hotel has a terrace solarium with swimming pool. The restaurant and many rooms give onto a charming garden. Private garage. AE, MC.

Jolly Carlton, Piazza Vittorio Veneto 4a (tel. 27.70). 140 rooms. At the edge of the Cascine park, easily reached by car. Ultramodern member of the famous Jolly chain, with efficient service, rooftop swimming pool, and large restaurant. AE, DC, MC, V.

Kraft, Via Solferino 2 (tel. 284.273). 66 rooms. Spanking modern hotel with charming sunny rooms in quiet residential neighborhood. Rooftop pool and snack bar; good restaurant; garage service. A Best Western hotel. AE, DC, MC, V.

Loggiati dei Servi, Piazza SS. Annunziata 3 (tel. 219.165). 20 rooms. With entrance under Renaissance loggia, on quiet and beautiful square in central location, it has authentic Florentine feel, modern comforts, tasteful decor. No restaurant.

Lungarno, Borgo San Jacopo 14 (tel. 264.211). 71 rooms. Rooms with terraces have views of Palazzo Pitti and the Boboli Gardens. On the Oltrano side of Ponte Vecchio. Modern, efficient and friendly. AE, DC, MC, V.

Monna Lisa, Borgo Pinti 27 (tel. 247.9751). 21 rooms. Sumptuous period decor in patrician building built partly before the 14th century. Modern baths; ask for a room on quiet 17th-century courtyard, especially the one with a delightful balcony. Parking; garden bar. Prices include a lavish buffet breakfast. Book well in advance for this very special pension. AE, DC, MC, V.

Plaza Lucchesi, Lungarno della Zecca Vecchia 38 (tel. 264.141). 97 rooms. In a handsome old palace on the Arno. Completely renovated, rooms now have contemporary decor and are soundproofed to keep traffic noise out. Elegant ambiance, bar, and restaurant. AE, DC, MC, V.

Principe, Lungarno Vespucci 34 (tel. 284.848). 21 rooms. Modern rooms with antique furnishings in lovely former home of a countess. Peaceful garden; some rooms with terraces. Spectacular views of Florence and the Arno from the loggia bar. Garage service. AE, DC, MC, V.

De la Ville, Piazza Antinori 1 (tel. 261.805). 71 rooms. Just off Via Tornabuoni, convenient to the elegant designer shops. Access to private swimming pool; own minibus to and from the station; restaurant and piano bar. AE, DC, MC, V.

Moderate

Albion, Via Il Prato 22r (tel. 214.171). 23 rooms. Modern rooms, some with balconies, in a neo-Gothic mansion near the river. Restaurant; family-run, garage nearby. AE, DC, MC, V.

Annalena, Via Romana 34 (tel. 222.402). 21 rooms. Many rooms have wood-burning fireplaces; all overlook charming quiet garden. Clean, newly renovated pension in magnificent former Medici residence across the street from rear entrance to the Boboli Gardens. Breakfast on terrace. Book in advance. MC, V.

Aprile, Via della Scala 6 (tel. 263.147). Ask for a room overlooking Santa Maria Novella or the quiet garden. This comfortable hotel is in the 15th-century Palazzo del Borgo, a former Medici residence. No restaurant. AE, MC, V.

Balestri, Piazza Mentana 7 (tel. 214.743). 49 rooms. Top-floor rooms have private balconies overlooking the Arno. Pleasant, family-owned hotel near Santa Croce. Minimum 3-day stay. Parking facilities. AE, V.

Beacci Tornabuoni, Via Tornabuoni 3 (tel. 212.645). 29 rooms. Some old baths, but plenty of European atmosphere. Florence's best-known pension in 14th-century palazzo on the chic shopping street. Elegant breakfast room; fabulous roof garden; warm sitting rooms. AE, DC, V.

Bonciani, Via Panzani 17 (tel. 210.039). 65 rooms. Pleasant blend of modern and antique, only 100 yards from the station. Restaurant and cocktail lounge. Own garage. AE, DC, MC, V.

Byron, Via della Scala 49 (tel. 216.700). 50 rooms. Near the rail station, this pleasant hotel is filled with antique furniture and fittings, modern baths. Garage nearby.

Calzaioli, Via Calzaioli 6 (tel. 212.456). 37 rooms. Basic modern comforts between the Cathedral and the Signoria, on a pedestrian-only street. AE, DC, MC, V.

Cavour, Via del Proconsolo 3 (tel. 287.102). 96 rooms. An unusually high number of suites. Wonderful views of the Cathedral from many rooms. Half- or full-pension rates available. A blend of modern comforts and extravagant 13th-century palace. AE, DC, MC, V.

Chiari Bigallo, Vicolo Adimari 2 (tel. 216.086). 27 rooms. Some rooms have spectacular views, but those over the courtyard are quieter. Simple pension in ancient building near the Cathedral.

Duomo, Piazza Duomo 1 (tel. 219.922). 15 rooms. Some rooms have balconies. Modern hotel across the street from the Cathedral. This is the closest view you'll ever get of Brunelleschi's dome; but the rooms at the back are quieter. AE, DC, V.

Golf, Viale Fratelli Rosselli 56 (tel. 293.088). 39 rooms. Easily reached from the autostrada, this small modern hotel has its own parking lot. AE, DC, MC.

Hermitage, Vicolo Marzio 1 (tel. 287.216). 14 rooms. Some rooms overlook a quiet courtyard. Lovely small hotel with sitting room and terrace smack over the Arno and Ponte Vecchio. Book well in advance.

Pendini, Via Strozzi 2 (tel. 211.170). 37 rooms. Front rooms are noisy, so ask for back. Clean, simple pension with sunny rooftop breakfast room. Ask for minibar in your room if you want it. Garage services. AE, DC, MC, V.

Pitti Palace, Via Barbadori 2 (tel. 282.257). 40 rooms. Near Ponte Vecchio, it combines Old World warmth with modern comfort. Roof terrace overlooking the city from beyond the Arno. AE, V.

Porta Rossa, Via Porta Rossa 19 (tel. 287.551). 71 rooms. Huge, well-furnished rooms, many with fireplaces, frescoes or casement ceilings. An old favorite, slightly tattered, but a unique find in the heart of town. Breakfast only. For two couples: the suite in the 13th-century tower has a breathtaking 360° view. AE, DC, MC, V.

La Residenza, Via Tornabuoni 8 (tel. 284.197). Elegant little pension with many rooms overlooking the roofs of Florence; front rooms are noisy. Delightful roof garden; garage service; friendly atmosphere. Bed and breakfast allowed, but half-pension is preferred.

San Giorgio & Rex, Via S. Antonio 3 (tel. 284.344). Most rooms are quiet. Completely renovated hotel near station and the straw market; parking facilities. DC, V.

Silla, Via de' Renai 5 (tel. 284.810). Modest but clean and friendly establishment below Piazzale Michelangelo. Roof garden with magnificent views of the river nearby.

Inexpensive

Alessandra, Borgo SS. Apostoli 17 (tel. 283.438). Huge old-fashioned pension furnished with massive antiques. Simple but clean. Ask for a room overlooking the Arno.

Boboli, Via Romana 63 (tel. 227.169). Good value for rooms without bath, as each has its own just down the hall. Simple pension near back entrance to Boboli Gardens. A favorite with Italian groups; ask for a room on quiet garden.

Bretagna, Lungarno Corsini 6 (tel. 263.618). 16 rooms. Old-fashioned but clean; all rooms are on back courtyard except one on the river (noisy, but what a view!). Frescoed breakfast room. Midnight curfew.

Costantini, Via Calzaioli 13 (tel. 215.128). 9 rooms. Rooms with bath are better here, as ten or more people use each public facility. Lively pension at the bottom of its category for price. Half- or full-pension terms available.

Cristallo, Via Cavour 27 (tel. 215.375). 17 rooms. Ask for quieter rooms overlooking the courtyard. Family-style in aristocratic old palace. Some rooms have casement ceilings, frescoes or balconies; massive antique furniture. Old but clean. AE, DC, MC, V.

Europa, Via Cavour 14 (tel. 210.361). 8 rooms. All new baths. Modern, clean and quiet hotel in Renaissance building with charming courtyard. Good value. MC.

Nizza, Via del Giglio 5 (tel. 296.897). 17 rooms. All new baths. Breakfast not included in price. With rates at the bottom of the category, this simple hotel is a very good bargain. Garage facilities. v.

Palazzo Vecchio, V. Cennini 4 (tel. 212.182). 8 rooms. 18 rooms in an immaculate 19th-century villa. Back rooms overlook private garden. Around the corner from the station, but like staying in a country home. Own parking lot. Best buy near the station. AE, DC, MC, V.

Rigatti, Lungarno Diaz 2 (tel. 213.022). 28 rooms. Charming rooms with new baths in a genteel 16th-century palace. Some rooms overlook the Arno, but others in the back over a delightful garden are quieter. Stunning loggia for breakfast or afternoon drinks. Book well in advance.

La Scaletta, Via Guicciardini 13 (tel. 283.028). 11 rooms. Some rooms overlook the Boboli Gardens; hold up to 5 beds. Splendid roof garden for breakfast. This genteel pension in a quiet 16th-century palace is a wonderful bargain. Reserve well in advance.

La Terrazza, Via Taddea 8 (tel. 294.322). 37 rooms. Ask for a room with airconditioning in summer. A bit threadbare but clean. Frescoed restaurant. Garage facilities.

Versailles, Via Martelli 3 (tel. 287.575). 9 rooms. Simple pension just 20 yards from the Cathedral.

Rock-Bottom

Casci, Via Cavour 13 (tel. 211.686). 14 rooms. Just down the street from the Cathedral, this pension has some rooms with balconies and others overlooking a quiet garden. Friendly, helpful management. AE, DC, MC, V.

Donatello, Via Alfieri 9 (tel. 587.521). 10 rooms. Cheerful, quiet and clean; neatly furnished. Popular with American students.

Esplanade, Via Tornabuoni 13 (tel. 287.078). 24 rooms. No frills, but all rooms have new baths. Cheapest buy on fashionable Via Tournabuoni.

Fiorentino, Via degli Avelli 8 (tel. 212.692). 11 rooms. At the bottom of the category for price; simple and stark but clean. No breakfast.

Firenze, Piazza Donati 4 (tel. 214.203). 48 rooms. Some rooms with 3, 4 and 5 beds. Simple, but very clean and quiet pension not far from Cathedral. Best buy in this category.

La Locandina, Via dei Pepi 7 (tel. 240.880). 10 rooms. All rooms with bath give onto a delightful courtyard. No singles. Slightly tattered but immaculate pension in 15th-century patrician palace. Good value.

Margareth, Via della Scala 25 (tel. 210.138). 9 rooms. Some rooms overlook a private garden. Bare essentials; no breakfast.

Regina, Borgo la Noce 8 (tel. 292.346). Near San Lorenzo; cordial owner and brand-new bathrooms. Good value.

Universo, Piazza Santa Maria Novella 20 (tel. 211.484). 53 rooms. Simple favorite with students and backpackers. Skip breakfast if you want, but be sure to get a room on the back, where it's quiet.

Apartments

If you're on an extended stay in Florence, you might want to check into a furnished apartment. Any of these agencies can lend a hand, for a fee.

Adams, Via Romana 32 (tel. 222.401);

American Agency, Via del Ponte Rosso 33r (tel. 495.070);

Roma, Via delle Pallottole 1 (tel. 288.648);

Soggiorno Italia, Via dei Servi 38 (tel. 284.828);

Solemar, Via Cavour 80 (tel. 218.112);

Or try a residence, where you'll find fully furnished mini-apartments with daily maid and switchboard service:

Firenze Nova, Via Panciatichi 5 (tel. 477.851), has 1-, 2- and 3-room modern apartments and a bar downstairs. Minimum one month.

Palazzo Ricasoli, Via delle Mantellate 2–6 (tel. 352.151), is a refurbished 16th-century palace near Piazza della Libertà. An average apartment rents for about 500,000 lire per week.

Porta al Prato, Via Ponte alle Mosse 16 (tel. 354.951), has comfortable mini-apartments in a modern building near the Cascine. 500,000 lire per week and up.

Youth Hostels

Ostello Europa Villa Camerata, Viale Augusto Righi 2–4 (tel. 600.315). Not very conveniently located and sleeps up to 100 in a room, but there are quiet gardens and optional dinner. Take bus 17B from the station; I.Y.H.F. card required. You can also get the *Guide to European Hostels* here.

Pensionato Pio X-Artigianelli, Via dei Serragli 106 (tel. 225.044). Smaller and cleaner than the others, but it's much harder to get a room here.

Santa Monaca, Via Santa Monaca 6r (tel. 268.338), in a former monastery near the Carmine church. Crowded but clean, showers free, also kitchen privileges. Ask about discounts at nearby restaurants. From 9:30 A.M. to noon, drop any ID card in the box, then return between 4 P.M. and midnight.

Camping

Florence has several organized camping grounds. For information on all camping facilities write to Federazione Italiana del Campeggia, Casella Postale 649, 50100 Firenze.

Italia & Stranieri, Viale Michelangelo 80 (tel. 681.1977). The closest to town; reached by the 13 bus from the station. Open to midnight, Apr. to Oct.

Mugella Verde, S. Piero a Sieve (tel. 848.511), is farther from town but very luxurious, with pool, tennis courts, riding and bungalows. Take the Barberino exit off the Autostrada del Sole and follow the signs.

Panoramica, Fiesole (tel. 599.069). Also offers bungalows, kitchens, ironing facilities and a playground for the kids. Take the 7 bus from the station, get off at Fiesole and follow the signs for a 15-minute walk. Open Easter to Oct.

Villa Favard, Via Rocca Tedalda 527, Rovezzano (tel. 652.520). For those needing only a place to stretch out in their sleeping bags under cover; showers and toilets.

Eating and Drinking

FOOD AND DRINK. For many years Italian restaurants abroad have tended to specialize only in southern Italian fare, so Tuscan food may hold a great many surprises in store for you. Simple and basic, liberally splashed with the excellent local olive oil and washed down with good red Chianti, it is served you in countless *trattorie* and *ristoranti* throughout Florence. Here you'll find genuine Tuscan recipes prepared with good, fresh ingredients and served with care.

Be adventurous and try some of the small, unpretentious neighborhood places suggested on the restaurant list below. You'll be eating with the locals, who tend to be demanding. In Florence, paying more doesn't necessarily mean eating better. Tuscans are generally parsimonious people who have carefully maintained their family fortunes, unlike the southern Italian aristocrats whose romantic extravagance has often brought them to ruin. As a result, the food in a modest trattoria may be inexpensive *and* delicious. Service in the various *bucas* and rustic trattorias often borders on the brusque, but don't be put off. Waiters in such places are known for their rudeness; it's part of the Florentine character and atmosphere.

A typical Florentine breakfast is a cappuccino (half coffee and half milk) and *brioche* (Italian croissants filled with cream or jam or chocolate or *semplice*—plain), consumed standing up at the bar. Later in the morning one might have a slice of salami, a *crostone* (toasted bread slathered with paté or tomatoes) or *prosciutto di cinghiale* (wild boar ham) with a glass of wine. Pizza is very un-Tuscan, but a few small shops sell it in take-out size squares.

Any self-respecting Florentine meal begins at the *antipasti* table. Some restaurants really specialize in these *hors d'oeuvres,* which can range from simple pickled vegetables to the most sophisticated dishes. When the table in the middle of the dining room holds up to 50 tempting selections, join the Italians and make a meal of *antipasti,* perhaps finishing up with a dessert. For some real Tuscan specialties, try any kind of *crostino* (toasted homemade bread spread with liver, meat or olive paté, among others), *fettunta* (garlic bread made with first-run olive oil), *panzanella* (a salad of tomatoes, red onions, basil and bread), *porrata* (leek pie), *torta di carciofi* (artichoke pie), *trippa in insalata* (tripe salad, with garlic and parsley).

Soup is a favorite, especially on blustery winter evenings. Any Florentine will tell you that *carabaccia* was the model for the famous French onion soup. *Minestra di pane* (a spicy bean soup), classic *minestrone* and *pappa al pomodoro* (tomato soup thickened with bread) are generally more faithful to the original versions than *ribollita,* which has evolved into a delicious vegetable soup with bread added. *Pasta e ceci* (pasta with chick peas) and *pasta e fagioli* (pasta with navy beans) are two of the best ways to eat beans.

The Florentines have their own pasta specialties. *Crespelle alla fiorentina* are light and airy crepes filled with spinach and ricotta cheese; *tortelle* or *topini* are similar to ravioli and may be filled *al magro* (with spinach and ricotta) or *alla carne* (with meat). *Pappardelle alla lepre* are flat noodles with wild hare sauce. You'll find *penne* (quill-shaped tubes of pasta) served in all kinds of ways. A wonderful—and costly—treat is *pasta al tartufo* (sprinkled with white truffles from Alba). For a first course that will really pre-empt the second, have *timballo alla fiorentina,* a rich pie made of pasta, a pastry crust, meat sauce and mushrooms.

This is a meat town, and its favorites are pork and beef. Most meat is grilled over an open fire with a few herbs and a drop of oil. *Arista* is pork roast; it is prepared *alla fiorentina* with garlic, rosemary and oil. Florence is one of the few places in Italy where you can get a good steak, and the *bistecca alla fiorentina* is a huge T-bone. Most often, it's served for two; its cost is determined by its weight, and it will increase your dinner bill considerably. However, if you're dying for a good piece of meat, this is the one to get. Smaller steaks are called *bistecchine* or *braciole*. *Pollo alla diavola* is a whole chicken that is split, flattened and grilled with lots of black pepper. Or try *fegatelli* (skewered pork livers). *Involtini al carciofo* (boned pork chops rolled around artichokes and *mortadella*) are a change from grilled meats; *scaloppine* may be served *alla fiorentina* (topped with spinach, ham, cheese and white sauce) or *al limone* (in a lemon sauce). *Stracotto* is the closest you'll get to pot roast; *cibreo* is an age-old concoction of livers, kidneys and sweetmeats served with a lemon-and-egg sauce. Florentines are very fond of innards, especially tripe, which almost every typical restaurant serves *alla fiorentina* (in a light tomato sauce). And try some of the wonderful wild game brought in from the Tuscan woods. *Coniglio alla cacciatora* (stewed rabbit with vegetables in tomato sauce) was invented here, as was *anatra all'arancio* (duck with orange sauce), although the French claim it as theirs.

Although you will find excellent restaurants specializing in fish, there is not a wide variety of it in Florentine cooking. For something different, try *anguilla alla fiorentina* (eels in a sauce of red wine, garlic, sage and lemon). *Baccalà alla fiorentina* is salt cod in tomato sauce; *baccalà e ceci* (codfish with chick peas) is another old favorite. *Seppie ripiene* (cuttlefish filled with spinach, ricotta and vegetables) are a local invention, while *sogliola alla fiorentina* is sole with spinach and parmesan cheese. If you like such things, try *ranocchi all'ortica* (frogs in nettle sauce) or *chiocciole in umido* (stewed snails).

As elsewhere in Italy, you'll find plenty of fresh vegetables served in restaurants. *Asparagi alla fiorentina* are buttered asparagus topped with fried eggs and parmesan; *carciofi alla fiorentina* are artichokes with spinach, lemon, parmesan and white sauce. *Cavolo strascicato* (cauliflower with tomatoes, black olives and sausage) is a delicious side dish, as are *fiori fritti* (fried zucchini flowers, stuffed with anchovies), *piselli alla fiorentina* (fresh peas with bacon and garlic), *piselli al prosciutto* (peas sautéed with ham) and *spinaci alla fiorentina* (spinach with parmesan and white sauce). But the Tuscan side dish par excellence is beans, usually white *cannellini*. *Fagioli al fiasco* are simply beans cooked in a sealed bottle to preserve their flavor; *fagioli all'uccelletto* (with tomatoes, sage, rosemary and garlic) is one of Tuscany's star dishes.

The best way to end a meal in Florence is also the simplest. Ask for *biscotti di Prato* or *quadrucci*, hard, dry almond biscuits that turn into heavenly delicacies when dipped into *vin santo*, a sweet white dessert wine. In the fall, try *castagnaccio* (chestnut custard pie). *Cremetta al mascarpone* is a sinfully rich pudding laced with rum. *Frittelle alla fiorentina* are crepes filled with raisins and served in a *vin santo* sauce. *Pandiramerino* is a traditional sweet bread, and *schiacciata alla fiorentina* is a cake flavored with orange and saffron.

Generally, drinking water in Florence is perfectly safe. Public drinking fountains, where some inhabitants still draw their daily water, come from natural springs. If you don't want to take any chances, stick to *acqua minerale*, either *gassata* (sparkling) or *naturale*.

RESTAURANTS. Florentines are fairly early eaters, by Italian standards. Lunch is served from 12:30 until 2:30; dinner from 7:30 until 10:30 or 11. Rare is the restaurant that stays open later; if you're on the prowl after midnight you'll have to head for a beerhall, pub or night club. Almost all eating establishments close one day a week and for a few weeks' vacation, as listed here. It's a good idea to have your hotel concierge check that these dates haven't changed in the meantime.

Our restaurant listings give details of which of the major credit cards are accepted by each restaurant we list. These appear as AE for American Express, DC for Diners Club, MC for MasterCard (incorporating Access, Cartasi, and EuroCard), and V for Visa.

Restaurant Prices. We have divided all the restaurants in our listings into price categories. Prices, per person, including wine are, in lire:

Expensive	60,000–95,000
Moderate	30,000–55,000
Inexpensive	20,000–25,000

Expensive

Enotecha Pinchiorri, Via Ghibellina 87 (tel. 242.777). Near Santa Croce. In the lovely Renaissance home of Giovanni da Verrazzano, this exclusive restaurant serves the best nouvelle cuisine in town, along with first-class wines. One of Italy's top restaurants. Reserve ahead. Closed Sun., Mon. lunch, and Aug. AE, DC, MC, V.

Il Cestello, Piazza Ognissanti 3 (tel. 294.301). The city's poshest restaurant, in the famed Excelsior hotel. Magnificent surroundings, whether on rooftop terrace overlooking the Arno (May to Sept.) or in posh *Renaissance* salon in winter; impeccable service, top-notch international and Tuscan cuisine. Reserve ahead. AE, DC, MC, V.

La Grotta Guelfa, Via Pellicceria 5r (tel. 210.042). Across from the main post office. Low on romantic atmosphere, but the food here is tops. Try for a table outside in the loggia. Closed Sun. and in Dec. and Jan. AE, DC, MC, V.

Harry's Bar, Lungarno Vespucci 22r (tel. 296.700). Impeccable service in a relaxed but sophisticated setting. Americans love it; it's the only place in town for a decent martini and club sandwich. Some well-prepared international dishes, too. The bar is open for drinks from late afternoon to midnight. Closed Sun. and mid-Dec. to mid-Jan. AE.

Il Lorenzaccio, Via B. Rucellai la (tel. 217.100). Fine international and Tuscan cooking in luxurious surroundings. Connected with the hotel Villa Medici. Reserve ahead. AE, DC, MC, V.

Nandina, Borgo SS. Apostoli 64r (tel. 213.024). This elegant restaurant is a favorite with the designers and owners of the chic boutiques around the corner on Via Tornabuoni. Good imaginative Tuscan cooking. Closed Sun. and in Aug. AE, DC.

La Posta, Via Pellicceria 28r (tel. 212.701). Charming restaurant across the street from the main post office, with large rooms and a few tables on a terrace. Florentines love the fish here; also *topini,* as the locals call *gnocchi;* and the *porcini* salad. Closed Tues. AE, DC, MC, V.

Le Rampe, Viale Giuseppe Poggi 1 (tel. 681.1891). Charming location in the woods below Piazzale Michelangelo (take a taxi!). Eat out on the terrace for a pleasant view. AE.

Relais Le Jardin, Piazza Massimo D'Azeglio 5 (tel. 587.655). International and traditional Tuscan food in a refined setting. Impeccable service. By reservation only. Closed Sun. AE, DC, MC, V.

Sabatini, Via Panzani 9a (tel. 282.802). Near Santa Maria Novella, this is one of Florence's most famous restaurants. International and Tuscan cooking in an elegant setting. Reserve ahead. Closed Mon. AE, DC, MC, V.

Silvio, Via Parione 74r (tel. 214.005). Near Via Tornabuoni and the designer shops, this big fish restaurant has lots of atmosphere and plenty of local devotees. Reserve for dinner. Try the *tartufi di mare* (raw sea truffles) or *aragosta* (lobster). Closed Sun., Mon. and mid-July to mid-Aug. AE, DC, MC, V.

Terrazza Brunelleschi, Piazza dell'Unità Italiana 6 (tel. 215.642). Rooftop restaurant of the Hotel Baglioni, it has marvelous views of the cathedral dome. Elegant empire decor, outdoor dining in summer. Fine Tuscan cuisine. Reserve. Open daily. AE, DC, MC, V.

Lo Zodiaco, Via delle Casine 2 (tel. 234.0984). Seafood and Sicilian cooking. Evenings only. Reserve ahead. Closed Sun. and in Aug. AE, DC, MC, V.

Moderate

Alfredo sull'Arno, Via dei Bardi 46r (tel. 283.808). This bustling modern restaurant is near Ponte Vecchio. Get here early to sit outside overlooking the Arno. Closed Sun. and half of July. AE, DC, MC, V.

La Barcaccia, Via Lavatoi 3 (tel. 283.958). Near Santa Croce, this rather haughty establishment is a favorite with Italian show people, whose photos plaster the walls. Try the *taglierini alla Beatrice,* with a delicate lemon sauce. Closed Mon., Jan. and Feb. V.

Il Bargello, Piazza Signoria 4 (tel. 214.071). For a relaxed meal outdoors in this famous square, this is probably the best bet. Closed Mon. and Nov. to Mar. AE, DC, MC, V.

Il Barone, Via Romana 123 (tel. 220.585). Near the Pitti Palace, this international restaurant has a garden for summer evenings. Closed Mon. AE, DC, MC, V.

Bibò, Piazza Santa Felicità 6r (tel. 298.554). Just around the corner from Ponte Vecchio, a simple neighborhood place with delicious spaghetti *al granchio* (with crab). Closed Tues. AE, DC, MC, V.

Buca dell'Orafo, Via dei Girolami 28r (tel. 213.619). Traditional Tuscan cooking in a small cellar restaurant with typical Florentine atmosphere. Near the Signoria. Closed Sun., Mon. and Aug.

Buca Mario, Piazza Ottaviani 16r (tel. 214.179). Uninspired surroundings downstairs, but good Tuscan cooking. Near Santa Maria Novella. Closed Wed. AE, V.

Buzzino, Via de' Leoni 8r (tel. 298.013). Pleasant, old-fashioned atmosphere with attentive service and good Tuscan specialties. Closed Thurs. DC, V.

Camillo, Borgo San Jacopo 57r (tel. 212.427). Excellent Tuscan cooking, served in a charming atmosphere. Very popular with the owners of the area's expensive antique shops. Closed Wed., Thurs. and Aug. AE, DC, MC, V.

Cantinetta Antinori, Piazza Antinori 3 (tel. 292.234). The Tuscan meals and snacks served in this small, elegant wine cellar are really only an excuse to taste the famed Antinori wines, some of which are true rarities. Be sure to ask the waiter's advice. Closed Sat., Sun. and Aug. AE, MC, V.

Cibreo, Via dei Macci 118 (tel. 234.1100). Near the Sant'Ambrogio market, it presents updated versions of Florentine classics in an upscale trattoria-style dining room or outdoors in summer. Inventive cooking; no pasta. Reserve. Closed Sun., Mon. and Aug. 1 to Sept. 10. AE, DC, MC, V.

Coco Lezzone, Via del Parioncino 26r (tel. 287.178). An earthly, crowded trattoria with whitewashed walls, red-checked tablecloths and ebullient international clientele, it serves classic Florentine fare. Closed Tues. eve. and Sun. (Sat. and Sun. in summer).

Da Noi, Via Fiesolana 46r (tel. 242.917). Near Santa Croce, it has a reputation for creative cuisine, served in an intimate dining room. Call at least 3 days ahead for reservations. Closed Sun., Mon., and Aug.

Dino, Via Ghibellina 51r (tel. 241.452). Quiet wine cellar near Santa Croce, with cordial and competent family in charge. Choose between good regional meals or a wide variety of cheeses and wines. Closed Sun. eve., Mon. and Aug. AE, DC, MC, V.

Le Fonticine, Via Nazionale 79r (tel. 282.106). Excellent Tuscan food and homemade pasta in a characteristic setting. Try the *tortellini*. *Porcini* mushrooms are always on the menu in season. Closed Sat. and Aug. AE, V.

Latini, Via Palchetti 6r (tel. 210.916). Good simple Tuscan cooking in an old-fashioned *fiaschetteria*. Near Via Tornabuoni, good for a quick lunch after the shops close for the midday break. Closed Mon. and Aug.

Leo, Via Torta 7r (tel. 210.829). Small and elegant, this friendly restaurant near Santa Croce specializes in *grancrostone alla piercapponi:* mozzarella, mushrooms, tomato and truffles served *au gratin* on a large slice of country bread. Closed Mon. and for two weeks in Aug. AE, DC, MC, V.

La Loggia, Piazzale Michelangelo 1 (tel. 287.032). Large bustling restaurant overlooking the famous square and Florence below. Don't come here for a romantic dinner, as it's usually crowded with tourists. Closed Wed. and in Aug.

Mamma Gina, Borgo San Jacopo 37r (tel. 296.009). Near the Ponte Vecchio on the Oltrarno side, this quiet restaurant has vaulted ceilings and an excellent *costola alla valtellina:* rib roast stuffed with mushrooms, ham and cheese. Closed Sun. and the first half of Aug. AE, DC, V.

Maria da Ganino, Piazza dei Cimatori 4r (tel. 214.125). Very central, informal and cheerful, this rustic trattoria offers homemade pastas and heavenly cheesecake for dessert. It's tiny and popular, so reserve. Closed Sun. and Aug. 15–25. AE, DC.

Natale, Lungarno Acciaioli 80r (tel. 213.960). Near Piazza Santa Trinita. You'll find this simple neighborhood haunt full of habitués, who like the friendly waiters and good wholesome food. Try the rich *tiramisù* (literally, "pick-me-up") for dessert. Closed Tues. and Aug. MC, V.

Nello, Borgo Tegolaio 2r (tel. 218.511). Good Tuscan food in a rather dark wine cellar. Try *fricandò* (roast veal stuffed with pistachios). Closed Mon. and half of Aug.

Osteria del Cinghiale Bianco, Borgo San Jacopo 43r (tel. 215.706). Very popular restaurant near the Ponte Vecchio. The local antique dealers feel at home with its old statues and marble pieces, so be sure to reserve ahead. Try the wonderful *cinghiale con polenta* (wild boar with corn mush). Closed Wed. and in Jan.

Il Paiolo, Via del Corso 42r (tel. 215.019). Near the Cathedral, a small restaurant full of pretty plants, with friendly service, a good selection of *crostini* and wonderful *costoletta di maiale:* pork chop with olives and rosemary. Closed Sun. and Mon. lunch. AE.

La Pergola, Via Sant'Antonino 10r (tel. 298.917). Good wholesome food from the nearby Central Market. Try the *scallopine* with *porcini* mushrooms. Closed Sun.

Sasso di Dante, Piazza Pallottole 6r (tel. 282.113). In a quiet square off to one side of the Cathedral, this tiny restaurant is best in summer, when you can eat outside. Closed Thurs., Fri. and Jan. AE, DC, MC, V.

Sostanza, Via del Porcellana 25 (tel. 212.691). Locally known as Il Troia, loved by generations of Florentines and frequented by enterprising tourists, this characteristic restaurant near the Ognissanti church has the very best *bistecca fiorentina* in town. Get there early or be prepared to wait, and don't plan to linger, for the blustery waiters won't let you. Closed Sat. eve., Sun. and Aug.

Vecchia Firenze, Borgo degli Albizi 76r (tel. 294.163). Near the Bargello Museum, this pleasant eatery is in a patrician palace. Closed Mon. AE, DC, MC, V.

Inexpensive

Acqua al Due, Via dell'Acqua 2 (tel. 284.170). Near the Signoria, its traditional Tuscan cooking and imaginative new fare are very popular with the young. Try the mixed pasta: five different varieties. Closed Mon. and Aug.

Angiolino, Via Santo Spirito 36r (tel. 298.976). This charming restaurant on the Oltrarno side of the river has vaulted ceilings, an open fire and brick floors. Sit by the stove in winter. Food is simple but excellent. Closed Sun. eve., Mon. and in July.

Bordino, Via Stracciatella 9r (tel. 213.048). Near Ponte Vecchio, this is a favorite with local shop people and is always crowded. Special limited-choice menu at a rock-bottom fixed price. Closed Sun., Mon. and Aug. AE, DC, MC, V.

Break, Via delle Terme 17r. A fun place for an easy-going snack or light lunch, near Ponte Vecchio. Excellent *crostoni,* pasta and crepes at rock-bottom prices. Closed Sun., Nov. and Dec.

Il Caminetto, Via dello Studio 34r (tel. 296.274). Near the Cathedral. Good Tuscan specialties in a characteristic setting. Try the *maccheroni alla Maremmana* with sausage, tomatoes and black olives. Closed Tues., Wed. and July.

Cantinone del Gallo Nero, Via Santo Spirito 6r (tel. 218.898). This Oltrarno wine cellar is run by the classic Chianti vineyards, whose symbol is the black rooster (*gallo nero*). Needless to say, wine is the star here, but simple Tuscan soups, pastas and pizzas are perfect sidekicks. Closed Mon. and in Aug. AE.

Casa del Vinsanto, Via Porta Rossa 15–17 (tel. 216.995). A bustling combination restaurant-pizzeria-tavola calda in the heart of town, this is a great place for a quick meal of any kind. No frills, but consistently good food. Closed Mon. AE, DC, MC, V.

Da Cesarino, Via dei Pepi 12 (tel. 241.756). In the Santa Croce area, this small, unpretentious family restaurant serves delicious homemade pasta. A real bargain. Closed Thurs. AE, DC, V.

Del Fagioli, Corso Tintori 47 (tel. 244.285). Near Santa Croce. Small and friendly, with a great *antipasti* table. Closed Sun., Sat. and Aug.

Gabriello, Via Condotta 54r (tel. 212.098). Good Tuscan food in a pleasant wood-paneled dining room, near the Signoria. Closed Sun. and in Aug.

La Galleria, Via Guicciardini 48r (tel. 218.545). In the heart of the shopping district, with uninspired decorations but good, imaginative food. Specializes in fish. Closed Sun., Jan. and Feb.

Giglio Rosso, Via Panzani 35r (tel. 211.795). Near Santa Maria Novella. This popular neighborhood place is crowded and noisy, but that's because the food is excellent. Closed Sun. AE, DC, MC, V.

Nella, Via delle Terme 19r (tel. 218.925). A quiet, small neighborhood place near Piazza Santa Trinita, serving good Tuscan specialties. Closed Sun.

Pinocchio, Via della Scala 28r. Near Santa Maria Novella. An unpretentious local place with delicious *sfoglia alla pistolese,* flaky pastry stuffed with *porcini* mushrooms, cheese and tomatoes. Closed Sat. and Sun. AE, DC, MC, V.

Quattro Leoni, Via Vellutini 1r (tel. 218.562). Near the Pitti Palace, this very simple neighborhood eatery has a few tables outside. Cozy in winter, with the open fire blazing. Rock bottom prices. Closed Sun. and Aug.

San Niccolò, Via San Niccolò 60r (tel. 282.836). At the very bottom of the price category, this delightful, tiny osteria is always full of cheerful young people. Share a big marble table and have simple but delicious food with excellent local wine. A great bargain, if you're not looking for luxury. Closed Sun. and half of Aug.

La Verandina, Via Cavalieri 2 (tel. 293.048). Locals come here to eat at long wooden tables under an awning in a quiet courtyard. The selection is small, but food is excellent and prices are rock bottom. Closed Sat., and Nov. to Mar.

Zi' Rosa, Via dei Fossi 12r (tel. 287.062). Plenty of truffles and *porcini* in a large pink dining room. Closed Thurs. and in July. AE, DC, MC, V.

Trattorias

Moderate

Del Carmine, Piazza del Carmine 18r (tel. 218.601). This small neighborhood trattoria has a few tables outside on a beautiful square. Try the delicious *cremino* for dessert. Closed Sat. eve., Sun. and Aug.

Il Che C'è C'è, Via dei Magalotti 11 (tel. 262.867). A tiny trattoria near Santa Croce specializing in spicy foods. Try *riso alle rose* (rose-flavored rice) for something unique. Closed Mon. and July.

Pennello, Via Dante Alighieri 4 (tel. 294.848). Between the Signoria and the Cathedral. You may have to wait for a seat in this lively trattoria, a favorite with locals. Try the excellent antipasti, or crepes on Sun. Closed Mon., Sun. eve. and in Aug.

Totò, Borgo San Jacopo 6 (tel. 212.096). Unpretentious trattoria on the Oltrarno side of the river with a huge open grill and a large selection of *antipasti.* Closed Wed. AE, DC, MC, V.

Inexpensive

Baldini, Via Panzani 57r (tel. 283.331). Near the station and low on atmosphere, but the wide range of *antipasti* is excellent. Try *fazzoletti alla nonna:* flaky pastry filled with ricotta cheese and spinach and served with meat sauce. Closed Wed. AE, DC, MC, V.

Buca Poldo, Chiasso degli Armagnati 2r (tel. 296.578). Tiny, top-value trattoria near the Signoria. Three tables outside in a quiet courtyard. Friendly and reasonable. Closed Thurs. and Jan.

La Casalinga, Via dei Michelozzi 9r (tel. 218.624). In the Santo Spirito area, and a favorite with locals. Service is casual, but the food is good, especially the huge salads. Very inexpensive. Closed Sun. and half of Aug.

Da Marco, Via dei Benci 13r (tel. 214.162). Between Santa Croce and the Arno. Eat downstairs or outdoors at this typical trattoria. Closed Mon.

Pasquini, Via Val di Lamona 2r (tel. 218.995). Tiny but with a real family atmosphere. Near the straw market. Closed Sat. eve., Sun. and Aug.

Pizzerias

Pizza is not as popular in Florence as in many other Italian cities, but there are a few regulation pizzerias, which means they cook their fare in wood-burning ovens, but only in the evening. These places are usually noisy, entertaining and filled with young people. Prices are low and closing time generally later than for restaurants. A few of the above restaurants also serve pizza.

Il Boccale, Via SS. Apostoli 33r (tel. 283.384). As well as pizza, this informal eatery also offers a good selection of *antipasti* and salads. The mixed grill for two is a specialty. Closed Mon. and July.

Il David, Via Rondinella 95r (tel. 604.565). So popular with Florence's young that it spawned a David 2 on the Via Aretina. Also serves cold plates and *antipasti.* Closed Sun., and Nov. to Mar.

Dante, Piazza N. Sauro 12r (tel. 293.215). At the Oltrarno side of Santa Trinita bridge. Always full of students, who like the modern plastic decor. Reasonable prices; also specializes in *penne.* Closed Wed.

Nuti, Borgo San Lorenzo 34r (tel. 210.410). It bills itself as the original old pizzeria Nuti, for there's another by the same name on this street. Closed Sun.

La Rosy, Viale Fratelli Rosselli 45r (tel. 475.991). Lots of pastas and pizzas and occasional live music at this popular meeting place. Closed Mon.

I Tarocchi, Via dei Renai 12–14r (tel. 217.850). You share your table in this large noisy pizzeria. A good meeting place for students. Not far from Palazzo Pitti. Only at night, until 1. Low prices; menu prices include tax and cover charge. Closed Mon.

Fast Food

In the San Marco area, the take-out **pizza stand** at Via Cavour 112r has sandwiches, calzoni and slices of pizza for an on-the-road snack. Down the street at 61r, **Money, Money** has typical fast food with tables. Or try **Le Colisée,** at 52r, for pastries and snacks at a few tables.

If you're near the station, the **self-service bar** at Via Nazionale 17r is unusually clean and has a good selection of ready-made sandwiches and snacks. And if you're having McDonald's withdrawal shock, try **Italy, Italy,** the big splashy fast food place at Piazza della Stazione 36r, on the left of the station. The usual, plus a nice salad bar and a few uninspired pastas.

The closest to the Cathedral is **Bottegone,** across the street at Via Martelli 6r, with a good selection of sandwiches, ice cream and fruit desserts; tables upstairs and down. **Marchetti,** at Via Calzaioli 100–104r, has a good selection of snacks, sandwiches and salads, with plenty of tables.

Near the Central Market and San Lorenzo flea market, the **Stuzzichino** at Piazza San Giovanni 24r has a wide selection of sandwiches. Near Piazza della Repubblica, **Hot Pot,** in Via Calimala, has a good *tavola calda,* lots of sandwiches and snacks, and three rooms of tables. Be careful if you're on a budget; this can be pricey.

At Piazza Santa Croce 11, **Don Burger** has fast food with outside tables in the sun. And the bar in the square has a good selection of pizzas, sandwiches and ice cream desserts, with a few outside tables.

Ponte Vecchio is a great area for quick snacks. The bar at the Oltrarno end of the bridge has pizza, sandwiches, shrimp cocktails and salads, with a few tables inside and out. To the left, at Via dei Bardi 64r, **Kenny's** has typical McDonald's-type fast food in a psychedelic atmosphere; the tables by the plateglass window have one of the choicest views of the Arno. Across the river on Por Santa Maria, **Queen Victoria** is a big clean place with one of the best selections of salads, pastas, cold meats and ice creams, plus plenty of tables, both inside and out in the garden. There's also lots of room at **Self-Serve,** up the street on the corner of Via Lambertesca. The bar at Por Santa Maria 26r has a good selection, with tables hidden in a tiny garden facing onto Santo Stefano church. Across the street, **La Borsa,** at 55r, has lots of the usual fare, with tables in a covered gallery. And finally, around the corner at Volta dei Mercanti 7r, **Niccolino** serves excellent sandwiches and salads at tables in a quiet courtyard.

Around the corner from Palazzo Vecchio, at Piazza San Firenze 1r, the **Badia** serves good snacks at pleasant tables, outside.

Wine Bars. The venerable old Florentine response to fast food, these charming places usually have a faithful local clientele, always a good sign.

Near the Duomo, try the tiny bar at Via Sant'Antonino 45r, where you can have a salami or cheese sandwich made to order, with a glass of excellent local wine. Across the river in Borgo San Jacopo 19r, sit at the bar and have delicious salami sandwiches or hamburgers made to order. Near the Signoria is **Piccolo Vinaio,** on Via dei Castellani, just behind Palazzo Vecchio, with tables on the charming square. Rock-bottom prices; closed in the cold months. The **Fiaschetteria,** on Via dei Neri, between the Uffizi and Santa Croce, serves tasty *antipasti* and sandwiches made to order.

CAFES. Italians love to pass the time by sitting at a sidewalk table while sipping coffee or an aperitif, reading the paper or simply gazing at the world. And there's no more entertaining way to rest your weary feet. Remember, however, that you cannot order at the bar and carry your own food outside. Table service is more expensive but it buys you the right to linger as long as you like.

In the San Marco area, **Le Colisée,** Via Cavour 52r, has a comfortable tea room.

To the left of the station the **Bar le Rose,** Piazza dell'Unità Italiana, has tables on the street and a good selection of cocktails or sweets. Or try the **Antico Caffé del Moro,** Via del Moro 4r, a charming old cafe.

Piazza Repubblica is known for its cafes. Try **Gilli** for a relaxed breakfast; have the best brioche in town as you plan your day's activities. Next door, **Paszkowski** has live music on summer evenings (and a cover charge). **Donnini** and **Giubbe Rosse** are across the square. But whichever you choose, watch out for the bold pigeons, which will nibble your toes to get the crumbs you may drop.

Behind the Baptistery, **Scudieri,** at Piazza San Giovanni 18–19r, has some of the very best pastries in town, in a posh setting. **Café de la Paix,** Piazza del Duomo 19r, is the only outdoor cafe in the square. Satisfy your eyes and your sweet tooth in one fell swoop.

Behind Palazzo Vecchio, **Fratelli Bronzi,** Via Gondi 2r, is a charming tea room with candies and cakes. Or sit on the square, at **Rivoire,** Piazza della Signoria 5r, famous for its hot chocolate (there's a chocolate *factory* in the basement!).

On fashionable Via Tornabuoni, **Procacci,** at 64r, has tiny tables in the characteristic setting of an old specialty shop. Try their truffle or salmon canapés. **Giacosa,** at 83r, is another smart cafe. **Caffé Strozzi,** Piazza Strozzi 16–17r, is a sophisticated, up-market cafe with tables in the relatively quiet square.

Some of Florence's most pleasant cafes are at Piazzale Michelangelo. Several can be found in the shade of trees above the famous square, both to the right and left. Or walk down the hill and stop in at **Il Rifrullo,** Via San Miniato 1–3r, where heavenly crepes are served on a leafy terrace in front of one of Florence's medieval gates.

Ice Cream and Pastry Shops.
Near the station, **Bondi,** at Via Nazionale 61r, has a good selection of ice creams. In the San Marco area, **Bamboo 2,** Via Cavour 65r, has about 50 flavors to choose from. Down the street at 30a, **Petrucci** has a large and scrumptious selection of pastries. The **Pasticceria,** at 102r is a pleasant place with a few tables.

The area around the Cathedral rewards diligent sightseers with a great choice of ice cream at **Florence,** Via Martelli 13r; **Duomo,** Via dell'Oriuolo 57r; and **Stuzzichino,** Piazza San Giovanni 24r, also good for snacks. **Romoli,** Via dei Servi 85r, and **Robiglio** at 21r (also on the other side of the Cathedral, at Via de Tosinghi 9–11r) are renowned for their pastries.

The bar in Piazza Santa Croce has lots of ice cream, including fabulous gelato-filled *cannoli.* **Gelatino,** at Via de' Neri 20r, and **Vivoli,** Via Isola delle Stinche 7r, also have a great selection.

Near the Santo Spirito or Carmine church, try **Ricchi,** Piazza Santo Spirito 9r, for ice cream, or **Cennini,** Borgo San Jacopo 51r, an elegant old-fashioned pastry shop.

In the vicinity of Ponte Vecchio your best bet is **Old Bridge,** Via dei Bardi 64r, where you can choose from crepes, 30 flavors of ice cream or a few wild concoctions and sit with a view of the Arno, the Uffizi, Palazzo Vecchio and the Cathedral dome.

Across the river and near the Signoria, **La Bottega del Gelato,** Via Por Santa Maria 33r, has a wide selection of flavors. For candy, stop in at **Migone,** Via Calzaioli 85r. Try the *torrone, sflogliata* (something like peanut brittle), and *panforte,* an incredibly rich Tuscan fruitcake.

PUBS AND BEER HALLS. There aren't many pubs in Florence, but you're bound to hear English spoken in these two: **BeBop,** near the Cathedral, at Via dei Servi 76c, is a steak house and pub as well as something of a music hall; or drop in at **Borgo Antico,** Piazza Santo Spirito 6r (tel. 210.437); closed Sun. and Mon. lunch.

Italian beerhalls are a good bet for the late-night crowd, since most of them stay open until 1 or 2 A.M. **Birreria Centrale,** Piazza Cimatori 1 (tel. 211.915) serves all kinds of beer, including special "ecological" varieties, and light snacks; closed Sun. **63 Rosso,** Via San Zanobi 63r (tel. 471.490) has low-priced crepes and *focaccie farcite* (something like hot pitta sandwiches); closed Sun. **Tally Ho,** Via Condotta 7–9r (tel. 296.804) has lots of beer, great pastas and sandwiches until 2 A.M. A favorite with Florentine teenagers. **I Due Amici,** Borgo San Frediano 102r (tel. 295.181), near the hostels, serves sandwiches and beer at rock-bottom prices until 2 A.M.; closed Sun.

PICNICS. If you're planning an excursion to Boboli or the Cascine park, or going out of town for the day, why not pack a light lunch to save time? Stop in at any *alimentari* shop, where you'll find cold cuts and cheese, to be bought by the *etto* (100 grams; about three and a half ounces). Most grocery stores will have a few drinks in the cooler, too. Pick up some fresh bread from the *forno* and you're all set. For special delicacies, try the shops listed here.

Norcineria, Via Sant'Antonino 21r, has a fabulous selection of salami, sausage, ham, in a wonderful old-fashioned store. **Azzarri,** Borgo San Jacopo 27cr, sells salamis, hams, sausages, cheese, wines and specialty foods. **Pomo Doro,** Via Lambertesca 15r, has a mouth-watering array of delicatessen delights in a beautiful shop near the Uffizi. And for the largest selection of all, head for the **Mercato Centrale** in the square of the same name, open from early in the morning to 1 P.M., and from 4 to 8:30 P.M., Oct. to May.

Shopping

For most people, a trip to Italy wouldn't be complete without a good shopping spree. Florence, with its age-old tradition of fine craftsmanship, is the place to find special mementoes, unique gifts and unabashed extravagances. Practically every street has at least one enticing workshop or boutique, and the city still offers some of the best bargains in Italy. You would be wise to have a good look around first, perhaps as you walk from one museum to another. What you see may help you decide what to buy, and you can make a note of addresses and prices, for later comparison.

Remember that bargaining is a thing of the past. You may have luck at the outdoor markets, but Italian shops and department stores stopped playing with prices long ago. As a rule of thumb, *prezzi fissi* means that no amount of savoir faire will get you a discount; *saldi* are seasonal sales, which can be excellent, if you keep your eyes open. Be sure you are buying what you want, as most stores will not refund purchases. And think twice before you have anything shipped by the store: it may never get there. You will find many shops that honor your credit cards or accept dollars and pounds, but if you pay with cash be sure to get a receipt. You may need it for customs back home.

What will you be seeing in all those masterfully decorated shop windows? Leather goods are certainly Florence's great shopping attraction. Smart suits and jackets, unusual bags, sophisticated footwear and sleek gloves are all over town. Then there are the world-famed Italian fashions. Even if you can't afford a one-of-a-kind evening gown, you can browse in the same famous-name boutiques used by princesses and movie stars—there's always a chance you might pick up an initialed coin purse or handkerchief at an affordable price. Ties, scarves and hats are also first-rate bargains.

Florence is known the world over for wonderful jewelry, both old and new. Some of the most interesting places for jewelry are the workshops themselves, where you can watch craftsmen create settings, filigrees or cameos. Prato, one of the great fabric centers of the world, is just a few miles away, so it's no wonder that fine linens, laces and upholstery fabrics abound in Florence. If you're planning to re-do your living room soon, keep an eye out for material that might be extravagant at home. And don't forget that Italy's hi-tech lamps are the most sought-after in the world.

In this city, the only problem with souvenirs is that there are too many. Whether it's straw hats and bags, alabaster or leather chess sets, gilded wooden frames or trays, fine prints, hand-painted ceramics or marbled-paper desk items, you'll have a hard time deciding what to buy. And if you like antiques, this is the city for you. Florence has a fabulous selection, from inexpensive knick-knacks to the finest 15th-century furniture and paintings. Experts might want to check into some of the antique fairs scheduled each year; novices should avoid expensive purchases, which may not be as authentic as the salesperson avows.

For inexpensive gifts, try an open-air market. San Lorenzo is the biggest and has the widest choice, including straw bags, gloves, leather wallets, scarves, coral and just about anything else. The straw market in Piazza del Mercato Nuovo specializes in souvenirs and leather and straw goods. For a combination of acceptable quality and low prices, this is definitely your best bet. The flea market in Piazza dei Ciompi, near San Lorenzo, sells antiques (many overpriced), miscellaneous junk and a good range of copperware. And there's a lively street market every Tuesday in the Cascine park just down the river from Ponte Vecchio. Try bargaining at these outdoor markets. It's fun, and you just might save a few dollars!

Almost all shops in Florence close for lunch from 1 to 3:30 or 4. You'll find that a lot of the smaller shops open at 9:30 or even 10 in the morning. Everything closes at 7:30 or 8 P.M. and most shops close on Monday morning. In July and August, shops close on Saturday afternoon; food shops close on Wednesday afternoon, except for July and August when they, too, close on Saturday afternoon. August is the most frustrating time to shop, with a great many shops locked up tight for the month.

Leather Goods. For glamorous designer boutiques, you can't beat Via Tornabuoni. Start at **Gucci** world headquarters, in two stores at 59r and 71–79r. Here, you'll find everything from a 22-piece set of handmade luggage to an enameled key ring. Join the crowds and browse: you're sure to find something. Next door at 61–63r, **Celine** has refined bags, shoes and women's fashions. **Maria Valentino**, at 65–67r, is one of Italy's most successful shoe designers, vying for sales volumes with **Ferragamo,** just down the street at 12–16, where there's a splashy array of styles to choose from. Along with **Gucci, Vuitton** makes the world's most-copied bags and suitcases. Stop in at # 49r and you're bound to recognize their renowned signature. If it's more trendy designers you're after, try **Orangi** at 17; **Desmo** at 18r; **Gherardini,** at 27r; or **Casadei,** at 33r. Around the corner at Via della Vigna Nuova 62–66r, **Etienne Aigner** has classic bags, shoes and women's wear. A few blocks away at Piazza Del Duomo 21–22r, **Piero Generini** has a smashing collection of leather goods; another must is **Beltrami,** whose lavish stores at Via Calimala 11r and at Via Calzaioli 44r and 31r draw shoppers like a magnet.

Tanino Crisci, at Via Tornabuoni 43–45r, makes shoes to order and also has a handsome collection of ready-made shoes. At Via Calimala 12r, on the corner of Via Lamberti, **Pollini's** top-notch styles are impeccable. In the Cathedral neighborhood, **Di Varese,** at Via Cerretani 49–55r, and **Bata,** at Via Martelli 31r, have a wide range of good quality shoes. For less expensive footwear, try **Asso,** nearby at Via Panzani 32r; **Proposta,** at Via del Corso 50r; **Gori,** at Piazza Santa Croce 14r; or the leather factory outlet around the corner at Corso Tintori 19–21r. Across the river, **Rive Gauche,** at Borgo San Jacopo 46r, and **Smalto** next door at 42r, also have low-priced shoes. And don't miss **Santini & Dominici,** at Via Calzaioli 95r, for the most imaginative footwear in town, *and* at reasonable prices.

Florence has Italy's widest selection of purses, beginning with the designer boutiques and continuing with such luscious handbag shops as **Franco Pugi,** in Via SS. Apostoli 48r, or **Bojola** at Via Rondinelli 25r, both just off Via Tornabuoni. Near the straw market, **Alessandrini,** at Via Vacchereccia 17r, sells Emmy bags, billed as the world's softest leather purses. Around the corner from Ponte Vecchio at Lungarno Archibusieri 12r, **Papini** has a wide selection; nearby at Via Parione 35r, **Il Bisonte's** bags are more trendy but every bit as luxurious. **Cellerini,** at Via del Sole 37r, has more of the same exquisite wares. For a famous signature at lower prices, try **Mandarina Duck's** off-beat plastic bags, travel bags and wallets, at Por Santa Maria 15r. In Piazza Santa Croce, **Leather Guild** at 20r and many other shops in the area have a good collection of inexpensive bags for women of all ages and tastes.

Not even Italy produces good leather clothing at low prices any more. But you can find some good buys if you look carefully. Try the shop at Via Guelfa 1D, near San Marco; or **Renard,** at Via Martelli 21–23r. At Lungarno Corsini 4r, **Gandola** sells classic styles at reasonable prices; **Dalexander,** around the corner at Via SS. Apostoli 15, has similar offerings. Smart Florentines buy their gloves at **Ugolini's** elegant little boutique in Via Tornabuoni, 20r. Or if you're heading for Palazzo Pitti from the Ponte Vecchio, stop in at the **Madova** glove factory outlet, Via Guicciardini 1r.

Boutiques. Florence's elegant shopping district has a full complement of top Italian designers. On Via Tornabuoni you'll find **Gianni Versace** (# 13–15) and **Giorgio Armani** (# 37r), both with fashions for men and women; **Daniel Hechter** (# 4), with more casual sportswear; and **Trussardi** (# 34r), the king of Florence's renaissance as a fashion center. Around the corner, **Enrico Coveri's** smart shop is at Via della Vigna Nuova 21–29r; # 47r is **Valentino's** emporium. Near Piazza della Repubblica, **Beltrami** has a vast selection on two floors at Via Calimala 44–50r; **Eredi Chiarini's** rigorously classic styles for men are at Via Porta Rossa 42r (their other shop is at Via Roma 18–22r). In the same area, **Marina Rinaldi** has stunning women's wear for large sizes, at Via Calzaioli 14r.

For less expensive high fashion, the selection is just as good. Off the beaten path at Borgo Pinti 65r, **Zavota** is as small as it is chic. Nearby, **La Mela** at Via della Pergola 43r will make women's apparel, using your own fabric or design, if you can wait ten days for delivery. **Diavola Rosa,** at Via Strozzi 11–19r, has a big selection of wild sportswear. Nearby at Piazza Limbo 2r, **Giorgio Vannini** has women's fashions. **Fiorucci's** famed whacky ideas for guys and gals are at Piazza Strozzi 12–13r. **Alex's** store at Via della Vigna Nuova 17–19r, has more offbeat styles by such designers as Basile and Les Copains; **Happy Jack** has men's wear at # 7–13r; **Emanuele Zoo** has wild originals at # 16–20r.

Via Roma is another good street for high-quality fashions: both **Raspini,** at # 25–29r, and **Carrano,** at # 6–10, have clothes for men and women; **Ermanno Daelli** has slightly more trendy men's fare, at # 12r; **Luisa,** at 19–21r, has a long list of offbeat designers including Kenzo, Gautier and Byblos (her other store is at Via del Corso 54r). **Romano** is a few feet away, at Piazza della Repubblica 46r. If your taste tends toward the old-fashioned, try **Chiffon** for charming lace dresses, lingerie and blouses, across the river at Via Romano 134. And for children, the shop at Borgo San Jacopo 5r has delightful styles.

Of course Florence has plenty of inexpensive sportswear to offer, too. **Benetton** is king in this area, with three shops (Via Sant'Antonino 39, Via Calimala 2–6, Por Santa Maria 66–68) full of clever mix-and-match separates. **Stefanel,** at Via Roma 15–17r, is as much like **Benetton** as you can get. Yet another spinoff is **Sisley,** at Via Tornabuoni 24r, Via Roma 7r and Piazza Mercato Nuovo 34r. Still more inexpensive sportswear can be found at **Niagara,** Via del Corso 50r; **Kermess,** Via Proconsolo 5r; and **Last Cry,** Via Romano 39.

Shirts, blouses and accessories are classic Florentine purchases. For a little of everything, go where the natives go: **Dalmassa** (Via Tornabuoni 81r). **Bertelli,** at # 30r, has a wide selection of silk ties and will make shirts to order; more ties are on sale at **Roxy,** Via Cerretani 33r. For the best-quality straw hats in town, head for **Paoli** (Via della Vigna Nuova 26r). **Stagnanini,** at Piazza Santa Croce 26r, has oodles of silk ties and scarves; if you're across the river, try **Piera & Bruna,** at Via Guicciardini 6r. Near the Cathedral, **Cambini,** at Via Calzaioli 22r, has lots of hats, including the famous Borsalino for men.

Jewelry and Handicrafts. You can go haywire buying jewelry in Florence, so look around a bit first. Via Tornabuoni has **Cascio's** splashy fake baubles at # 32r; **Manfredi's** trendy designs at # 6; **The Shabby Shop's** priceless antique wares at # 38r; and **Cartier's** mainstream gems at Piazza Santa Trinita 1. Around the corner at Lungarno Corsini 16r, **Botteguccia** sells sumptuous cameos and corals; more of the same is on sale at **Sebastianelli** (# 30r). Of course the heaviest metal concentration is downriver at Ponte Vecchio. **Gherardi,** at # 8r, has antique corals and cameos; **Mannelli,** at # 14, is more contemporary than the rest; **Tozzi** (# 19), **Vaggi** (# 20) and **Cardini** (# 34) have a lovely selection of delicate gold necklaces, bracelets and rings; **Rajola** (# 24) and **Burchi** (#

54) have extravagant styles; **Pacci** (# 42) and **Melli** (# 46) have exquisite antique jewels, tableware and instruments. Nearby, at Vicolo Marzio 2r, the **Casa Artigiana dell'Orafa** is a workshop where you can see things being made. At the other end of the bridge, **Giuggiu** has great jewels and accessories made exclusively from synthetic fabrics (Borgo San Jacopo 82r). In the Piazza della Repubblica area, **Gabriella Nanni** has gorgeous contemporary jewelry made with silver, lapis lazuli and turquoise (Via Lambertesca 28r); and **Rocca,** at Via Roma 2–4, has classic designer pieces.

You'll find plenty of shops selling gorgeous hand-embroidered linens along with smart modern sheets and towels. In the Via Tornabuoni area, browse at **Industrie Femminili Italiane,** at Lungarno Corsini 34r; **Baroni** and **Cesari,** at Via Tornabuoni 9r and 2 respectively; or **Bruno Spadini,** at Lungarno Archibusieri 6r. Near Ponte Vecchio there's **Taf,** at Por Santa Maria 17r. **Pratesi,** at Lungarno Vespucci 84, is the most famous of them all; **Ghezzi,** at Via Calzaioli 108r, is less expensive.

Sumptuous upholstery fabrics that would be prohibitive at home are affordable in Florence, so don't be afraid to ask prices. **Rubelli** is at Via Tornabuoni 3r; **Valli** is at Via Strozzi 4–6r; **Antico Setificio Fiorentino,** at Via della Vigna Nuova 97r, displays the fabulous silk fabrics handmade at the museumlike workshop in the San Frediano district at Via Bartolini 4; **Casa dei Tessuti,** Via dei Pecori 20, near the Cathedral, has a good selection of high fashion fabrics; and **De Angelis** has slick postmodern fabrics at Piazza Santa Trinita 3r. Behind the Cathedral, **Cecchi** has a luscious selection at Piazza San Giovanni 13–14r. **Blue Home** is nearby at Via Porta Rossa 56r. Also for the home, have a look at the wonderful ultra-modern lamps that no one makes quite like the Italians. **Artemide,** at Piazza del Duomo 41r; and **Flos,** at Borgo San Jacopo 62r, have a great selection.

Another Florentine specialty is hand-marbled paper. **Papiro,** with shops at Via Cavour 55r and Piazza del Duomo 24r, takes first prize, using its fanciful papers to cover all manner of desk items; they also have clever papier-mâché animals. On Piazza Pitti, at 37r, **Giannini** is one of the city's oldest purveyors of paper goods. **& C.,** at Via S. Egidio 22r, has unusual notebooks and cards. **Bottega del Libro,** on Lungarno Corsini 40r, adds papier-mâché carnival masks to its collection. **Oli-Ca,** nearby at Via SS. Apostoli 27r, also has all sizes of boxes. **Pineider** stationery shops can be found around the world, but the one at Piazza della Signoria 14r is the original; kings and presidents have their calling cards made up here (there's another store at Via Tornabuoni 76r).

Antiques. Florence is one of Italy's greatest centers for antiques. Most of the dealers are concentrated in two areas near the Arno: Borgo San Jacopo and Borgo Ognissanti. In Borgo San Jacopo, just off Ponte Vecchio, browse through **Mirna Gabellieri's** antique frames and statuettes (# 80r); stop in at **Lo Spillo** (# 72r) for a charming selection of antique jewelry, frames, boxes, bottles, and pins; enter the impressive portal at 70r for knick-knacks, furniture, toys and glassware. **Cose del '900** (# 45r) has admirable art deco glassware; the little girl's dream attic at # 68r has an incredible hodge-podge of junk and jewels; the shop at 64r has priceless one-of-a-kind furniture. Farther on, you'll find less expensive shops such as **Camiciotti** (Via di Santo Spirito 9r) or **Confetti** (Borgo San Frediano

12r). Across the river on Borgo Ognissanti, each shop is a display of exquisite taste. Particularly impressive are **Hall** (# 58r); **Baroni** (# 52r); **Pietro
Betti** (# 44–46r); **Fioretto** (# 43r); **Pierini** (# 22r); **Romano** (# 20r)
and **Ventura** (# 14–16r). **Pino Marletta,** around the corner in Via Mazzetta 2r, has priceless antique ceramics. Nearby Via dei Fossi is another
gold mine: **Noel Dutilleul** (# 10r) has instruments and ceramics; **Griffo**
(# 19r) and **Ottaviani** (# 44r) have high-quality furniture; **Antonio Frilli**
(# 26r) has marble and bronze statues. For more art, try **Peter Bazzanti
& F.,** Lungarno Corsini 46r, with reproductions of statues from the Greeks
to Matisse; **Moscardi,** down the street at 36r, for tasteful antique frames;
Margua Antichita, at Via Magliabecchi 1r (near Santa Croce); or **An-
dreini,** at Via Proconsolo 63r, for antique statues and ceramics. **Bellini,**
slightly out of the way at Lungarno Soderini 5, is one of the most prestigious of all.

Souvenirs. Florence is a good place to stock up on inexpensive gifts.
You'll find them all over town, especially near the Cathedral, Palazzo Vecchio, Santa Croce and San Lorenzo. For a bit of everything, try Piazza
Santa Croce 8r; **Cellini,** next door at # 12; **Aram,** across the square at
27r; **Giorgi,** nearby at 32r. Across the bridge, there are two all-purpose
shops in Via Proconsolo, at # 3r and 13r. At Lungarno Acciaiuoli 40,
The Little Shop has plenty of variety. Nearby on Via della Vigna Nuova,
you'll find **Baccani** at # 75r and **Vexus** at # 15.

Hand-painted pottery is another Tuscan specialty, beautiful to look at
if impractical to carry home. For a good selection, try **Sbigoli,** at Via S.
Egidio 4r. You can watch the artist at work in the window of **Ceramica,**
at Borgo Pinti 40r; the shop at Via dei Benci 39 (near Santa Croce) has
excellent pottery at slightly higher prices; **Galleria Macchiavelli** at Via
Guicciardini 18a has a vast selection (their other shop is at Via Porta
Rossa 13r). Near Ponte Vecchio, a shop at Via dei Bardi 65r has especially
lovely wares. Straw products are best bought at open-air markets, but
you'll find a wide selection at **Piero,** Via della Scala 21r.

If you like art books, prints or posters and know how to evaluate what
you're seeing, you've got a good chance of coming away with a true find.
Try **Campani,** near the Cathedral at Via dei Servi 22r; **Cose del Passato,**
at Via dei Fossi 3r; or **Sarti,** at Borgo San Jacopo 40r. For books on art
in general and that of Florence and Tuscany in particular, go to **Salimbeni,**
Via Matteo Palmieri 14r. **Alinari,** at Via della Vigna Nuova 46–48r, has
wonderful old photos of the town and its inhabitants, taken through the
years by the famed Alinari brothers.

The crafty Florentines have all kinds of ideas for your gift list. **Sughero,**
around the corner from the Cathedral at Via dei Servi 9r, sells clever
knick-knacks made of cork and unpainted pottery; **Domo,** at Via della
Scala 21r, has alabaster gifts. And what about stunningly designed house-
hold gadgets? **Proforma,** at Via Tornabuoni 47r, has a good selection; **La
Porcellana Bianca,** just off Ponte Vecchio at Via dei Bardi 53r, has more,
along with a pristine array of pure white ceramics. The little shop at Via
del Parione 32r sells those wooden Pinocchios that delight children of all
ages.

Department Stores. If you find yourself wandering aimlessly through
blistering streets while the rest of Florence has an afternoon siesta, head

for Piazza della Repubblica 2r, where you'll find the big **UPIM** store, which stays open from 9 A.M. to 8 P.M. Browse through the inexpensive range of goods and try the third floor for unusual housewares, linens and yarns. And if you've bought so much you need an extra suitcase, pick one up on the mezzanine. **Principe,** which takes up an entire block between Via Tornabuoni and Piazza Strozzi, is a different kind of store, with several designer boutiques and a vast array of fine apparel.

Entertainment

Florence's Maggio Musicale festival in May and June offers a program of world-class musical events at the big Teatro Comunale, the elegant little Teatro della Pergola, and at other venues in the city. For a program and tickets, write to the Biglietteria del Teatro Comunale, Corso Italia 16, 50123 Firenze (tel. 277.9236) and order by mail. Last-minute tickets are usually scarce.

Throughout the summer, the Teatro Comunale stages ballet, concerts and opera in the courtyard of the Pitti Palace. The Estate Fiesolana, Fiesole's summer festival, has a full program of concerts, opera, ballet, theater and movies. Book through Globus, Piazza Santa Trinita 2r (tel. 214.992). The best all-round guide to the many, many events held in and around Florence is the magazine, *Firenze Spettacolo;* it's in Italian, but you'll be able to understand the programs. Pick it up at newsstands.

Concerts. The regular music season is particularly rich in Florence, with all sorts of formal and informal concerts held all over town. Check *Firenze Spettacolo* (or ask at your hotel) for special events, scheduled in palazzi, churches, villas and museums. The *Amici della Musica* (tel. 608.420) organize excellent musical events most of the year. The Lyceum, at Via Alfani 48, also has a busy season. Most important musical events are held at the Teatro Comunale; box office is at Via Solferino 15 (tel. 277.9236). For information on the Tuscan Regional Orchestra's concerts in churches and palazzi, call 242.767.

Opera and Ballet. Everything takes place at the Teatro Comunale (see above). You'll find most programs rotate for several months, except special recitals or guest performances. Check for world premieres: they're not unusual. The opera season in Florence is usually the earliest of the year in Italy, opening at the end of September or beginning of October.

Movies. Florence has one English-language cinema, the **Astro,** in Piazza San Simone, near Santa Croce (tel. 222.388). There are usually two evening shows; admission 4,000 lire; closed Mondays and July. Occasionally, film clubs may show English-language films in the original; check the *Spettacoli* section of the newspaper. In summer, the city sets up two outdoor screens at Fort Belvedere; the setting is delightful and some films are shown in English. You'll find a program at the tourist offices.

Nightlife. Il Barretto, Via del Parione 50 (tel. 294.122) is a popular spot for drinks and piano music.

Caffè, Piazza Pitti 9 (tel. 296.241), gets a fairly sophisticated, international crowd. A pianist is usually on hand.

Loggia Tornaquinci, Via Tornabuoni 6 (tel. 219.148). A sophisticated cocktail lounge with a fabulous view.

Pintor's Blue Pearl, Piazza Strozzi 3 (tel. 298.745). This elegant little boite, located in the cellars of an aristocratic old palazzo, is a seemingly endless string of tiny rooms.

Poggetto, Via Michele Mercati 24B (tel. 460.127). Dancing to a live orchestra on Fri., Sat. and Sun. A pizzeria provides sustenance.

River Club, Lungarno Corsini 8 (tel. 282.465). In a lovely winter garden, with a large dance floor.

The Red Garter, Via de' Benci 33r (tel. 263.004). Occasional live music, but mainly canned banjos in this friendly, informal place, which looks exactly like you think it would, and is a tourist rendezvous.

Verde Luna, Viale Michelangelo 84 (tel. 68–127.917). Dancing indoors and out at this favorite old Florentine night spot nestled into the hillside overlooking the city.

Discos. Andromeda, Piazza dei Cerchi 7A (tel. 292.002). One of the largest in town; open every night.

Full-Up, Via della Vigna Vecchia 21r (tel. 293.006). A perennial favorite. Choose between service at the bar or at a table. Closed Tues.

Jackie O, Via dell'Erta Canina 24b (tel. 216.146). Refined and slightly more expensive than other clubs. The local jet set comes here. Closed Wed.

Space Electronic, Via Palazzuolo 37 (tel. 293.082). Ultramodern psychedelic disco with music as up-to-the-minute as you're likely to hear in this town. A lively dance floor, or quiet rooms for chatting. Closed Mon. in winter.

Tiffany, Lungarno Colombo 23 (tel. 676.912). This spacious locale also has a charming piano bar, with well-known Italian guest singers. Open Thurs. to Sun.

Yab Yum, Via Sassetti 5 (tel. 282.018). A favorite with the young international set. The whole elegant show, closed Mon., moves to **Central Park,** (tel. 356.723), just inside the entrance to the Cascine park, for the summer.

Miscellaneous

CHILDREN. Having trouble interesting your children in the historical glories of Florence? Take a deep breath and climb with them to the top of Giotto's Campanile (Belltower), next to the Cathedral. They'll love the climb and the bird's-eye view of the city. For less strenuous entertainment, take them to see the fully-armed cavalry battalion at the Stibbert Museum.

All kids love a fort, and Florence has two: Fortezza da Basso and the Belvedere. Each has plenty of ramparts, moats and lawn areas for picnics.

There are fairly well-equipped playgrounds—and lots of other kids—in the Cascine park (take bus 17C from the station or San Marco), and at the Rifredi play area (bus 28 from the station), where puppet shows are sometimes staged. In winter months, the Teatro Artigianelli at Via dei Serragli 105 (tel. 225.057) has colorful antique puppets and similar entertainment that transcends the language barrier, on Saturdays and Sundays. If you're still desperate, check the papers for the circus, or take them bowling or skating (see "Sports," below).

CLOSING TIMES. Normal business hours are generally from 9 or 9:30 A.M. to 1 P.M. and from 3:30 to 7:30 P.M. (winter) or 4 to 8 P.M. (summer). The UPIM department store at Piazza della Repubblica is a notable exception, staying open from 9 A.M. to 8 P.M. All shops are closed on Sunday. Non-food shops take Monday morning off (September–June 15) or Saturday afternoon off (June 15–September). Food shops close on Wednesday afternoon (Saturday afternoon in the summer). Hairdressers and barbers are closed Sunday and Monday. In August, only the most tourist-oriented shops stay open; even a great many restaurants close for the month.

CONVENIENT CONVENIENCES. Hotels and restaurants have public W.C.s, although many proprietors won't be pleased to let you use them if you aren't a customer. But don't despair. Few bars would begrudge the use of their facilities. In addition, you'll find public toilets in Piazza San Marco, Piazza dell'Indipendenza, upstairs at the Mercato Centrale, in the underground passage near the station and in the Fortezza da Basso parking lot, as well as in all the museums. Where there's an attendant, tip 100–200 lire.

The *Albergo Diurno* (day hotel), downstairs at the station, is a bit spartan, but it has toilets, bath tubs, showers, Turkish baths, plus a barber, hairdresser, manicure and pedicurist, dry cleaning and ironing services, even a shoeshine boy. There's another of these on Via Sant'Agostino, open Tues., Thurs. and Sat.

PARKS AND GARDENS. Florence has almost no small neighborhood parks. The great Renaissance families had large private gardens within the confines of their palazzi, and most are still inaccessible to the public. Still, there are a few spots where you can relax in sylvan surroundings.

Boboli Gardens. Created for Eleonor of Toledo, Cosimo I's Spanish wife, they cover the hillside behind the Pitti Palace and stretch all the way to Porto Romana. The gardens were the setting for lavish spectacles under the Medici Grand Dukes and the French princes. When Victor Emmanuel became Italy's first king, his official residence was Pitti Palace, but he preferred to live in a house in the Boboli, far more peaceful and private. Star attractions of the park include Buontalenti's grotto, where Michelangelo's *Slaves* once stood; the Roman Amphitheater, graced by a 3,500-year-old obelisk from Luxor; the Porcelain Museum, chock-full of priceless tableware used by the owners; a close-up view of Michelangelo's fortifications and a charming Coffee House. Picnicking is allowed only on the green in front of the Coffee House.

Cascine. This huge park was once Medici farmland. To get there, take bus 17C from the station to Piazzale delle Cascine, where you'll find a statue of George Washington (donated by Florence's American colony), a well-equipped playground and some refreshment stands. This spot is exactly at the park's halfway point. If you have a bicycle or moped you might like to make the excursion all the way to the end of the park, where you'll come across a Renaissance amphitheater, and the lovely little monument to Rajaram Cuttraputti, a 20-year-old Indian prince who died while visiting Florence in 1870. This half of the park is not recommended for pedestrians, as it is really a wild forest where you'll be alone and unguarded. For a pleasant stroll, take the shady bike paths or broad jogging track back to Piazza Vittorio Veneto, past the outdoor pool, race track, tennis courts, the Medici outbuildings and fragments of ancient marbles. On Tuesday mornings a lively street market lines the jogging track. On the feast of the Ascension (May or June) Florentines celebrate the Festa del Grillo (Cricket Day), enjoying huge picnic lunches in the park; for good luck, children buy caged crickets which they then set free.

Fortezza da Basso, Viale Strozze. A small quiet park with a lovely artificial pond. Children will love the huge swans.

Orto Botanico, Via Micheli 3. This botanical garden was founded by Grand Duke Cosimo I in 1545. Along with a majestic old yew tree planted in 1720, countless firs shade this quiet garden, next door to Italy's largest Botanical Museum. The garden is open Mon., Wed., and Fri. 9–12.

Orti Oricellari, Via della Scala 85. This is a private garden, dating back to the 15th century. But if you ring the bell and offer the concierge a small tip, he'll let you in to see the statue of Polyphemus, over 7½ meters (25 ft.) tall, by a student of Giambologna.

PHARMACIES. At the **International Pharmacy,** Piazza della Repubblica 23r, the attendants speak English and have a variety of British and American products. Most pharmacies are open from 8:30–11 and 4–8, but there are 24-hour pharmacies inside the station (tel. 263.435), in Via Calzaioli 7r (tel. 263.490) and at Piazza San Giovanni 20r (tel. 284.013).

Emergency Care. The only city hospital in the center of Florence is Santa Maria Nuova, around the corner from the Cathedral. The **Piccola Compagnia di Maria** hospital in Via di Villa Cherubini (tel. 572.556) is run by Irish nuns, who can help you arrange for medical treatment or find an English-speaking specialist. For 24-hour home visit service, call 475.411 and ask for English-language assistance.

POST OFFICES. The main post office is the Palazzo della Posta, which occupies an entire block of Via Pellicceria between Via Porto Rossa and Via degli Anselmi. Postal services, including the *Ferma Posta* (poste restante) are open here from Mon. to Fri., 8:15–7 and on Sat., 8:15–12 noon. For packages, around the back at Via de' Sassetti 4.

Other post offices, which stay open Mon. to Fri., 8:15–1:40, and Sat., 8:15–12 noon, are at Viale Belfiore 36 (Via Il Prato area) and Via Maso Finiguerra 15r (Borgognissanti area).

You can buy stamps at *Tabacchi* shops throughout the city, distinguished by black signs bearing a large white "T."

Telegrams. The *Telegrafi* offices in the Via Pellicceria post office and at the station are open around the clock seven days a week.

READING MATTER. Paperback Exchange, Via Fiesolana 31r (tel. 247.8154) has new and used English-language paperbacks for sale, in the Santa Croce area. The **BM** shop at Borgognissanti 4r has a good selection of American and English books. **Feltrinelli,** in Via Martelli 20r, near the Cathedral, has a small selection of best sellers and classics in English. Beautiful **Baccani,** at Via Porta Rossa 99r, also has fashion and a good selection of magazines. For art books, guide books, modern prints and fun posters of Florence, try **Becocci,** at Canto dei Nelli 10r (tel. 212.478), near the San Lorenzo market. At the straw market, **Del Porcellino** has some English paperbacks and guide books (Piazza del Mercato Nuovo 6–8r).

The *International Herald Tribune* and British papers are available at large central newsstands, where you'll also find English-language magazines. For the best selection of English-language reading matter, go to any of the three newsstands in Piazza della Repubblica.

Libraries. The **American Library** at Via San Gallo 10 (tel. 296.114) is open Mon. to Fri., mornings, 9–12:30. The **British Institute's** library, at Lungarno Guicciardini 9 (tel. 284.031) is open Mon. to Fri., 9:45–12:25, 3:15–7:15. Both have periodicals; the latter has a good selection of literature on Tuscany.

RELIGIOUS SERVICES. Services are held in English at the following locations. **Anglican:** St. Mark's, Via Maggio 18 (tel. 294.764); Holy Communion at 9 A.M. on Sunday and 8 P.M. on Friday. **American Episcopal:** St. James, Via Rucellai 9 (tel. 294.417); services on Sunday at 9:30 and 11 A.M. **Jewish:** The main Synagogue is at Via Farini 4 (tel. 245.252).

SIGHTSEEING TIPS. Museums. Museum hours may change with the season or with the whims (and budget) of custodians and authorities. Generally museums are open at least from 9–2 on weekdays and 9–1 on Sunday. In peak tourist season hours may be extended. It is always wise to check before planning your day. The city has recently set up videoscreens in the lobbies of the large museums with an up-to-date list of shows and hours. Try to get to the important museums before 9 or risk finding nightmarish lines. Save the small, lesser-known places for the mid-morning hours, hectic in larger museums.

State museums charge from 1,000 to 5,000 lire for admission. The old practice of free admittance on Sundays has been abolished. Remember that ticket offices close 30 to 60 minutes before closing time.

State and city museums are closed on January 1, Easter, April 25, May 1, the first Sunday in June, August 15 and December 25.

What to do on Monday. In a country where all national museums are closed on Mondays, Florence provides welcome exceptions. Try the Casa Buonarroti, Casa di Dante, Firenze Com'era, Museo Bardini, Museo Ebraico, Museo Horne, Museo dell'Opera del Duomo, Museo dell'Opera di Santa Croce, Museo Stibbert, Opificio delle Pietre Dure, Ospedale degli Innocenti, Palazzo Medici-Riccardi, Palazzo Vecchio, and the Santa Maria Novella museum.

Churches. Most churches are open from 7–12 and from 3–6, and you can expect to find almost all of them open on Sunday morning. Bear in mind that you'll miss much of their splendor on winter afternoons when sunlight is weak. The best time to visit a church is on your way to a museum in the morning, when there will be few tourists about. Have plenty of 100-lire coins ready and keep an eye out for littles boxes on chapel walls and at points of interest to drop them in to turn on the illumination.

SPORTS. Bowling is just starting to catch on here. You'll find a no-frills establishment half hidden in the courtyard at Via Faenza 71 (tel. 261.380), open every day, 3 P.M.–midnight. This isn't the world's best bowling alley, but it's a fun place to meet Italian youngsters.

Golf. The lovely club at *Golf dell'Ugolino,* Via Chiantigiana 1A (tel. 205.1009), is one of Florence's oldest sports landmarks. To get there, take the Strada Statale Chiantigiana from Piazza Franco Ferrucci for 11 km. (7 miles). The club has an 18-hole course shaded by olive, cypress and pine trees, plus a 9-hole putting course, a pool and tennis courts.

Horse Racing is a big event at the Cascine park. *Ippodromo della Mulina,* on Viale Pegaso, has harness races (tel. 411.130); *Le Cascine,* at Piazzale Le Cascine (tel. 353.394) has flat racing.

Riding. Tuscany is horse country. The sturdy local Maremmana mounts and softly rolling countryside make for a wonderful outing. *Centro Ippica Toscana,* Via de' Vespucci 5a (tel. 372.621) has horses and instructors; *Montefreddi,* on the Via Bolognese (tel. 813.435), is further from town but closer to the country.

Roller Skating. The rink at Viale Michelangelo 61r (tel. 681.1880) is open 9–12, 3–7 and 9–midnight. Skates are included in the fee.

Swimming. Most Florentine pools are private, but the city has a few, all charging 3,500 lire. The most extravagant is at *Costoli,* Viale Paoli (tel. 675.744), where you'll find three outdoor pools (covered in winter), a kiddie pool and high diving board. It's near Campo di Marte. The outdoor pool at *Bellariva,* Lungarno Colombo 6 (tel. 677.521) is smaller and not as clean, but *Le Pavoniere,* Viale degli Olmi in the Cascine park (tel. 367.506), is the most beautiful of them all, shaded by the park's ancient elm trees. It's usually open until midnight, and is normally less crowded than the others. Another indoor pool open to the public is *Amici del nuoto,* Via Romito 38b (tel. 483.951).

Tennis. The big club at Viale Michelangelo 64 (tel. 681.2686) rents courts from 8 A.M. to midnight; instructors are available, but you'll have to bring your own racket. Take the 13/ bus from the station. Another possibility is *Poggetto,* at Via Michele Mercati 24B (tel. 460.127). Courts are open 8:30 A.M.–11:30 P.M. and again, there are no rentals. Maximum advance reservations five days before. This club also has an outdoor pool, open Sat. and Sun. 9–6:30.

TELEPHONES. The Florentine area code is 055. Most phones have six numbers in Florence, but don't be surprised if some have seven, four, or even eight. At the railway station and a few other places you can use the brand-new *scheda* phones, which use cards instead of tokens. Buy your card at the baggage deposit window, for a value of 3,000, 6,000 or 9,000 lire. Tear off the perforated corner. Lift the receiver and insert the card with the corner (and arrow) facing down. You will now see your card's value in the window. After the call, hang up and the card will be returned at the bottom of the phone. You can continue to use it until it runs out.

Remember that it may cost much more to place a long-distance call from your hotel room. There's no extra charge at the SIP *Telefoni* offices at Via Cavour 21r, near San Marco (open 9–8), in the front wing of the railway station (open 7:30 A.M.–9:30 P.M. every day) and at the Via Pellicceria post office (open 24 hours). These offices have phone books for all

Italian cities. To place an international call, give the number to the operator behind the counter, then wait to be assigned a booth.

Emergency Calls. Police, fire or ambulance—call 113; Highway emergency and repairs—116; Main police station, foreigners' bureau, stolen cars—49.771 (English-speaking personnel from 9 A.M. to 2 P.M.); Red Cross—215.381.

USEFUL ADDRESSES. Consulates. *American,* Lungarno Vespucci 38 (tel. 298.276); *British,* Lungarno Corsini 2 (tel. 284.133).

Airlines. *Alitalia,* Lungarno Acciaioli 10–12r (tel. 263.051); *British Airways,* Via Vigna Nuova 36r (tel. 218.655); *British Caledonian,* Via Palestro 4 (tel. 262.380); *Pan American,* Lungarno Acciaioli 4 (tel. 263.804); *TWA,* Piazza Santa Trinita 2r (tel. 296.856).

Travel Agents. *American Express,* Via Guicciardini 49r (tel. 278.751); *CIT,* Via Cavour 56 (tel. 294.306) and Piazza della Stazione 51 (tel. 284.145); *Wagons Lits,* Via del Giglio 27r (tel. 218.851); *STS Student Travel Bureau,* Via Zanetti 18r (tel. 292.067); *Student Travel Bureau,* Via dei Ginori 11r (tel. 263.570).

VENICE

VENETIAN HISTORY

The date traditionally ascribed to the foundation of Venice is 421. But why anyone should have chosen to settle in the swampy malarial marshes of the Venetian lagoon in the first place, which hitherto had been the site only of a few communities of fishermen and salt gatherers—and the weekend homes of a small number of rich Romans with a passion for hunting—is easily answered. By the 5th century A.D., as what remained of the Roman empire rapidly disintegrated, successive waves of invading Huns, Goths and other marauders, sweeping south into Italy from central and northern Europe, repeatedly forced the peoples of the mainland cities around the lagoon, principally Aquileia and Padua, to take refuge among its dismal but defensible islands until the danger passed. Each time a few stayed on, hence, the traditional foundation of the city in 421. By 466 the little lagoon community had established itself enough to elect a government of sorts, the Tribunes.

However, it was only in 568, over 100 years later in other words, following the brutal invasion of northern Italy by the Lombards, that the settlement of the lagoon achieved much real momentum. It was then that the mainlanders finally threw in the towel and settled permanently in the lagoon.

Foundation and Growth

7th century. The island communities (who make their living trading salt) ally themselves with the Italian part of the Byzantine empire, the increasingly independent eastern half of the by now all but defunct Roman empire. In 697 the Byzantines replace the Tribunes with a new system of government centered around the Doge (from the Latin *dux,* meaning leader). They do this to ensure the city's continued defense against the Lombards. The effect is to promote Venice—though the city still won't be given this name for several centuries—high on the ladder of the Byzantine hierarchy, allowing the city to claim a relative degree of self-government. The Venetians will push for complete autonomy and the chance to become a sovereign state from now on.

8th century. Charlemagne's expansionist Frankish empire, centered in much of present-day France and Germany, takes over from the Lombards in Italy. Venice, caught between her links with Byzantium and a pragmatic desire for good relations with the Lombards, undergoes a minor civil war. With loyalties divided and the city weakened by factional in-fighting, she is wide open to attack by the Franks.

809. Pepin, Charlemagne's son, homes in on the lagoon from the sea, taking island after island. The inhabitants of the main island, Malamocco, escape, however, and retreat to the group of islands in the center of the lagoon called Rivo Alto (now the Rialto). From here, as Pepin's forces get stuck in the mudflats, they successfully ambush and defeat the Franks. This victory ensures that Venice is gradually recognized as a partner of Byzantium rather than a mere subject state.

829. The body of St. Mark the Evangelist is stolen from Alexandria in Egypt by the Venetians. They smuggle it out in a barrel of pork, safe from probing Moslem hands. St. Mark then replaces St. Theodorus as patron saint of Venice—he is considered very much more prestigious and thus more in keeping with the city's growing importance—and a new church (San Marco) is built.

9th and 10th centuries. Despite vicious bouts of fighting between powerful Venetian families, a gradual consolidation of the city's position takes place. Trade links are set up with the Germans; the Byzantines are squeezed out of certain traffic routes; punitive expeditions are mounted against the Slavs on the Dalmatian (Yugoslavian) coast; the fleet becomes more and more powerful; wealth is accumulated . . . Venice lines her nest.

976. Much of Venice is burnt (including St. Mark's) in a civil revolution.

997. Victory against the Dalmatians, thereafter celebrated annually as the Wedding with the Sea (Venice symbolically marrying the Adriatic).

1082–5. Victory in the Balkans over the Normans from south Italy, removing yet another obstacle on the Adriatic route to the Orient.

Toward the Apex of Venetian Power

12th century. Venice becomes involved with the Crusades (Christian Europe against the Moslems in Palestine) rather than with the struggle between the Papacy—centered in Rome—and the Holy Roman Empire—based in much of central Europe—which is tearing the rest of Italy apart. The reasons for this are financial: it has interests to maintain in the Middle East.

1202–4. The scandalous Fourth Crusade. The Frankish Crusader army fails to come up with payment for ships and provisions supplied by Venice. The blind 90-year-old Doge Dandolo skillfully obliges the Franks to subdue rebellious Venetian colonies on the Dalmatian coast and then to storm Byzantium (Constantinople) itself as compensation. The Crusaders never in fact get to the Holy Land, and the Moslem cause is actually reinforced by the temporary fall of Byzantium. Venice, on the other hand, comes out of the venture with the Cyclades, Durazzo, Lacedaemon, Crete and the Sporades under her dominion.

1256. Marco Polo born (died 1324). Travels to the Far East and brings back, as well as fabulous tales, precious jewels and spices, the secrets of how to make silk, and spaghetti (this last hotly contested by patriotic Italians).

1295. A street fight in Constantinople turns into a general attack by the Genoese on the Venetians and ends with the Venetian Governor being thrown out of a window and the wholesale massacre of the inhabitants of the Venetian colony.

1297. Change in constitution, concentrating the power in the hands of a few aristocratic families.

1298. Following the events of 1295, preparations for war with Genoa have been made and a battle is now fought off the island of Curzola. The Venetians lose disastrously and thousands are taken to Genoese prisons, including Marco Polo who, in order to relieve the boredom, dictates his adventures to a fellow prisoner.

1299. Venice makes a treaty with Turkey to ensure protection for pilgrimages to the Holy Land under its auspices, thereby gaining the monopoly of the lucrative tourist traffic for the Republic.

1310. Plot by the Tiepolo and Querini families to overthrow Doge Gradenigo, whereby Tiepolo hopes to rule as "Signore" in a type of government similar to that of other Italian city-states. It is foiled by an old woman who drops a heavy stone on the head of the rebel standard-bearer, causing the rebels to retreat in havoc and disorder.

1335. The narrow escape from the attempted coup of 1310 has persuaded the Venetians that it is necessary to change the constitution. A new, mind-bogglingly complex system is set up to "defend the freedom and rights of the people." It involves an elaborate procedure to elect, from the Grand Council, the Doge (just a figurehead), the elite Council of Ten (which is the real executive) and later, from 1539, the even more select Council of Three, which makes final decisions. Each of these is strictly rotated, the shortest term of office being one month for the Three. The Council of Ten employs its own secret agents, but can act on anyone's anonymous denunciations that are posted into the stone Bocca del Leone (Lion's Mouth). It is a ruthless, highly efficient body. Not only can it summon, interrogate, torture, accuse, try and execute a person in the course of a single day, or hire assassins to travel hundreds of miles to dispose of a victim, it can have people thrown into prison (the dreaded Pozzi, or the Piombi where Casanova spent 15 uncomfortable months) without telling them why, and even find them guilty for an *intention* to commit a crime. It has powers of intervention in every field of life: "public morals," occultism, science (Galileo came up against them on account of his discoveries), the arts and religion, as well as politics. In all Europe it is spoken of in hushed tones; in Venice the mere sight of the Inquisitor's gondola with its red flag makes citizens go white and cross themselves.

1355. Doge Marin Falier is beheaded after a plot to make him absolute ruler is discovered.

1373. Immigration of Jews to the city from the mainland. Originally they are made to live on the island of Giudecca but in the 16th century they will move to the Ghetto—a Venetian word—in the northwestern part of the city. (It will be abolished by Napoleon in 1797.) Although Jews are highly taxed and their freedom of movement limited, their position is safer here and generally more prestigious than almost anywhere else in Europe.

The Beginning of the End

The civil unrest of the 14th century is in part due to the aftermath of the terrible battles with Genoa, which has steadily been growing as a rival sea-power. It takes decades for each side to recover after each round. The end of this bitter duelling comes with the battle of Chioggia in 1380, at which the Genoese surrender. Genoa will never again be a serious threat to Venetian supremacy, but the victor is left too exhausted to resist the advancing tide of Turkish conquest.

1403–5. A remarkable recovery has been made since the costly (in terms both of lives and resources) victory over the Genoese, and Venice is in a position to be able to expand further. This time it looks to mainland Italy and conquers Bassano, Belluno, Padua and Verona.

1423. Under Doge Francesco Foscari, Venice eats its way west into Lombardy, north into the Trentino and south into the Dalmatian coast with the help of notorious *condottieri* (gentlemen mercenaries) such as Francesco Sforza (who has fought on the opposite, Milanese, side, and will do so again), Gattamelata, Colleoni, and Carmagnola (who is rewarded for resigning his services too early with torture and decapitation in 1431).

By 1454 the city has acquired more mainland territories: Ravenna, Treviso, Vicenza, Friuli, Brescia, Bergamo, Crema and Feltre, making Venice possessor of most of northern Italy. Thirty years of warring have taken their toll, however, and it is this, together with the appalling news that Constantinople has fallen to the Turks (1453), that persuades Venice in 1455 to join an alliance with its former enemies Florence and Milan against any power that might disturb Italy's peace.

At home, meanwhile, the ducal Foscari family have been in trouble. In 1445 Jacopo, the Doge's son, was charged with accepting bribes and condemned to exile. He refused to play ball and the case dragged on for six years with Jacopo behaving badly in exile at Trieste and Treviso (not far from Venice). In 1447 he had received a present of 2,000 ducats from Venice's then enemy, Duke Filippo Maria Visconti of Milan, which was confiscated. Now exiled to Crete as punishment, he writes a letter, which is intercepted by the Venetian authorities, to the Turkish sultan begging him to send a ship to take him away from the island. Jacopo narrowly misses a death sentence for this treacherous move (the Turks being Venice's arch-enemy) and is rebanished to Crete where he dies six months later. His father collapses into an almost catatonic state of grief. Urgent affairs of state are ignored and the Doge is necessarily, but humiliatingly, deposed in 1457. The legacy of his otherwise glorious reign is increased taxation, forced loans, national default, non-payment of salaries, depreciation of real estate, depression of industry and reduction in population.

It is the beginning of the end for Venice. The great economic and political power that had been built up since the 9th century, reaching its apex in the 13th and 14th centuries, now begins to crumble.

1463. For a century consuls have been warning the leadership about the Turkish peril but none of the Doges has taken any notice. This year the Turks conquer the Morea (in northwest Greece) and Epirus (in the Peloponnese).

1470. Venice loses the island of Negroponte (off eastern Greece).

1471. The Turks enter Istria and Friuli (northeast and due north respectively of Venice) and raze the provinces as close as Udine. Not one Italian state raises a hand to help.

1479. Venice surrenders to the Turks, giving up huge chunks of territory and agreeing to pay an indemnity and an annual tax for its trading privileges. The whole of Italy is suspicious of Venice's motives in agreeing to these demands and unites against her. Driven into a corner, the Republic resorts to inviting the king of France to claim Naples as his by right, and the duke of Orléans to take Milan, as a diversionary tactic.

The years that follow are a maze of political back-stabbing and chicanery, secret pacts, further defeats by the Turks, plans to slice up the Papal states on the death (in 1503) of Pope Alexander VI (of Borgia fame). Venice, however, is in an unfortunate position since France, by now involved to the hilt in Italian politics, decides that on balance it would be more sensible to join Spain, the Papacy, the Holy Roman Empire, Mantua and Ferrara in the League of Cambrai (1508) than stick with Venice. They form a quasi-crusading League, dedicated to fighting the enemies of Christianity, and go on to excommunicate the Venetian Republic which, as always in the history of its wranglings with the Church, Venice ignores.

Decline and Fall

16th century. In the last years of the 15th century Venice's mercantile supremacy, which had already been eroded by Turkish conquests, was further threatened by the Spanish and Portuguese discoveries of America and India. With the new century the center of the commercial world moves from Venice to the Iberian peninsula. The Venetian nobility lose interest in commerce and discovery and choose instead to live on their invested capital and the revenues of their mainland estates. In the whole of Italy there is a general turning inwards. Gradually, the Spanish and Austrians force the French out and establish themselves as the ruling power (Treaty of Château-Cambrésis in 1559).

1509. Venice temporarily loses her entire mainland dominion to the League. Soon, however, internal quarrels break up the League and over the next six years the Serenissima manages to cobble together a sizeable state in the north and east Italy again.

The tenacious Turks, after a brief respite, take to the warpath again, reclaiming colonies in the eastern Mediterranean (Egina, Paros and Syra in 1535, Malvasia and Nauplia in 1540, Cyprus in 1570) but are resoundingly defeated by the allied fleets (Venice, the Papacy and Spain) at Lepanto in 1571. The victory is greeted with enthusiasm by the Christian world with the exception of Spain, anxious not to see Venice grow as a power again. Split from within, the Christian forces fail to press home their advantage over the Turks. As a result, demoralized Venice withdraws from the war and signs a separate, crippling peace treaty.

1606. Relations with the Papacy have become increasingly strained since Lepanto. Venice, though religious up to a point, has always been adamant that the Church should not interfere with the running of the government. Quibbles with the Popes as to taxation of Church property, inspection of monasteries, the right of the Republic to try law-breaking clergy, turn into fierce disputes and finally to excommunication (once again) in 1606. In this long drawn-out quarrel, the Republic is defended by the highly intelligent theologist Paolo Sarpi, who becomes known in all Europe as a champion of national liberty against Papal aggression. Three attempts are made to assassinate him (in 1607, 1609 and 1610) but he is still advising the Senate on his deathbed in 1623.

1618–22. The blackest years of a black period. Paranoia sweeps the city as accusations of treason are made almost daily against hundreds of Venetians, all of whom are believed to be in the pay of the Austrians and Spanish plotting to seize the city. Numerous arrests are made and those found guilty are strangled and hung head downwards.

1644, 1657, 1669. More defeats by the Turks, with accompanying losses of territory.

1683–1703. Some territories are won back under the leadership of Doge Francesco Morosini. For a time it seems that Venice will return to her former glory as a great maritime power, but it proves an illusion. Fifteen years of truce are followed by the peace of Passarowitz (1718), secretly drawn up between Austria and the Turks. The age-old enmity draws limply to a close, all parties exhausted.

18th century. The Venetian Republic is used as a battle-ground for the great powers of Europe (Spain, Poland, Austria and France), against which it has no redress for the colossal damages inflicted on it. The government, which has not changed substantially for 1,000 years, is outmoded and incompetent; the ruling class lurches towards complete decadence. The Serenissima turns into a tourist curiosity, renowned for its wild parties, casinos, brothels and extravagant Carnivals. A member of the Gradenigo family writes in 1779 that Venice "seems to have become a puppet-theater." This is the era of the notorious playboy/philosopher/diplomatist/scientist/occultist Casanova (1725–98). But it is also—as if to refute the theory that great art flourishes only in times of economic stability—a period of extraordinary fertility in the arts, especially the theater and painting.

1797. Venice is in no fit state to put up any opposition to Napoleon's occupation, which has already been planned with the Austrians. The last Doge wearily takes off his horned cap and hands it to an attendant saying "Take this away, it won't be needed again." It is the first time Venice has ever been captured in its 1,000-year history. Over the next 40 years it is passed from hand to hand like a toy between the Austrians and the French. The Austrians are given the city, they lose it again after the battle of Austerlitz, and regain it after the battle of Waterloo.

19th century. In spite of its complete decline, Venice still attracts travelers (especially Romantic poets and Victorian novelists) like bees to a honeypot, such as Byron, who studies Armenian here, George Eliot, whose husband falls out of their hotel window into the Grand Canal, Shelley, Ruskin, George Sand, Mark Twain, the Brownings, etc., etc.

1846. A railway causeway is built to join Venice to the mainland.

1848–9. The Venetians, in a swansong of national pride, rise against the Austrians and expel them. Under the courageous Daniele Manin, they resist an Austrian siege, in which explosives attached to balloons are floated over the city (the first air raid in history). But it is the galloping epidemic of cholera, and the severe shortages of food and ammunition that force them to surrender in 1849. Venice remains under Austrian rule even after most of the rest of Italy has been liberated under Garibaldi in 1860.

1866. At last Venice becomes part of Italy and as such subject to Italian government.

World War I. Over 600 bombs are dropped on Venice but no great damage is done to artistic monuments.

1931. A road causeway connecting Venice with the mainland is built.

1945. The British army enters Venice.

1960. Marco Polo airport is built.

VENICE—ART AND ARCHITECTURE

From the fall of the Roman empire until well into the Middle Ages all Italian art was more or less an offshoot of Byzantine art. This was especially so in Venice since the city was directly linked by trade to Byzantium. The city was—and still is—crammed with darkly glittering Byzantine mosaics, altarpieces, carvings and precious stones. The colorful, decorative style of these art objects had a powerful effect on Venetian artists. Some were still making icons well into the Renaissance.

THE MIDDLE AGES AND THE RENAISSANCE

They were not all so conservative. In the 14th century there was a move away from the formal rigidity of Byzantine art to the new, more intimate International Gothic. Naturalistic elements—landscape, details of clothing, animals—were introduced into the backgrounds of paintings. Colors became brighter, figures more three-dimensional. Toward the end of the 15th century the way was clear for the spread of Renaissance art, already well established in many other parts of Italy, pre-eminently Florence of course. The new realism of Renaissance painting rapidly found a sympathetic reaction among Venetian painters. Gentile Bellini and Antonio Carpaccio, to name only two, took to covering their canvases with crowd scenes, buildings, canals, processions, dogs, ships, budgerigars, chimneys. . . . These were generally narrative paintings, telling the story of a saint's life, or simply everday scenes recording a particular event.

142

It was emphasis on color, though, that really made Venetian art Venetian, and it was the 15th-century masters of color, pre-eminently Giovanni Bellini and Giorgione, who began to use it no longer as decoration but as a means to create a particular atmosphere. Imagine how different the effect of Giorgione's *Tempest* (in the Accademia) would be with a sunny blue sky instead of the ominous grays and dark blues which fill the background. For the first time, the atmosphere and not the figures became the central focus of the painting. Titian, in the next generation, followed this line in his early paintings but soon shifted the emphasis some way back onto the figure, and—in his portraits—onto the expression of his figures' personalities.

Titian's younger contemporaries (he lived to a ripe old age), Veronese, Tintoretto and Bassano foremost among them, wanted to make names for themselves independently of the Grand Old Man. They started using huge canvases, giving themselves more freedom of movement. In their earlier works at least they played all sorts of visual games, juggling with viewpoints and perspective and using dazzlingly bright colors. There's a sense here of these painters painting simply for the sheer pleasure it gave them. This visual trickery suggests a natural parallel with the self-conscious artifice of Florentine painting of the same period—Mannerism—but the exuberance of these Venetian painters, and the increasingly emotional quality of their work, chiefly their mysterious and subtle use of color, always remained significantly more vital than the arid and ever more sterile products of central Italy toward the end of the 16th century.

In the same way that Venetian painting retained a strong individuality, so did Venetian architecture. This was partly for the same reasons (the strong Byzantine influence), and partly for obvious physical reasons such as the lack of land and the fact that there was virtually no need for fortification. At the same time, however, Venetian architecture follows no tidy line of development. The strong Byzantine influence gave way gradually in the 16th century to a flamboyant version of Gothic with pointed arch windows, a strain of which continued right through to the 18th century. Otherwise, the buildings are in a mixture of styles, sometimes even in the same building, with Renaissance architects making additions to Gothic buildings which in turn have Byzantine elements in them.

The same was true of sculpture, which invariably went hand-in-hand with architecture, since builders were usually sculptors as well, who would decorate the facades of palaces and churches with carvings, reliefs and, sometimes, statues in the round. Jacopo Sansovino, for example, during his stay in Venice not only designed the Libreria Vecchia (also known as the Libreria Sansovino) but also sculpted the imposing statues at the head of the Scala de' Giganti. Another famous architect—in many ways even more famous—who built in Venice was Palladio, whose grandiose churches in his influential classical mode added yet another style to those already existing here.

Medieval and Renaissance Painters

Paolo Veneziano (?–before 1362). Founder of the Venetian school. Painted panels in a mixture of Byzantine and the new Gothic styles. (Museo Marciano, Museo Correr, Accademia, Frari).

Lorenzo Veneziano (worked 1356–1372). More decisively Gothic, i.e. more three-dimensional, brighter colors, less gold. (Museo Correr, Accademia, San Giacomo Dell'Orio).

Gentile da Fabriano (c. 1370–1427). Not a native Venetian, but nonetheless painted frescoes in the Doge's Palace in 1409 in the International Gothic style.

Jacopo Bellini (*c.* 1400–c. 1470). Father of Gentile and Giovanni (see below). Few works surviving. Style founded in International Gothic but shows a new naturalism and humanity. (Accademia, Museo Correr).

Gentile Bellini (*c.* 1429–1507). Worked on cycle of history pictures in the Doge's Palace in 1474 and on return from Constantinople but all were burnt in 1577. Best-known for the narrative paintings (e.g. the *Procession in Piazza San Marco,* 1496) in which he recorded in a highly detailed, anecdotal way special occasions in Venice.

Giovanni Bellini (c. 1430–1516). The best-known of the family, famous for his Madonnas, portraits, intense color and dramatic, evocative lighting. Influenced by Mantegna (his brother-in-law) but later developed his own individual style. (Museo Correr, Doge's Palace, San Zaccaria, Santi Giovanni e Paolo, Accademia, Frari, San Giovanni Crisostomo, Ca' d'Oro).

Cima da Conegliano (*c.* 1459–1517). Arrived in Venice around 1490 and over the next 30 years produced a considerable output of naturalistic paintings with Veneto landscape backgrounds. Very popular in his time. (Museo Correr, San Giovanni in Bragora, Accademia, Carmini, Manfrediniana, Madonna dell'Orto).

Vittore Carpaccio (active 1490–d. 1523/6). Like Gentile Bellini, devoted himself mostly to narrative works (such as the San Giorgio degli Schiavoni and Santa Ursula cycles). Still, dream-like paintings, often inspired by the city of Venice, with a profusion of architectural and topographical detail. (Museo Correr, Doge's Palace, San Vitale, Accademia, Ca' d'Oro, San Giorgio Maggiore).

Giorgione (Giorgio da Castelfranco, 1477/8–1510). Creator of a new genre of painting, the *poesie,* in which the figures portrayed are less important than the poetic mood of the landscape they are in. Few works still extant. (Ca' d'Oro, Accademia).

Sebastiano del Piombo (*c.* 1485–1547). The least important of the three founder figures of the Venetian High Renaissance since he left Venice as early as 1511. Early works show influence of Giorgione; later moved to a more monumental style. (San Salvatore, Accademia, San Giovanni Crisostomo).

Titian (Tiziano Vecellio, *c.* 1487–1576). Spent most of his long career in Venice, though the greater part of his vast output of portraits, religious and mythological paintings was commissioned by patrons abroad. A winning combination of Venetian color and Central Italian/classical Roman figure style. (Doge's Palace, Libreria Sansovino, San Salvatore, Accademia, Santa Maria della Salute, etc.).

Palma Vecchio (Jacopo Palma, *c.* 1480–1528). Pupil of Giovanni Bellini, much influenced also by Titian and Giorgione. Specialized in attractive blonde female saints, e.g. *St. Barbara and other Saints* in Santa Maria Formosa (also Querini-Stampalia, Accademia).

Schiavone (Andrea Meldolla, *c.* 1510/15–63). Mannerist painter of small horizontal narrative scenes: high contrast between light and shadow, and large gaps between foreground and background. (Biblioteca Nazionale Marciana, Querini-Stampalia, Accademia, Carmini).

Jacopo Bassano (*c.*1510/18–92). Though trained in Venice worked mostly in Bassano. Influenced at first by the Central Italian Mannerists, later toned his colors down and innovated a genre of (relatively) realistic pastoral scenes, practised also by his sons Francesco and Leandro. (Doge's Palace, San Giorgio Maggiore).

Jacopo Tintoretto (1518–94). Aiming at the Mannerist ideal (with Titian and Michelangelo as his starting point), specialized in visual tricks, unexpected movement, sharp dazzling colors and dramatic foreshortening. Decorated the entire Scuola di San Rocco. (Works in at least a dozen churches, plus Accademia).

Paolo Veronese (c.1528–88). Came to Venice in 1533. Went in for huge allegorical, historical and Biblical pictures but got into trouble with the Inquisition for his flippant approach to sacred subjects. See his ceilings in the Doge's Palace for their daring perspective and nude figures in elaborate Mannerist poses. (Also Santi Giovanni e Paolo, Manfrediniana, San Sebastiano and other churches, plus Accademia).

Medieval and Renaissance Architects and Sculptors

Lombardo family—**Pietro** (c.1435–1515) plus sons **Antonio** (c.1485–1516) and **Tullio** (c.1455–1532). Pietro settled in Venice after 1467, built Santa Maria dei Miracoli, a successful blend of Veneto-Byzantine and Renaissance styles. (Also San Giobbe, Palazzo Dario, facade of Scuola di San Marco).

Mauro Codussi (*c.*1440–1504). Settled in Venice around 1469. Rival of Pietro Lombardo and architect of the finest early-Renaissance buildings in Venice: San Michele in Isola, San Salvatore, San Giovanni Crisostomo, Santa Maria Formosa, Palazzo Corner Spinelli and Palazzo Vendramin-Calergi.

Jacopo Sansovino (1486–1570). Fled in 1527 to Venice from Rome where he had worked mainly as a sculptor. Became the leading architect (in the High Renaissance style) in Venice until the arrival of Palladio. Buildings include the Library and Mint (Zecca), the Loggetta, San Francesco della Vigna and the Palazzo Corner della Ca' Grande.

Michele Sanmichele (c.1484–1559). Often compared with Palladio. Most famous buildings in Venice are the Palazzo Corner at San Polo, and the Palazzo Grimani.

Andrea Palladio (Andrea della Gondola, 1508–80). Described as "the first great professional architect." Fascinated by ancient Roman architecture, symmetry and "harmonic proportions." Famous particularly for his villas on mainland Veneto, he also worked on San Francesco della Vigna and built San Giorgio Maggiore and the church of the Redentore in Venice. His classicizing theories had a profound effect on generations of architects in Italy and abroad, viz Palladianism.

Antonio da Ponte (*c.*1512–97). Architect of the Rialto bridge.

Alessandro Vittoria (1525–1608). Pupil of Sansovino from 1543 but worked successfully on decorating buildings with his friends Titian and Tintoretto and the architect Palladio. Best known for his portrait busts. (Frari, San Salvatore, San Zaccaria, San Moise, Santi Giovanni e Paolo, Ca' Rezzonico, Manfrediniana, Ca' d'Oro, etc.).

Antonio Scamozzi (1552–1616). The most important of Palladio's immediate followers, he nevertheless tended to be conservative and derivative. What's more, he spent most of his career finishing buildings begun by other architects such as the Procuratie Nuove and the Libreria Sansovino.

THE 17TH AND 18TH CENTURIES

With the deaths of Palladio, Titian and Tintoretto, Venice spiralled quite suddenly into a startling artistic decline. Right through the first half of the 17th century uninspired workshops made efforts to continue the great masters' traditions, producing hack, assembly-line imitations of their art.

It was three non-Venetians—Strozzi, Lys and Fetti—who injected some life into Venetian painting when they brought to the watery city the Baroque style they had seen in the work of Caravaggio, Elsheimer and Rubens. Baroque was an emotional and heroic style, designed to overwhelm the spectator through its visual illusion, dramatic lighting, strong colors and violent movement. Strozzi, Lys and Fetti each took certain of these characteristics and blended them with Venetian color technique, dragging Venice into the 17th century and ensuring that its art didn't degenerate completely into an increasingly dreary series of ham-fisted pastiches.

The situation as regards architecture and sculpture was similar. Sansovino's and Palladio's style continued to be influential but, other than Longhena's dramatically impressive churches and palaces, the only noteworthy activity in this field were versions (and even straight copies) of Bernini's works in Rome, especially his statues. In fact, during this period, statuary began to assume a disproportionate importance to the building it was decorating, so that a nightmarish topheaviness was achieved.

Although by the 18th century Venice was nearing the last stages of its political decline, there was still immense wealth in the city, mostly in the hands of families who, typically Venetian, wished to make sure the world knew about it—and what better way than through vast, dazzling Rococo canvases, reassuringly stylized and removed from reality? Venetian art now underwent a revival, beginning with Sebastiano Ricci and expertly elaborated by Piazzetta and Giovanni Battista Tiepolo. But this revival could never have taken place had there not been a return to the city's great artistic traditions of the past. Late 16th-century color technique and expertise was drawn on and fused with what had been learnt from the Baroque to create the breathtaking, magical, decadent world of the Venetian Rococo.

Another strand from the tapestry of Venetian art was taken up at this time. Scenes of Venice, whether in the form of artistic *vedute,* or views (by Canaletto and Guardi), or as records of everday events (Pietro Longhi, Gian Domenico Tiepolo, Gabriel Bella), became extremely popular and were in great demand as tourist souvenirs, particularly among the English.

This was the final flowering of Venetian painting. The death of Francesco Guardi in 1793, compounded by the fall of the Republic in 1797, marked the effective end of the city's artistic life. Neo-Classicism found no champion here, except for the sculptor Canova who in any case did his finest work once he had left Venice. Architecture went in two directions in this period: back towards Rococo, with the extravagantly ornate churches of Domenico Rossi, and backwards further again to the 16th century, and even to ancient Rome with the severe, cold designs of Giorgio Massari.

17th- and 18th-Century Painters

Palma Giovane (1544–1628). Palma Vecchio's grand-nephew. Worked with Titian in his last years on the *Entombment*, intended for Titian's own tomb. Borrowed greatly from both Tintoretto's and Bassano's styles but repeated himself endlessly. (Almost everywhere, including Doge's Palace).

Domenico Fetti (*c.*1589–1623). Born in Rome, worked in Mantua and settled in Venice in 1621, though was already painting in a Venetian style before he arrived. Very small paintings, using soft, feathery brushwork. (Accademia).

Bernardo Strozzi (1581–1644). A Franciscan friar from Genoa, heavily influenced by Rubens, and by Caravaggio's dramatic realism. Moved to Venice in 1630 and was the first to practise Caravaggio's style here. (San Benedetto, Accademia, Santa Nicola da Tolentino).

Johann Lys (or Jan Liss, *c.*1595–1629). Moved from Germany to Venice around 1620. One of the more original foreign artists in the city, and might have advanced the development of Venetian painting significantly if he had not died of the plague—always a hazard—before he really got going. (Accademia, Ca' Rezzonico, Santa Nicola da Tolentino).

Francesco Maffei (*c.*1600–38). Famous mostly for his *St. Tobias and the Angel* in the church of Santi Apostoli, but something of a Lys-and-Fetti clone. (Also Ca' Rezzonico).

Sebastiano Mazzoni (1611–78). An original, not to say eccentric, Florentine artist working in Venice in the first half of the 17th century. His taste for *sotto-in-su* perspective—literally, "from below upwards," meaning that the action in the picture takes place above you with figures, buildings and landscapes correspondingly foreshortened—and for frantic movement make his series in San Benedetto positively tiring to look at. (Also Carmini, San Giorgio Maggiore).

Sebastiano Ricci (1659–1734). Key figure in the 18th-century revival of Venetian art. Widely traveled, he successfully combined Venetian love of color with developments taking place in Baroque painting elsewhere in Europe. Strongly influenced by Veronese (whose work he sometimes pastiched so well as to cause a number of scandals). The first touches of Rococo frivolity (fluffy cherubs, sentimental and pouting expressions) can be seen here, see *Madonna and Child with Nine Saints* in San Giorgio Maggiore. (Also Doge's Palace, St. Mark's, Querini-Stampalia, Accademia, Manfrediniana, San Stae, San Rocco, San Marciliano).

Marco Ricci (1676–1730). Nephew of Sebastiano, a master of the picturesque ruin-in-a-landscape kind of *capriccio,* or imaginary landscape. (Accademia).

Giovanni Battista Piazzetta (1683–1754). An intense, melancholy man who produced an introverted style of painting, starting out from moody Baroque chiaroscuro and moving to a more flowing Rococo technique. (La Pietà, Santi Giovanni e Paolo, Santa Maria della Fava, Accademia, Carmini, Ca' Rezzonico, Gesuati, San Stae).

Giovanni Battista Tiepolo (1696–1770). Internationally famous—and indeed much of his most famous work was done away from Venice—for his grand, illusionistic fresco decorations of palace ceilings and walls (such as the ones in the Ca' Rezzonico or Palazzo Labia) but capable of dealing equally well with a vast range of subjects from landscapes to Bible scenes. (Doge's Palace, San Francesco della Vigna, La Pietà, Scuola Grande di San Marco, Santa Maria della Fava, Accademia, Scuola Grande dei Carmini, Gesuati, San Stae and other churches).

Gian Domenico Tiepolo (1727–1804). Son of Giovanni Battista. Similar style to his father's in his religious paintings but found his own voice in the satirical scenes of contemporary life in Venice. *Il Riposo di Pulcinella* in the Ca' Rezzonico (Commedia dell'Arte masked figures posed as if they were Greek gods) is sinister in a Goyaesque way. (Also San Lio, San Polo, Scuola di San Giovanni Evangelista, San Francesco di Paola, San Michele in Isola).

Pietro Longhi (1702–85). Painter of everyday aristocratic dalliance, and correspondingly popular with Venetian society, which he gently satirized, for instance *The Rhinoceros,* in which the plodding bulk of the animal is amusingly contrasted with the delicate, sophisticated men and women looking at it. (Large collection in the Querini-Stampalia, also Accademia and Ca' Rezzonico).

Alessandro Longhi (1733–1813). Pietro's son and one of the best portrait painters of his time. (Querini-Stampalia, Accademia and Ca' Rezzonico).

Rosalba Carriera (1675–1757). Gained fame originally with her ivory miniatures and then with her exquisite, light, pastel portraits. Immensely popular and influential, too, in the Paris art world after she moved there in 1720. (Accademia, Ca' Rezzonico).

Antonio Canaletto (1697–1768). His views (or *vedute*) of Venice with their almost photographic clarity became so famous that a market was set up to export them (especially to England). As a result, few are left in Venice. (Accademia).

Francesco Guardi (1712–93). Another Venetian *veduta* painter whose freer, more impressionistic canvases had less of a reputation at the time than Canaletto's but still sold well. Fond of pale, bright colors: the fact that Tiepolo was his brother-in-law may have some connection . . . (Accademia plus several attributions elsewhere).

Gabriel Bella (1730–1800). Native painter who depicted fascinating scenes of everyday life and local festivities in Venice. (Querini-Stampalia).

17th- and 18th-Century Architects and Sculptors

Baldassare Longhena (1598–1682). The only great Venetian Baroque architect. Trained under Scamozzi. Imposing, complex works (Santa Maria della Salute) using vast domes, huge scrolls, double staircases to achieve a theatrical effect. Occasionally goes right over the top, as with the superabundance of giant heads and lion masks on the facade of the Ospedaletto. (Also Ca' Rezzonico, Ca' Pesaro and others).

Giuseppe Sardi (c. 1621–99). Took over from Longhena as Venice's leading architect, but stylistically added very little. He concentrated on statuary to decorate his buildings (Santa Maria Zobenigo, San Salvatore, Santa Maria degli Scalzi, ex-Scuola di San Teodoro and others) to the detriment of the structural whole.

Giorgio Massari (1687–1766). The most important architect of the 18th century in Venice. Derived his style from Palladio and the classical canons of Vitruvius. (La Pietà, Palazzo Grassi, part of the Gesuati).

Antonio Canova (1757–1822). The celebrated neo-Classical sculptor was born in Venice and worked here for a while before going to Rome, Vienna and Paris. His early work (e.g. *Daedalus and Icarus,* Museo Correr) is still typically 18th-century in its smiling, almost bashful, softness.

EXPLORING VENICE

It is called La Serenissima. The literal translation of this name is ungainly: "the most serene." The term "Serene Republic" more successfully suggests the monstrous power and majesty of this city that was for centuries the unrivaled mistress of trade between Europe and the Orient and the staunch bulwark of Christendom against the tides of Turkish expansion. It suggests too the extraordinary beauty of the city—and surely Venice is the most beautiful city in the world?—and its lavishness and fantasy, the result not just of its remarkable buildings but of the very fact that Venice is a city built on water, a city created more than 1,000 years ago by men who dared defy the sea, implanting their splendid palaces and churches on mudbanks in a swampy and treacherous lagoon.

It is a unique city, small but disorientating in its complexity, a labyrinth of narrow streets and waterways opening now and then on to an airy square or broad canal. You must walk almost everywhere in Venice. And where you cannot walk you must board a boat of some kind. In Venice, almost everything is extraordinary.

The Venetians have mastered the art of living well in their singular city. You'll see them going about their daily affairs in *vaporetti* and along the *calli.* They are a purposeful and voluble people, generally courteous and helpful, only occasionally grumpy. Although Venice is faced with some serious problems, there's a cautious optimism in the air. The plan adopted in 1985 to build movable barriers across the entrances to the lagoon to hold back dangerously high tides will, they hope, be implemented without further delay. Pollution from the industrial area so shortsightedly installed on the mainland at Marghera should soon be largely eliminated. And they are being encouraged by state subsidies to renovate their Venetian homes, rather than leave the city to live and work on the mainland, a trend that has hitherto drastically reduced Venice's population.

Then there are the mixed blessings of tourism. The Venetians are nothing if not skilled in dealing with the veritable armies of visitors that descend on their city. Tourism has been their most important industry for several hundred years. But even they blanched at the crowds of merrymakers who, one Shrove Tuesday a few years ago, outnumbered the population of the entire city.

You, too, will have to come to terms with the crowds. Get away from the Piazza San Marco. Stride off into the districts of Cannaregio or Castello, or into the refreshingly unaffected areas of Dorsoduro, San Polo and Santa Croce. Get to the museums before or just after the tour groups. And look for the little cafes and *trattorie* where the Venetians go. You will find a city of unexpected pleasures, easy grace, and incomparable beauty.

Before launching into our description of the city, however, it is essential to say something about the layout of Venice. Venice is an immensely complicated city to find your way around. Indeed it is doubtful if in any other city in the world you can become quite as lost quite as quickly. A further twist is added when you consider that very few areas of Venice stand out as natural units. Rather, they tend to form an amorphous mass, with a hundred different ways in and out and a multitude of routes running through them. There are, it's true, certain exceptions to this general rule. St. Mark's Square is the most obvious. Likewise, the areas to the north of the city are reasonably self-contained, by Venetian standards anyway, as are those to the east. And the city is divided into a series of administrative districts or *sestiere*. But their importance is as much historical as geographical and the boundaries between them are in any case blurred and indistinct.

In dividing up our "Exploring" chapters therefore, we have necessarily had to be somewhat arbitrary. Where a natural unit exists we have taken advantage of it. But for the most part our descriptions of the city have been based on the geographical proximity of places of interest. In some cases, this has given us reasonably short chapters. In others, it has meant very long chapters. Those possessed of unusual stamina might well be able to walk these longer chapters: the routes they describe are perfectly feasible. But more ordinary mortals will probably prefer to take little bites out of them, coming back for more as circumstance and mood permit. But whether human or super human, it is essential that you obtain as complete and detailed a map as you can. It will speed your way immeasurably. Further hints on exploring Venice are given in the *Practical Information for Venice* under "Getting Around."

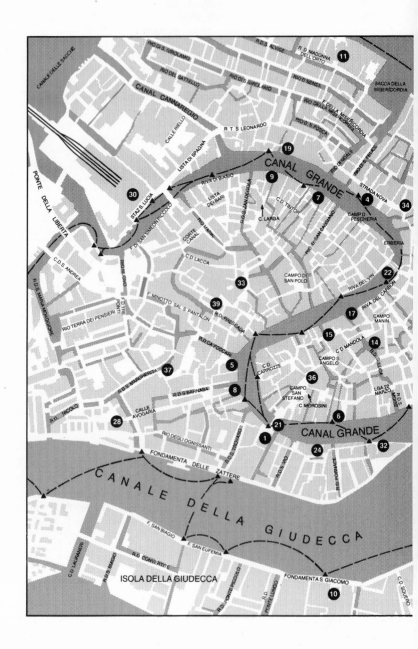

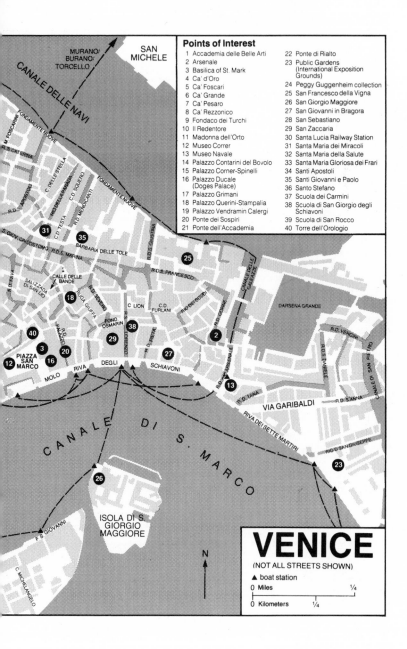

Points of Interest

1 Accademia delle Belle Arti
2 Arsenale
3 Basilica of St. Mark
4 Ca' d'Oro
5 Ca' Foscari
6 Ca' Grande
7 Ca' Pesaro
8 Ca' Rezzonico
9 Fondaco dei Turchi
10 Il Redentore
11 Madonna dell'Orto
12 Museo Correr
13 Museo Navale
14 Palazzo Contarini del Bovolo
15 Palazzo Corner-Spinelli
16 Palazzo Ducale
   (Doges Palace)
17 Palazzo Grimani
18 Palazzo Querini-Stampalia
19 Palazzo Vendramin Calergi
20 Ponte dei Sospiri
21 Ponte dell'Accademia

22 Ponte di Rialto
23 Public Gardens
   (International Exposition
   Grounds)
24 Peggy Guggenheim collection
25 San Francesco della Vigna
26 San Giorgio Maggiore
27 San Giovanni in Bragora
28 San Sebastiano
29 San Zaccaria
30 Santa Lucia Railway Station
31 Santa Maria dei Miracoli
32 Santa Maria della Salute
33 Santa Maria Gloriosa dei Frari
34 Santi Apostoli
35 Santi Giovanni e Paolo
36 Santo Stefano
37 Scuola dei Carmini
38 Scuola di San Giorgio degli
   Schiavoni
39 Scuola di San Rocco
40 Torre dell'Orologio

VENICE
(NOT ALL STREETS SHOWN)

▲ boat station

0 Miles ¼
0 Kilometers ¼

Piazza San Marco

A vast open space enclosed by an orderly procession of arcades marching towards the fairytale cupolas and marble lacework of the Basilica di San Marco, the Piazza San Marco is the heart of Venice, permanently animated and lively, crowded with people and pigeons. In summer, cafe tables cluster around bandstands and weary tourists rest their feet, sipping drinks and listening to the little orchestras. In winter, the piazza is magically melancholy, as mists swirl around the lamp-posts and fog rolls in from the lagoon to envelop the Doge's Palace, the Palazzo Ducale.

Historically and geographically, the Piazza San Marco is the logical place to start your visit to Venice. From its earliest days, the city's administrative and religious life was centered here, in the Palazzo Ducale and the basilica. These were the splendid seats of proud faith and oligarchic power, symbols of the Republic itself, embellished and enriched with the treasures the city's ships brought from the East. The piazza remained the focus of Venetian life throughout the protracted decline that began with the fall of Constantinople to the Turks in 1453, was hastened by the discovery of America in 1492 and ended when Napoleon's troops entered the city in 1797. It was the scene of legendary carnivals, of debauched revelries, of extravagant processions, of betrayals and executions. Its splendor may today exist chiefly for the benefit of tourists, but it is real enough for all that.

Around the Piazza

Napoleon called the piazza "Europe's most beautiful drawing room," though this did not prevent him from promptly redecorating it. His architects demolished a church that stood at the southeast end of the piazza, opposite the basilica. In its place they put up a new building, the Ala Napolonica or Fabbrica Nuova, to unite the two Procuratie, the elegant arcaded buildings that run down either side of the piazza. The Procuratie Vecchie, the "Old" Procuratie, on the right of the piazza if you stand with your back to the basilica, was built in the early 16th century by the Florentine architect Jacopo Sansovino. This housed the offices and homes of the Procurators, administrators of the Republic's finances. The Procuratie Nuove, on the left of the piazza, was begun in 1582, and largely repeats Sansovino's design.

At the eastern end of the Procuratie Nuovo is the Campanile di San Marco, the great brick bell tower of St. Mark's, an instantly recognizable Venetian landmark. The campanile was begun in the 10th century, completed in the 12th and restored in the 16th. Just as today's visitors climb

PIAZZA SAN MARCO
(NOT ALL STREETS SHOWN)

0 miles ⅛
0 kilometers ⅛

PIAZZA SAN MARCO

Porta della Carta

Piazzetta

Molo

S. Marco Giardinetti

Bacino di San Marco

S. Marco Vallaressa

Campo S. Gallo

Mercerie

C. d Specchier

Rio Giudra

Mercerie

C. Frubera

Calle d. Rio Terrà d. Colonne

Calle d. Fabbri

C. larga S. Marco

Piazzetta dei Leoncini

Rio Palazzo Paglia

Salizz. S. Provolo

Calle Albanesi

Calle Rasse

Riva degli Schiavoni

Frezzeria

C. dell'Ascensione

Calle Vallaresso

C. Ridotto

Rio Zecca

Points of Interest
1 Ala Napoleonica:
   Museo Correr
2 Basilica di San Marco
3 Campanile di San Marco
4 Libreria Vecchia
   (Sansovino): Museo
   Archeologico;
   Biblioteca Marciana;
5 Palazzo Ducale
6 Ponte dei Sospiri
7 Prigioni Nuove
8 Procuratie Nuove
9 Procuratie Vecchie
10 San Giuliano
11 Torre dell'Orologio
ℹ Tourist Information

to its summit for the view over Venice and the lagoon, so visitors in the past, from the humblest traveling merchant to the grandest foreign potentate, climbed it, and for much the same reason. Its summit was sheathed in brass to act as a beacon for ships, and for centuries its six great bells summoned the Venetians to worship in St. Mark's. Weakened by lightning, damaged by earthquakes and undermined by floods and fires, it collapsed, practically without warning, on the morning of July 14, 1902, crumbling into a heap of rubble. No one was hurt—though a cat was rumored to have been killed—and remarkably the basilica and the Procuratie Nuove were undamaged. Even more symbolically, its great bell, the Maragona, 600 years old, was found intact in the rubble. Heartened by these discoveries, the Venetians immediately set about rebuilding this venerable symbol of their city, determined to create an exact replica. This they did, though prudently strengthening the original foundations and reducing the weight of the tower in the process. In April 1912, exactly 1,000 years after the original tower was begun, the new campanile was opened.

At its base is a small loggia, the Loggetta, built by Sansovino. Though badly damaged when the campanile fell down, it has been successfully restored. Originally, the Loggetta was used as a meeting place for Venetian nobles. Later, it came to be employed as a guard house during meetings of the Great Council in the Doge's Palace opposite. Its pretty bronze gates are an 18th-century addition. Niches in its marble facade house fine statues, also by Sansovino, of Pallas, Apollo, Mercury and Peace. Above, are sculptured reliefs with Venice, here personified as Justice, a recurrent and

typically confident Venetian theme, presiding over Jupiter and Venus, the
latter pair representing Crete and Cyprus, both then Venetian possessions.
Just inside the Loggetta, which sometimes serves as the entrance to the
bell tower, is a pretty marble *Madonna and Child* by Sansovino, pieced
together after the collapse of the tower.

It's worth the entrance fee to take the elevator to the top of the tower.
The view over the city, the lagoon and, on clear days, to the distant Alps
is superb. Oddly, you can't see the myriad canals that snake through the
117 islets on which Venice is built. And you can barely make out the rift
in the red tiled roofs created by the broad loops of the Grand Canal. As
you descend, give a thought to those 15th-century clerics, found guilty
by the Republic of immoral acts and suspended in wooden cages from the
tower, sometimes to subsist on bread and water for as long as a year, sometimes to starve to death.

The Piazzetta

Running south from the campanile out of the piazza is the Piazzetta,
literally the "little piazza." On one side of it is the Doge's Palace, on the
other Sansovino's arcaded Libreria Vecchia, the Old Library, begun in
1540. At its southern end, overlooking the Basin of St. Mark's, the Bacino
di San Marco, are two columns. If ever evidence of Venice's pragmatism
were needed, of the city's enduring ability to shape the works and artefacts
of others to her own ends and stamp on them a quintessentially Venetian
character, these lofty granite columns would more than suffice. The spoils
of some battle in the East, the columns lay in the piazza until, in the 12th
century, Nicola Starantonio, builder of the first permanent bridge at the
Rialto, raised them up. His ingenuity was rewarded by a concession—
typically Venetian—to run a gambling stand at their feet. Having put up
the columns, the city placed on one a lion, again brought from the Orient,
on which they stuck wings and, under a paw, a stone Bible, thus converting
him into the symbol of St. Mark, the city's patron saint. On the other,
they put a statue of St. Theodore. He was the original patron saint of the
city, until, in the 9th century, St. Mark the Evangelist, an altogether
grander saint, was adopted as patron saint and his corpse, stolen from
Egypt, brought to the city. Here, St. Theodore stands on what is thought
to be a dragon, though it bears a marked resemblance to a crocodile.

The Torre dell'Orologio

Across from the Piazzetta, on the northern side of the piazza, the Torre
dell'Orologio, the Clock Tower, marks the start of the Mercerie, the city's
principal commercial thoroughfare. This leads to the Rialto district.
Erected in the late 15th century by Mauro Codussi, Venice's finest early-
Renaissance architect, the Torre dell'Orologio is a decorative piece of
work, bright with enamel and gold. During Ascension Week—La Sensa
in Venetian dialect—and at Epiphany, figures of the Magi emerge from
the doors which normally show the hours and make a circuit of homage
in front of the Madonna above the clock. There's a handsome gilded lion
too, and, crowning the lot, a great bronze bell with two Moors who strike
the hour. The entrance to the tower is under the arch. Try to time your
visit to see the Moors in action.

One final sight is worth mentioning before heading into the mysterious darkness of the basilica itself. These are the graceful red flagstaffs, tapering above their 16th-century bronze pedestals, that stand in front of the basilica. Huge flags sometimes fly from them, but their role has not always been merely decorative. From ropes stretched between them, misdoers were hung, chilling reminders of the Republic's implacable severity. Sometimes the corpses appeared overnight: no one asked who they were, or what crime they had committed. Certainly, no Venetian would linger in the piazza in the dead of night when these grisly bundles emerged from the torture chambers and dungeons of the Doge's Palace. (On one memorably shocking occasion, two of these unknown victims were found buried head first in the piazza itself, their legs protruding from the dislodged flagstones.)

The Basilica di San Marco

Now turn your attention to the basilica, a cluster of Byzantine bubbles and spires over lacy stonework and broad arches. The facade is a marvelous aggregation of rounded and pointed arches, sheaves of columns, gleaming mosaics, graceful statues and decorative reliefs. For much of its history, for all its splendor, the basilica was no more than the chapel of the doges, an annex of the Doge's Palace and site of state ceremonies. Interestingly, it became the cathedral of Venice only in 1807, after the fall of the Republic. Until then, San Pietro di Castello, away to the east of the city, had served as Venice's cathedral.

The genesis of the church came about in the 9th century. At that time Rivo Alto, the group of islands in the center of the lagoon (the future Venice) was being settled, and it was decided to build a new church there to house the remains of St. Mark which had lately been filched from Alexandria in Egypt. (The story goes that the two agents of the doge who stole the saint's remains hid them in a barrel under layers of pickled pork, safe from probing Islamic hands.) When the saint's corpse arrived in Venice, a legend was fortuitously remembered—or invented. It was said that during St. Mark's return from preaching the gospel on the shores of the upper Adriatic, the saint was resting in his boat, anchored off the Rivo Alto. An angel appeared to him in a dream and announced that his final resting place would be here. To the Venetians this story was sufficiently convincing for them to oust St. Theodore as the city's patron in favor of St. Mark.

The great basilica you see today is the third built on the site. It dates from 1063. The first was destroyed by fire and the second demolished to make way for the magnificent edifice that would, according to the doges, outshine the Romanesque cathedrals then being built throughout Italy and the Byzantine basilicas of the East. Consecrated in 1093, St. Mark's is indeed something of a synthesis of Byzantine and Romanesque. Yet at the same time it manages to transcend its models, creating a rich, frothy impression quite unlike any other church in Christendom.

Over the years it has been endowed with all the riches Venetian admirals and merchants could carry off from the Orient. The four gilded bronze horses; the Pala d'Oro; precious columns and rare marbles; the porphyry Tetrarchs on the exterior; the gem-studded icons seized in the sack of Constantinople in 1202: all this and much more was carried to Venice and St. Mark's. Perhaps as significantly, the highly skilled *magistri de muxe,* the mosaicists of Byzantium, were also persuaded to come to Venice as honored guests and to decorate the basilica. They began the immense task of covering the interior with superb gleaming mosaics of biblical scenes. These master craftsmen in turn sparked off the formation of a native Venetian school of mosaicists, who carried on and completed the mosaic decoration of the interior, introducing more obviously Western styles, yet never completely abandoning the Byzantine influences of their teachers. At the same time, a native school of sculptors was growing. They were responsible for many of the statues of the exterior and much other carving, all of which proclaims the flowering of the distinctive Venetian-Gothic style.

The overwhelming elaboration of the facade is too much to take in at once. It's best to stand some distance away, toward the other end of the piazza. From there the harmonious lines of the building are more easily seen, its rounded arches and domes echoed in the arcades of the Procuraties on either side. Nearer the church, the larger details come into focus: five arches below, five above; the rich sculptural and mosaic decoration, especially in the beautiful central arch. Closer still, these sculptures reveal more of themselves. Venetian trades—boat-building and fishing—are here, as are the months and the Virtues, Christ and the Prophets, the Earth, the Oceans, various animals and scenes of the Ages of Man. In the first lunette to the right of the main arch, the story of St. Mark's dream is shown.

Inside the Basilica

Step into the dark narthex, or atrium, and pause while your eyes become accustomed to the half light. Here, on the domes and arches, there are 13th-century mosaics representing scenes from the Old Testament. Niches in the bay in front of the main door are decorated with the oldest mosaics in the basilica, figures of Mary and the Apostles executed in the 11th century. Note the contrast between these hieratic figures and the full-blown representation of St. Mark in Ecstasy in the half-dome, done about 1545 and probably based on a cartoon, a preparatory drawing, by Venetian-born painter Lorenzo Lotto.

In front of the main door a white marble disc set in a slab of red marble marks the spot where the Emperor Frederick Barbarossa reluctantly knelt before Pope Alexander III one muggy July day in 1177 to seal a truce negotiated by the Venetians. The event is depicted in many a celebrative canvas in the Doge's Palace. On the left of the main entrance look for the charming mosaic of the Tower of Babel.

To enter the basilica you must pass the critical gaze of a liveried custodian who singles out and courteously but firmly turns back anyone, male or female, wearing shorts, sundresses or other inappropriate clothing.

Inside the basilica, dust stirred by milling feet floats in hazy beams of sunlight that set the golden mosaics agleam, mingling with the smoke of votive lamps suspended from the arches. Curving cupolas shimmer with color. Distant figures blur in the shadowy light. The inlaid marble pavement is strangely uneven, seeming to move under your feet as if the basilica itself were afloat. Much like St. Peter's in Rome, San Marco doesn't really seem to be a church. It's usually full of tourists tagging behind guides who hiss explanations. The people seated in the few pews in front of a side chapel are there not to pray but to rest their feet. But more unusually, the dim

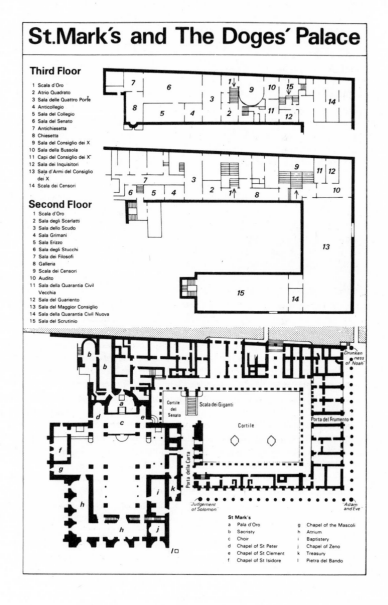

St. Mark's and The Doges' Palace

Third Floor

1 Scala d'Oro
2 Atrio Quadrato
3 Sala delle Quattro Porte
4 Anticollegio
5 Sala del Collegio
6 Sala del Senato
7 Antichiesetta
8 Chiesetta
9 Sala del Consiglio dei X
10 Sala della Bussola
11 Capi del Consiglio dei X
12 Sala dei Inquisitori
13 Sala d'Armi del Consiglio dei X
14 Scala dei Censori

Second Floor

1 Scala d'Oro
2 Sala degli Scarlatti
3 Sala dello Scudo
4 Sala Grimani
5 Sala Erizzo
6 Sala degli Stucchi
7 Sala dei Filosofi
8 Galleria
9 Scala dei Censori
10 Audito
11 Sala della Quarantia Civil Vecchia
12 Sala del Guariento
13 Sala del Maggior Consiglio
14 Sala della Quarantia Civil Nuova
15 Sala del Scrutinio

St Mark's

a Pala d'Oro
b Sacristy
c Choir
d Chapel of St Peter
e Chapel of St Clement
f Chapel of St Isidore
g Chapel of the Mascoli
h Atrium
i Baptistery
j Chapel of Zeno
k Treasury
l Pietra del Bando

light, glowing mosaics, the galleries high above the naves—they served as the *matroneum,* the women's gallery—the massive altar screen, or iconostasis, the single massive Byzantine chandelier, even the Greek cross ground plan, give St. Mark's an exotic aspect quite unlike that of most Christian churches. The effect is remarkable. Here the pomp and mystery of Oriental magnificence are wedded to Christian belief, creating an intensely awesome impression.

The dim light makes it hard to see much of the interior. But it is sometimes fully lit during services, providing a memorable and magnificent spectacle. The upper walls and domes are entirely sheathed in mosaics on a shimmering gold ground. Largely completed by the end of the 13th century, the mosaics were extensively restored in the 16th and 17th centuries, and again in the '70s. Those in the Baptistery and other chapels were added in the 14th and 15th centuries. Those on the great domes date back to the 12th and 13th centuries, from the Pentecost in the first dome as you enter to the Ascension in the central dome. The mosaic of four saints in the dome over the right transept was executed in the early 13th century, the Greek cross with scenes from the life of St. John in the left transept a century earlier, as was the dome mosaic over the presbytery. Be sure to see the monumental early 13th-century figures of Mary and the Prophets on the right-hand wall of the nave and, above them, the splendid scene of the Agony in the Garden. Interspersed among these venerable productions are 15th-, 16th- and 17th-century mosaics based on works by such masters as Titian, Tintoretto and Palma Giovane, easily distinguishable by their movement and color.

To the right of the polygonal pulpit, where the doge used to appear to the public after his consecration in the sanctuary, you can buy a ticket (500 lire and well worth it; it's also valid for entrance to the Treasury) to see the Pala d'Oro, an incredibly opulent golden altarpiece encrusted with precious gems and cloisonné enamels. It's a stupendous work, epitome of the riches that were brought to Venice from Constantinople. This glittering masterpiece of the goldsmith's art was executed in the first half of the 14th century, but it incorporates enamels from earlier altarpieces, some dating back to the 11th century. Before Napoleon partially despoiled it, the Pala d'Oro had 1,300 pearls, 300 emeralds and an equal number of sapphires, 15 rubies, 400 garnets and 90 amethysts. Also in the sanctuary are the sculptured Oriental alabaster columns supporting the baldachin, a magnificent ornamental canopy, over the main altar; their relief carvings of New Testament scenes are of great historical and artistic interest. The bronze figures of the Evangelists on the left altar rail are by Sansovino. On top of the iconostasis, the altar screen separating the sanctuary from the nave, stand some fine Gothic sculptures by the Masegne brothers, the foremost sculptors in Venice at the beginning of the 15th century. The large chapel in the left transept holds a much-revered icon of the Madonna of Nicopeia. In the 17th century a men's confraternity met in the small rectangular chapel in the same transept. Known as the chapel of the Madonna dei Mascoli (of the Men), it has a decorative Gothic altarpiece and 15th-century mosaics in the vault based on cartoons by the Florentine Andrea del Castagno.

Now cross the nave to the right transept and the entrance to the Treasury, where you can admire a 6th-century marble throne known as the Chair of St. Mark, and some gorgeous icons, including an exceptional

10th-century icon of St. Michael. Here you will find also precious chalices, reliquaries and caskets, and an unusual Armenian medieval silver-and-gilt coffer in the form of a five-domed church. As you emerge from the Treasury, note the door on your right, through which the doge entered the basilica directly from his palace next door.

Head for the Baptistery, off the right aisle of the church. Closed for restorations, and not likely to be reopened for a year or so, the Baptistery has a large font designed by Sansovino, who is buried in front of the altar. But its most noteworthy features are the mosaics on the walls and ceiling. The light from the tall windows illuminates these mosaics, scenes from the life of St. John the Baptist and the life of Christ, much more clearly than those in the basilica proper. The figure of Christ in the dome over the baptismal font is encircled by figures of the Apostles baptizing the gentiles. The mosaic of the Banquet of Herod above the door into the basilica was based on designs by Paolo Veneziano and is particularly effective. Next door is the Zen Chapel, originally part of the narthex. It was closed off in 1504 to create this chapel and fulfill the terms of the bequest of Cardinal Zen, who left his fortune to Venice on the condition that he be buried in the basilica. As in other circumstances, notably that of Colleoni's equestrian statue, the Republic happily complied. The chapel contains some handsome bronze sculptures by Antonio Lombardo, of the important family of sculptors headed by Pietro Lombardo. Antonio's brother Tullio designed the chapel.

The Quadriga

Before you leave the basilica climb the steep stairs to the gallery and Museo Marciano, St. Mark's Museum. Fragments of 12th-century mosaics are displayed in the first rooms. There are ecclesiastical vestments trimmed with exquisite lace and a soulful gilded wooden lion of St. Mark, a 16th-century work. From the organ gallery, with its view of the interior of the basilica and the dome mosaics, you step out onto the loggia, a narrow balcony on the basilica's facade. Here, there are airy vistas of Piazza San Marco, the Piazzetta, the Campanile and the Torre dell'Orologio. Examine the marble Gothic traceries of the facade, the statues, the lead roofing of the domes, the odd crosses topping the parasol-shaped lanterns over the domes. From one side of the loggia you can get a good look at the Porta della Carta, entrance to the Doge's Palace. At its apex, a serene figure of Venice as Justice sits firmly on two of the 75 lions that decorate the portal. You have to squeeze past the four bronze horses, dull copies of the original quadriga inside, to get to the other side of the loggia. Inside the organ gallery, turn left into the brick-vaulted room where the original steeds of St. Mark's stand in vigorous glory. They are splendid, gleaming animals of weathered green bronze streaked and brushed with gold. The only quadriga—technically, a team of four horses yoked together—to survive from ancient times, they were probably cast in Constantinople in the early 4th century. It is believed that they were taken from Constantinople to Rome to adorn an imperial arch and then transported back to Constantinople to stand in the Hippodrome. From there they were shipped to Venice as booty, and placed in the Arsenal. Later hoisted to the loggia of the basilica, they remained there for five centuries until Napoleon carried them off to Paris in 1797. He had them placed above the Arc du Carousel.

Returned to Venice in 1815, they were removed to Rome for safekeeping during the two World Wars. Several years ago the quadriga was removed for good, restored, and taken on a world tour before being installed in the museum.

As you leave the basilica turn right into Piazzetta dei Leoncini where at the height of the season tourists and pigeons jostle for room to rest on the steps surrounding the fine old wellhead. Few manage to gain a place of honor on the long-suffering red marble lions at the corners, which serve as hobby horses for Venetian children after the tourists have gone. This side of the basilica bears some interesting reliefs and a sculptured nativity scene in the prettily carved arch over the last door on the left. The other side of the basilica is decorated with booty from the Orient. At the corner is the Pietra del Bando, a fragment of a column from Acre in the Holy Land. From the mid 13th century all official decrees were proclaimed here. The taller, intricately carved freestanding columns just beyond it probably were "liberated" in Constantinople but are Syrian handiwork of the 5th or 6th century. The charming dark red porphyry figures of the Tetrarchs, also called Moors, on the corner of the wall near the Porta della Carta are Egyptian. They date back to the 4th century and probably represent Diocletian and other Roman emperors. The Byzantine relief panels on the walls were carved sometime in the 9th century and, like so many other works of art, were carried off from Constantinople for the greater glory of San Marco.

The Palazzo Ducale

The next building of the great complex in and around St. Mark's Square is probably also the most important. This is the Doge's Palace, the Palazzo Ducale. Its importance is two-fold. First, it is by any standards a supremely beautiful building. It may lack the exuberant fantasy and mysterious potency of St. Mark's, but its extraordinary, almost eccentric architecture—simultaneously delicate and sturdy, yet above all massively confident—allied to its unrivaled location overlooking the Basin of St. Mark's, make the Doge's Palace one of the great buildings of Europe. Secondly, and in some ways more significantly, the palace was also the very epicenter of the Serene Republic's great empire, a veritable symbol of Venice and all it stood for. The building was thus much more than just a palace. Rather it was a sort of combination White House, Senate, Supreme Court, torture chamber and prison rolled into one. It was here that the Great Council met and the laws of the Republic were determined. It was here that the doges were elected—by a process of quite staggering complexity—and here, surrounded by luxury but politically well-nigh impotent, that they lived. And it was here that prisoners were tried and, if guilty, tortured— very often to death—and incarcerated.

Today's building is the successor to a number of other, earlier palaces. The first, a fortress more than a palace, was built in the 9th century at the time of the original settlement of the Rivo Alto. This and a number of later buildings were all destroyed over the years by fire. The present building went up in the 14th century. It too burnt down, in the 16th century, but an exact copy was constructed almost immediately, the Venetians having by then become conservative in their tastes, or perhaps they had simply grown fond of their palace. The design of the 14th-century building was the work of architect and sculptor Filippo Calendario, who was subsequently hanged in 1355 for his part in the infamous plot led by Doge Marin Falier to overthrow the Great Council. Construction continued into the following century with the addition of the Scala dei Giganti (the Stairway of the Giants) and the Arco Foscari, the arch in the courtyard, both the work of Veronese sculptor Antonio Rizzo. He too had a checkered career and fled to the Papal States in 1498, accused of embezzling public funds.

Externally, the most remarkable feature of the building is the apparent inversion of the upper story and the two lower stories. These two lower stories consist of two rows of delicate, almost flimsy arches. Above them is a massive pink and white marble wall, whose solidity is barely interrupted by its six great Gothic windows. It should look top-heavy, but it doesn't. It is worth pointing out, however, that the lower arcade has acquired a progressively more stunted look over the years. Every time the piazza was repaved, so its level rose, hiding little by little the bases of the columns of the arcade, giving them their somewhat squat look. (Interestingly, this arcade, where merchants, princes and politicians met to gossip and intrigue, is called the "broglio," a word that has been passed down to us as "imbroglio," a fitting Venetian inheritance.) The interior of the palace is a fascinating and magnificent maze of vast halls, monumental staircases, secret corridors and peepholes, state apartments and cramped wood-paneled offices, and the sinister and gloomy prison cells and torture chamber.

Inside the Doge's Palace

The entrance to the palace is through the Porta della Carta, a highly decorative Gothic gateway. Its name—*carta* means paper—is derived either from the decrees that were posted here for all to read, or from the archives kept in the palace. It is the work of Bartolomeo Bon. With his father, Giovanni, he was also responsible for the Ca' d'Oro, one of the Grand Canal's most sumptuous buildings. Beyond, the palace courtyard is fittingly impressive. You enter under the Arco Foscari, for which Rizzo executed some fine sculptures. Ahead is the same architect's Scala dei Giganti, named after the colossal statues of Mars and Neptune, by Jacopo Sansovino, that decorate it.

You can choose between two tours of the palace (and you may find a special exhibit here, too; entrances and admission fees are all separate). You can do the classic tour on your own. Alternatively, you can take the *Itinerari Segreti* tour, the Secret Itinerary, though this is unfortunately given only in Italian: it takes place four times daily, but you will need to reserve ahead. This will take you behind the scenes, up and down inner staircases to stuffy offices and lavishly decorated private apartments, where the day-to-day business of the Republic was carried on for centuries. You visit the doge's private apartment, where you may be surprised to find a group of paintings by Hieronymus Bosch, strange bedfellows among the Bellinis and Carpaccios. You climb to the attic, where Casanova was imprisoned in the Piombi prison, so-called because of the lead *(piombo)* plates on the roof. From a cat-walk over the ceiling of the immense Sala del Maggior Consiglio, the meeting place of the Great Council, you can see the enormous tree trunks used as roof beams by Venice's master builders, who applied their art to palaces and ships alike.

The classic tour starts as you climb the Scala d'Oro, known as the Golden Staircase for its richly gilded stucco decorations. It's a long climb up yet another flight of stairs to the third floor of the palace, where state ceremonies were held. At the top, sit for a moment in the Atrium to catch your breath and look for the Tintoretto painting of *Justice* on the ceiling, due to be back in place after restoration. On the right you enter the Sala delle Quattro Porte, decorated in the 16th century. Here ambassadors waited to be received and could while away the time by studying the opulent ceiling designed by Palladio, with some (now much-restored) frescoes by Tintoretto and larger-than-life stucco figures.

Next door in the Anticollegio, you'll find a huge mantelpiece and Veronese's *Rape of Europa,* opposite the window, in which a rosy-breasted Europa looks rather apprehensive as the taurine Jove licks her sandal in anticipation. On the end walls are paintings of four mythological subjects by Tintoretto. Next, you enter the Sala del Collegio, where the doge and his counsellors met and where they received ambassadors. The massive carved and gilded ceiling is breathtaking, even dizzying, as you wheel around searching for the best vantage point from which to admire Veronese's frescoes, splendid after recent restoration revived their marvelous colors. That in the center at the far end is considered the best; it shows Justice and Peace offering sword, scales and olive branch to Venice. Above the throne Veronese painted Doge Sebastiano Venier offering thanks for the Republic's great naval victory over the Turks in the Battle of Lepanto in 1571. Next door is the Sala del Senato, where the doge and the senators sat; it's a large hall with a fine ceiling. The ceiling centerpiece is by Tintoretto, the paintings on the left and end walls by Palma Giovane. Many works in this room are, however, gradually being restored and may not all be in place.

As you go back through the ambassador's waiting room and adjacent corridor, pause at the window for a good view of the upper facade of San Zaccaria. Then you enter the Sala del Consiglio dei Dieci, where Venice's forbiddingly severe Council of Ten met and passed judgment on political prisoners. In the ceiling are Veronese's *Old Man in Oriental Costume,* in the far right-hand corner, and *Juno Offering Gifts to Venice,* in the left center. The latter is a masterful example of Veronese's command of pictorial illusionism; the gold coins, crowns and doge's cap seem literally to be falling through the air. Napoleon liked these paintings too, and carried them off to Brussels in 1797. These two were returned in the 1920s, but several others remained in the Louvre, where they can still be seen today.

In the Sala della Bussola, next door, you'll find a *bocca di leone,* or lion's mouth, a stone plaque with a slot that served as a sinister mailbox for anonymous denunciations. There were many of these throughout the palace. The windows here and on the adjacent landing look out onto the lead-sheathed roof of the Piombi prison, over which Casanova scrambled in a successful escape, and over to the venerable Hotel Danieli's modern wing, an eyesore still deeply resented by many Venetians. Stairs here lead up to the Armory. It has a good collection of antique arms and armor, but annoyingly is often closed.

Descending the Scala dei Censori to the second floor of the palace, you enter the Andito del Maggior Consiglio, an ante-chamber. Peek into the second room on the left, where you'll see two huge globes and some fragments of the large 14th-century fresco by Paduan artist and pupil of Giotto, Guariento di Arpo. Originally it decorated the end wall of the immense Sala del Maggior Consiglio next door. Ruined by fire in 1577, what was left of it was hidden by Tintoretto's vast canvas until its rediscovery in 1903. On the enclosed verandah at the end of the antechamber the members of the Great Council used to stretch their legs between sessions. The statues here are the originals from the Arco Foscari; the Adam and Eve are among Antonio Rizzi's finest works, and the statue of Francesco Maria I della Rovere, duke of Urbino and a commander of the Venetian armies, is a worthy portrait by Florentine sculptor Giovanni Bandini.

From here you'll enter the largest and most imposing room in the palace, the Sala del Maggior Consiglio, where the Great Council, once composed of as many as 1,000 patricians, met to ratify laws and elect the doges. The hall was built in 1370 and later decorated by such esteemed artists as Guariento, Gentile da Fabriano, Pisanello, Vivarini, Bellini, and Carpaccio. All their work went up in smoke in a terrible fire in 1577. The hall was quickly and faithfully reconstructed by Antonio da Ponte, who later built the Rialto Bridge. Tintoretto, by now an old man, and Veronese were called upon to replace the destroyed frescoes. Tintoretto seized the opportunity to produce a *summa* of his art, a vast work for a vast hall, the largest oil painting in the world. His rendition of *Paradise,* recently restored, is a dark, dynamic, crowded masterpiece in which the artist painted his own daughter at the feet of St. Christopher. The only other really important work here is Veronese's *Apotheosis of Venice,* an oval panel in the heavy, carved ceiling near the *Paradise.* Veronese's decorative, illusionist style and subtle effects of light and color contrast markedly with the vibrant power of Tintoretto's work. The historical paintings around the walls are generally dreary and uninteresting. A frieze above them presents the portraits of the first 76 doges, with the grim exception of Marin Falier; under a black void near the left-hand corner of the wall opposite the *Paradise* a Latin inscription bluntly explains that Falier was executed: for treason in 1355. *Hic est locus Marini Falethri decapitati pro criminibus,* it reads (Here is the place of Marin Falier, beheaded for his crimes). The plot in which he had involved architect Filippo Calendario had been discovered, and the Republic was never to forgive him. Even if you have to wait your turn to do so, be sure to step out onto the balcony for a wonderful view of busy St. Mark's Basin and San Giorgio Maggiore across the channel. If it's clear you'll see the Lido in the distance. Below, the water churns with the wake of myriad craft.

On your way to the exit you pass through the Sala dello Scrutinio, where the Great Council's votes were counted and recorded. This room has a full complement of paintings, though none is outstanding in comparison with those in other rooms. The exit is under a pompous triumphal arch honoring late 17th-century Doge Francesco Morosini, remembered mainly for having blown up the Parthenon in Athens along with a Turkish powder magazine installed there. From the hallway step out onto the loggia that runs the length of the facades on the Piazzetta and St. Mark's Basin. On the far right end you'll have another close-up view of the Porta della Carta and the relief in which Doge Francesco Foscari looks very old (he was forced to abdicate at 84), while the winged lion is clearly still young and vigorous. At the seaward end of the loggia, several dusty busts of past doges look out disapprovingly at the hectic motorboat traffic on the lagoon.

On your way to the exit on the ground floor you can see the Pozzi prison, 18 dark cells on two levels that were set aside for the most hardened criminals. On an upper landing is the entrance to the Bridge of Sighs and Prigioni Nuove, the New Prison. Not always open to the public, the Bridge of Sighs served as a passageway for prisoners and authorities between the prison and the courts in the palace. The usual exit from the palace takes you through the courtyard, where you can sit for a while under the portico and admire the towering Baroque facade at one end and the two lovely old wellheads.

The Libreria Vecchia and the Museo Correr

The Libreria Vecchia, or Old Library, sometimes also called the Libreria Sansovino after its architect, Jacopo Sansovino, stands opposite the Palazzo Ducale and forms the western wall of the piazzetta. Sansovino's building, begun in 1540 and completed in 1588, eight years after the architect's death, is generally considered the first Renaissance, or classical, building in Venice. This is not altogether surprising given that the Florentine Sansovino was not only familiar with the latest developments in the rapid rediscovery of classical Roman architecture then still taking place in his native city, but had spent much time in Rome itself, which he fled in 1527 following the sack of that city. Thus he brought to Venice, still at that time distinctly parochial in regard to architecture and still somewhat in thrall to Gothic and Byzantine styles, a new and fresh architectural vision. Flattering the Venetians' love of opulence and display, Sansovino made his library a considerably more ornate building than might have been deemed fitting in Rome or Florence, for example, but with its magnificent and stately classicism it heralded a new and influential architectural language for Venice.

There are in fact two libraries in Sansovino's magnificent building, as well as the Archeological Museum, the Museo Archeologico. The principal library is the Biblioteca Marciana, the city's main public library. Its reading rooms are housed in the Zecca, originally the city mint, where sequins—*zecchini* in Italian—were made; the entrance is at no. 7. Above the Marciana library is the main library itself, simply known as the Biblioteca. It is not generally open to the public but may be visited by appointment; the entrance is at no. 13a. Here paintings and frescoes by Tintoretto, Veronese and Titian among others decorate a dusty treasure house of ancient manuscripts and books, ample proof of Venice's significant contribution to the development of printing. The Archeological Museum is at the northern end of the building. It contains fine collections of ancient Greek and Roman statues, especially the 5th-century B.C. Greek statues of Persephone, Hera and Athena in Room IV.

Fronting the Piazzetta, with the Doge's Palace to one side and the Libraria Vecchia to the other, is the Molo, an elegant waterside terrace. If you walk west here, toward the Grand Canal, past the garden laid out early in the 19th century on the site of what were originally the city's granaries, you soon come to the San Marco landing stage. In addition to catching the *vaporetto* you can also, if you desperately want one, buy a plastic gondola from one of the many souvenir vendors hawking their cheap and garish wares here. There are also public pay toilets on the Molo, housed in an inconspicuous building (closed in the winter).

If you turn the corner into Calle Valleresso you'll find the humble door of a very unhumble watering place, Harry's Bar, traditional Venetian hangout of such as Hemingway, Maugham and Onassis, not to mention Barbara Hutton, Peggy Guggenheim and Orson Welles. Now the tourists far outnumber the celebrities, but Harry's is still known for the best and driest martinis in town, at appropriately stiff prices. Now, for the Museo Correr. Head back to Piazza San Marco, turning left at the end of Calle Valleresso.

The Museo Correr, Venice's historical museum, is in the Procuratie Nuove on the southern side of the piazza. This building too was designed by Sansovino, as an extension of his Libreria Vecchia, though it was completed by the Venetian architect Longhena in the 17th century. You enter the museum from the Ala Napoleonica, the wing that Napoleon added to link the Old and New Procuratie. A monumental marble staircase leads up to the second floor, decorated in the neo-Classical style popular at the time when Napoleon transformed the building into a royal palace.

Room I, the Throne Room, has some early works by Hayez and Canova, one of Napoleon's favorite sculptors. The other rooms on this floor are given over to the historical collections: paintings, documents, reliefs and ceremonial robes and portraits of the doges. In a display case you'll find an example of the grotesquely high-soled shoes—some a startling 20 inches high—much favored by fashionable Venetian ladies in the 16th century. So precariously were they perched on these creations, they could get about only with the help of two servants.

The picture gallery on the third floor has a section on the Risorgimento, Italy's 19th-century independence and unification movement (usually and unhelpfully closed), and another, of much greater interest to foreign visitors, containing Gothic and Renaissance paintings. In Room I are works of the Venetian-Byzantine period, while Room II holds altarpieces, some by Paolo Veneziano. Room III is devoted to the works of Lorenzo Veneziano, a contemporary but no relative of Paolo. Room IV contains Gothic sculptures; the most noteworthy piece is the little kneeling statuette of Doge Antonio Venier by Jacobello delle Masegne, dating from around 1400. The works in Room VI are given over to the International Gothic style, a decorative, highly gilded style that preceded the advent of the Renaissance in Italy. See the music-making angels by Stefano da Verona and the *Madonna* by Jacobello del Fiore.

The Flemish paintings in Room X are not particularly noteworthy, but next door there's a fine *Madonna* by Bouts, a *Crucifixion* attributed to Hugo van der Goes, author of the *Portinari Altarpiece* in Florence's Uffizi, and a deteriorated but impressive *Christ Supported by Angels* by Antonello da Messina, a Sicilian artist who came to Venice in the late 15th century. Antonello's influence on early-Renaissance Venetian painting was decisive. Having encountered—and mastered—the oil painting techniques then being developed in Flanders, Antonello introduced them to his colleagues in Venice. The new methods were immediately adopted by Giovanni Bellini, the leading painter of the time. Bellini's striking use of color and light, opulent and rich, was equally important for the later development of Venetian painting. His *Crucifixion* and *Transfiguration* in Room XIII are marvelous examples of the positively luxurious qualities of much Venetian painting in the Renaissance. Also in Room XIII are a *Crucifixion* by Jacopo Bellini, Giovanni's father, and the *Portrait of Doge Giovanni Mocenigo* by Gentile Bellini, Giovanni's brother.

Rooms XV and XVI contain several Carpaccios, among them the well-known *Two Venetian Ladies* painted around 1500. The picture was long assumed to be of two courtesans. Recent research has indicated, however, that these two rather bored looking women, playing with a motley menagerie of birds and dogs, are probably the wife and daughter of an important Venetian, a far cry from two ladies of easy virtue.

The Mercerie

You may wish that you were back in the quiet halls of the Museo Correr as you make your way through the hectic Mercerie, the narrow, crowded commercial artery that cuts through the San Marco district to the Rialto. Still, your visit to Venice would not be complete without a walk along these shop-lined streets. The church of San Giuliano offers an oasis of calm along the way. It was rebuilt in 1553 by Jacopo Sansovino, who honored the project's financial backer, Tommaso Rangone, with a seated statue on the facade. Stop in to see the fine ceiling by Palma Giovane and the *Pietà* by Paolo Veronese over the first altar on the right.

Back in the mainstream, continue along the Mercerie, cross the canal and turn right. Beneath the portico at # 4939 is the notorious Ridotto Venier, gambling hall and meeting-place of 18th-century Venetian society. Only aristocrats or those wearing masks were allowed to enter. The Republic finally closed it down because the Venetians were losing exorbitant sums there to foreign gamblers. The interior is decorated with some extravagant Rococo stucco work; ring the doorbell and ask the porter if he'll let you take a look. Guardi's painting, *Il Ridotto,* in the Ca' Rezzonico also will give you an idea of what these gambling halls looked like in their heyday. From the Ridotto Venier just follow the Mercerie to the Rialto.

SIGHTSEEING DATA. For general information on museum and church opening times and entrance prices, see "Sightseeing Tips" under *Miscellaneous* in the *Practical Information for Venice.*

Basilica di San Marco, Piazza San Marco. You will not be admitted to the Basilica if you are wearing shorts or otherwise revealing clothing. Open from early morning, but tourists are asked to observe the following hours: Mon. to Sat. 9:30–5:30, Sun. 2:30–5:30. **Pala d'Oro and Treasury,** Mon. to Sat. 10–5, Sun. 2–5. Admission 500 lire. **Gallery and Museum,** daily 10–5. Admission 500 lire. Free guided visits in English Mon. to Sat. 11 A.M.; groups form in atrium.

Campanile di San Marco. Open daily Apr. to Oct. 9:30–7:30, Nov. to Mar. 10–4. Admission 1,500 lire.

Museo Archeologico, Libreria Sansoviniana, Piazzetta San Marco 17 (tel. 522.5978). Open Tues. to Sat. 9–2, Sun. 9–1. Closed Mon. Admission 2,000 lire.

Museo Correr, Central portico, Ala Napoleonica, Piazza San Marco (tel. 522.5625). Open Mon., Wed. to Sat. 10–4, Sun. 9–12:30. Closed Tues. Admission 3,000 lire.

Palazzo Ducale (Doge's Palace), Piazzetta San Marco (tel. 522.4951). The Secret Itineraries tour takes you behind the scenes. Open daily 8:30–7. Admission 5,000 lire.

Torre dell'Orologio (Clock Tower), Piazza San Marco (tel. 523.1879). Closed for restorations in 1988; reopening date unknown at presstime.

The Grand Canal

The Venetians call it the Canalazzo, but to the rest of the world it's the Grand Canal, Venice's main thoroughfare, a two-mile-long ribbon of water that loops through the city. When it is busiest, large and small craft criss-cross in its waters, creating a maelstrom that sets gondolas rocking and sends green waves slapping at the seaweed-slippery foundations of the palaces. You should see it once when traffic is at a peak, preferably from a vantage point on the Rialto or Accademia bridges, or, if you're lucky enough to have one, from a window overlooking the canal. The action starts at about 7 or 8 in the morning and continues well into the afternoon. But the early hours are undoubtedly the busiest. Barges laden with food-stuffs for the hotels or piled with bricks and sand for a construction job chug purposefully by. In another a deckhand sits atop a mountain of packing cases reading the morning paper while the helmsman steers the barge with a tanned and confident foot on the tiller. *Vaporetti* from the railway station are crammed with excursionists from the mainland and Venetians on their way to school or work. The post office boat drops off mailmen at strategically located landings to begin their rounds. The *vigili urbani* (city police) in their small blue and white boats keep a stern eye on the fast, sleek motorboats that carry visiting dignitaries and wealthy tourists to the luxury hotels. Garbage barges rendezvous with the garbage collectors who trot through the streets with metal carts, picking up the bags of refuse.

On Saturdays and Sundays you may be lucky enough to see a wedding party in a flower-bedecked gondola, the gondoliers dressed in ceremonial satin suits of white and yellow or red and gold. You'll see the bride's precarious descent into the gondola, a flash of leg as hovering aunts and cousins hold her crinolines high above the water until she settles down and is rowed grandly off, her veil a puff of white at the center of the black crescent. Her relatives follow in a cortege of motorboats. She'll be met by her groom at the church, and afterwards they will glide off together to some rustic restaurant on the lagoon for a rousing wedding party.

Or you may see a funeral in gondolas, a somber affair, as the black-draped boats pass silently through the city and cross the lagoon to the cemetery island of San Michele, where the dead are laid to rest under the cypresses. Then there are the fireboats that roar out of their boathouse near the Ca'Foscari with sirens wailing, a churning wake of white foam stretching behind them. The ambulance boats wail, too, and in the quieter hours you can hear them coming from a long way off. They are equipped with barrow-like stretchers with front wheels and handles so that the attendants can transport patients over the humpbacked bridges. And in the midst of it all, in the roll and pitch of crossed wakes and boiling water, imperturbable gondoliers steady their fragile-looking craft so that their passengers can snap photos of them, of each other, of the boats and palaces along the canal, of the weddings, the funerals and all the other everyday events that, simply because they're in Venice, are extraordinary.

The quietest and most romantic time to take a ride in a gondola along the Grand Canal is late afternoon or early evening, ideally around sunset. And be sure to let your gondolier know that you want to see the *rii*, the smaller canals, too. You'll get an entirely different perspective of life in Venice. However, for an overall sightseeing tour of the Grand Canal, you'll get a better view from the *vaporetto*, which is both higher in the water and very much less expensive. Use Vaporetto Line 1, which takes about 45 minutes between San Zaccaria and the station, making all the stops and allowing you plenty of time to ogle the palaces. You're more likely to find one of the coveted seats in the prow if you go against the tourist tide, i.e., toward the station in the morning, away from it in the evening. The stern seats also give you an unobstructed view to the rear.

The Grand Canal has an average depth of about nine feet and varies from 40 to 76 yards in width. It follows the course of a river channel that cut through the islands of Rivo Alto (Rialto), where Venice was founded by settlers from other islands in the lagoon who had fled the mainland as refugees centuries earlier. Most of the palaces along the canal were built between the 14th and 18th centuries, though some date back to the 12th century. Each rests on a thicket of wooden piles driven into the clay canal bed. A foundation of bricks was built up over the piles and several courses of Istrian stone then laid over the bricks more or less at the waterline. This Istrian stone is highly resistant to water erosion and forms a waterproof base for the brick walls of the palace, though these were sometimes faced with stone.

For many centuries the canal could be crossed only by boat or over its single bridge, the Ponte di Rialto. Eventually two more bridges were built, the wooden Accademia Bridge and the Scalzi Bridge near the railway station. But to get from one side of the canal to the other the Venetians rely mainly on the *traghetto*, a two-man gondola that leaves from various wooden landing stages, and for a few hundred lire ferries people from shore to shore. It's the cheapest and shortest gondola ride in Venice, and it can save an enormous amount of walking. As you ride up and down the Grand Canal on the *vaporetto*, look for these *traghetto* stations. Sooner or later you will find them very useful (there's a list of the stations in *Practical Information for Venice*).

Along the Grand Canal

The Grand Canal was, and to some extent of course still is, the Fifth Avenue of Venice. It was here that the city's leading families lived, building for themselves a series of magnificent palaces, remarkable even by the standards of this remarkable city. Any building is enhanced by the presence of water. Here, the combination of water and the most opulent, luxurious and fantastical efforts of a people obsessed with opulence, luxury and fantasy, has created a seemingly endlessly unfolding panorama of unique architectural richness. The sheer numbers of these buildings can produce a sort of cultural shell-shock, particularly if you attempt to identify each

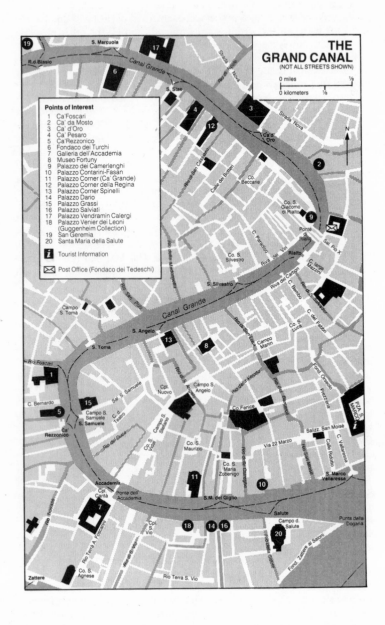

THE GRAND CANAL
(NOT ALL STREETS SHOWN)

0 miles   ⅛

0 kilometers   ⅛

Points of Interest

1	Ca'Foscari
2	Ca' da Mosto
3	Ca' d'Oro
4	Ca' Pesaro
5	Ca'Rezzonico
6	Fondaco dei Turchi
7	Galleria dell'Accademia
8	Museo Fortuny
9	Palazzo dei Camerlenghi
10	Palazzo Contarini-Fasan
11	Palazzo Corner (Ca' Grande)
12	Palazzo Corner della Regina
13	Palazzo Corner Spinelli
14	Palazzo Dario
15	Palazzo Grassi
16	Palazzo Salviati
17	Palazzo Vendramin Calergi
18	Palazzo Venier dei Leoni (Guggenheim Collection)
19	San Geremia
20	Santa Maria della Salute

i   Tourist Information

✉   Post Office (Fondaco dei Tedeschi)

and every one, to left and to right, as you head up the canal. Accordingly, it makes sense to attempt little more at first than to sample, to breathe in, the unparalleled magnificence of the Grand Canal, letting it wash over you (only metaphorically, of course; it may not be deep but it's very dirty). Then once you've begun to acclimatize, come back for more. For those who feel ready to begin the considerable business of identifying all the major buildings we have provided a fairly comprehensive listing here. A number of the more important are also covered in the appropriate "Exploring" chapter.

Start your tour of the Grand Canal from the San Zaccaria landing stage on the Riva degli Schiavoni, just to the west of the Doge's Palace. Take a line 1 *vaporetto* headed toward the right and the Grand Canal. You'll see the Bridge of Sighs—the Ponte dei Sospiri—the Doge's Palace itself, the Piazzetta and the Zecca on the right. Away to your left across St. Mark's Basin are Palladio's imposing church of San Giorgio Maggiore, the island of Giudecca and, marking the left-hand entrance to the Grand Canal, the Punta della Dogana. There has been a maritime customs house at Punta della Dogana since the early 15th century, though the classical building there today, with its golden sphere and weathervane, was put up in the 1670s. This was the strongpoint in Venice's defense. An enormous iron chain could be stretched across the mouth of the Grand Canal from Punta della Dogana to prevent enemy ships from entering the city. Next to the customs house is a 17th-century seminary and the great white-domed Baroque church of Santa Maria della Salute, one of the most striking and memorable sights of the Venetian skyline. Built between 1635 and 1687 by the Venetian architect Baldassare Longhena, it commemorates a plague that struck the city in 1630. On the right, beyond the Hotel Monaco et Grand Canal, is the 15th-century Gothic Ca' Giustinian, with its graceful windows and loggias. This now belongs to the city of Venice. The luxurious hotel Bauer Grunewald is in a 19th-century Gothic building, while across Rio San Moisè is the sober, classical facade of the 17th-century Palazzo Treves dei Bonfili, and the contemporary Palazzo Tiepolo, now the Hotel Europa. Three palaces beyond, you'll see the tiny Palazzo Contarini-Fasan, a charming 15th-century Venetian Gothic palace with three windows on the main floor and a tracery balcony; it is known as the House of Desdemona. The 15th-century Palazzo Pisani is now the luxurious Gritti Palace Hotel, probably the city's most famous hotel.

In the little square by the hotel, a vine-covered wooden hut marks the Santa Maria del Giglio *traghetto* station. On the left, across the canal, you can't miss the flashy modern mosaic facade of Palazzo Salviati, an imitation Renaissance building in which the well-known glass blowers have a showroom. Just beyond a side canal and the 16th-century Palazzo Barbaro is the charming Palazzo Dario, built in the 15th century in the style promulgated in Venice by Pietro Lombardo and his followers. It has pretty multicolored marble decorations in geometric forms and many chimney pots, always a highly distinctive feature of Venice. The walls of this venerable palace lean at an angle over the canal. Beyond it is Palazzo Venier dei Leoni, begun in 1749 and never completed. The palace gets its name from the frieze of lion heads (*leoni*) just above water level. For 30 years it was the home of American heiress and patroness of the arts Peggy Guggenheim, who died in 1979, and it still houses her collection of modern art. Across the canal, on your right, is the imposing Palazzo Corner, known as the Ca' Grande, a huge and handsome classical Renaissance stone building designed by Jacopo Sansovino. It is now the Prefecture of Venice, an administrative body. The little garden next door half conceals the Casetta delle Rose, or Cottage of the Roses, where the neo-Classical sculptor Antonio Canova had his first studio, and where the extravagant Italian poet, revolutionary and fascist Gabriele d'Annunzio lived during World War I.

On the left side of the canal you'll see the beautiful old Palazzo Da Mula, a Gothic building with a three-story loggia, and, next to it, the rather garish late 19th-century mosaics on the facade of Palazzo Barbarigo, adjoining the pretty little Campo San Vio. Just beyond is the garden and graceful facade of Palazzo Contarini dal Zaffo, which bears the polychrome marble motifs that were the hallmark of the style introduced by the Lombardos.

Opposite, on the right side of the canal, the striking Palazzo Cavalli-Franchetti is a grandiose 15th-century building in an ample garden; it was rebuilt in the late 19th century, and its facade intentionally echoes that of the Doge's Palace. On the right of this elegantly showy palace is the much smaller Palazzo Barbaro, a Gothic building in which Whistler, Sargent, Monet, Henry James and Robert Browning, among many others, were entertained.

Past the Accademia

Now you pass under the Accademia Bridge, the Ponte dell' Accademia. Built in the '30s, it was intended as no more than a temporary replacement for the early 19th-century Accademia Bridge which had been declared unsafe. Temporary structure or not, it's still here today. On the left is the Galleria dell'Accademia, housed in the former church and Scuola of Santa Maria della Carità. Also on Campo della Carità, a coat-of-arms marks the British Vice-Consulate in Palazzo Querini. On the left-hand corner of Rio Trovaso, look for Palazzo Contarini degli Scrigni, a twin edifice made up of a 15th-century building decorated with motifs in polychrome marble and another built in 1609 by Vincenzo Scamozzi, with a rusticated stone base and classical-looking windows.

On the right, directly across the canal, you can distinguish Palazzo Giustinian-Lolin, built by Longhena in 1623, with its rusticated stone foundation and two stories of airy loggias. It's owned by a music foundation. Next to it is the 15th-century Palazzo Falier, which has two of the few surviving *liagos,* open terraces, once typical of Venetian palaces. Across Rio del Duca the rusticated stone construction on the corner was to be part of the massive base projected for Ca' del Duca, begun by Bartolomeo Bon for the Cornaro family in the mid-15th century but never completed. It was owned by Francesco Sforza, duke of Milan, whose troops fought for Venice. Just beyond Campo San Samuele is Palazzo Grassi, restored by a Fiat-led consortium and reopened in 1986 as a prestigious venue for art exhibitions and other cultural events. It's a fine 16th-century classical building by architect Giorgio Massari. The stone facade has been cleaned and is now a gleaming ivory color.

Directly across the canal is the Ca' Rezzonico, a huge palace begun by Longhena in 1660 and completed by Massari. It houses a very good museum of 18th-century decorative arts. Look beyond the two small palaces on the right of Ca' Rezzonico to the twin facades of Palazzi Giustinian, the earlier of which was built in the 15th century. In the far palace Wagner lived during the winter of 1858–59, composing the second àct of *Tristan and Isolde*. Next door, the magnificent Ca' Foscari is one of Venice's most beautiful Gothic palaces, with intricate tracery windows and loggias. Built for Francesco Foscari, the doge who was deposed after 34 years, it is now occupied by Venice University's Institute of Economics.

At this point there is a bend in the canal known as the *Volta del Canal;* the finish line of regattas is usually established here, partly because the canal is wide enough at this point to accommodate floating grandstands. Just across Rio Foscari, a canal that flows into Rio Nuovo to form a direct route to the railway station, you'll see the 16th-century Palazzo Balbi, seat of the regional government. Opposite it, on the right side of the canal, look for Palazzo Contarini delle Figure, a 16th-century Lombardesque building, named after the caryatids, the supporting figures—*figure* meaning "figures"—over the portal. Next door are the four Mocenigo palaces, marked by the blue and white poles in the canal. These poles, or *pali,* can be seen in front of many palaces. Painted in the colors of the family that owns the palace, they also serve as mooring posts. In one of the Mocenigo palaces Giordano Bruno was betrayed by his host in 1592 and handed over to the Inquisition; in another Byron began writing *Don Juan* in 1818.

Glancing to the left side of the canal you'll see a succession of 15th- and 16th-century palaces, but keep your eyes peeled on the right for the splendid Renaissance Palazzo Corner Spinelli, designed by Mauro Codussi, with its rusticated ground floor, beautiful windows and balconies. Opposite, on the corner of Rio San Polo, is Palazzo Capello Layard. Next door are Palazzo Grimani, with a rich Lombardesque facade of the early 16th century, the 18th-century Palazzo Querini and, beyond it, Palazzo Bernardo, one of the best preserved Gothic palaces in Venice, with exceptionally beautiful tracery windows. There's another Palazzo Grimani on the right side of the canal, across Rio di San Luca. Designed by Sammicheli, it's now the seat of the Court of Appeals.

The Rialto

The pace of the canal quickens as you near the Rialto. The Riva del Vin on the left is lined with characteristic Venetian dwellings resembling those painted by Carpaccio. Opposite, on the Riva del Carbon, are Palazzo Loredan, the city hall, and a number of *vaporetto* landing stages. There are gondola stations and moorings and a succession of snack bars and canalside restaurants. Gondoliers shout and boats blow their horns as they negotiate the blind turn under the massive white stone span of the Rialto Bridge. There has been a bridge over the canal here ever since the 13th century. At one time it was a wooden drawbridge, as you can see in Carpaccio's painting of the *Miracle of the Cross* in the Accademia. In the 16th century Antonio da Ponte was commissioned to design and build a stone bridge on the site. Under his direction 6,000 piles were driven into the banks at either end to support its weight.

Just beyond the bridge on the right is the Fondaco dei Tedeschi, a massive 16th-century edifice that housed the trading center leased by the Venetians to German and Austrian merchants. In the Ca' d'Oro you can see fragments of the frescoes by Giorgione and Titian that once covered the facade of the building, now used as the main post office. On the other side of the canal at the foot of the Rialto Bridge is the large Palazzo dei Camerlenghi, a Renaissance building in white stone. It was an administrative office of the Republic and its ground floor was used as a prison. This is one of the lowest points in Venice. Often at high tide the sidewalk between the bridge and the palace is awash. Normally the canal here is 13 feet deep. The palace is on the fringe of Venice's colorful market area. Fruit and vegetable stands spill out onto the piazza from the porticoes of the 16th-century Fabbriche Vecchie and Fabbriche Nuove, next door. The latter was built by Jacopo Sansovino and now houses judiciary offices. Opposite these two buildings on the right side of the canal, look for Ca' da Mosto, a Venetian-Byzantine palace built in the 13th century and decorated with arches and saucer-shaped ornaments called *paterae,* typical of Byzantine architecture. In the 15th century this was the home of Alvise de Mosto, who discovered the Cape Verde Islands; later it became a famous inn, the Leon Bianco. A *traghetto* plies the canal here, ferrying housewives with shopping bags to and from the market. The neo-Gothic arcade at the end of the market shelters the Pescheria, or fish market.

A House of Gold

On the right, look for the Ca' d'Oro landing stage. Next to it is the most magnificent palace on the Grand Canal, the fabulous Ca' d'Oro (the House of Gold, named after the gold that once accented the carved marble ornaments on its facade). The palace was completed about 1440. It has been extensively restored and now houses the Franchetti art collection. Across the canal, beyond Rio di San Cassiano, you'll see the classical facade, with loggias on two stories, of Palazzo Corner della Regina, built in 1724 and named after the Queen (*regina*) of Cyprus, Caterina Cornaro, who was born in an older palace on this site. The palace holds the Biennale's collections of contemporary art. Just beyond it you can't miss the imposing bulk of the splendid Baroque Ca' Pesaro, or Palazzo Pesaro, built by Longhena in 1710. The building is one of the noblest in Venice, far more impressive than the undistinguished collection of modern and oriental art that it houses. Look for the ornamental masks on the arches. Wealthy Venetians vied with each other for property along this stretch of the canal, where the waterway is wide enough to allow their sumptuous palaces to be properly seen and admired. Just beyond Ca' Pesaro on the left side of the canal you'll see the pretty Baroque facade of the church of San Stae (Sant' Eustachio), where pigeons roost among spanking-white statues.

Opposite San Stae on the right-hand corner of a small *rio* is 15th-century Palazzo Barbarigo, the only palace on the canal that still bears the faint traces of fresco decoration, on the lower facade. On the same side of the canal you can't miss Palazzo Vendramin Calergi, a large, beautiful Renaissance building designed by Codussi and completed by the Lombardo family's workshop about 1509. In a wing of this palace Richard Wagner died one blustery February day in 1883. During the winter its sumptuous salons play host to Venice's municipal casino. Just beyond it is the landing stage of San Marcuola, named after the little church with its unfinished brick facade and square in which numerous cats and pigeons live in happy coexistence. Practically opposite Palazzo Vendramin Calergi is the Fondaco dei Turchi, originally a 13th-century Venetian-Byzantine structure but entirely rebuilt in the 19th century, and not very authentically according to many. Once the property of the dukes of Ferrara, it became a commercial center for the Turks who came to Venice to trade. The ground here is very low; at high tide the water often laps at the sarcophagi under the portico. One of these is without an inscription but is notorious as that of Marin Falier, the doge who was beheaded in 1355 for treason. His corpse was put on display for 24 hours, with the head between the feet, and was then enclosed in the sarcophagus and taken to San Zanipolo. When the sarcophagus was opened in 1812, the skull was still lying between the leg bones. The unforgiving Venetians used the sarcophagus as a cattle trough for a while, then relented enough to have it placed under the portico of Fondaco dei Turchi as a decorative element.

At the next curve of the Grand Canal, another canal branches off into the Cannaregio district. You can see the back of the church of San Geremia on the left of the canal of Cannaregio and get a glimpse of Palazzo Labia and the Ponte delle Guglie. Along the Grand Canal a few old palaces alternate with newer ones, some grouped around pretty little tree-shaded *campielli* on the canal's edge. You pass under the Scalzi Bridge, built in the '30s to create a direct pedestrian route between the center and the station. On the right the Baroque facade of the church of the Scalzi contrasts with the sweeping horizontal lines of the railway station. Until the Austrians built the railway bridge across the lagoon from the mainland in 1846 (providing it with 48 chambers for explosives in case it had to be demolished in a hurry) the only way you could arrive in Venice was by boat.

Opposite the station, across the canal, is the green-domed church of San Simeone Piccolo, an 18th-century edifice. The smallish Papadopoli public gardens are at the end of the Fondamenta and just beyond them is the entrance to the Rio Nuovo, the canal cut in 1933 to create a direct water route to San Marco. Beyond is the landing stage for Piazzale Roma, the terminus of the causeway to the mainland and the garages and parking lots where Venetians and visitors alike must leave their cars when they arrive in the city.

SIGHTSEEING DATA. For general information on museum and church opening times and entrance prices, see "Sightseeing Tips" under *Miscellaneous* in the *Practical Information for Venice.*

Galleria dell'Arte Moderna, Ca' Pesaro (tel. 721.127). Closed indefinitely.

Museo Fortuny, Tio Terrà della Mandorla, San Beneto (tel. 520.0995). Open Tues. to Sun. 9–7. Closed Mon. Admission 5,000 lire.

Museo Orientale, Ca' Pesaro (tel. 524.1173). Open Tues. to Sat. 9–2, Sun. 9–1. Closed Mon. Admission 2,000 lire.

West of St. Mark's

Takes in much of the *sestiere* of San Marco, a district off the heavily beaten tourist track from the Piazza to the Rialto. Head out of Piazza San Marco under the portico of the Ala Napoleonica and follow Salizzada San Moisè to Campo San Moisè, where the tourist tide is still strong and where you'll find the American Express office, the posh old Bauer Grunewald Hotel and a busy gondola station across the canal. The facade of the church of San Moisè is overwhelmingly Baroque, heavy with statues and carved reliefs. Inside is an equally overpowering sculptured altarpiece of Moses receiving the Ten Commandments.

Crossing the bridge you enter a broad thoroughfare, Calle Larga XXII (Ventidue) Marzo, named after the date of the Venetian uprising led by Daniele Manin against the Austrians in 1848. Follow this street of banks, shops and good hotels around the corner into Calle delle Ostreghe and continue into Campo Santa Maria Zobenigo, which opens onto the Grand Canal and is bordered to its east by one side of the Gritti Palace Hotel. The church here, variously known as Santa Maria Zobenigo and, less commonly, Santa Maria del Giglio, looms on the right. Built under the auspices of the Barbaro family in the 17th century, the church has an interesting Baroque facade that is singularly lacking in religious motifs—the great 19th-century art pundit, John Ruskin, was accordingly deeply distressed by it. Rather, it is a paean to the military accomplishments of the Barbaros. Look at the unusual and charming stone reliefs showing three-dimensional plans of Zara, Crete, Padua, Rome, Corfu and Split; they commemorate victories won by various Barbaro commanders. You can clearly discern the landmarks in each plan, and you can't miss Rome's Colosseum. The church's vast rectangular interior is similar to that of San Moisè. It has a full complement of 17th- and 18th-century paintings, including a *Visitation* by Palma Giovane in the third chapel on the right and portraits of the Evangelists by Tintoretto below the organ in the sanctuary.

Campo Santo Stefano

Continuing in the same direction, you cross the bridge into Campiello della Feltrina, where the Piazzesi shop, an institution in Venice, makes and sells hand-printed paper and papier-maché objects that make easy-to-pack gifts to take home. Crossing the next bridge, continue on into Campo San Maurizio. On the left is the Gothic Palazzo Zaguri, on the right the neo-Classical church of San Maurizio. From here you can see the tipsiest bell tower in Venice, that of Santo Stefano. Now take Calle del Piovan

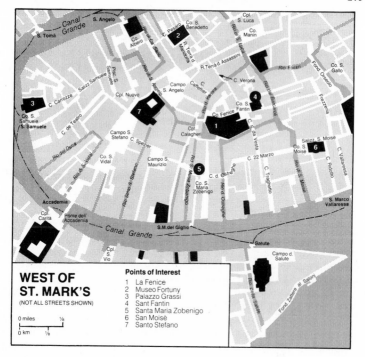

WEST OF ST. MARK'S

(NOT ALL STREETS SHOWN)

0 miles   ⅛
0 km   ⅛

Points of Interest

1   La Fenice
2   Museo Fortuny
3   Palazzo Grassi
4   Sant Fantin
5   Santa Maria Zobenigo
6   San Moisè
7   Santo Stefano

and Calle del Spezier into the vast Campo Santo Stefano—also confusingly known as Campo Morosini after Doge Francesco Morosini, who lived in the palace at # 2802. Campo Santo Stefano has a pleasant, relaxed atmosphere. It also has the Cafe Paolin—which makes some of the best ice cream in Venice—several fine old palaces and a steady stream of pedestrians heading for the Accademia Bridge just beyond the church of San Vitale at the end of the piazza.

The church of Santo Stefano has a brick facade and an unobtrusive but handsome Gothic portal. Make it a point to visit this church to see its large, shadowy Gothic interior, where tall columns support a beautiful wooden roof reminiscent of an inverted ship's keel, one of several in Venice. There are a number of works by masters of the Lombardo school scattered throughout the church. A big Renaissance portal leads to the sacristy, now used as a chapel. Here, feed a coin into the light machine to get a better look at the three Tintorettos on the right wall. In the pavement at the center of the nave, a huge bronze funeral slab conspicuously marks the tomb of Doge Francesco Morosini, buried here in 1694, who has been called one of the great fighting doges (and who accidentally blew up the Parthenon in Athens).

Now make a tour of the campo to see the remodeled Gothic Palazzo Loredan on the right, just this side of San Vitale, a deconsecrated church that is used as an art gallery. On the left, a stone wall delimits the gardens of Palazzo Cavalli-Franchetti. Behind it, on a smallish campo, Palazzo Pisani was built in the 17th and 18th centuries and was one of the largest private palaces in Venice; now it's the Music Conservatory.

At this point you could cross the Accademia Bridge to visit the Accademia, Venice's most important picture gallery, which we cover in our "West of the Grand Canal" chapter. Alternatively, if you want to continue your tour of the San Marco district, leave Campo Santo Stefano by way of Calle Fruttarol and continue more or less straight ahead. Emerging from the calle—a plaque here proclaims the birthplace in 1725 of Casanova—you'll be in Campo San Samuele, an attractive little square on the Grand Canal. To one side is the entrance to Palazzo Grassi, recently restored by the Fiat organization as a cultural center, to the other, the Palazzo Malipiero. Between them is the former church of San Samuele, with its 12th-century bell tower. If Palazzo Grassi is open, step in to have a look at the illusionistic frescoes of carnival revelers over the staircase. Campo San Samuele has a landing stage for the Line 4 *vaporetto* and for the gondola *traghetto* as well.

Now take Calle delle Carrozze into Salizzada San Samuele, where Veronese died in 1588. Cross a canal and continue in the same direction to Corte dell'Albero, where the ACTV office, half-hidden in a garden, sells discount passes (the "Carta Venezia") and blocks of tickets for the *vaporetto*. Take Calle Pesaro to Campo San Benedetto and turn the corner to Palazzo Fortuny, a 15th-century palace with a picturesque exterior wooden staircase and loggia. This was the home of Mariano Fortuny, eclectic Spanish-born genius known for his sumptuous fabric and costume designs and artistic photographs. The museum, a fascinating place with a rather eccentric atmosphere, contains a wealth of curios and mementoes.

Campo Sant' Angelo and La Fenice

Now take Rio Terrà della Mandorla and turn right into Campo Sant'Angelo, a large, attractive square just a few steps from Campo Santo Stefano. It is surrounded by some fine palaces, has a miniscule Oratory smack in the middle and offers another good view of Santo Stefano's leaning tower. From here you can head directly to La Fenice, taking the narrow Calle del Caffettier into Campo Fenice before turning left and then right. Or you could backtrack on Calle del Spezier and turn right into Rio Terrà degli Assassini, a name common to several Venetian streets and a reminder of the times when violence and betrayal were everyday occurrences. Because of the dastardly deeds committed under its beautiful roof, the nearby church of Santo Stefano had to be reconsecrated no less than six times. Present-day Venice, however, holds no such threats for the visitor. It is one of the safest of all Italian cities.

From the street of the assassins, Calle del Verona to the right leads to Campo San Fantin. The classical lines of the simple Renaissance church of Sant Fantin are repeated in its beautiful domed sanctuary, probably designed by Sansovino. San Fantin is a bit too large for its own little campo, and it seems to steal some of the limelight from the neo-Classical facade of La Fenice, Venice's famous opera theater, and scene of many memorable operatic premiers, including, in 1853, the dismal first night flop of Verdi's *La Traviata*. The theater was originally built in the 1790s, when fun-loving, libidinous, pleasure-crazed Venice had more theaters than Paris. Razed by fire in 1836, it was rebuilt, rising from its own ashes like the phoenix after which it was named. Today it possesses a delightful early 19th-century interior, all gilt carving and stuccoes. Theater-goers arriving by gondola have a special entrance directly from a side canal. If there are no rehearsals going on, you may be able to visit the theater. Inquire at the box office, which is open every weekday.

To return to San Marco from here, take Calle del Veste, where there's a nice wine shop that offers buffet meals, continuing into Calle Larga XXII Marzo and turn left for San Moisè.

North and East from St. Mark's

This chapter has been arranged as two separate walks from St. Mark's. Though geographically close to each other, the two areas we describe have few other obvious points of overlap. Nonetheless, given that any division of this tangled maze of a city into "Exploring" areas must necessarily be arbitrary, they form reasonably convenient units. As usual, however, with each walk containing a number of outstanding highlights, you may prefer to make straight for any one (or more) of these rather than follow the precise sequence we list.

Walk One—St. Mark's to the Rialto

Heading north from St. Mark's to the Rialto takes you through some of the busiest areas of central Venice, as well as past a number of lesser but nonetheless intriguing attractions. Its principal goal, other than the Rialto itself, is the market just on the other side of the Grand Canal, reached by the Rialto Bridge. It's important that you attempt this on a weekday morning when the market is in full swing.

From the Piazza di San Marco the walk to the Rialto is easily done, if complex to describe. Head through the portico of the Ala Napoleonica (at the eastern end of the piazza) and bear left into Bocca di Piazza. Turn right into Calle Frezzeri, left into Calle dei Barcaroli and right into Calle Fuseri. Here, take the second on the left into Calle Contarini del Bovolo. This will lead you to the Palazzo Contarini del Bovolo. Signs direct you to a narrow alley from where the Scala del Bovolo is visible in the courtyard of the palace. This is one of the most remarkable and fantastic constructions in the city, a spiral staircase, built a little before 1500, set in a brick and marble tower with a charming three-story brick loggia attached to it. Much of the fantasy and quirkiness of pre-Renaissance Venetian architecture is eloquently expressed by this delightfully eccentric tower. Its nickname—"del Bovolo"—means "of the snail." Unfortunately, though the staircase has been restored, its setting is in a sad state of neglect.

From here, take Calle della Vida into Campo Manin, where one of Venice's innumerable churches was torn down to make room for a modern bank. There's also the statue of Daniele Manin here, the patriot who led Venice's rebellion against the occupying Austrians in 1848. At Manin's feet lolls a large and shiny lion that children love to climb on. In the far corner of the square take Salizzada San Luca into Campo San Luca and the heart of Venice's central shopping district. Continue along Calle dell'Oro and cross the bridge into Campo San Salvador. While the tower-

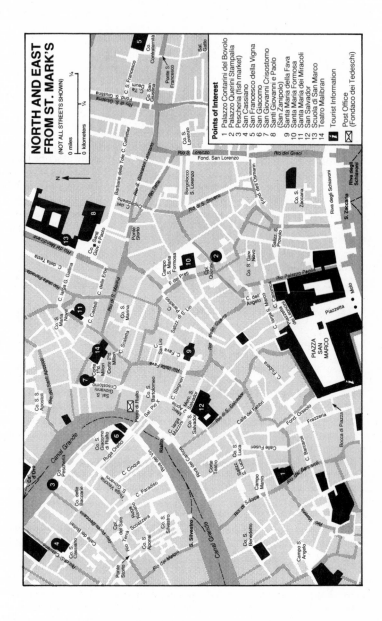

NORTH AND EAST FROM ST. MARK'S

(NOT ALL STREETS SHOWN)

Points of Interest

1 Palazzo Contarini del Bovolo
2 Palazzo Querini Stampalia
3 Pescheria (fish market)
4 San Cassiano
5 San Francesco della Vigna
6 San Giacomo
7 San Giovanni Crisostomo
8 Santi Giovanni e Paolo
   (San Zanipolo)
9 Santa Maria della Fava
10 Santa Maria Formosa
11 Santa Maria dei Miracoli
12 San Salvador
13 Scuola di San Marco
14 Teatro Malibran

ℹ️ Tourist Information

✉ Post Office
   (Fondaco dei Tedeschi)

ing Baroque facade of the church of San Salvador—San Salvatore as it is sometimes called—is undergoing restoration the entrance is from the side, on the Merceria San Salvador.

Though the facade of the church is late 17th century, the interior is much earlier, begun in fact in 1506 by a little known Venetian architect, Giorgio Spavento, and completed, under the direction of Sansovino, in 1534. The church is calm and harmonious inside, typical of the restraint and balance of much mid-Renaissance architecture. Gray mouldings on plain white halls reinforce this placidity. There's much in the way of painting and sculpture to see here. There's a *Transfiguration* by Titian over the altar and a better, but still very dark, *Annunciation* over the third altar in the right aisle, where there's a light machine. A window in the pavement in front of the main altar gives you a view of a recently discovered tomb that was probably frescoed by Titian's brother, Francesco Vecellio. Caterina Cornaro, queen of Cyprus, who ended her days in opulent exile in Asolo on the mainland, is entombed over the sacristy door in the right transept. A relief shows her relinquishing the crown of Cyprus into the hands of the doge (1489). In the chapel to the left of the apse, the *Supper at Emmaus* is a 16th-century copy of a work by Giovanni Bellini. Before you leave the church, see the monument to Doge Francesco Venier between the third and fourth altars in the right aisle; it's by Sansovino, who also executed the statue of *Hope* when he was 80 years old.

Now take Merceria 2 Aprile into the elongated Campo San Bartolomeo, junction of the various currents of pedestrian traffic that swirl and eddy at the feet of the statue of 18th-century Venetian playwright and man about town, Carlo Goldoni, who whimsically surveys the scene. Fondaco dei Tedeschi, now the main post office, is in one corner of the campo; step inside to see its imposing courtyard. Then head for the Rialto Bridge, passing through Salizzada Pio X. The bridge is divided into three lanes by two rows of shops. Pause here for the view of the Grand Canal and its traffic, then descend into the colorful chaos of the fruit and vegetable market.

The Rialto

The Rialto district was the site of one of Europe's greatest commercial exchanges, where bankers, moneylenders and merchants financed adventurous trading enterprises throughout the Mediterranean and into the Orient. After a disastrous fire in the early 16th century devastated the area, it was rebuilt to a plan that has remained substantially unaltered over the centuries. At the same time the palaces here were rebuilt with arcades that could serve as shops. Likewise, large open spaces for market stalls and broad quays along the Grand Canal were created, the latter to facilitate loading and unloading. Where cabbages and carrots are sold today, gorgeous silks, teas and spices were once traded.

The church on the right of the campo is San Giacomo, reputedly one of Venice's oldest. It is plain and unassuming, its only ornament a large clock on the facade that never seems to tell the right time. Like the market, it is open in the mornings. On the side of the church toward the bridge you can see an inscription admonishing merchants to be fair, and give true weight and keep their promises.

Opposite the church, at the other end of the campo, is a little statue, the Gobbo di Rialto—the Hunchback of Rialto—often hidden by crates of fruit or vegetables. The Gobbo is bent under the weight of a rostrum of Egyptian granite from which laws and decrees were read, as at the Pietra del Bando near the Basilica. In the 16th century the Jews who had sought refuge in Venice from mainland wars and who had managed to gain a precarious foothold here in the Rialto district, earning the grudging tolerance of the Venetians, heard the crier on the rostrum proclaim their banishment to a tiny island in the Cannaregio district that was to add the word "ghetto" to the world's vocabulary.

Wander about the Rialto district at will. You'll find excellent shopping and good places for snacks or complete meals. Stroll over to the right to see the Pescheria, the fish market, where silvery piles of fish are subjected to the exacting scrutiny of Venetian housewives. From the Pescheria turn into Campo delle Baccarie, cross the canal and follow the *sottoportego* to Calle dei Bottari, where you turn left and then right on Calle del Cristo into Campo San Cassiano. The church of San Cassiano, rebuilt in the 17th century, has retained its 13th-century bell tower and harbors a number of important works of art, especially the three Tintorettos in the apse.

Outside the church, take Calle Muti in the far left corner of the Campo and cross the bridge on Calle del Rasoio. Turn right onto Calle del Sale, which leads to Campo Sant'Aponal. On the right side of the campo you'll find Calle di Bianca Capello and Ponte Storto, where the early 16th-century Palazzo Capello at # 1280 was the birthplace of the beautiful Bianca Capello, who eloped to Florence in 1563 with a bank clerk and later became mistress, then wife, of Francesco Medici. From here follow the curving Rio Terrà di Scoazzera and turn left into Ruga del Ravano. From here you can take Ruga Vecchia San Giovanni, where you'll find plenty of interesting shops, back to the Rialto Bridge.

San Giovanni Crisostomo and Marco Polo

Cross the bridge and turn left into Salizzada San Giovanni Crisostomo as far as the church of the same name, a gorgeous example of Venetian architecture, designed by Mauro Codussi in the late 16th century. Step inside to see Giovanni Bellini's altarpiece with three saints on the first altar on the right; the light machine is indispensable here, for the church is quite dark. On the main altar, Sebastiano del Piombo's *St. John Chrysostom* was painted about 1508; diffused with soft light, it shows the influence of Giorgione. The exquisite high relief of the *Coronation of the Virgin* on the second altar on the left has the distinctive delicacy and precision of Tullio Lombardo's work.

Outside, circle the church and step into Marco Polo's neighborhood. He was born in one of these narrow calli, and the two Corti del Milion bear his nickname, "Il Milion," bestowed on him by his fellow Venetians who thought his stories of Oriental opulence exaggerated. The Corte Seconda del Milion is especially picturesque. Here, too, is the Teatro Malibran, where one of Handel's works, *Agrippina,* had its premiere in 1710.

Cross Rio di San Lio and Ponte Marco Polo and take Calle Scaletta, pausing to glance at the Gothic Palazzo Bragadin-Carabba on the curve of the canal. Take the first calle on the right and continue straight ahead to Campo San Lio. If you continue in the same direction on Calle della Fava, you'll come to the campo and church of Santa Maria della Fava. This small 18th-century church has a dramatic *Madonna with St. Philip*

Neri by Piazzetta over the second altar on the left and Tiepolo's later and more poetic *Education of the Virgin* over the first altar on the right. From the bridge outside the church you get a good view of some deliciously decadent Gothic palaces. You can continue on Calle Stegneri into Campo San Bartolomeo and on to the *vaporetto* landing stage at Rialto. Or, if you wish, you can return to San Lio and make your way from there back to San Marco.

Walk Two—To Santa Maria Formosa

This itinerary takes you to a small picture gallery and three very different churches in the area behind St. Mark's Square. And, if you wish, you can continue on to yet another church on the edge of the Castello district, where tourists are few and far between.

From the Piazzetta dei Leoncini next to the basilica, take Calle Canonica and turn left onto Calle dell'Angelo. Cross the bridge on the right into Campiello Querini, a pretty little square at the junction of two canals. A bridge gives access to Palazzo Querini-Stampalia, which houses a library and picture gallery bequeathed to the city in 1868 by a wealthy Venetian. The ground floor was restored in the '60s. Take the elevator to the Pinacoteca, the picture gallery, on the third floor. Rather dusty, ill-kept and low-key, the gallery contains some interesting works, starting with the sizeable collection of 18th-century genre scenes by Gabriel Bella in Room 1 and by Pietro and Alessandro Longhi in Rooms XI-XIII. There's a *Conversion of St. Paul* by Andrea Schiavone in Room V; a *Presentation in the Temple* in Room VIII, perhaps a copy by Giovanni Bellini of a painting by Mantegna now in Berlin; Palma Vecchio's unfinished portraits of Francesco Querini and his wife Paola Priuli, also in Room VIII; Vincenzo Catena's *Judith* in Room IX—possibly a copy of a lost work by Catena's friend Giorgione—and Tiepolo's impressive full-length portrait of *Doge Giovanni Dolfin* in Room XVII.

Just to the north of the Palazzo Querini-Stampalia is Campo Santa Maria Formosa, a lively square with a number of sidewalk cafes and a small vegetable market on weekday mornings. Dominating it is the lovely white marble church of Santa Maria Formosa, built by Mauro Codussi in 1492 over the site of a much earlier church. Its name recalls a vision in which Mary appeared to St. Magnus in the form of a buxom woman (or possibly a beautiful woman, depending on the exact nuance you give to the Italian word *formosa:* perhaps "comely" would be best, if a trifle old-fashioned). A similar vision of pulchritude inspired Palma Vecchio's *St. Barbara;* the artist's daughter, Violante, was his model for the figure of the saint in a reframed altarpiece in the right transept. There's a glowing 15th-century altarpiece of the *Madonna of Mercy* by Bartolomeo Vivarini in the first chapel on the right.

Santa Maria dei Miracoli

If you have time to make a brief detour to see some picturesque byways, stroll along Fondamenta dei Preti and cross the bridge to Calle del Paradiso. Returning to Campo Santa Maria Formosa, pause for a look at the two large palaces at the end of the square opposite the church, then cross the bridge between them and follow Calle Borgolocco to Campo Santa

Marina. On the right is the large white Palazzo Marcello Papadopoli, probably designed by Longhena. Just beyond it, across the canal, Palazzo Pisano is a 15th-century Gothic building with lovely balconies. Cross Ponte del Cristo at the junction of three canals, then turn left onto Calle Castelli past the Gothic Palazzo Soranzo-Barozzi to the jewel-like church of Santa Maria dei Miracoli. A small, perfectly proportioned structure sheathed in marble and harmoniously decorated by marble reliefs, it was built in the late 15th century by Pietro Lombardo. It exudes all the classical serenity of the early Renaissance. Pay the small entrance fee and get a close look at the exquisite marble reliefs and carvings on the interior, especially those on the balustrade and raised sanctuary, the work of Pietro Lombardo and his son, Tullio. See the pillars supporting the nun's choir over the entrance, the early 15th-century *Madonna* on the high altar and Tullio Lombardo's relief of the Last Supper in the crypt, inspired by Leonardo da Vinci's painting. The coffering in the vault frames 50 portraits of prophets and saints.

The Scuola di San Marco

Now retrace your steps along Calle Castelli and cross the bridge into Calle delle Erbe, following the signs for "SS. Giovanni e Paolo." The majestic church of Santi Giovanni e Paolo, or San Zanipolo in the slurred Venetian dialect, stands on its own large campo facing a canal. On the left of the church is the Scuola di San Marco, on the right the powerful equestrian monument of Bartolomeo Colleoni by Verrocchio, a touchstone of early-Renaissance sculpture. Colleoni had served Venice well as a *condottiere,* or commander of mercenary troops (the Venetians preferred to pay others to fight for them, and had the money to do it). On his death in 1475 he bequeathed his considerable wealth to the city on the condition that a statue be elected in his honor "in the piazza before St. Mark's." The Republic's shrewd administrators coveted the ducats but had no intention of honoring anyone, no matter how valorous, with a statue in Piazza San Marco. So they commissioned Florentine sculptor Andrea del Verrocchio to make an equestrian statue of Colleoni and they did indeed place it "in the piazza before St. Mark's"—in the piazza before the Scuola di San Marco. And until 1866, when the unification of Italy spawned countless statues of kings and patriots, Colleoni stood alone, strong and defiant on his great bronze steed, the only outdoor monument in all of Venice.

The Scuola di San Marco is one of several such *scuole* in the city. These were the headquarters of confraternities devoted to charitable works, much given to beautifying their private chapels and meeting halls with works by the finest artists they could command, employing figures such as Carpaccio for the Scuola di San Giorgio degli Schiavoni and, most famously, Tintoretto for the Scuola di San Rocco. The Scuola di San Marco is now part of a city hospital, but you can still go inside to see the shadowy columned hall on the ground floor, and you may be able to see the hospital chapel, the 17th-century church of San Lorenzo dei Mendicanti, by Scamozzi. It contains a painting of *St. Ursula* by Tintoretto and a *Crucifixion* by Veronese. But by far the best feature of the Scuola is its facade, executed in the 15th century by Pietro Lombardo and his sons. Look at the richly decorative floral motifs on the portal and the illusionistic trickery in the high reliefs on the marble panels.

San Zanipolo

Now you can concentrate on San Zanipolo itself, tall and graceful, the chief Dominican church in Venice and twin—or rival—of the Frari, the great Franciscan church on the other side of the Grand Canal. It took about a century to build, and was consecrated in 1430. Its facade has remained unfinished to this day. Plan to devote a half-hour or more to this church, the pantheon of the doges. Twenty-five are buried here and all the doges' funerals from the 16th century on were held here. Entering, you'll see massive but perfectly proportioned columns of Istrian stone, slender arches and an unusually luminous apse. Just inside the main portal are two large funeral monuments by the Lombardo family. The doorway itself is surmounted by the colossal monument to Alvise Mocenigo and his wife. On the wall between the confessional and the two altars on the right, a bust of Marcantonio Bragadin is the focal point of this monument; the small urn contains a chilling relic of this heroic Venetian admiral who defended Famagusta in Cyprus in 1571 during its long siege by the Turks. Forced to surrender, he was horribly tortured before being flayed alive. The urn, in fact, contains his skin, bought or stolen from the Turkish Arsenal in Constantinople, where his victors kept it as a trophy. Above the second altar on the right is the glowing altarpiece of *St. Vincent Ferrer* by Giovanni Bellini, in its original frame (1469). The tombstone of Doge Diedo in the pavement in front of the next chapel is a fine example of *niello* work (a special technique for engraving metal) and contrasts with the stunning polychrome pavement in the chapel. Next door, the little chapel of the Madonna della Pace has a 14th-century Byzantine icon of the Virgin Mary, and the adjacent chapel of St. Dominic boasts a fine illusionistic ceiling painting by Piazzetta done in 1727.

In the right transept, Alvise Vivarini's *Christ Carrying the Cross* is a moving, straightforward work, and Lorenzo Lotto's painting of St. Antonio, archbishop of Florence, shows the prelate being counseled by angels while acolytes accept petitions for alms. The stately gilt armchair that occupies a place of honor here was used by the doges during ceremonies in the church. Note the delicate embroidery in the *baldachino,* the great canopy over the altar. The four monumental tombs flanking the main altar are splendid works of various periods of the Renaissance. The most noteworthy is Tullio Lombardo's tomb of Andrea Vendramin on the left wall, near the window. Its smooth and rather formal aspect contrasts with the more vigorous, expressive works of this kind produced by contemporary 15th-century Florentine artists. Oddly, the effigies on these tombs all look uneasy, as if they were about to roll off into the choir stalls. The Venier doges and family members have their tombs on the wall of the left transept, surrounding the door to the Rosary Chapel. This was built in the 16th century in commemoration of the victory of Lepanto and was gutted by fire in 1867. Paintings by Titian and Giovanni Bellini were lost in the blaze but others were moved in to take their place and the chapel was finally restored and reopened in 1959. It is a sumptuous study in decoration, in which a great variety of materials are used, from the silky carved wooden surfaces of the choir stalls and the gleaming golden cherubs' heads and tragic masks in the ceiling to the marvelous ceiling paintings, including a fine *Annunciation* by Veronese, and the stone choir and tabernacle. There are marble reliefs around the sanctuary and huge statues above, a terracotta Madonna and a polychrome marble pavement.

In the left aisle of the main church, busts of Titian, Palma Vecchio and Palma Giovane appear on the funeral monument that Palma Giovane designed for himself to honor his masters. Along the aisle are sculptured tombs and monuments to various doges; some, such as Florentine sculptor Lamberti's tomb for Tommaso Mocenigo, were taken as models by later artists. The figure of St. Jerome over the altar nearest the door in the left aisle is a 16th-century work by Vittoria, who succeeded Sansovino as Venice's most important and active sculptor. Outside the church, note the relief of *Daniel in the Lion's Den* on the corner of the church and the original level of the campo, visible next to the apse wall.

San Francesco della Vigna

Continue along the Salizzada to the Ospedaletto, originally an orphanage, with its heavy Baroque facade by Longhena. Now you can choose whether to cut your itinerary short, taking Calle dell'Ospedaletto and following the signs back to San Marco by way of Santa Maria Formosa, or to continue as far as the church of San Francesco della Vigna. If you opt for the second, follow Barbarie delle Tole and Calle Caffettier, both refreshingly domestic neighborhood thoroughfares. Continue in the same direction and you'll emerge in Campo San Giustina, where an impressive Renaissance facade is all that's left of the church, long since converted into a school. Behind the school, take Calle Te Deum and turn right. You'll see San Francesco della Vigna straight ahead, its mid 16th-century austere Palladian facade often a backdrop for a gaggle of boys playing soccer in the campo.

Quite bare, with a severely simple gray-and-white interior, the church is often empty. Not many tourists find their way here, and the Venetians frequent it only on Sundays. Yet there's plenty to see. On the right as you enter is an altarpiece by Antonio Vivarini in a dark frame. The *Madonna and Child* in the right transept is a pretty composition by Antonio da Negroponte painted in 1450, and there's an impressive tombstone marking Marcantonio Trevisan's grave in front of the sanctuary. The Giustiniani Chapel is lined with lovely 15th-century marble reliefs by Pietro Lombardo and his school. In the left transept the sacristy opens onto one of the monastery's lovely little 15th-century cloisters, this one paved with the tombstones of the Franciscan friars and their benefactors. In an adjacent chapel there's a *Madonna and Saints* attributed to Giovanni Bellini. Use the light machine on the left of the door and you'll find a disconcertingly detached St. Sebastian coolly eyeing you.

Outside the church turn left, crossing Campo della Chiesa and Ponte San Francesco, where laundry is usually strung across the winding canal. A few steps beyond you'll come upon an authentically Venetian venetian-blind shop. Continue straight ahead into Salizzada delle Gatte, turn right into Campo Foscolo, bear left and then right into Calle Furlani and cross the bridge into Calle Lion. From here you can turn left and continue in the same direction to Riva degli Schiavoni and the San Zaccaria landing stage, or cross the bridge to Fondamenta San Lorenzo, turning left into Borgolocco San Lorenzo and continuing toward Santa Maria Formosa.

SIGHTSEEING DATA. For general information on museum and church opening times and entrance prices, see "Sightseeing Tips" under *Miscellaneous* in the *Practical Information for Venice*.

Pescheria (Fish Market), Rialto. Every morning except Sun.

Pinacoteca Querini-Stampalia (Querini-Stampalia Picture Gallery), Campiello Querini, Santa Maria Formosa (tel. 522.5235). Open Tues. to Sun. 10–3. Closed Mon. Admission 5,000 lire.

West of the Grand Canal

This chapter covers almost all the major places of interest to the west of the Grand Canal, among them the Accademia, the Friari and the Scuola San Rocco. It includes not only a substantial area of the city, but many of its most important treasures. Much of it is well off the beaten track and, in places very hard to find your way through, far from the Venice most tourists see. Before launching yourself into it, however, it is as well to point out that only the most determined or foolhardy could hope to take it all in on one visit. Not only is it a fairly sizeable area, the sheer volume of things to see will have you begging for mercy before too long (added to which the erratic opening times of museums and churches would make such a marathon impractical). The reason for including such a surfeit of riches in one chapter is simply that they fall naturally into one geographical unit. To break this chapter anywhere would be to do so purely arbitrarily. The best and most rewarding way to visit it is probably to select any of the numerous attractions it boasts and make straight for it, ignoring the others. Alternatively, you could perhaps decide to take in two or three places close by one another. To attempt more is to risk serious over-exposure to culture with a capital "C." It's as well also to remember that as with so much of Venice, there are numerous ways in and out of this area, and it is of course not necessary to visit anywhere here in the sequence we have used.

The Accademia

Early one morning—for the Gallery is open only until 2 P.M. (the ticket office closes earlier and at 12:15 on Sundays)—walk, or take the *vaporetto,* to the Accademia landing stage. The Accademia, or Academy of Fine Arts, was founded in 1750 and had Piazzetta and Tiepolo as its first directors. Since the early 19th century it has been housed in the monastic complex of Santa Maria della Carità and over the years has accumulated what is unquestionably the most extraordinary collection of Venetian art in the world, all attractively displayed and well lit. You should allow about two hours for a leisurely visit, though you can see the highlights (but little else) in about an hour. Alternatively, make several visits, sampling just a few pictures at a time. Indeed, it's no exaggeration to say that the richness, diversity and scale of the collections are such as to make return visits essential for anyone seriously intent on doing justice to this magnificent gallery. We have attempted here little more than to highlight a few of the Accademia's most famous pictures. Good guides detailing the art collection are available at the gallery; likewise all the works are well labeled.

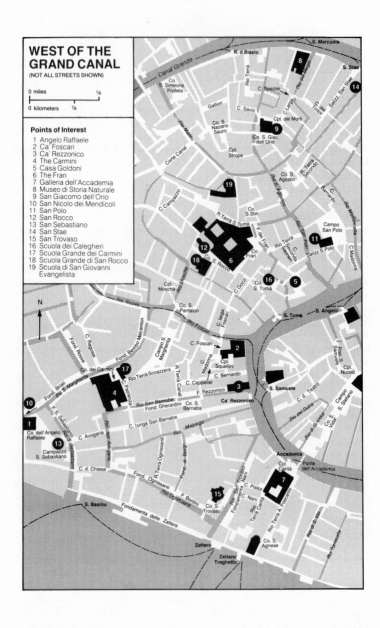

WEST OF THE GRAND CANAL

(NOT ALL STREETS SHOWN)

0 miles ⅛

0 kilometers ⅛

Points of Interest

1 Angelo Raffaele
2 Ca' Foscari
3 Ca' Rezzonico
4 The Carmini
5 Casa Goldoni
6 The Frari
7 Galleria dell'Accademia
8 Museo di Storia Naturale
9 San Giacomo dell'Orio
10 San Nicolo dei Mendicoli
11 San Polo
12 San Rocco
13 San Sebastiano
14 San Stae
15 San Trovaso
16 Scuola dei Calegheri
17 Scuola Grande dei Carmini
18 Scuola Grande di San Rocco
19 Scuola di San Giovanni Evangelista

Around the Accademia

From the entrance climb the stairs to Room I, former chapter house of the Scuola della Carità, and prepare yourself to be awestruck by the impact of the Accademia's big guns: an opulent carved and gilded wooden ceiling of the 15th century, from which a host of cherubs and a ceiling painting of the *Holy Father* by Alvise Vivarini look down on an array of splendid Venetian Byzantine and Gothic paintings that send flashes of gold and brilliant color dancing across the room. Among the most important of these works is Paolo Veneziano's *Coronation of the Virgin,* in the center of the hall. At the top of the stairs is Jacobello del Fiore's triptych of *Justice,* with a vigorous figure of St. Michael. On the right, look for Lorenzo Veneziano's *Annunciation,* and study the elaborate composition of the large *Coronation of the, Virgin* attributed to Jacobello. At the end of the room is another *Annunciation,* part of a splendid polyptych by Veneziano.

Behind Veneziano's large altarpiece at the end of the room are stairs leading to Room II. This contains a series of large altarpieces. The most important is on the right wall. This is the *San Giobbe Altarpiece* by Giovanni Bellini. Dated about 1485, it shows the Madonna and sleeping Child with saints and three charming music-making angels at Mary's feet. Note the foreshortening of the figures and the architectural details, painted so as to create the illusion that the architectural background of the work was actually a continuation of the church in which it stood. There's another delightful music-making angel in Carpaccio's *Presentation of Christ in the Temple* opposite the entrance. Most noteworthy of an impressive trio of altarpieces by Cima da Conegliano are the *Madonna of the Orange Tree* and the *Incredulity of St. Thomas* in Room III.

There's usually a crowd in Room IV, for it contains some small but exquisite 15th-century paintings. From left to right, counterclockwise, look for Hans Memling's *Portrait of a Young Man,* and Giovanni Bellini's masterpiece, the *Madonna and Child with Sts. Catherine and Mary Magdalene,* one of the most important works in the Accademia. Then there's Cosimo Tura's *Madonna and Child,* Piero della Francesca's badly deteriorated *St. Jerome* and Andrea Mantegna's soulful *St. George.* Room V next door holds one of the gallery's most famous paintings, Giorgione's *Tempest,* a work that has consistently baffled art historians as to its meaning, while charming by its magical painterly qualities and exquisite landscape, visual "poetry" of the most captivating and alluring kind. The work is nothing if not ambiguous, but with a haunting melancholy and a distinct sense of threat created by the gathering summer storm in the background. In the foreground a naked woman suckles a child, watched impassively by a young soldier. Next to this tantalizingly beautiful picture is another Giorgione, the *Old Woman,* painted about 1508. The woman holds a piece of paper on which the words *col tempo* ("with time") appear, an allusion to the inevitability of old age. The painting is in what was probably its original frame. Room V contains a further series of pictures by Bellini, including a charming series of Madonnas.

Room VI ushers you firmly into the 16th century and the Venetian High Renaissance, a period of remarkable richness, almost glamor, that reflects accurately the Venetians' love of rich color, grand scale, heroic drama and, above all, great opulence. Tintoretto's *Madonna of the Chamberlain* is the most dominating work here. The apogee of this love of richness is found in Room X, the grandest room in the gallery, one entire wall of which is taken up by Veronese's immense *Feast in the House of Levi*. The work, originally intended as *The Last Supper*, was painted for the refectory of the monastery of Santi Giovanni e Paolo. But Veronese's almost carnival-like atmosphere was considered too worldly by the ecclesiastical authorities, then in the midst of the Counter Reformation. Indeed, Veronese's splendid banquet, set in a Renaissance Venetian loggia, so scandalized the clergy that the painter was summoned to appear before the Inquisition to answer accusations of blasphemy. His judges particularly objected to the presence of dwarfs, clowns and the dog in the foreground, considered irreverent in a holy picture. Veronese was ordered to paint over some of the offending elements, but he merely changed the title and left the painting as it was. That's his own self-portrait in the head against the pillar in the left foreground. Restored not too long ago, this gorgeously theatrical work glows with color; take a few minutes to enjoy it.

On the adjoining wall are some large canvases by Tintoretto illustrating the *Legend of St. Mark*. Titian's *John the Baptist* stands on an easel nearby, while the artist's last work is on the left wall. It's a *Pietà* that he painted for his tomb in the Frari, and it was completed by Palma Giovane. A powerful and daringly conceived work, it illustrates to perfection both the dramatic, almost Impressionistic quality of the aging Titian's finest work. In Room XI, another large hall, you'll find biblical scenes by Tintoretto on the right and a lovely ceiling painting, an allegory of Venice by Veronese, at the end of the room. Tiepolo's *Discovery of the True Cross* shows his dizzy mastery of Renaissance illusionistic techniques.

In the adjoining wing, a long corridor with a view of the courtyard flanks a series of small rooms (restrooms on the right) containing 17th- and 18th-century works, some quite pretty but mostly of minor artistic interest. The *Rape of Europa*, a favorite Renaissance subject, appears several times. Look for Zuccarelli's decorative version in the corridor, in which Jove is the tamest bull you've ever seen and Europa is not at all unhappy over her fate. By contrast, in Tiepolo's picture, in Room XVI, Europa has a much more solemn mien and an impish cherub pees off a cloud in the sky above. Rooms XVII and XVIII hold 18th-century landscapes, including some noteworthy ones by Guardi, a less well known painter than his contemporary Canaletto yet, with his light, shimmering brushwork, probably very much more in tune with modern tastes than the faintly pedantic, always faithful and carefully constructed views of Venice that Canaletto painted in such quantities.

Around the corner is a portrait gallery, which also serves as a vestibule for various other rooms. On the right is the entrance to Room XXIII, which traces the outlines of the church of Santa Maria della Carità, with its three apses. Among the collection of late 15th-century works here, you should see the altarpieces by Carlo Crivelli, Giovanni and Gentile Bellini, and Bartolomeo and Antonio Vivarini. The vestibule also opens onto Room XIX, of little interest, and Room XX, with charming depictions by various artists of the *Miracles of the Relic of the True Cross* from the Scuola di San Giovanni Evangelista. That by Carpaccio depicts the old wooden drawbridge at the Rialto. Gentile Bellini's depiction of the recovery of the relic from the canal contains a portrait of Caterina Cornaro,

Queen of Cyprus. She's the first lady on the left. Giovanni Bellini's picture shows Piazza San Marco as it was in 1496, with the members of the artist's family kneeling on the right. The other paintings are similarly interesting for their views of 15th-century Venice.

Room XXI displays the St. Ursula cycle painted by Carpaccio in 1490–96 for the Scuola di Sant'Orsola. Recently restored, these paintings tell the story of the life of the saint with such careful attention to detail and atmosphere that they have considerable historical as well as artistic merit. The cycle begins with a painting of *Ursula in Glory* accompanied by the 11,000 virgins whom she led on a pilgrimage to Rome, a legend whose basis in historical fact is tenuous, even by the accommodating standards of early-Christian mythology.

Room XXIV is the old council room of the Scuola della Carità. Here your tour of the Accademia ends with yet another of its star attractions, the *Presentation of the Virgin*, painted by Titian in 1538 precisely for the wall where you see it today. Against a lovely mountain landscape, the luminous, solitary and vulnerable figure of the infant Mary ascends the steps of the temple. Take a good look at the painting, as you may wish to compare it with Tintoretto's *Presentation* in the Church of Madonna dell'Orto. The brilliant triptych by Antonio Vivarini and Giovanni d'Alemagna was also painted expressly for this room.

San Sebastiano

After the rarefied delights of the Accademia you are faced with a choice (though those determined to leave no stone unturned may be tempted to take in both options, albeit not necessarily one after the other). The first route takes you west from the Accademia deep into the heart of the Dorsoduro. Outside the gallery turn left onto Rio Terrà della Carità and right on either Calle Pistor or Calle dei Nani. You'll come to Rio San Trovaso, where from Fondamenta Nani you can see one of Venice's few remaining *squeri*, the boatyards where gondolas are built and repaired. On the same fondamenta, cross the little bridge to Campo San Trovaso, beside the church of the same name. Trovaso is the typically abbreviated Venetian dialect corruption of Santi (Saints) Gervasio and Protasio. In the church's dim interior you may be able to make out the *Birth of the Virgin* and *Deposition* by Palma Giovane over the third altar on the left, a *Last Supper* by Tintoretto in the left transept, and two of his last works on either side of the main altar.

In front of the church is Rio Ognissanti, where you should turn right and follow Fondamenta Bonlini and Fondamenta Ognissanti. This is an attractive and interesting walk past old palaces with walled gardens, *campielli* and another boatyard on Rio dell'Avogaria. Continue straight ahead past the diminutive houses on Calle della Chiesa and turn onto Fondamenta San Sebastiano, crossing over to the church, one of Venice's outstanding sights, despite its unpretentious exterior.

Built in the early 16th century, the church was decorated over a period of 15 years, starting in 1555, by Paolo Veronese, who lived nearby and is buried here. Inside you will find a profusion of gloriously vibrant frescoes, alive with color and movement. Sumptuous and immensely accomplished, they make very clear the Venetian love of finery and display. Use the light machines to get an adequate view of the *Story of Esther* on the ceiling, the scenes from the *Life of St. Sebastian* in the sanctuary, the organ panels, the ceiling in the sacristy and the frescoes in the choir and gallery. This delightful place is well worth going out of your way to see.

And while you're here, go around the corner into the next campo for a look at the church of Angelo Raffaele, where the Angel Raphael appears with Tobias and his dog in a sculptural group over the main door. Tobias also appears inside on the organ panels by Gianantonio Guardi.

If you have the time and energy (but remember that churches close about noon) you could cross the canal in front of the church of Angelo Raffaele and go left to San Nicolo dei Mendicoli, a charming 12th-century church rebuilt in 1977 by the British Venice in Peril Fund. If you have ventured this far and want to take the *vaporetto* home, you will have to return to San Sebastiano and then go on to the San Basilio landing stage on the Fondamenta delle Zattere. Alternatively, if you think you can make at least part of the way home on foot, cross the bridge in front of San Sebastiano and take Calle Avogaria and Calle Lunga San Barnaba—where there are a few restaurants—continuing straight ahead to the Ca'Rezzonico landing stage on the Grand Canal. On Calle Lunga San Barnaba you'll pass the Ponte dei Pugni—the Pugni bridge. Here white stone footprints mark the starting points of the traditional free-for-alls that used to be held when the bridge had no parapet. Just beyond is Venice's last floating vegetable market.

Ca' Rezzonico

The other option from the Accademia takes you north towards the Scuole di San Rocco and the Frari, via the Ca'Rezzonico and the Carmini. This is essentially a route for the committed art and architecture sightseer. Anyone who feels he or she has had his or her fill of culture should bow out now, coming back for more later if desired. Assuming, however, that you can take more, catch the Line 1 *vaporetto* from the Accademia one stop north to the Ca'Rezzonico.

The beautiful Baroque palace that is the Ca'Rezzonico was begun by Longhena in about 1667, though not completed for almost 100 years. From the *vaporetto* landing stage, follow the signs into Campo San Barnaba. Cross the *rio* and turn right onto Fondamenta Rezzonico. A monumental gateway and a fountain bearing the Rezzonico coat of arms mark the entrance. Climb the broad marble staircase to the marvelous ballroom with its highly polished floors, remarkable carved furniture by 17th-century craftsman Andrea Brustolon, and gilt 18th-century chandeliers suspended below a lavishly frescoed ceiling. Step out onto the balcony for the view of Rio San Barnaba, with the bell towers of San Barnaba and the Carmini a bit farther away, and the twin domed towers of the church of Angelo Raffaele in the distance.

The door on the right leads to Room II, where a Tiepolo allegory on the ceiling celebrates the marriage of Ludovico Rezzonico and puts a coy idea of a baby over the bridegroom's head. The stairs here descend to the apartments on the mezzanine floor, where Robert Browning died in 1889 and where Carlo Rezzonico, who later became Pope Clement XIII, lived for a while. The apartments are unfortunately closed indefinitely. The next rooms are smallish, and pleasingly decorated with portraits, tapestries and bright stuccoes and lacquer work. The so-called throne room in the corner overlooking the Grand Canal also has a ceiling by Tiepolo. The *portego,* a hall running the length of the palace, a feature typical of Venetian palaces—they were designed to admit light and air into the otherwise dark central areas—has a splendid view of the Grand Canal and overlooks the courtyard on the other side. The black box-like structure here is a *felze,* a wooden shelter that was put on gondolas to protect their passengers from inclement weather. Casanova relates that on occasion they also served to create cozy alcoves for clandestine amours. The corner room opposite the throne room has a Longhi portrait and another Tiepolo ceiling, an allegory of *Strength and Wisdom,* in which the artist playfully painted an upside-down cherub toying with a bat. A passage leads into the dark, wood-paneled library, with dusty 18th-century tomes and a simple Murano chandelier. In Room XII there's some more intricately carved furniture by Brustolon.

From the *portego* head up to the second floor, where there are some good paintings, especially the *Death of Darius,* a typically convoluted work by Piazzetta, and two Canalettos (you'll find very few Canalettos in Venice; most are in England). On the right of the *portego* is a charming 18th-century boudoir—Room XV—decorated in typical Venetian style. Room XVIII is the so-called Green Drawing Room, decorated with chinoiseries, lacquer furniture and a ceiling attributed to Francesco Guardi. The corner room boasts Venice's largest collection of genre scenes by Pietro Longhi—a relatively little-known 18th-century Venetian painter who specialized in scenes of the fossilized and corrupt Venetian aristocracy—and a ceiling painting by Tiepolo in which the sensuous, rosy-fleshed figure of Flora is embraced by a gossamer-winged Zephyr. On the other side of the *portego* are more works by Antonio and Francesco Guardi. Look for the rosary-maker's shop sign by Francesco Guardi, showing the skulls and bones from which the beads were made. A series of rooms (XXIII–XXVI) on the courtyard end of the palace reconstruct the fresco decorations of the little country villa that the Tiepolos bought in 1753 in Zianigo on the mainland. In *The New World* Tiepolo painted himself in an odd pose on the right, looking through a monocle, with his father in front of him. The carnival scenes and clowns in the other rooms are rather melancholy, the satyrs and centaurs typically rowdy. The third floor of the palace has a puppet theater and an old pharmacy, but has been closed for years.

The Carmini

Leaving Ca' Rezzonico, take Fondamenta Rezzonico and cross the bridge back into Campo San Barnaba, continuing along the canal on Fondamenta Gherardini, past the vegetable barge, heading for your landmark, the 17th-century bell tower of the Carmini. Cross the bridge at the end of the fondamenta into Calle Pazienza, which skirts the side of the church of the Carmini—more correctly known as Santa Maria del Carmelo—with its Romanesque porch and Byzantine mosaics. You can enter the church from its more recent facade on the Campo dei Carmini. The interior is dark and has heavy carved and gilded wood panels below the 17th- and 18th-century paintings that cover its walls. The best paintings here are the earlier ones, the *Adoration of the Shepherds* by Cima da Conegliano over the second altar in the right aisle, and Lorenzo Lotto's *St. Nicholas with John the Baptist and St. Lucy* with its fine landscape, over the second altar in the left aisle. Use the light machines to get a better look at these works. The large singing galleries over the choir were decorated by Andrea Schiavone in his bold and lavish style.

Next to the church is the Scuola Grande dei Carmini, a late 17th-century building by Longhena where the Carmelite confraternity met. It's known particularly for the fine ceiling paintings by Tiepolo on the second floor. Chief among them is that representing St. Simon Stock, 13th-century prior general of the Carmelite order, receiving the "scapular" of the Carmelite order from the Virgin Mary, the scapular—two simple squares of cloth tied together—guaranteeing a swift passage for heaven for all who wore it. Tiepolo has transformed this distinctly unpromising subject matter into his usual breathtaking riot of color, movement and virtuosity, a major work by the foremost Italian painter of the 18th century. The mirrors thoughtfully provided on the benches make it easy to study these delightful paintings.

Toward the Frari

From here, you can turn the corner into Campo Santa Margherita, one of the down-to-earth neighborhood squares that many tourists in Venice never see. There's a small outdoor market here, and a few trees at one end where mothers sit and watch their children cutting loose in what must seem to them an endless space. There's a good restaurant and a modest wineshop, some interesting shops on the square and a mask shop just around the corner. The little building in the campo is the Scuola dei Varotari, where the tanners' confraternity met; there's a centuries-old relief of the Virgin on the wall. Now the workers and old men meet for a glass of wine and game of cards behind the storefront with the Communist Party posters in the window.

At this point you can leave the campo on the left at the end opposite the Carmini, passing the stump of an old bell tower and crossing the bridge to Campo San Pantalon, from where you bear right to get to the Frari. Alternatively, you can make a short detour into the narrow *calli* behind Ca' Foscari, seat of the university. From Rio Terrà Canal in one corner of the square, go left into Calle della Madonna, which curves into Calle Cappelier. This brings you to the charming Campiello Squellini, where the roots of the plane trees push the herring-bone brick pavement into hillocks beneath your feet. Over in the corner an old wall is inset with bright modern mosaics, presumably by the artist who lives behind the garden gate. Follow Calle Foscari past the courtyard entrance of the university's Institute of Economics and pause as you cross the bridge to look down at the fireboats. Then continue along Calle Larga Foscari and over another bridge into Calle Gozzi. Turn left and you'll find yourself face to face with the massive brick walls of the church of the Frari.

The Frari

The best approach to the Frari—and the neighboring Scuola di San Rocco—for anyone who wants to visit it without having first taken in any of the other sites in this chapter is to take the *vaporetto* to the San Tomà landing stage on the Grand Canal. From here, make your way to the Campo San Tomà. The Frari is no more than a step away. The Campo

San Tomà is itself of interest, not for its church, which has been closed for years, but for the Scuola dei Calegheri, a small 15th-century building and seat of the shoemakers' confraternity. Look for Pietro Lombardo's relief of St. Mark healing the cobbler Ananais on its wall, along with a Madonna della Misericordia.

Before heading in to the Frari itself, it's as well to say something about the districts of San Polo and Santa Croce in which it stands. These are among the most labyrinthine areas of Venice, and accordingly ignored by many tourists. It's a certainty you'll get lost at least once or twice, for the *calli* and canals crisscross here in a hopelessly confusing way. But you will be rewarded for your trouble by views of Venice that many never see. Moreover, you'll find some authentic Venetian restaurants along the way.

Begun in 1330, though taking more than a century to complete, the Frari is the principal church of the Franciscans in Venice, *frari* meaning "friars." It is often compared with the Dominicans' contemporary church of Santi Giovanni e Paolo (San Zanipolo) away on the other side of the Grand Canal. But there are important differences between these two Venetian-Gothic wonders. Where both internally and externally San Zanipolo is lavishly decorated, the Frari is deliberately austere and plain, befitting the simplicity of the Franciscans' lives, where spirituality and poverty were key tenets of the order. Paradoxically, however, the Frari also contains a number of the most sumptuous and brilliant pictures in any Venetian church, far outweighing anything in San Zanipolo. Chief among them are the magnificent Titian altarpieces, arguably the most dazzling works that prolific artist produced.

From the outside, the most striking feature of the church is its bell tower, standing high above the massive brick facade. It's the second highest building in the city, topped only by the bell tower in St. Mark's Square. Enter the church by the door in the side of the left door. There's a small charge to help defray lighting expenses, or at least that's what the sign says. Your eyes are drawn immediately to Titian's immense *Assumption of the Virgin* over the main altar. As you make the rounds of the church to examine the other works of art that it contains you can see how completely Titian's work dominates the vast interior, and how effectively the painting is framed by the chancel arch between the crossing and the choir.

Around the Frari

Start your visit at the main door on the end wall, where there are Renaissance marble tombs on either side. Between the first and second altars on the right is a large and rather ugly 19th-century monument to Titian, built on the site where he is believed to have been buried. Titian died at 88 during the plague of 1576. It is claimed that he was the only one of its 70,000 victims who was allowed to be buried in a church. On the third altar Alessandro Vittoria's beautifully modeled marble statue of *St. Jerome* is said to portray the aged Titian. Titian was the master of Palma Giovane, who painted the *Martyrdom of St. Catherine* over the fourth altar on the right. Now you can step to the middle of the nave and take a closer look at the choir screen, faced with marble reliefs by sculptors Bartolomeo Bon and Pietro Lombardo. Then go on to the right transept, where the sacristy door is flanked by impressive 15th-century Gothic tombs. The sacristy contains another of the Frari's treasures, the Giovanni Bellini altarpiece of the *Ma-*

donna and Child with Sts. Nicholas of Bari, Peter, Mark and Benedict. Bellini's work, painted in 1488 for precisely this spot, is noteworthy for its still beauty and mellow luminosity. The contrast with the heroic energy of Titian's works here—painted little more than 30 years later—is startling, and illustrates clearly the immense and rapid development of Venetian Renaissance painting. From the sacristy you can enter the chapter house, next to the cloister of the Franciscan monastery adjacent to the church. On the wall of this room the Gothic funeral monument of Doge Francisco Dandolo is surmounted by a lunette of the doge and his wife being presented to the Virgin. Painted by Paolo Veneziano about 1339, it is the earliest such dedication picture in existence.

The chapel on the far right of the main altar holds a very fine altarpiece of the *Madonna with Saints* by Bartolomeo Vivarini, dated 1482, in its original frame. In the third chapel from the right you'll find a wooden statue of St. John the Baptist, one of the first works Donatello did in the Veneto. Now you can observe Titian's *Assumption* more closely. The altarpiece caused a sensation when it was unveiled in 1519 and was immediately acclaimed for its heroic forms and brilliant colors, especially the glowing reds. The *putti,* or cherubs, are among the most beautiful ever painted in Italy, and they were taken as models by later artists, notably Tiepolo. Interestingly, though the friars initially voiced fears over Titian's positively revolutionary work, they quickly came to realize that "art was not their profession, and that the use of the breviary did not convey a knowledge of painting."

The tombs on either side of the main altar evoke sorrowful stories. On the right lies Francesco Foscari, deposed in 1457 after 34 years as doge; he died of a broken heart only a few days after his son was executed for treason. Opposite, an exceptionally fine Renaissance tomb by Antonio Rizzi honors Doge Nicolo Tron, who is shown with the bushy beard that he grew and kept through life as a sign—bizarre to modern tastes—of mourning for the death of a favorite son.

Among the works of art in the chapels on the left, the altarpiece by Bartolomeo Vivarini that can be seen through the grill of the chapel at the end of the left transept is worth a second glance, if for no other reason than that the enthroned St. Mark is without his faithful lion. You should step into the choir enclosure at the center of the church for a close look at the fascinating details of the decorations of the 15th-century choir stalls. Over the first altar on this end of the left nave is another powerful and revolutionary work by Titian, the *Pesaro Madonna,* painted in 1526. Here Titian placed his subject off center, a daring break with tradition and an innovation that set a trend for numerous later Baroque altarpieces. The model who posed for this handsomely naturalistic Madonna was Titian's wife, Celia, who died shortly afterwards in childbirth. You can't miss the huge Baroque tomb of Doge Giovanni Pesaro, whose sarcophagus is supported by 20-foot-tall statues of Moors. Next to these colossal figures the pure, neo-Classical lines of Canova's somber funeral monument present a striking contrast. The 18th-century sculptor Canova had designed this tomb, with its spooky half-open door and despondent lion, as a funeral monument for Titian, but Canova's pupils chose to carry it out for their own master. Toward the end of his long life Titian had worked on plans for his own tomb, but the plague precipitated his demise and he was hastily buried in the Frari.

Adjacent to the Frari is the Archivio di Stato, the State Archives, where some 15,000,000 volumes documenting the history and minutiae of the Venetian Republic fill about 300 rooms in the former Franciscan monastery known as Ca'Grande. Parts of the Archives are occasionally opened to the public for special exhibitions; if you have a chance to see it, don't pass it up.

The Scuola di San Rocco

Behind the apse of the Frari, the white stone facades of the church and Scuola di San Rocco bear witness to Venice's attachment to St. Roch, protector against plagues. The Venetians invoked the saint during the repeated outbreaks of pestilence that afflicted them, probably borne from the Orient on the same ships that brought them wealth and opulence. To ensure St. Roch's direct intervention, the Venetians, acting with typical unscrupulousness, stole his body from Montpellier in France and built a church in his honor. But church and *scuola* are first and foremost of interest for the vast series of paintings by Tintoretto they contain. Indeed this is by far the largest collection of Tintoretto's work in Venice, all moreover painted specifically for the church and *scuola*. In the church are an *Annunciation* and a *St. Roch* on either side of the door. Two more Tintorettos hang between the first and second altars on the right, several more on the wall of the sanctuary. But the most extraordinary of all decorate the Scuola di San Rocco, next door. In 1564 Tintoretto beat the other artists competing for the commission to decorate the building by submitting not a sketch but a finished work, which he additionally offered free of charge. This was the *St. Roch in Glory,* now on the ceiling of the Albergo, or committee room of the *scuola*. This subterfuge earned him the animosity of his fellow artists but it ensured him the commission. The work took him a total of 23 years to complete. Several years ago an American fund financed the restoration of the more than 50 Tintorettos in the *scuola*.

In the hall on the ground floor, the paintings illustrate the Life of Mary, from the *Annunciation* on the left of the entrance to the *Assumption,* now unfortunately somewhat spoiled by unsympathetic restoration. Upstairs, Tintoretto's startling light effects create dark explosions in the canvases on the wall and ceiling of the dimly lit great hall. (For a small fee you can rent a mirror in order to get a better view of these ceiling paintings.) The ceiling is covered with scenes from the Old Testament, the walls with scenes from the New Testament. The most striking of these are the *Agony in the Garden,* the resplendent *Resurrection,* and the *Ascension.* The walls are hung with ceremonial lanterns and lined with dark wooden benches carved with grotesque figures by master woodcarver Francesco Pianta, who supposedly included a caricature of Tintoretto in the bench near the altar, usually roped off.

The Albergo, the room off the end of the great hall, contains what is held to be Tintoretto's masterpiece, the dramatic *Crucifixion.* The *Road to Calvary* also is remarkable for its unusual composition.

Campo San Polo

After the dark, oppressive dynamism of the huge canvases in the Scuola di San Rocco, you need a change of pace. Consequently, you'll be glad to learn that the nearby Scuola di San Giovanni Evangelista, decorated mainly by Domenico Tintoretto, Jacopo's son and disciple, is closed for restorations. Instead, reluctantly or otherwise, head for Campo San Polo for some fresh air and a cup of coffee. Cross the bridge in front of the Frari and turn right onto Fondamenta dei Frari, then left into Rio Terrà and right into Calle Seconda Saoneri. Take a left at the end of this street and cross the bridge into Salizzada San Polo, which leads to Campo San Polo, one of Venice's largest squares.

Lined with handsome palaces, the square is today a favorite playground for children. Until 1802, it was also the scene of bull-baiting, a cruel but popular sport that pitted snarling dogs against tethered bulls. There are interesting old sculptural reliefs on the church of San Polo, the Venetian corruption of San Paolo. But the church is also interesting for its dark wooden roof, in the form of an inverted ship's keel. The church further rewards you with an antidote to an overdose of Tintorettos. Go into the little Oratory of the Crucifix at the end of the church, opposite the altar, where Gian Domenico Tiepolo's *Stations of the Cross* throbs with color and movement. And in the church you'll enjoy the delicate altarpiece by Gian Domenico's father, the great Gian Battista, over the second altar on the left. By the way, you really should take a look at the dramatic *Last Supper* on the left of the Oratory door. Its startling light effects stamp it as, of course, another Tintoretto.

San Giacomo dell'Orio and San Stae

From Campo San Polo take Calle Bernardo at the far corner of the square. Turn left on Rio Terrà Secondo and right onto Calle del Tintor, which leads to Campo San Giacomo dell'Orio, another pretty square, again with an old church and a 13th-century bell tower. Neighbors sit chatting on its few, scattered benches, giving the campo a homey, comfortable air. The church of San Giacomo dell'Orio is one of Venice's oldest, and though rebuilt in the 13th and 16th centuries it has kept much of its aura of antiquity. The low, 14th-century ship's keel ceiling in aged wood rests on massive Byzantine pillars. Successive reconstructions have created a number of oddly placed chapels and sacristies, decorated with crucifixes and paintings of various epochs. In the apse are a *Madonna* by Lorenzo Lotto and a *Crucifixion* by Lorenzo Veneziano.

On the right, behind the church (where there's a good pizzeria), cross the bridge and take Calle Savio, following the signs to the *vaporetto* landing stage at Riva di Biasio, or make your way to San Simeone Grande and the bridge to the railway station. Alternatively, you can take Calle Larga out of the far end of the campo toward the Fondaco dei Turchi for a quick visit to the modest Natural History Museum (Museo di Storia Naturale), or you can cross Ponte del Megio at the end of Calle Larga and take Calle Spezier and Calle Tintor, following the *vaporetto* signs to Salizzada San Stae.

The church of San Stae (Venetian dialect corruption of Sant'Eustachio) has a finely proportioned Baroque facade on the Grand Canal studded with statues and dotted with pigeons. Both the facade and its bright interior have been restored and deserve your attention. The series of paintings of the Twelve Apostles in the sanctuary constitutes a survey in a nutshell of the leading lights of early 18th-century painting in Venice. Look for the *Martyrdom of St. James* by Piazzetta on the lower left, the *Liberation of St. Peter* by Sebastiano Ricci next to it, and the *Martyrdom of St. Bartholomew* by Gian Battista Tiepolo on the lower right.

There's a *vaporetto* landing stage at San Stae, and while you're waiting for the boat you can study the noble facade of Palazzo Vendramin-Calergi on the left, across the Grand Canal.

SIGHTSEEING DATA. For general information on museum and church opening times and entrance prices, see "Sightseeing Tips" under *Miscellaneous* in the *Practical Information for Venice.*

Accademia (Galleria dell'Accademia), Campo della Carità (tel. 522.2247). Open Tues. to Sat. 9–2, Sun. 9–1. Closed Mon. Admission 4,000 lire.

Casa Goldoni, Calle dei Nomboli 2793, San Tomà (tel. 523.6353). Open Mon. to Sat. 8:30–1:30. Closed Sun. Admission free.

Ca' Rezzonico (Museo del Settecento Veneziano), Fondamenta Rezzonico (tel. 522.4543). Open Mon. to Thurs. 10–4, Sat. 10–4, Sun. 9–12:30. Closed Fri. Admission 3,000 lire.

Museo di Storia Naturale (Natural History Museum), Fondaco dei Turchi (tel. 524.0885). Open Tues. to Sat., 9–1:30, Sun. 9–12. Closed Mon. Admission 3,000 lire.

Scuola Grande dei Carmini, Campo dei Carmini (tel. 528.9420). Open Mon. to Sat. 9–12, 3–6. Closed Sun. Admission 2,000 lire.

Scuola Grande di San Rocco, behind the Frari (tel. 523.4864). Open daily 10–1, 3:30–6:30. Admission 5,000 lire.

Cannaregio

A walk through the sestiere of Cannaregio in the north of the city takes you into the hidden corners of Venice, well away from the crowds. For the sake of convenience, we've divided this chapter into two walks, one short, the other rather longer. But there's no reason, stamina aside, why you shouldn't combine them if you want. Equally, the first in particular could easily be tacked on to a tour of the Rialto.

WALK ONE—the Ca' d'Oro

The fabulous palace of the Ca' d'Oro is the highlight of this brief itinerary. Standing on the Grand Canal, and with a *vaporetto* landing stage directly outside, the gorgeous Gothic facade of the Ca' d'Oro has long been one of the most celebrated sights of this most celebrated city. Its name—the House of Gold—spells out the reason for this fame. For the palace was originally decorated with an opulence remarkable even by Venetian standards, with golden objects of every kind set off against a richly painted background. Very little of this remains today, but there is enough to give at least a suggestion of its former splendor. It would be a mistake to imagine that the facade is the only reason for seeing the Ca' d'Oro, however, for the palace also contains a fine collection of Renaissance art, bequeathed to the Italian state by the palace's last owner, Baron Franchetti.

The Ca' d'Oro was built between 1420 and 1435 by Giovanni Bon, who also created another Gothic masterpiece, the Porta della Carta in Palazzo Ducale. The entrance to the Franchetti Gallery is on the narrow *calle* leading to the Ca' d'Oro landing stage. Inside are a pretty little entrance court and a larger main courtyard with a magnificent well-head by Bartolemeo Bon, Giovanni's son. Along with the impressive interior of the palace, considerably altered by recent restorations, you will see some fine works of art here. Outstanding among them is Mantegna's expressive *St. Sebastian,* on the first floor, on the right as you enter. Mantegna had just put the finishing touches on the work when he died in 1506; in a corner of the painting, next to an allusive snuffed-out candle he added a Latin inscription: "Only God endures, the rest is smoke." The *portego,* or large hall opening onto the Grand Canal, holds some fine Venetian sculptures, both large works and small. More of the same, plus some 15th-century paintings and an exhibit illustrating the history of the building and its restoration, are in smaller rooms on this floor.

A beautiful 15th-century wooden staircase from another palace leads to the second floor and more paintings: Titian's *Venus,* a Van Dyck portrait, and a series of frescoes painted by Pordenone in the 1530s for the

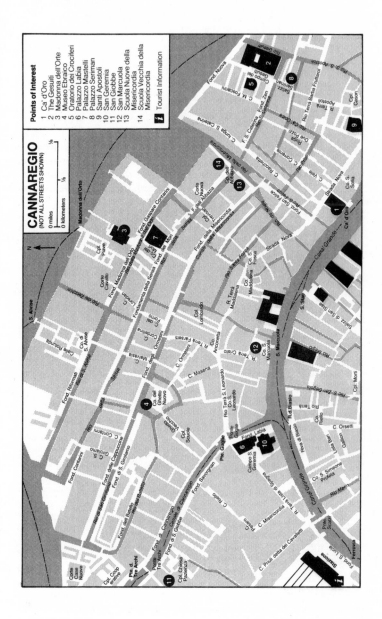

CANNAREGIO
(NOT ALL STREETS SHOWN)

0 miles ⅛
0 kilometers ⅛

Points of Interest

1 Ca' d'Oro
2 The Gesuiti
3 Madonna dell'Orte
4 Museo Ebraico
5 Oratorio dei Crociferi
6 Palazzo Labia
7 Palazzo Mastelli
8 Palazzo Seriman
9 Santi Apostoli
10 San Geremia
11 San Giobbe
12 San Marcuola
13 Scuola Nuova della Misericordia
14 Scuola Vecchia della Misericordia

ℹ️ Tourist Information

cloister of Santo Stefano and subsequently brought here. There are some more very interesting fragments of similarly "detached" frescoes at the end of the *portego*. These were executed by Giorgione (possibly) and Titian for the facade of the Fondaco dei Tedeschi, from which they had to be removed for preservation.

The Gesuiti

From Ca' d'Oro turn left to the Strada Nuova, a shopping street that is also one of the main pedestrian routes between the station and San Marco. You'll find plenty of shops, cafes and pastry shops to distract you here. But turn into Fondamenta San Felice on the other side of the bridge and follow it along the pretty canal, lined with walled gardens. Pass one bridge and take the next one into Sottoportego dei Preti, continuing into Calle della Racchetta, where you turn left. Cross the bridge here and turn right onto Fondamenta Santa Caterina, named after the church, which has been closed for ages and is now being rebuilt.

This is a peaceful and pleasant walk; in spring and summer the walled gardens overflow with bignonia and wisteria. At the end of Fondamenta Zen turn left into Campo dei Gesuiti, ample and placid, and little changed over the centuries. You'll have to back up one of the alleys in front of the church of the Gesuiti to get a good view of its towering white facade, with its massive columns and multitude of statues. Its bulk seems incongruous in this neighborhood of low, brightly colored houses.

One of Venice's most imposing and emphatically Baroque churches, the Gesuiti was built in the 18th century over an existing 12th-century building. The most striking thing here, aside from the facade, is the gray-and-white marble decoration that covers the walls like brocade and is draped around the pulpit on the left. The ceiling is equally ornate, studded with medallions set in gold-and-white frames. The colossal *baldachino* over the high altar, with its ten twisted marble columns, is a close runner-up as far as theatricality goes. However, the most important single work of art in the church is Titian's highly dramatic *Martyrdom of St. Lawrence* over the first altar on the left. In natural light the painting is so dark as to be almost invisible, but when you turn on the light switches (marked *lux*) on either side of the chapel, you'll see the piercing effects of light and the force of movement that make this one of the most powerful of Titian's late works.

On Campo dei Gesuiti, a pale yellow building with four tall chimneys houses the Oratorio dei Crociferi, founded as a hospital for returning Crusaders. The chapel is covered with a glowing cycle of paintings by Palma Giovane that was seriously damaged by the 1966 flood and has been restored by a British-based fund. The Oratory is open either in the morning or afternoon, depending on the season.

Santi Apostoli

Now you can stroll past the inviting trattoria at the other end of the campo to the Fondamenta Nuova, from where the *vaporetto* to Murano leaves. Or you can continue your walk through some interesting *calli*. From Campo dei Gesuiti cross the bridge and take Salizzada Seriman. The 15th-century Palazzo Seriman is now a school, but the custodian may be moved to let you in to see the staircase and frescoes by an artist of Tiepolo's school. The little wrought-iron Ponte Sartori gives you a view of the palace's canal facade and a close-up of a wooden *altana,* or roof terrace, across the way. Straight ahead, in Calle Spezier, there's an artisan who sells Venetian lamps and fixtures in brass or wrought iron.

Continue in the same direction along Rio Terrà Santi Apostoli and turn right at the end to the church of Santi Apostoli, which contains a hodge-podge of art, including some 14th-century frescoes on the right of the main altar, Renaissance marble sculpture scattered throughout and Tiepolo's painting of the *Communion of St. Lucy* in the Corner Chapel. Outside Santi Apostoli you can opt to head left on foot toward the Rialto and San Marco or take the Strada Nuova on the right to the Ca' d'Oro landing stage.

WALK TWO—the Palazzo Labia

This second walk around Cannaregio takes you to one of the quietest areas of Venice. Equally unusually, the area has the nearest thing to a regular layout of streets the city can boast, interspersed with reasonably wide canals. All of which tends to make this northernmost area both easy of access and distinctly soothing to walk through.

Start from the landing stage at San Marcuola on the Grand Canal. On the right is pretty Casa Gatti Casazza, restored as it probably was in the 18th century with a typical *altana,* or roof terrace, laden with plants and flowers. The unfinished brick facade of the church of San Marcuola (the Venetian dialect for Santi Ermargora and Fortunato) faces the Grand Canal across a square full of strutting pigeons and cats in various stages of lethargy. In the church are two unusual depictions of Christ over the side doors: one a painting of Christ as a child with St. Catherine and St. Andrew; the other, a head of Christ between two male portraits. On the left of the main altar is an early *Last Supper* by Tintoretto, and on the right a copy of a Tintoretto.

Rio Terrà Cristo takes you into Campo Anconetta, a crossroads on the busy pedestrian route between the station and San Marco. To make the so-called Strada Nuova (New Road) along this route, several canals were filled in during the 1870s, some years after the railway bridge had enabled trains to arrive in Venice itself. Turn left onto Rio Terrà San Leonardo, where there are shops, a few restaurants catering to the tourist trade and a small morning market. Cross the 16th-century Ponte delle Guglie, named for its *guglie,* or spires, pausing for a look at the attractive 17th-century canal facade of Palazzo Labia.

Today the palace is the headquarters of R.A.I., the Italian radio and T.V. monopoly. It is hard to imagine a broadcasting company in any other country in the world establishing itself among such opulent splendor. The Palazzo Labia, built in the early 18th century, contains one of the supreme examples of 18th-century illusionistic fresco painting. Heroic, accomplished and breathtaking in their imagination and assurance, they are by Tiepolo, and illustrate scenes from the lives of Anthony and Cleopatra (set, as with almost all Tiepolo's history painting, in 16th-century Italy). The building is not generally open to the public but the ballroom, site of the frescoes, can sometimes be visited—book ahead—on Wednesday, Thursday and Friday afternoon. It is also used for concerts.

To one side of the Palazzo Labia is the ungainly pile of the church of San Geremia, a cluster of seemingly disparate elements. The interior is more harmonious, with a tall, airy dome over the crossing. In a chapel in the left transept a gold altar framed by flickering vigil lights holds the relics of St. Lucy, whose body was filched in 1204 (shades of St. Mark) by the Venetians from Constantinople. The sacristan will invite you into a room behind the altar where there are some more relics, vestments and a painting of the saint by Palma Giovane. St. Lucy was martyred in Syracuse, in Sicily, and the Syracusians have always hotly contested Venice's claim to her relics. Not too many years ago, in emulation of the Venetian crusaders, Sicilian raiders stole St. Lucy's relics and carried them off to Syracuse. The good offices of eminent ecclesiastics were required to soothe the irate souls and settle the dispute.

San Giobbe

Off to the left, Lista di Spagna leads to the railway station. It's lined with a plethora of shops selling garish souvenirs, tiny trattorias specializing in leathery prefab pizza, and other emporia catering to the needs of mass tourism. Instead, you should go in another direction, perhaps making a detour along the Cannaregio Canal, second widest in the city, to the church of San Giobbe, easily reached on the left of the Ponte dei Tre Archi. (Check beforehand, as the church may be closed for repairs.)

Built in the 15th century in thanksgiving for the end of a plague (as were so many of the city's churches), San Giobbe has a fine sculptured doorway and sanctuary, both by Pietro Lombardo. The marble frame on the second altar on the right contained Bellini's celebrated *San Giobbe Altarpiece* before it was removed to the Accademia. In the center of the pavement in front of the main altar a beautifully carved tomb slab (sometimes covered) marks the resting place of the church's founder, Doge Cristoforo Moro, and his wife. Legend has it that Doge Moro was the original Moor of Venice, Shakespeare's Othello. On the French ambassador's tomb (the French Embassy was nearby) are two rather ludicrous crowned lions by French sculptor Perrault. The second chapel on the left has a distinctly Tuscan aspect; it was built for a family of textile workers from Lucca in the 15th century and its colorful terracotta decorations are the only works by the Della Robbias, the Florentine sculptors, in Venice.

The Ghetto

From San Giobbe cross Ponte dei Tre Archi and follow the canal to the right as far as Sottoportego del Ghetto, which leads into the heart of the Jewish Ghetto. In the early 16th century, the Venetian mainland was a permanent battleground on which the Venetian forces were engaged in defending their territories against the troops of the League of Cambrai. Among the refugees from the terra firma were many Jews, who set up their small businesses around the Rialto. But in 1516 Venice's Great Council ordered that all Jews be confined to a small island in the *sestiere* of Cannaregio. The island, which had been the site of a foundry, a *geto* in the Venetian dialect, was to be closed off by huge gates that were barred from sunset to dawn. The Jewish community had to pay the expenses of the Christian crews who manned the boats that patrolled the canal at night.

No Jew was allowed to leave the island after sunset, with the exception of their medical doctors, who were highly esteemed by Venetian aristocrats. All were required to wear yellow caps.

As the community grew, the houses on the island grew ever taller to accommodate new arrivals from all over Europe and the Middle East. The first Ghetto quickly assumed its distinctive atmosphere, spreading in 1541 and in 1633 to include the adjacent areas of the Ghetto Vecchio and the Ghetto Novissimo. Each time the gates were moved accordingly. The Ghetto became a microcosm of Jewish culture, its population reaching a peak of 5,000 in 1630, then declining steadily until Napoleon's troops threw open its gates in 1797 in the name of the rights of man.

You can see the hinges of the original gates to the Ghetto in the Sottoportego del Ghetto. And here there's also an old stone plaque on the left that lists the restrictions to which the Ghetto's inhabitants were subjected.

Continue into Campiello delle Scuole, where the Levantine Synagogue was founded in 1538 and the Spanish Synagogue in 1555. Cross the canal onto the island and enter Campo del Ghetto Nuovo. One of the most pleasing little corners of Venice, the campo has a splashing water fountain, a few trees, some benches and well-heads and tall, 17th-century houses. On one side a movingly simple monument evokes the horror of the Nazi concentration camps, in which 200 Venetian Jews, out of the Ghetto's total population of 1,200, perished. Next door is a home for the elderly. On the opposite side of the campo you can see the arcades where the pawnbrokers had their establishments. Every day when the Ghetto's gates swung open a stream of Venetians flowed in seeking loans and credit.

Over in the corner is the Museo Ebraico, or Jewish Museum, restored and modernized in 1986. Small and well organized, it has displays of splendid silver and gold ritual objects and precious textiles. But the highlight of a visit is the guided tour of the synagogues offered several times a day by English-speaking guides. The German synagogue, the oldest of the five built here, is part of the museum. After an explanation of the Ghetto's history, the guide will take you to Campiello delle Scuole to see the Spanish and Levantine synagogues, with especially beautiful interiors. The Levantine synagogue, in particular, is decorated with elaborate woodcarving by Andrea Brustolon, whose work you may have seen in Ca'Rezzonico.

Return to Campo del Ghetto to admire the beautiful ritual glass objects created by a soft-spoken artist in his little shop just across from the museum. Then roam about, passing under the Sottoportego into the Ghetto Nuovissimo. Again, you'll see the hinges of the gates and more tall houses, linked by lines of laundry strung over the canal that separated the Ghetto from the rest of the city.

From Campo del Ghetto Nuovo or from Calle Ormesini cross Rio della Misericordia, where there's a good view of the onion-shaped dome on the bell tower of Madonna dell'Orto. Go right on Fondamenta degli Ormesini, where there are a couple of modest trattorias. Beyond, on Fondamenta della Misericordia, several metalworking shops continue the centuries-old traditional business of Cannaregio. Turn left into the narrow Calle del Forno and cross the quiet Rio della Sensa, continuing into Calle Loredan. Directly across the bridge is Corte Cavallo (Horse), named after the steed on Verrocchio's monument to Colleoni, cast in a foundry here.

Madonna dell'Orto

From here, turn right to the lovely Gothic church of Madonna dell'Orto on the placid *rio,* where a few funeral boats are usually moored. The facade is one of the purest examples of Venetian Gothic in the city, and the interior is suffused with light that takes on the pinkish tones of the brick. This was Tintoretto's parish church, and he contributed mightily to its decoration before his death in 1594. He is buried under a simple stone on the right of the main altar. Over the first altar on the right as you enter, Cima da Conegliano's *St. John the Baptist* is, quite simply, a masterpiece. Beyond the fourth altar on the right you'll find Tintoretto's *Presentation of the Virgin.* Compare its dynamic movement and twisting perspective with the calmer, more majestic *Presentation* by Titian in the Accademia. Even more tumultuous are Tintoretto's two huge canvases on either side of the main altar, the *Last Judgement* and the *Adoration of the Golden Calf,* in which the artist is supposed to have painted his own black-bearded face on one of the pagans holding up the golden calf, adding his wife, in blue, nearby. There are two more Tintorettos in the apse, the *Vision of St. Peter* and the *Beheading of St. Paul,* flanking an *Annunciation* by Palma Giovane. The aged artist also painted the figures of the Virtues on either side of the central figure in the apse. And he contributed still another work to the Contarini Chapel, at the head of the left aisle. The painting shows St. Agnes bringing the son of the Roman prefect back to life before a crowd of astonished onlookers. Step into the first chapel at the other end of this aisle to admire a pretty *Madonna* by Giovanni Bellini.

Camels and Moors

When you leave the church make a brief detour, crossing the bridge in front of the church into Campo dei Mori. The Venetians have invented various legends to explain the presence of the weatherbeaten statues of three Moors in the wall of Palazzo Mastelli. And they have thoughtfully given the Moors new stone turbans. The figures are said to represent members of the Mastelli family, wealthy merchants who traded in the Orient, hence the turbans. Right around the corner on Fondamenta dei Mori, at # 3399, is the building that was Tintoretto's home from 1574 until his death.

Now return toward Madonna dell'Orto and turn onto Fondamenta Gaspare Contarini. On the canal side of Palazzo Mastelli you can see the charming relief of a man with a camel that is undoubtedly another reference to the trade with the East that made the family's fortunes. You'll pass a modern foundry on the *fondamenta* and some old palaces before you reach the end of the canal, from where there is a fine view north over the lagoon. You'll see San Michele and its cypress trees and Murano's lighthouse and bell towers a little farther away. Cross the bridge and continue in the same direction to the next canal. The ramshackle wooden buildings on the right belong to a *squero,* or boathouse, where gondolas are made and repaired.

Now turn to the left on Fondamenta dell'Abbazia, where a sculptured Gothic portal opens onto the countrified-looking courtyard of the old poorhouse that was supported by the Confraternity of the Misericordia.

You pass under an early 16th-century portico into Campo dell'Abbazia, a little-known but appealing place. The austere Gothic entrance of the Scuola Vecchia della Misericordia stands cheek-by-jowl with the ornate Baroque facade of the church. A worn well-head sits on an even more decrepit brick pavement, laid heaven knows how long ago. The Scuola is used sporadically as a center for restorations—the church was deconsecrated long ago—and the massive brick walls of the second Scuola della Misericordia across the canal seem to be crowding this forgotten corner of Venice into the lagoon. And you wonder if anyone would notice that it's gone, cut off as it is from the rest of Venice by the huge brick bulk of the newer Scuola, begun by Sansovino in 1532 and now used as a gymnasium.

Assassins and Pharmacists

Now you can make a choice. You can cross the Rio de Noale and the next canal, heading for Calle della Racchetta, where there's a pleasant trattoria, and from there on to the church of the Gesuiti. Otherwise you can take Fondamenta della Misericordia, head left over the first bridge and continue straight ahead into Campo Santa Fosca. You'll cross another Ponte dei Pugni, one of those bridges where marble footsteps in the pavement mark the starting point of battles between rival districts. Standing tall and somber on its pedestal in Campo Santa Fosca, a statue of Paolo Sarpi honors the monk who was an advisor to the doges and who eloquently championed Venice's cause in the Republic's tense power struggle with the Papacy in the early 17th century, when Venice was on the brink of accepting Protestantism as its state religion. Sarpi was assaulted near here one night by hired assassins, agents of the pope. He was stabbed repeatedly and left for dead with a dagger embedded in his cheekbone. Miraculously, he survived and hung the dagger as an *ex voto* in his monastery church.

The church of Santa Fosca is smallish and of little interest. More noteworthy are the Gothic Palazzo Correr across the street, with its 11 balconies, and the pharmacy nearby, which preserves the solid walnut woodwork, antique ceramic jars and bronze mortars of a centuries-old apothecary shop. In shops like these throughout Venice a potion, known as *teriaca,* the so-called penicillin of the Middle Ages, was dispensed as a panacea for all ills.

From here you can head for the *vaporetto* landing stage at Ca' d'Oro or San Marcuola.

SIGHTSEEING DATA. For general information on museum and church opening times and entrance prices, see "Sightseeing Tips" under *Miscellaneous* in the *Practical Information for Venice.*

Galleria Franchetti, Ca' d'Oro, Calle della Ca' d'Oro (tel. 523.8790). Open Tues. to Sat. 9–2, Sun. 9–1. Closed Mon. Admission 2,000 lire.

Museo Ebraico (Jewish Museum), Campo del Ghetto Nuovo (tel. 715.359). Also, guided tours to the Ghetto's various synagogues. Open mid-Mar. to mid-Nov., Mon. to Fri. 10:30–1, 2:30–5, Sun. 10:30–1. Closed Sat. and Jewish holidays. Mid-Nov. to mid-Mar., same days 10–12:30. Admission 2,000 lire.

Oratorio dei Crociferi, Campo dei Gesuiti, Cannaregio. Open July to Sept., Fri., Sat. and Sun. 4:30–6:30; Apr., May, June and Oct., Fri., Sat. and Sun. 10–12.

Toward the Arsenale and Castello

The broad, breezy quay of the Riva degli Schiavoni looks out over the Bacino di San Marco, St. Mark's Basin. Its name comes from the Slavs, or Slavoni, from the Republic's territories in what is now Yugoslavia. There are posh hotels and sidewalk cafes on one side, landing stages and tugboat moorings on the other. The tugboats ride high in the water, waiting for a call to prod and pull some huge ship through the Canale della Giudecca, the Giudecca Canal.

The Riva is usually crowded with people embarking and disembarking, people waiting to go somewhere and see something, people sunning themselves on the stone benches. In the winter a carnival comes to the quay; the colored lights of its Ferris wheel and carousel give it the air of a fairyland that has sprung up for the pleasure of the city's children. The Riva, like the Zattere on the Giudecca Canal and the Fondamente Nuove on the other side of Venice, offers airy relief from the city's somewhat claustrophobic *calli* and *rii*. Even the Grand Canal can sometimes seem hemmed in by its magnificent palaces, and the eye welcomes the distant horizons of the lagoon.

San Zaccaria

From the Molo, the quay in front of the Piazzetta and the Doge's Palace, you cross Ponte della Paglia, with its view of the Bridge of Sighs, onto the Riva proper. Continue on, crossing Ponte del Vin and pausing to admire the splendid lions on the equestrian monument to King Victor Emmanuel, 19th-century king of Italy. The second *calle* on the left, Sottoportico San Zaccaria, leads under an arch into quiet Campo San Zaccaria, site of the stately church of San Zaccaria, a successful blend of Gothic and Renaissance styles.

Completed in the late 15th century by Mauro Codussi, San Zaccaria is known for the famous and very beautiful altarpiece by Bellini over the second altar on the left, conveniently equipped with light machine. Painted in 1505, the picture was recently restored, and once more dazzles with the brilliance of its original coloring and luminosity. At the end of the right aisle, you pay a few hundred lire for admittance to the chapel of Sant'Atanasio, with an early Tintoretto over the altar. The ceiling of the apse of the adjacent chapel of San Tarasio was frescoed by Florentine painter Andrea del Sarto in 1442. These frescoes, now in poor condition, are among the earliest properly Renaissance works in Venice, though their full significance was evidently lost on local artists at the time. Antonio and Giovanni d'Alemagna, for example, painted the attractive pictures on

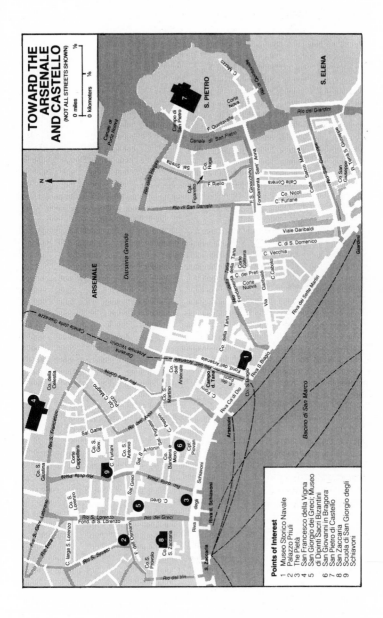

TOWARD THE ARSENALE AND CASTELLO

(NOT ALL STREETS SHOWN)

0 miles   ⅛

0 kilometers   ¼

Points of Interest

1 Museo Storico Navale
2 Palazzo Priuli
3 The Pietà
4 San Francesco della Vigna
5 San Giorgio dei Greci; Museo di Dipinti Sacri Bizantini
6 San Giovanni in Bragora
7 San Pietro di Castello
8 San Zaccaria
9 Scuola di San Giorgio degli Schiavoni

either side of the altar some years after Andrea del Sarto completed his labors here. Yet these native Venetian works still look back to Gothic models rather than forward to the naturalism of the Renaissance.

Over the Gothic arch at the corner of Campo San Zaccaria is a lovely marble Madonna in relief.

San Giorgio dei Greci

In tiny Campo Provolo, turn right to Fondamenta dell'Osmarin. This is a pretty little corner of the city, where vines spill out of a walled garden on a small canal. Here Palazzo Priuli, on the corner of the *rio* opposite, has lacy 14th-century Gothic windows and balconies. Pause as you cross the bridge over Rio dei Greci and look to your right. The bell tower that slants so alarmingly is the campanile of the church of San Giorgio dei Greci, center of Venice's once sizeable Greek colony. Venice's ties with the east made the city a natural refuge for well-to-do Greeks and Armenians when the Turks invaded their lands. Indeed for centuries Venice was the most important center of the threatened Greek and Armenian cultures. The Armenians still have an active printing establishment in Venice, and a monastery on the island of San Lazzaro degli Armeni where precious volumes in Armenian are preserved. At one time there were about 10,000 Greeks in Venice. Like the Jews and the Armenians, they were merchants and moneylenders, and their activities were a mainstay of the city's commercial successes. Today the Greek colony has dwindled to a mere handful, but services are still held in the interesting church that they built, San Giorgio dei Greci, with its gleaming icons, characteristic iconostasis and Byzantine decorations.

Next door is the Scuola di San Nicolo dei Greci, designed by Longhena in the late 17th century for the prospering Greek community. Here there's also a small Museum of Icons (Museo di Dipinti Sacri Bizantini), most from the 16th and 17th centuries.

Scuola di San Giorgio degli Schiavoni

From the bridge, follow Calle della Madonna and Salizzada dei Greci to the next canal, where you cross the bridge and turn left, following the faded sign to the Scuola di San Giorgio degli Schiavoni on the next corner. This small 16th-century building was the seat of the confraternity founded by the Dalmatian community. Like the Slavs, the Dalmatians came from parts of what is now Yugoslavia. Behind the heavy curtain at the door is a smallish room decorated by Carpaccio with episodes from the lives of three saints especially revered by the Dalmatians: St. Jerome, St. Tryphon, and St. George. After collecting the admission fee, the custodian will leave you in peace to admire them.

On the left wall is the best known, *St. George and the Dragon,* a meticulously composed scene of carnage. Next to it is the *Triumph of St. George.* On the end wall are *St. George Baptizing the Gentiles,* a *Madonna and Child* attributed to Carpaccio's son, Benedetto, and the *Miracle of St. Tryphon,* which shows the saint exorcizing the devil, who here takes the form of a basilisk, from the body of a daughter of the Emperor Giordanus. On the right wall are two subjects evidently unsuited to the artist's sunny, rational style: the *Agony in the Garden* and the *Calling of St. Matthew.*

Next is a delightful picture of St. Jerome leading his faithful lion into the monastery as the terrified monks seem literally to fly in fear. The *Funeral of St. Jerome* and the masterful *St. Augustine in his Study* are among Carpaccio's best works. The upstairs rooms, where the paintings were originally hung before being moved downstairs in about 1551, is rich in 17th-century decorations.

If you didn't take in San Francesco della Vigna on your walk to San Zanipolo, this is your chance to do so. In front of the Scuola di San Giorgio go left along Calle Furlani, turn left at the end and left again into Salizzada delle Gatte, continuing more or less straight ahead to San Francesco. Afterwards, retrace your steps to San Giorgio degli Schiavoni and continue the itinerary from there.

Toward the Arsenale

From San Giorgio degli Schiavoni, return to the Ponte dei Greci and turn left into Salizzada Sant'Antonin. At the end of this street turn right into Campo Bandiera e Moro. This peaceful square is only a few steps from the bustle of the Riva degli Schiavoni yet seems miles away. On one side a beautiful Gothic palace harbors a good pension, while in the corner of the Campo is the ancient church of San Giovanni in Bragora. Its facade is comparatively recent, dating from the 15th century. But the body of the church is probably 8th century. Stop in to see the fine *Baptism of Christ* by Cima da Conegliano over the main altar, painted in about 1495. There's another Cima on the right of the door to the sacristy, and some more or less contemporary works by Bartolomeo and Alvise Vivarini.

At the end of the left nave is a red marble font in which composer Antonio Vivaldi was baptized in 1678. Vivaldi was a priest as well as a composer—he was known as the "red priest" on account of his flaming red hair—and served as violin teacher and, later, concert master in the Pietà, a music conservatory for orphaned girls on the Riva degli Schiavoni. The church of the Pietà is open a few mornings a week, and is worth visiting for its sumptuous 18th-century decorations, which include a splendid ceiling fresco by Tiepolo. Vivaldi composed many of his finest works for the soloists and choir of the Pietà, and it can be a thrilling experience to hear a concert of his music here. They are held fairly frequently.

Continuing your itinerary from San Giovanni in Bragora, turn right into Calle dei Preti and left into Calle del Pestrin. Follow it into Calle della Crosera. Turn right at the end and follow Rio San Martino, crossing the bridge into Campo San Martino. There's a church with a good selection of 17th-century art here. From San Martino follow the *fondamenta* along the canal into Campo dell'Arsenale.

The Arsenale

The shipyards of the Arsenale cover an area of about 80 acres. Here the Republic built, armed and equipped the ships that made her unrivaled Queen of the eastern trade routes and scourge of the Turks. Crenellated walls encircle the Arsenale, while two sturdy towers protect its seaward entrance. Two huge lions from Piraeus, spoils of war, guard the Renaissance arch that forms its gateway. The bald lion sitting upright on the left bears a Runic inscription on its haunch, carved by the Byzantine emperor's Viking bodyguards. The smaller lions probably came from the Lion Terrace at Delos. Inside the arch is a Madonna by Sansovino.

For centuries, the Arsenale was the greatest shipyard in the world, the symbol of Venice's economic and military power. At its height it employed 16,000 workers. It is said that the Arsenale could equip a ship in one day. Certainly, during the wars against the Turks in the 16th century a new ship sailed out of its yards every day for 100 days. As the ships headed through the canal into the lagoon supplies were handed to those on board from windows in buildings along the way; arms from one window, ammunition from another, cordage and foodstuffs from others. By the time it reached the Riva the ship was fully supplied and equipped. One of the *fondamenta* along the canal is still known as Fondamenta dei Forni ("of the Bakeries"). While on Riva Ca' di Dio around the corner you can see a marble frieze marking the 15th-century bakeries that supplied the ships.

Behind the Arsenale there are still working shipyards, but the Arsenale itself is no longer used for important jobs. It was militarized by the Austrians during their occupation of the city after the fall of Napoleon in 1815 and is still military property, off-bounds to private boats. Proposals are afoot to convert the Arsenale into a cultural center and yacht marina.

At this point you can stop in at the Museo Navale, the Naval Museum, though note that it is open only in the mornings. Alternatively, if you've had your fill of sightseeing for the time being, you can head back along the Riva degli Schiavoni to St. Mark's.

The Museo Navale and Castello

Located in Campo San Biagio, the Museo Navale was originally the city's granary. It is essential viewing for anyone with a taste for things maritime and/or history. Kids usually love it. There are four floors of ship models and full-scale boats of all kinds and sizes, ranging from gondolas and Chinese junks to the ornate *Bucintoro,* the doges' ceremonial boat. There are models of ocean liners and warships too, all in no particular chronological order.

By now you are deep in the heart of Castello, Venice's easternmost district. Across the Rio delle Tana, which skirts the Arsenale, is Via Garibaldi, a street bearing the distinctly un-Venetian appellation of "via." As you can guess from its pavement, it's actually a filled-in canal, laid out by Napoleon. Before heading down it, glance at the first house on the right. It belonged to John and Sebastian Cabot, intrepid explorers of the New World in the 15th and 16th centuries.

Via Garibaldi is the scene of a busy morning market and home to a number of good little restaurants and snack bars; useful for lunch. Wander off into the side streets, especially to the left to Fondamenta della Tana and Corte Coltrera and to the right into Corte Caboto. Opposite the neo-Classical church of San Francesco di Paolo is the gate to the public gardens, another of Napoleon's good works. They were laid out by the busy Frenchman in 1812. The gardens extend through to the grounds where the Biennale art exhibition is held every other year in June and July. Except for the time of this great arty shindig, this part of the city is normally blessedly free of tourists, and a pleasure to wander through.

San Pietro di Castello

At the end of Via Garibaldi the canal reappears, dividing the street into two *fondamente*. Continue along Fondamenta San Gioacchino, then cross the bridge and bear right to get to Fondamenta Riello, a small canal lined with modest homes, an antidote to—and antithesis of—the Grand Canal. Cross the bridge to the arcade on the other side and turn left for Campiello del Figaretto at one end of Campo della Ruga (site of a number of simple eating places). Take Salizzada Stretta toward the wall of the Arsenale and turn right onto Calle Larga. This leads to the workaday Canale di San Pietro, lined with boatyards. A bridge crosses the canal to grassy, tree-shaded Campo di San Pietro, where the freestanding 15th-century bell tower lists conspicuously to one side.

The church of San Pietro di Castello was Venice's cathedral for centuries, though it strikes many as odd that such an important function should have been relegated to such an unimportant backwater. The present church was built in the 16th century on the site of a very much earlier building. It's a typically Palladian structure, airy and luminous. Its chief treasure is a bishop's throne from Antioch in the Middle East, inscribed with a quotation from the Koran. It's in the right aisle.

If you have time, you may like to wander along the few *calli* on the island before crossing the bridge from Fondamenta Quintavalle to Fondamenta Sant'Anna. Here, the former church of Sant'Anna is now part of an abandoned naval hospital. It may be converted into a youth hostel. Continue straight ahead to Via Garibaldi and its *trattorias*. You can end this walk at the Arsenale landing stage or, if you prefer, delve even deeper into the *sestiere* of Castello, turning left on Calle Correra. You'll pass ranks of dull 19th-century houses before turning right into the more interesting Calle Secco Marina. Follow Rio San Giuseppe to reach the landing stage at Giardini where you can catch the line 1 *vaporetto*.

Sant'Elena

If you choose to continue by boat to the Lido you'll get a view of the new district of Sant'Elena. The church of Sant'Elena is ignored in most guide books, with some reason. But if you can't resist the impulse to see another church, get off the *vaporetto* at the Sant'Elena landing stage, follow the *fondamenta* around the end of the island and cross the second bridge you come to. Founded in the 13th century and rebuilt in the 17th, the church was turned into an iron foundry in the last century. It was reconsecrated in the '20s. Its most noteworthy work of art is the sculpture on the facade showing Admiral Vittorio Capello kneeling before St. Helena, a 15th-century work by Antonio Rizzi.

SIGHTSEEING DATA. For general information on museum and church opening times and entrance prices, see "Museums and Churches" under *Miscellaneous* in the *Practical Information for Venice.*

Museo di Dipinti Sacri Bizantini (Museum of Icons), Scuoletta di San Nicolò dei Greci, Calle dei Greci (tel. 522.6581). Open Mon. and Wed. to Sat. 9–1, 2–5, Sun. 9–1. Closed Tues. Admission 2,000 lire.

Museo Storico Navale (Naval Museum), Riva San Biagio (tel. 520.0276). Open Mon. to Fri. 9–1, Sat. 9–12. Closed Sun. Admission 1,000 lire.

Scuola Grande di San Giorgio degli Schiavoni, Calle Lion, Castello (tel. 522.8828). Open Tues. to Sat. 9:30–12:30, 3:30–6:30, Sun. 10–12:30. Admission 3,000 lire.

The Palace of the Lions and the Plague Churches

You can choose to start this walk at the Accademia landing stage and take in at least one art collection as you stroll through the *sestiere* of Dorsoduro on your way to the church of the Salute. Alternatively, you can start directly at the Salute landing stage. If you choose the Accademia, take Rio Terrà Sant'Agnese on the left of the gallery and go left again into Calle Nova Sant'Agnese, where there are interesting shops. Continue along Piscina Forner to the entrance, on the left, of 16th-century Palazzo Loredan-Cini on Rio San Vio. The palace houses the small private art collection of the Giorgio Cini Foundation, well worth seeing for its fine Tuscan works. Look for the early 14th-century *Maestà* and the Daddi *Madonna* in Room I; Botticelli's *Judgment of Paris* in Room III, where there are also an outstanding *Madonna* by Piero di Cosimo and a *Madonna* attributed to Piero della Francesca; and a portrait by Pontormo in Room IV. On the second floor are illuminated manuscripts, prints and drawings.

From Palazzo Loredan-Cini cross the bridge into the attractive little Campo San Vio beside the Grand Canal. The Anglican church of St. George here has served Venice's once sizeable English colony for more than a century. From Calle della Chiesa flanking the church continue along Fondamenta Venier, which swerves left into Calle San Cristoforo.

The Guggenheim Collection

An unusual gate marks the entrance to the neo-Classical Palazzo Venier dei Leoni, home of the late Peggy Guggenheim, where she lived with her many cats and her discerning collection of modern art, obtained for the most part directly from the artists themselves, whom she coddled, financed, entertained, and on occasion, married. You will find most of the big names in modern art in her collection, from Picasso to the Abstract Expressionists, Pollock, Rothko and De Kooning. Their works are displayed under the auspices of the Solomon R. Guggenheim Foundation in the gardens and salons of the villa, surrounded by the massive walls of what was intended to be one of the grandest constructions on the Grand Canal, Palazzo Venier dei Leoni, begun in 1749 but never completed. The lions *(leoni)* that gave the palace its nickname can be seen at the base of the facade just above the waters of the canal. The paintings are put into storage from November to March, when temporary exhibitions are mounted, so their arrangement may vary slightly. The enchanting sculpture garden is dominated by a large Byzantine throne. Off in a far corner of the garden, Ms. Guggenheim's ashes are buried next to a plaque commemorating her beloved cats. On the terrace facing the Grand Canal, Marino Marini's emphatically virile horseman is entitled the *Angel of the Citadel.*

The collection includes a number of Cubist works that are hung in the former dining room, some fine Surrealists, a bedhead and mobile by Alexander Calder in what was the bedroom, and large works by Pollock, Bacon, Sutherland and other postwar artists in the Barchessa, or boat house.

The Salute

Now cross the narrow canal into pretty little Campiello Barbaro and continue along Calle Barbaro across Rio della Fornace, where you can make a brief detour to visit the glassworks along the *fondamenta,* if you wish. Continuing along Ramo Barbaro you will come to Campo San Gregorio, where the Gothic church is now a workshop for art restorations. The *calle* tunnels under the old monastery and emerges at Santa Maria della Salute, one of the five churches built by the Venetians in thanks for the end of a plague.

Santa Maria della Salute is a particularly beautiful white octagonal building by Baldassare Longhena, constructed after the plague of 1630–31 that killed more than 46,000 Venetians, about 30 percent of the population. Even before it was completed in 1687, the doges had instituted a procession of thanksgiving that is still held every year on November 21, when a bridge of boats is thrown across the Grand Canal. More than a million wooden piles were driven into the mud to form the foundations for this splendid building. Inside, light pours in from the large windows below the dome, illuminating the polychrome marble decorations and three paintings by Luca Giordano in the chapels on the high altar and Titian's Pentecost on the far left. For a few hundred lire you can enter the Sacristy and see Tintoretto's votive painting of *St. Mark* over the altar and three scenes from the Old Testament by Titian, noteworthy for the artist's evident mastery of foreshortening.

Ice Creams and Angels

Leaving the church, turn right along the *fondamenta* toward the Dogana di Mare, the 17th-century customs house, where gray patrol boats are anchored at the quay. On a clear day the view here takes in the whole of St. Mark's Basin. Turning into the Zattere, a promenade on the broad Guidecca Canal, you'll pass the Magazzini del Sale, the Republic's salt warehouses, originally headquarters of Venice's highly profitable salt monopoly. The building is now used as an exhibition hall in connection with the Biennale. You also pass the 15th-century church of Spirito Santo, which has a *Marriage of the Virgin* by Palma Giovane, and the Incurabili, once a hospital.

Continuing along the Zattere, you come next to the large 18th-century church of the Gesuati. It's dedicated to the Rosary, which Tiepolo's marvelous vault frescoes duly celebrate, setting a flock of angels soaring through mid-air. The lavish interior also contains a lovely, luminous *Madonna with Saints* by Tiepolo on the first altar on the right and darker, more intense altarpieces by Piazzetta in the next two chapels on the same side. The third chapel on the left holds a powerful *Crucifixion* by Tintoretto.

After your walk you have an excuse to pause for refreshments at Aldo or Nico cafes, both known for delicious ice cream and floating terraces on the canal. Now take the *vaporetto* across the canal to the Giudecca, looking to the left where you can see the Mulino Stucky, an immense imitation-Gothic factory built in the 19th century. It has been inactive for ages, but the Venetian authorities can't decide whether to tear it down or convert it into something. What, is the question.

La Giudecca

The Giudecca is a long, eel-shaped conglomerate of eight islands. Its name may have derived from the Jewish colony here in the 13th century. During the Republic's long and luxurious decline, it became the pleasure garden of the Venetians. Today it is rather humdrum. There's not much to hold your interest, with the exception of the wonderful views of Venice proper, the church of the Redentore and a few good eating places.

The Redentore, or church of the Redeemer, is a monumental edifice, certainly one of Palladio's most successful and harmonious constructions. It is very much part of the Venetian scene, yet oddly detached from the city's everyday activity, except on the Feast of the Redeemer, on the third Sunday in July, when the Venetians make amends for neglecting it. A temporary bridge of boats crosses the Giudecca Canal, and the Venetians flock to the church by boat or on foot. Picnicking and merrymaking continue into the night when there's an eruption of fireworks that lights up St. Mark's Basin as far as the Lido.

The church was begun in 1577 and completed 15 years later. Like Santa Maria della Salute, it was put up in thanks for the ending of a terrible plague (that of 1576 which carried off some 50,000 Venetians, among them the great Titian). The only noteworthy painting in the church is a *Madonna* by Alvise Vivarini in the sacristy. However, the harmony and proportion of this late-Renaissance masterpiece, both inside and out, make the Redentore an inspiring church to wander around, both deeply beautiful and with an almost tangible air of mysticism and solemnity.

San Giorgio Maggiore

From the Redentore landing stage take the *vaporetto* to San Giorgio Maggiore. On the way you'll pass the Zitelle (literally, the "old maids"), where Palladio designed the church for an orphanage where young girls without dowries were taught how to make lace.

San Giorgio Maggiore takes its name from the Benedictine monastery established on the island in the 10th century. It was converted into a barracks during the 19th century, when the monastery was suppressed, and is now the headquarters of the Cini Foundation, which includes a cultural center and a naval training school. Its cloisters, refectory and dormitory are decorated with fine works of art and are often used for top-level international meetings. They are usually closed to the public, except when opened for exhibitions.

Nevertheless, the major point of interest here is of course the majestic church of San Giorgio Maggiore itself, built, like the Redentore, by Palladio. It was begun in 1566 and completed, some years after Palladio's death, in 1610. Again like the Redentore, Palladio imposed a double pediment on the facade, a characteristically brilliant solution to a problem that had long dogged Italian Renaissance architects. Their concern was to reconcile a classical Roman temple front—an essentially square shape—with the needs of a Christian church, with its high central nave and lower side aisles. Palladio's design incorporates a high central pediment, marking the nave, superimposed on a lower and squarer pediment, marking the aisles. Put like this, the answer seems clumsy. But Palladio was typical of his period also in his abiding interest in the application of mathematical proportion to building, his belief that exact mathematical relationships— making the length of a building exactly twice its height, to take a very simple example—would result in a harmonious relationship of parts not unlike that in music. And indeed it has been remarked that Palladio's buildings are as mathematically exact (and complex) and as harmoniously satisfying as a Bach fugue. The result in the case of San Giorgio Maggiore is unquestionably one of the most commanding and beautiful church fronts in Italy. Seen from a distance on a misty day it seems to float on the lagoon like a mirage, out of reach and alluring.

In comparison to the complexities of the exterior, the inside of the church is relatively austere, though no less beautiful. There are two important late Tintorettos: the *Shower of Manna* and the *Last Supper,* placed on either side of the high altar. Both were painted in 1594 and share the mystical, almost phosphorescent quality of the artist's later works. There are two further Tintorettos—the *Deposition* and the *Resurrection*—in the Chapel of the Dead, both probably painted partly by the artist's son, Domenico. The chapel also contains a photograph of Carpaccio's *St. George and the Dragon*—the picture is hung elsewhere in the monastery complex—a later and less successful version of that in the Scuola di San Giorgio degli Schiavoni.

If it's a clear day, make the easy ascent by elevator to the top of the slender bell tower for a breathtaking view of Venice, the lagoon, and the Dolomites in the distance.

From San Giorgio you can catch a *vaporetto* directly to San Marco.

SIGHTSEEING DATA. For general information on museum and church opening times and entrance prices, see "Sightseeing Tips" under *Miscellaneous* in the *Practical Information for Venice.*

Cini Collection, Palazzo Cini, Calle Nova Sant'Agnese 864, San Vio (tel. 521.0755). Open June to Oct., Tues. to Sun. 2–7. Closed Mon. Admission 4,000 lire.

Guggenheim Collection, Palazzo Venier dei Leoni, Calle San Cristoforo (tel. 520.6288). Open Wed. to Fri. and Sun., Mon. 12–6, Sat. 12–9 (admission free Sat. 6–9). Closed Tues. Admission 5,000 lire. (From Nov. to Mar. open for temporary exhibitions; check hours with AAST Information Office).

San Giorgio Maggiore, Campanile (Bell Tower). Open daily 9–12:30, 2:30–6. Admission 1,000 lire. An elevator whisks you up.

Around the Lagoon

An excursion to the islands of the Venetian lagoon can come as a welcome relief after the brooding, enclosed charms of the city itself. The closest of the major islands is Murano, known the world over for its glass. The line 5 *vaporetto*—faster than the other *vaporetti*—has regular services to it. You can catch it from the rail station or, if you prefer, from the San Zaccaria landing stage on the Riva degli Schiavoni.

SAN MICHELE

The first step on the way to Murano is San Michele, Venice's main cemetery. Here you'll see Venetians disembarking from the *vaporetto* to tend the flowers and vigil lights at the graves of their loved ones, moving quietly through the avenues of dark cypresses among tombs of all shapes and sizes. Join them to see the church of San Michele, the earliest Renaissance church in Venice. It was built by Mauro Codussi. You can enter the church from the Gothic gate on the right. There's a painting of *St. Margherita of Cortona* by Tiepolo in the chapel on the left of the apse. The adjacent Emiliani chapel is enriched with marble reliefs and inlays. On the other side of the 15th-century cloisters is the cemetery. Poet Ezra Pound is buried in the small Protestant graveyard in the far corner. The graves of Diaghilev and Stravinsky are in the Orthodox section. All those illustrious Venetians not buried in the city's churches have been entombed here, along with the countless Venetians who never owned a palace on the Grand Canal, never served as doge, and never painted a great picture. And periodically the bones of all of them are removed from their graves to be deposited in an ossuary—a depository for the bones of the dead—to make room for newcomers. The Jewish cemetery, by the way, is on the Lido.

MURANO

Catch the next boat to Murano and get off at the Colonna landing stage. Like Venice itself, Murano is made up of a number of smaller islands linked by bridges. It's known almost exclusively for its glassworks, but it also has two fine churches, one of which, Santa Maria e Donato, is alone worth the trip.

Murano became Venice's glassmaking center in the 13th century when the glassworks, always a fire hazard, were moved here from the city. The Venetians had jealously monopolized the secrets of making fine glass, especially mirrors, and clung to this primacy until well into the 16th century.

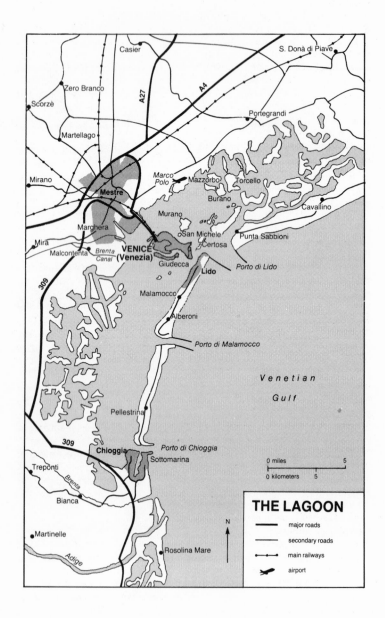

THE LAGOON

— major roads
— secondary roads
•—• main railways
✈ airport

So intense was their determination to guard their secret glass-making techniques that any glassworker who left the Republic to ply his trade elsewhere was, with characteristic ruthlessness, hunted down by agents of the Republic and murdered.

Like the island of Giudecca, Murano became something of a playground for Venice's aristocrats, a discreetly distant setting for dalliance. Gradually the brick walls of the glassworks crowded out the pleasure villas and the vineyards. There's little green left on Murano now, but although considerably built up it usually manages to look half deserted. But at certain times of day guides herd tourist groups off excursion boats into the glassworks where the promise of a demonstration of glassblowing is the pretext for a hard sell of what can be pretty hideous stuff. Don't be lured by the shills. Visit Murano on your own—perhaps planning to lunch in one of its trattorias—and visit the Glass Museum, which is usually open in the early afternoon. As for the pros and cons of purchasing glass here, see the "Shopping" section in *Practical Information.* You are perfectly welcome to stop in at any of the glassworks where signs indicate that demonstrations are given. Amid the roar and glow of the furnaces you can watch master craftsmen pick up a gob of molten glass on the end of a rod, then twirl, twist, snip and blow it into shape. There's usually a conspicuously placed receptacle for the few hundred lire you may care to leave as a thank-you for the hospitality. And of course the exit sign leads straight into the showroom.

There are plenty of glassworks along Fondamenta dei Vetrai and on either side of the broad Canale degli Angeli, which divides Murano in half. Toward the end of Fondamenta dei Vetrai is the church of San Pietro Martire, a Gothic building rebuilt in the early 16th century. In the right aisle is a splendid *Madonna and Child* by Giovanni Bellini, and on the left, over the sacristy door, a solemn *St. Jerome* by Veronese.

Cross the large bridge, the Ponte Vivarini, over Canale degli Angeli, looking back over your left shoulder to the Gothic Palazzo Da Mula, the large building with the elaborate windows. On the other side of the canal, turn right and follow Fondamenta Cavour to the Glass Museum, the Museo Vetrario. The collection, housed in the attractive Palazzo Giustinian, includes some pieces of Roman glass, but its most beautiful exhibits are such priceless 15th-century glass objects as the Barovier wedding cup, in Room II, and the collection of 16th-century glass, unique for its clarity and delicacy. A survey of the antique and contemporary glass on display may be useful in orienting your subsequent purchases.

Continue along the *fondamenta* to the lovely Romanesque basilica of Santi Maria e Donato. The apse on the canal is extraordinary, an intricate interplay of colonnades, arches and decorative brickwork, all on a perfectly proportioned, diminishing scale. The interior is charming, too, with a magnificent pavement, ancient columns and 15th-century ship's keel roof. The apse mosaic of the eminently serene and solitary Virgin was executed in the 12th century. The fine low relief of St. Donato in the left aisle was carved not much later, showing the donor and his wife as the tiny figures in the lower corners. The altarpiece of the *Dormition of the Virgin* on the same wall is attributed to Paolo Veneziano. Look behind the Baroque main altar for the most curious thing in the church—three large suspended rib bones, supposedly those of a dragon slain by St. Donato. Extensive restorations partly financed by a U.S.-based fund here in the mid-'70s saved the precious 12th-century mosaic pavement from irreparable damage caused by the infiltration of salt water from below.

You can roam at will about Murano, keeping in mind that the line 5 *vaporetto* stops at landing stages at Colonna: Fondamenta Venier, near the bridge over the Canale degli Angeli; Museo, near the glass museum; Navagero and Faro. From the Faro landing stage you can also catch a line 12 *vaporetto* for Burano and Torcello, though we don't recommend you visit these on the same day unless you're feeling exceptionally hale and hearty.

TORCELLO

You should allow four or five hours for a leisurely trip to Torcello and Burano, and you will surely find a suitable lunch spot on one or the other. Take the *vaporetto*—line 12—from Fondamente Nuove. This leaves every hour or so. The boats stop at Murano and then pass several deserted islands before arriving at Mazzorbo, a verdant island that is linked to Burano by a long footbridge. From here the boat may make its first stop at either Burano or Torcello. Hours and routes are posted at all landing stages. The trip one way takes about 40 or 50 minutes from Fondamente Nuove. If you plan to picnic on Torcello, a beautiful place to do so, bring provisions from Venice or stop off at Burano to buy food; there are no stores on Torcello.

From the 7th to the 13th century Torcello prospered under the impetus of settlers who had fled Altinum on the mainland in fear of the Lombard invaders from the north. The cathedral was founded in 639 as seat of the bishopric, and the island's population continued to grow even after some of its inhabitants moved to the islands of Rivo Alto, farther out in the lagoon, founding what was to become Venice itself. The people of Torcello, who numbered about 20,000 by the 16th century, had established a thriving wool manufacturing business, and boosted their economy with revenues from fishing and trade. They were able to allow themselves the luxury of building no less than ten fine churches. Eventually, however, the rivalry from increasingly powerful Venice and continued epidemics of malaria fatally weakened Torcello. Its inhabitants moved away and the Venetians began to use it as a quarry for building materials, carrying off a column here, a roof beam there. Now it is almost entirely deserted, an enchanted island in the far reaches of the lagoon.

From the landing stage a brick-paved lane follows the curve of a canal toward the center of the island. Nearby is the celebrated Locanda Cipriani, an inn famous for its good food and for Ernest Hemingway's erstwhile patronage. The inn's restaurant has expanded itself considerably. Still very fashionable and expensive, it has become perhaps a bit too popular with tourists, who can zip over on a fast speedboat direct from Harry's Bar, under the same ownership.

Just beyond this outpost of elegance, you come upon a small grassy square that holds the only surviving monuments of the island's past splendor. The low church of Santa Fosca on the right, the taller cathedral, the loggia of Palazzo dell'Archivio and the museum in Palazzo del Consiglio, on the left. The large stone seat at the center of the square is known as Attila's chair. The octagonal church of Santa Fosca was built in the 11th century; its strikingly spare and simple interior has 12 Greek marble columns with Byzantine capitals, and an interesting roof design.

The cathedral is an austere, 11th-century Venetian-Byzantine building, known for its exquisite mosaics. The vast mosaic on the interior of the facade represents the Last Judgement as the artists of the 11th and 12th centuries conceived it, a fearsome event that they imagined in obsessive, grotesque and sometimes ingenious detail. Opposite, in the 13th-century apse mosaic, a deeply touching figure of the Madonna stands alone on a field of gold, above a staunch array of Apostles. Take a close look at the four Byzantine reliefs of the 10th and 11th centuries in the iconostasis, or altar screen. Palazzo dell'Archivio is being renovated and will eventually house an archeological museum, while the Palazzo del Consiglio contains works of art and other objects from the churches that once stood on Torcello.

BURANO

The island of Burano presents a bright contrast to Torcello's haunting melancholy, a happy splash of color amid the gray and green of the lagoon. Its little houses—blue, yellow, pink, ocher and dark red—are picked out in white trim, with flowers spilling over the windowsills. Towering over them is a raffishly raked campanile. A toytown of colored blocks, crisscrossed by narrow canals, Burano is inhabited by a cheerful population of fishermen whose wives make lace while their men are out in the boats. Exhibits in the Lace Museum show the handiwork of Burano's lacemakers over the centuries. You'll find several trattorias in or near the main square, where shops and stalls sell lace that may have been made on the island (and if so it will be costly) together with bargain lace and embroidery that is "handmade." Yes, but in China.

THE LIDO

A flat strip of sand lying to the southeast of Venice proper, the Lido is the principal barrier between Venice and the sea. Its fame, still considerable, derives from the days, beginning at the end of the last century, when this was a fashionable sea resort that attracted the cream of European society, a state of affairs that lasted until well into the '60s. Gaming at the casino, lolling in the luxury of its palatial hotels or popping into a sleek motorboat to zoom over to Piazza San Marco for an aperitif were—indeed to some extent still are—the Lido's chief attractions. The Venetians continue to rent the comfortable beach cabanas at Des Bains or the Excelsior, where they socialize and take the sun. But, paradoxically for a beach resort, practically no one goes near the water itself, now perilously polluted.

Though the summer is still the principal high season, the Lido livens up considerably in September, when the annual movie festival draws celebrities by the bucketful and journalists by the plane load. Otherwise, aside from its few historical points of interest, there's little to see here: some handsome old villas, for example, and the likes of the marvelous Hotel Hungaria on Viale Santa Maria Elisabetta, gorgeously *art nouveau*. But the Lido is pre-eminently a good place to get a little fresh air or have a good lunch (but not on Sunday when the trattorias are filled to bursting and beyond, or on Monday when most of them are closed). And then there are the three *bocche di porto*, the three openings in the lagoon through which the tides flow in and out, flushing out Venice's congested canals, and sometimes flooding the lower sections of the city for a few hours during the winter months with the dreaded *acqua alta* or high tide.

Around the Lido

The Lido is easy to reach from Venice. *Vaporetti* lines 1 (quite slow) and 2 and 4 (faster) have frequent services to Piazzale Santa Maria Elisabetta. There's also a Casino Express—line 28—fast motorboats from the rail station and Piazzale Roma that stop off at the San Zaccaria landing stage on the Riva degli Schiavoni before cutting across St. Mark's Basin to the Lido and the casino's private landing stage. In July and August there's also a boat between the Riva degli Schiavoni and Chioggia right down to the southern end of the lagoon; this takes about two hours. If you're in a hurry, a bus service runs between Chioggia and Venice, via the mainland; this takes about 40 minutes. Finally, a regular boat service also links Pellestrina, about two thirds of the way down the outer islands of the lagoon, with Chioggia.

Arriving at Piazzale Santa Maria Elisabetta on the Lido, to get to the northernmost channel and the church and monastery of San Nicolò, take Bus. A. It leaves from just in front of the landing stage. San Nicolò, founded in 1044, was used by the doges to receive grandees sailing into the lagoon on state visits. Rebuilt in the 16th century, the church has a beautifully carved wooden choir. This is also the site of the symbolic wedding of Venice to the Adriatic, a ceremony dating back to 997. It takes place every year on the first Sunday after Ascension, usually in June. It's an occasion of considerable pomp, as the ecclesiastical and municipal authorities set off from St. Mark's over the lagoon.

Across the water from San Nicolò you can see the tipsy bell tower and the dome of San Pietro in Castello, and the island of Certosa, originally the site of a munitions factory but later abandoned, as have been so many other islands in the lagoon. Discussions as to the fate of these deserted islands have been proceeding fitfully for years. Some have been sold to individuals, most of whom have in turn been forced to abandon them again because of the enormous cost of maintaining them. Now the authorities are talking about using them for parks, hostels, cultural institutions and playgrounds for the city's children. Whether much will come of these good intentions remains to be seen. Close by San Nicolò, and the little airport here, is the Jewish cemetery, a melancholy spot granted to the Jews in 1386.

The tip of the Lido guards the main entrance to the lagoon, the Porto di Lido. Opposite, on the island of Certosa, is the great fort of San Andrea, built in the 16th century. It was from the fort that huge chains could be stretched, closing off the lagoon to enemy ships. Beyond it are Punta Sabbioni and Cavallino, once deserted sandy flatlands, now given over to beach establishments and camping sites. The line 14 *vaporetto* from San Nicolò serves them.

To get down to the southern end of the Lido you can take either Bus A or line 14 *vaporetto* back to Piazzale Santa Maria Elisabetta. Here, you change to Bus C, which takes you past the luxury hotels, the casino and the burgeoning residential districts to Malamocco, about two-thirds of the way down the Lido proper. It's one of the oldest settlements in the lagoon, inhabited as early as the 8th century. Today, it's a pretty village of little houses clustered around the unprepossessing 15th-century Palazzo del Podestà, the governor's residence, located on a small square.

From here, you can continue all the way down to the southernmost tip of the Lido and Alberoni, site of a golf course and the landing stage of the ferry that crosses Porto di Malamocco, the central entrance to the lagoon. Beyond is Pellestrina, a long thin island, little more than a sand bar reinforced by a dike. But there are some good trattorias in the little villages of Pellestrina and San Pietro in Volta. Beyond Pellestrina is the *murazzi,* the sea wall, an imposing structure built in the middle of the 18th century, proof that even during her decline the Venetian Republic was still able to command considerable technical resources.

You can continue on still farther south from here—though you must first backtrack to Pellestrina to catch the ferry—to Chioggia, at the very southern tip of the lagoon, really a part of the mainland. Chioggia was originally a fishing village, but it has become distinctly touristy in recent years, especially around its beach suburb of Sottomarina.

SIGHTSEEING DATA. For general information on museum and church opening times and entrance prices, see "Sightseeing Tips" under *Miscellaneous* in the *Practical Information for Venice.*

Museo dell'Estuario, Torcello (tel. 730.761). Open Tues. to Sun. 10–12:30, 2–5:30. Closed Mon. Admission 2,000 lire.

Museo Vetrario (Glass Museum), Fondamenta Cavour, Murano (tel. 739.586). Open Mon., Tues., Thurs., Fri. and Sat. 10–4, Sun. 9–12:30. Closed Wed. Admission 3,000 lire.

San Francesco del Deserto. Small boats ferry visitors from Burano. Visitors are welcome every day, 9–11, 3–5:30.

San Lazzaro degli Armeni (tel. 526.0104). Vaporetto Line 10 from Riva degli Schiavoni (15 minutes). The monks guide visitors through the monastery near the Lido. Open to visitors Thurs. and Sun. 3–5. Inquire at AAST Information Office for additional opening hours. A small donation is welcome.

Scuola dei Merletti (Lace School and Museum), Piazza Galuppi, Burano (tel. 730.034). Open daily 9–6. Admission 2,000 lire.

Torcello island. An hour by vaporetto. Cathedral open 10–12:30, 2–6:30. Admission 1,000 lire.

Excursions from Venice

The ideal way to break free from the claustrophobic charms of Venice is a trip to the mainland, the Veneto, as the plain west and north of the city is known. Venice's influence is evident throughout the region, but the principal cities here—Padua, Treviso and Vicenza—have an appeal of their own. Moreover, the Veneto is dotted with a series of magnificent villas, many the work of Palladio. It was in these handsome piles that the aristocractic families of Venice, a good number of whom had vast estates in the Veneto, vacationed and took their leisure in the long hot summers of the Venetian Republic's decline. Above the plain, vineyards and orchards outline the curving contours of the hills, while in the distance the Dolomites raise their craggy peaks.

We cover no more than the highlights of the Veneto here. Anyone interested in exploring the region further—or in information on the many excursions and tours that can be made from Venice—should head for the tourist office in Piazza San Marco. They will be able to supply full details.

PADUA

Padua, about 35 miles southwest of Venice, is a bustling city, centered around its two major institutions: the university and the basilica of Sant'Antonio, both of which date back to the 13th century. Padua is an ancient city, founded by the Romans under whom it became an illustrious center of learning and the arts. It was a free commune in the Middle Ages until, in 1405, it ceded to the overwhelming power of neighboring Venice. Today, the heart of Padua remains its medieval center, the narrow, winding streets of which, full of bicycles and bookshops, form a striking contrast to the unattractive, modern business district that surrounds them. Alongside the more cultural attractions of the city, shopping here ranks very high, and is in some ways superior to that in Venice.

Arriving in Padua by train, your visit starts at one of the city's most extraordinary monuments: the Scrovegni chapel. It was built at the end of the 13th century by a wealthy Paduan, Enrico Scrovegni, in honor of his deceased father. Scrovegni called on Giotto to decorate the chapel, a task that occupied the great artist and his team from 1303 to 1305. They created a magnificent fresco cycle, arranged in typical medieval comic-strip fashion, illustrating the lifes of Mary and Christ. Today the frescoes are beginning to show signs of deterioration, and conservation measures are being put in hand to reduce the damaging heat of the illumination, and the dust and humidity carried by visitors.

230

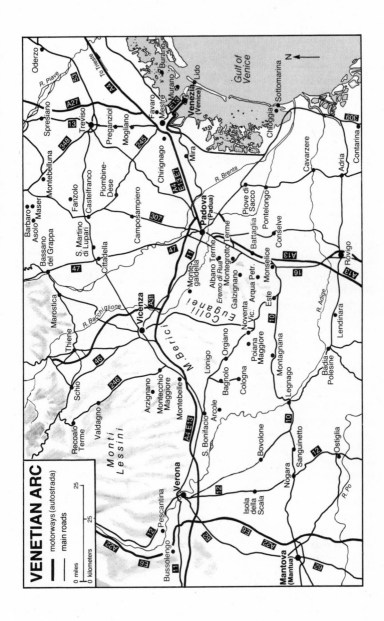

Just around the corner from the gardens that now occupy the area of the original Roman arena, next to which the Scrovegni chapel was built, is the 13th-century church of the Eremetani. It was decorated by Mantegna at the end of the 15th century, but suffered considerable damage in the 1944 bombing of Padua. The precious Mantegnas were all but obliterated. Though you can see what remains of them, it is a dispiriting experience. From here, follow Corso Garibaldi to Piazza Cavour, site of the historic 19th-century Cafe Pedrocchi. Pause for a coffee or *cappuccino* amid its neo-Classical columns.

The University building on Via VIII Febbraio is worth a visit to see the exquisite and perfectly proportioned 16th-century anatomy theater. Behind the Municipio, or city hall, are the three adjacent historic squares that form the heart of the city. These are Piazza della Frutta and Piazza delle Erbe—both, as their names suggest, originally market places, though only the latter is still used as such—and Piazza dei Signori. Separating the two old marketplaces is the 14th-century Palazzo della Ragione, seat of Padua's parliament. To the left of the imposing old Palazzo del Capitanio, in Piazza dei Signori, is the unfinished facade of the 16th-century cathedral with its Romanesque baptistery.

Cross Piazza Antenore and turn right into Via del Santo. This leads to Piazza del Santo and the huge basilica of Sant'Antonio, one of Padua's major attractions. It's somewhat reminiscent of St. Mark's basilica in Venice, with its eight Byzantine domes and slender, minaret-like bell towers. Standing in front of the cathedral is Donatello's magnificent equestrian statue of Gattamelata, the great Venetian soldier. Cast in bronze—itself a monumental technical achievement—in about 1450, Donatello's statue was to prove decisively influential on the development of Italian Renaissance sculpture, as witness for example Verrochio's Colleoni monument in Venice executed about 30 years later. The basilica itself has a suitably sumptuous interior, with marble reliefs by Tullio Lombardo as well as a striking series of bronze reliefs by Donatello illustrating the life of St. Anthony. Donatello was also responsible for the bronze statues of the Madonna and saints on the high altar, a superb ensemble, though their original, more tightly-grouped arrangement was more effective. On the right of the piazza are the Oratorio di San Giorgio and the Scuola del Santo, the former with some good 14th-century frescoes and the latter with 16th-century frescoes including three by Titian.

Also on Piazza del Santo is the Museo Civico. This contains a *Crucifixion* by Giotto removed from the Scrovegni chapel as well as works by various Venetian painters. Look for Bellini's *Portrait of a Youth* and Piazzetta's *Supper at Emmaus,* interspersed with a few energetic Tintorettos.

From the basilica, take Via Belludi to Prato della Valle, a lovely and unusual piazza laid out in 1775. In its center is a small oval park surrounded by a canal. There were in fact many canals in Padua, but they have been filled in over the years, principally to accommodate automobile traffic. At one end of the immense square is the 16th-century church of Santa Giustina, with its austere brick facade. In the apse you should see the finely inlaid choir stalls and Veronese's colossal altarpiece of the *Martyrdom of St. Justine.*

Close by the park—reached by Via Donatello—is the Orto Botanico, Europe's oldest botanical gardens. It was founded in 1545 and still boasts two of the original plants. One is a palm—known as Goethe's Palm after the great German man of letters wrote about it in the 18th century. Today it is protected by its own octagonal greenhouse. The other, a *vitex castus agnes,* or Chaste tree—so called because its scented blooms were believed to ensure chastity—still flowers every June.

PRACTICAL INFORMATION FOR PADUA

GETTING THERE. By Train. Padua is about 20 minutes from Venice's Santa Lucia rail station. Trains run every half hour or so, with some additional services during the rush hour.

By Bus. Buses leave for Padua from the bus terminal at Piazzale Roma, with departures every half-hour or so. The trip takes about 30 minutes. Most travel agencies offer a half-day coach tour of the Venetian villas between Venice and Padua, including a sightseeing tour of Padua. It's available from April through October and costs about 50,000 lire. It's a quicker, more economical version of the Burchiello tour (see below).

By Boat. An unusual all-day excursion to Padua (April through October) is offered by most travel agencies as the "Burchiello Tour" due to the Burchiello motor launch that leaves Venice three times a week at 9 (Tuesday, Thursday and Saturday) and heads along the Brenta Canal to Padua, stopping at Malcontenta, Oriago, Mira and Stra along the way. This is an all-day trip—the return to Venice is made by bus—and costs about 100,000 lire per person, with lunch and visits to a series of villas included. On Wednesday, Friday and Sunday the launch makes the trip in the opposite direction, from Padua to Venice in other words.

By Car. From Piazzale Roma or the Tronchetto parking lot in Venice, take the causeway to the mainland and follow the signs for the A4 *autostrada* Venezia–Milan. Get off the highway at the Padua Est exit and follow the signs for Via Venezia and the rail station. There is parking at the station and just outside the city walls near the Scrovegni Chapel.

LUNCH SPOTS. El Toulà (E), Via Belle Parti 11 (tel. 26.649). Book ahead for this small but elegant dining room in an historic palace in the center of town. It scores highly for service, atmosphere and food. Closed Sun., Mon. lunch and Aug. AE, DC, MC, V.
   Al Fagiano (M), Via Locatelli 45 (tel. 652.913). A busy, popular spot near the basilica with good regional food. Closed Mon. and July.
   Sant' Antonio (M), Piazza del Santo (tel. 875.0634). Restaurant of the Hotel Donatello. Scores for the view, with tables outside in the summer, overlooking the basilica. The food is otherwise entirely geared to the tourist trade. Closed Wed.

SIGHTSEEING DATA. Museo Civico, Piazza del Santo 10. Open Tues. to Sat. 9–1:30, Sun. 9–1; closed Mon. Admission 2,000 lire.
   Orto Botanico, Via Orto Botanico 15. Open daily, 9 to one hour before sunset.
   Scrovegni Chapel, Corso Garibaldi. Open daily May to Sept. 9–12:30, 2:30–5:30., Oct. to Apr. open Mon. to Sat. 9:30–12:30, 1:30–4:30, Sun. 9:30–12:30. Admission weekdays 2,000 lire, Sun. 1,000 lire.

Scuola del Santo. Open daily 9–12 and 2:30–6:30. If the door is closed during these times the sacristan will open it for you.

Tourist Office. APT, Rail Station (tel. 875.2077).

TREVISO

Less than 20 miles north of Venice, Treviso is a charming medieval city of arcaded streets, frescoed houses and rushing waterways. It has a prosperous and pleasant air, and some very good eating at its old inns.

Start your visit at San Niccolò, near the rail station and bus terminal. This impressive Gothic church, begun in the 13th century, has a beautifully simple interior with an interesting vaulted ceiling and a wonderful fresco of *St. Jerome* by Tommaso da Modena on the second pier on the left. Next to the church, in the chapter house of the seminary—ring the bell for the porter; entrance is free but an offering is appreciated—the same artist painted a masterful series of 40 portraits of famous Dominicans. They are remarkable for their psychological insight and realism, both significant innovations considering the works are signed and dated 1352.

From here it's a short walk across Viale Battisti and down Via Liberale to the Museo Civico on Borgo Cavour. The museum has some run-of-the-mill works by Bellini and Cima da Conegliano, and a couple of good portraits by Lotto and Titian. The 18th-century works are more interesting, with a Guardi landscape, a Longhi portrait and a series of pictures by Tiepolo.

Turn left from the museum on to Borgo Cavour and head right on to Via Riccati, a picturesque street lined with 15th-century houses, a number of them decorated with frescoes. You'll soon see the cathedral, built in a mixture of styles over many hundreds of years, from 12th-century Romanesque to 19th-century Gothic. Inside, head for the chapel on the right of the choir. Here, Titian's masterful *Annunciation,* painted in 1520, dominates. Unusually, Titian painted the picture in concert with Pordenone, author of the original fresco in the chapel dome. This showed the Holy Spirit about to descend on Titian's Virgin. Sadly, Pordenone's work was destroyed by a bomb in the war. In the apse, there are some fine marble carvings by the ubiquitous Lombardi family. If the medieval crypt is open, descend the stairs to see its veritable forest of columns.

From the cathedral, turn right into Via Calmaggiore, lined with arcades and 14th- and 15th-century houses. It leads to Piazza dei Signori. Both pretty and impressive, the piazza boasts a series of fine medieval buildings as well as a Renaissance loggia under which the people of Treviso meet to talk business and gossip before they make for one of the cafes on the piazza for an aperitif. On the square, in Palazzo del Monte di Pietà, the richly decorated 17th-century chapel of the Rettori has been restored and is worth seeing.

Ask to be pointed toward the Pescheria, a little island in one of the rivers that traverse the town. Stroll along the river and see how cleverly the town has been built around and over its rushing streams. From here it's not far to the former church of Santa Caterina where Tommaso da Modena's detached fresco cycle of St. Ursula can be seen by special request.

PRACTICAL INFORMATION FOR TREVISO

GETTING THERE. By Train. Treviso is about 30 minutes by train from Venice, and connections between the two are frequent, running every half hour or so.

By Bus. Buses leave Piazzale Roma for Treviso at least every hour. The trip takes about 30 minutes.

By Car. Follow the signs for the A27 *autostrada* from Venice, and take the first exit marked Treviso. This trip is a mite longer distance-wise than the old Route 13 through Mogliano Veneto but is faster in the long run. You can park near the rail station in Treviso.

LUNCH SPOTS. El Toulà (E), Via Collalto (tel. 540.275). One of the best restaurants in Italy—so be sure to reserve ahead—with superb food served in nostalgic surroundings. This is worth coming to Treviso for. Located in the center of town. Closed Sun. eve., Mon. and July 25–Aug. 25. AE, DC, MC, V.

Beccherie (M), Piazza Ancillotto 10 (tel. 540.871). An old inn in the town center with lots of atmosphere and delicious food from a menu based on traditional regional specialties. Closed Thurs. dinner, Fri. and July 15–31. AE, DC, MC, V.

Al Bersagliere (M), Via Barberia 21 (tel. 541.988). Personalized approach to regional and international cuisine. Pink-accented elegance in a 13th-century building. Closed Sun. and Aug. 10–25, Jan. 2–14. AE, DC, MC, V.

SIGHTSEEING DATA. Chapel of the Rettori, Palazzo del Monte di Pietà, Piazza dei Signori. Open Mon. to Fri. 9–12. Admission free.

Museo Civico, Borgo Cavour 22 (tel. 51.337). Open Tues. to Sat. 9–12 and 2–5, Sun. 9–12; closed Mon. Admission 1,000 lire.

Santa Caterina, Via Santa Caterina. Open on request; arrangements through Museo Civico (tel. 51.337). Admission 1,000 lire.

Seminario (Tommaso da Modena portraits), Via San Nicolò (tel. 542.322). Open daily 8–1 and 3:30–7. For admission, inquire at custodian's desk at Seminary entrace.

The churches and cathedral open early in the morning and close about noon for a couple of hours, opening again in the afternoon.

Tourist Office. Palazzo Scotti, Via Toniolo 41 (tel. 0422–547.632).

VICENZA

Vicenza, about 50 miles west of Venice, bears the distinctive signature of 16th-century architect Andrea Palladio, whose elegant villas and palaces were to prove so influential in propagating classical architecture throughout much of Europe, especially Britain and, later, America (as witness of course Palladianism). Vicenza suffered great damage in the mid 16th century during the bloody wars waged against Venice by the League of Cambrai. Palladio, actually a native of Padua, was given the opportunity to rebuild parts of the shattered city, imposing upon it his grandly Roman buildings—possibly rather overblown considering the town's provincial status—in 1549 when he began work on the basilica. His reputation was immediately ensured and he embarked on a substantial series of lordly buildings, all of which proclaim the same rigorously classical vision while yet remaining harmonious and elegant. The broad main avenue of Vicenza—Corso Palladio, named in honor of the great man—contains a succession of these handsome mansions, while the large square at its end, Corso Matteotti, contains two more of Palladio's most celebrated buildings: Palazzo Chiericati and the Teatro Olimpico.

A visit to Vicenza entails a fair amount of walking, so wear comfortable shoes. And plan to have lunch in town before heading out to see the villas. Remember, however, that one, Villa Valmarana dei Nani, is closed in the winter.

You will probably start your visit at the rail station. Take Viale Roma and turn right onto Corso Palladio, where you can admire Palladio's Palazzo Bonin-Thiene at # 13, two Venetian Gothic palaces at # 47 and 67, and Palazzo del Commune, built in 1592 by Vicenzo Scamozzi (who had the distinction of completing many of the buildings left unfinished at Palladio's death in 1580). Detour to the left onto Contrà Porti to see yet more splendid palaces. Follow this street round into Contrà Zanella and you'll emerge again onto Corso Palladio at Palazzo da Schio. This is also known as Ca' d'Oro, the House of Gold, and makes a natural comparison with the other, more famous, Ca' d'Oro in Venice itself. Be sure to stop in at the church of Santa Corona to see the magnificent *Baptism of Christ* by Bellini on the left just in front of the transept. Painted in 1500, it is an exceptionally fine work, with emphatic coloring and a sweeping, shimmering landscape.

At the end of the Corso stands Palazzo Chiericati, an exquisite building, unmistakably Palladian. Today it houses the Museo Civico, home of a representative collection of Venetian painting. On the other side of the piazza is the Teatro Olimpico, Palladio's last work, and based closely on ancient Roman theaters, complete with a cunningly devised perspective street as a permanent backdrop. The theater is almost as notable for its perfect acoustics as for its grandiose architecture.

Retrace your steps along Corso Palladio, turning into the elongated Piazza dei Signori, the heart of the city. This is the site of Palladio's basilica, a confusingly named building in that it is not actually a church but a court house, the Palazzo della Ragione, or Palace of Justice. Only the magnificent exterior is by Palladio, the earlier, Gothic, interior having survived the attentions of the League of Cambrai. Almost as remarkable as the splendid two-story galleries that dominate the exterior is the skill with which the architect wedded his exterior structure to the interior. Opposite, is the Loggia del Capitaniato, designed by Palladio but never completed. From here you can walk a block or two farther to the Gothic Duomo, the cathedral, which boasts a gleaming 14th-century polyptych by Lorenzo Veneziano in the fifth chapel on the right.

Two of the most interesting villas of the Veneto are within easy walking distance of the city, on the Este road, leading southeast out of Vicenza. Take Viale X Giugno out of the city center and follow it as far as Via San Bastiano. This leads to Villa Valmarana dei Nani. This fine 18th-century country house has a series of marvelous frescoes by Tiepolo, fantastic vi-sions of a mythological world, rendered in broad expressive strokes and heavenly colors. You will be given a card explaining the subjects of the frescoes. The Foresteria, or guest house, next door was decorated by Tiepolo's son, Gian Domenico.

From Villa Valmarana it's a short walk to La Rotonda, the most famous Palladian villa of them all. The house and grounds have very limited opening hours. The name La Rotonda is apt, for in addition to the shallow dome over the building, Palladio repeated his restrained, classical facade on each of the building's four exteriors, producing a perfect wonder of harmonious and exact symmetry. Probably the most famous building La Rotonda inspired was Thomas Jefferson's Monticello in Virginia, ample proof of Palladio's appeal to the man of reason and balance.

If you still feel like walking, you can follow the second stretch of Viale X Giugno, flanked with arcades and chapels, up to the Baroque basilica of Monte Berico, interesting mainly for the view from the terrace in front of the church and for Veronese's canvas in the refectory of the monastery. This latter is a huge painting of the *Banquet of Gregory the Great* and has evident affinities with the artist's *Feast in the House of Levi* in the Accademia, though this picture isn't in such good condition.

PRACTICAL INFORMATION FOR VICENZA

GETTING THERE. By Train. Trains for Vicenza leave Santa Lucia rail station every half hour or so. The journey takes around 50 minutes.

By Car. Take the Autostrada A4 (Venezia–Milano) from Venice and follow it to Vicenza, about an hour's drive. There is ample parking space near the rail station. To get to the villas by car, take Viale Risorgimento out of Vicenza, then Borgo Berge, following the signs to the villas.

LUNCH SPOTS. Gran Caffè Garibaldi (M), Piazza dei Signori (tel. 44.147). Good, centrally located restaurant. Closed Tues. dinner and Wed. AE, DC, MC, V.

Al Pozzo (M), Via Sant' Antonio (tel. 221.411). Pleasant spot near the cathedral serving good antipasto. Closed Tues. AE, DC, MC.

Scudo di Francia (M), Contra Piancoli 4 (tel. 233.368). Handsome Gothic setting and excellent food combine to make this an especially appealing haunt; book ahead. Closed Sun. dinner and Mon., and two weeks in Aug. AE, DC, V.

SIGHTSEEING DATA. Museo Civico, Piazza Matteotti (tel. 39.534). Open Tues. to Sat. 9:30–12 and 2:30–5, Sun. 10–12. Closed Mon. Admission 3,000 lire.

La Rotonda, Via della Rotonda 33. House open Wed. 3–6. Admission 5,000 lire. Grounds open Tues. to Thurs. 10–12 and 3–6. Admission 2,000 lire.

Teatro Olimpico, Piazza Matteotti. Open Apr. to Sept., Mon. to Sat. 9:30–12:20 and 3–5:30, Sun. 9:30–12:20.; Oct. to Mar., Mon. to Sat. 9:30–12:20 and 2–4:30, Sun. 9:30–12:20. Admission 3,000 lire.

Villa Valmarana dei Nani, Via dei Nani (tel. 21.803). Open Thurs. and Sat. ·10–12, Mar. to Apr. daily 2:30–5:30, May to Sept. 3–6, Oct. to Nov. 2–5. Closed Dec. to Feb. Admission 4,000 lire.

Tourist Office. Teatro Olimpico, Piazza Matteotti (tel. 528.944). The office will provide full lists of villas to visit in the area and itineraries for visits by car.

PRACTICAL INFORMATION FOR VENICE

Arriving in Venice

SECURITY. Venice—Venezia to the Italians—is possibly the safest city in Europe. But though dark and ill lit at night, with forbidding alleyways and *sottoporteghi* (little streets passing under buildings), it is perfectly safe to walk in at any time, and you need not be nervous about waiting on a deserted landing stage for a late-night *vaporetto*. Mugging is unheard of, and robbery takes the more subtle forms of overcharging and shortchanging. But you should watch out for pickpockets on the *vaporetto*, especially on the lines used by tourists, and at the station.

GETTING IN FROM THE AIRPORT. Venice's Marco Polo airport is at Tessera, about 10 km. (six miles) north of the city on the Italian mainland. Buses run by ATVO buses connect the airport with Piazzale Roma, where you can get a *vaporetto* (waterbus). The fare is about 4,000 lire. A taxi from the airport to Piazzale Roma costs about 40,000 lire. A taxi from the airport to Piazzale Roma costs about 35,000 lire. You can also take a watertaxi—a *motoscafo*—from the airport. This will run upwards of 100,000 lire for up to five people, but agree on the price before you leave; overcharging is common. If you are staying in a top hotel you can arrange to be met at the airport by the hotel launch, though you'll pay handsomely for the service. The best boat service into Venice, however, is that run by the Cooperative San Marco: economical and hassle free. The boat leaves from a landing stage near the terminal and goes all the way to the Zecca on Piazzetta San Marco. Buy your tickets at the desk at the airport. For the return trip you buy your ticket at the desk on the landing. Cost is 11,000 lire per person including baggage. These boats run more frequently during the morning.

ARRIVING BY CAR. If you can possibly help it, don't bring your car to Venice. You'll have to pay for a garage or parking space during your stay. If there's space you can park in one of the multi-story garages at Piazzale Roma or in the parking lot of Tronchetto. On holiday weekends traffic backs up on the causeway between Venice and Mestre, and electronic signs let you know if and where space is available. During the summer and at Easter and Carnival the parking areas of Fusina and San Giuliano on the mainland handle the overflow; they are connected to Venice by direct *vaporetto* service (about 30 minutes). If you park in a garage at Piazzale Roma, you walk to the *vaporetto* landing stages on the canal. If you park at Tronchetto you can walk the half kilometer (quarter of a mile) or take the A.C.T.V. bus 17 (ticket at information booth) to Piazzale Roma and the *vaporetti*, or take the Line 34 waterbus, direct to St. Mark's (every 10 minutes or so) from the Tronchetto landing stage.

You can take your car to the Lido. The car ferry (Line 17) leaves about every half hour from the terminal on Tronchetto.

ARRIVING BY TRAIN. Santa Lucia rail station is in the northeast corner of the city. In addition to the EPT-AAST Information Office—regularly ornamented with long lines of arriving tourists—there is an AVA Hotel Association booth where you can get last-minute hotel bookings. The *vaporetto* landing stages are strung along the canal outside. The station has a fair number of porters—they wear badges and, usually, blue overalls—who meet trains and will, if you want, take your luggage out to the landing stages. There's a kiosk at the far left of the quay outside the station where you may be able to get a porter to accompany you to your hotel, though it will cost you a pretty penny. Official rates are posted on the porters' kiosks. You can figure on about 8,000 lire for one or two pieces of luggage, and 2,000 lire for each additional piece. There are porters at some of the main landing stages along the Grand Canal, but a luggage cart can be a lifesaver if you can't find—or don't want to pay—a porter.

TOURIST OFFICES. The main tourist office in Venice (AAST) is at Calle Ascensione 71C, just off Piazza San Marco under the arcade in the far left corner opposite the Basilica; tel. 522.6356. There are also offices at the Santa Lucia rail station (tel. 715.016); at Piazzale Roma in the bus terminal (tel. 522.7402), open in summer only; and on the Lido at Gran Viale 6 (tel. 765.721). There is also an EPT-AAST desk at Marco Polo airport, and information booths at the three outdoor parking lots at Tronchetto, Fusina and San Giuliano. Finally, there are also information booths at Ca'Savio at Cavallino beach (tel. 966.010) and at the Marghera service area of the autostrada (tel. 921.638).

All will give you a general map of Venice—though it's not detailed enough to be useful in exploring the city—and a hotel list, but it's not a good idea to arrive in the city without having first made hotel reservations, although the AVA office at the station can work miracles. The AAST office in St. Mark's Square can also supply copies of the free weekly publication *Un Ospite a Venezia* ("A Guest in Venice"), full of useful information on transportation and current events. This is also available in many hotels.

CHANGING MONEY. There are exchange offices at the airport, rail station and Piazzale Roma, but you're likely to find long lines at them all. Try to have enough lire with you when you arrive to cover your first day's expenses. There are plenty of exchange offices throughout Venice. The following observe shop hours, all closing on Sun., most on Sat. afternoon.

American Express, San Moisè (tel. 520.0844).

Banco di San Marco, Bassani, Calle Larga XXII Marzo (San Moisè), (tel. 520.3644).

CIT, Piazza San Marco (tel. 528.5480).

Wagons Lits/Turismo, Piazzetta Leoncini (tel. 522.3405).

Banks. Bank hours are 8:30–1:30 and 3–4. They are closed on Saturdays and Sundays.

American Express, San Moisè (tel. 520.0844).

Banca d'America e d'Italia, Calle Larga XXII Marzo (San Moisè), (tel. 520.0766).

Banca Nazionale di Lavoro, Bacino Orseolo (tel. 667.511).

Banco di San Marco, Calle Larga San Marco (tel. 529.3711).
Credito Italiano, Campo San Salvador (tel. 957.600).

Getting Around Venice

ORIENTATION. Getting around in Venice presents some unusual problems. It's not just that all the main streets are filled with water and that the city buses are motorboats. Rather, that Venice is a city of quite astounding complexity, with no logic of any kind determining its layout. Its little streets and canals twist and turn at random. Apparently major thoroughfares turn into dead ends, narrow lanes turn out to be important arteries. Moreover, through the city is divided into districts, or *sestieri,* and has been since the 12th century, these districts are themselves sources of extra confusion. In each of them, buildings are numbered on a spiral pattern, making it practically impossible to tell on which street a given number is located. The post office does, it's true, issue a directory of these numbers, but it's really of use only to the mailman. An address such as Dorsoduro 2397 is unlikely to do anything other than add to the confusion. The trick is always to find out the name of the street that whatever you are looking for is located on, though the duplication of street names in the various *sestieri* does not help the bewildered tourist greatly.

The city is also obliged to cope periodically with flooding caused by high tides, despite millions of dollars spent on the problem over the years. This flooding generally occurs between November and April, and then only as a result of particularly bad weather. Only the lowest parts of the city are flooded, and normally for no more than two or three hours. A siren warns the Venetians to evacuate first-floor dwellings, and city workers put out duckboards for citizens and visitors alike to walk on. Nonetheless, a pair of rubber boots—not to mention a sense of humor—is essential. Anyone visiting the city in the winter should be very sure to forget neither.

Two other basic points are worth making. One, that you make sure you know how to get to your hotel before you arrive. Two, that you get hold of as detailed a map as you possibly can, one that includes transportation lines. If all else fails, however, have no hesitation in asking a native the way. The Venetians are renowned for their courtesy and consideration in directing visitors around, and though their directions can sometimes be irritatingly vague—*"sempre diritto"* is a stock response, generally accompanied by a happy smile; it means "straight on," which is not always exactly to the point—it is not unusual to find yourself escorted all the way to your destination.

Districts and Street Names. Venice is built on 120 islands, all of them connected by bridges. The main part of the city consists of the six districts mentioned above: San Marco, Castello, Cannaregio, Santa Croce, San Polo and Dorsoduro. In addition, there are the other islands of the Venetian archipelago: the Giudecca and the Lido are both fairly close to Venice proper; Murano, Burano and Torcello slightly farther away.

The only piazza in Venice is Piazza San Marco, St. Mark's Square. All other squares are known as *campi*—singular *campo*—unless they are very small, in which case they're a *campiello* or a *corte.* A street is a *calle,* or, if it's quite large, a *calle larga,* or a *ruga,* or sometimes a *salizzada* (these were originally the only paved streets). A *calletta* or *ramo* is an alley (no shortage of these in Venice). A *sottoportego* is a street that passes under buildings. A *fondamenta* is a street flanking a canal. A street formed by a filled-in canal is a *rio terrà.* A *lista* is a street that originally led to an ambassador's palace. All canals in Venice are called *rii*—singular *rio*— except the Canale Grande, the Canale di Giudecca and the Canale di Cannaregio.

CITY TRANSPORTATION. By Vaporetto.

A.C.T.V., the public transit system, runs the city's efficient *vaporetto,* or waterbus, service. To make the most of it, get hold of a good map of the system and a timetable. Both are on sale at newsstands, though timetables are also posted on all landing stages. Buy tickets from the booths at these landing stages, open from early to about 9 P.M. You can also buy tickets on the boats, but a small supplement is charged for this. You can either buy individual tickets or books of ten, but count your change: shortchanging is not unknown. Fares in 1988 were 1,500 lire for most lines and 2,000 lire for the Line 2 express between the rail station, the Rialto, San Marco and the Lido. Stamp your ticket in the yellow machine at the entrance to the landing stage. Alternatively, there are daily tourist tickets available for use on all lines. These cost 8,000 lire. However, anyone staying in Venice for more than three or four days should get a "Carta Venezia" pass. This offers substantial discounts on normal fares; 600 lire, for example, for most lines rather than the full 1,500 lire. To get a card, go to the A.C.T.V. office near the Sant'Angelo landing stage in a garden off Corte dell'Albero. It's open from 8:30 to 1. You'll need a passport-type photograph—there's a photo machine at the rail station—plus additional ID. A fee of 8,000 lire is also payable. The entire operation takes about five minutes. The pass is valid for three years. Carry it with you all the time as you'll need to show it to get your discount.

Vaporetti services are frequent, with boats running every ten minutes or so during the day. Lines 1, 2 and 5 run all night, with boats every hour between midnight and dawn. All landing stages are clearly marked with name and line number, and serve boats going in both directions. If you're in any doubt about which line you want, ask the conductor; though chronically lax at checking tickets, they're always happy to help.

By Gondola.

Gondolas aren't generally used for getting around any more. Before the days of motorboats every aristocratic family had its own gondola moored at the *pali* (poles) in front of their palace. Now they are strictly a tourist attraction, but a unique experience for all that, and one you shouldn't miss. However, choose the right time for your ride. The usual Grand Canal itinerary is too heavily trafficked to be pleasant during the morning and afternoon. Late afternoon and early evening hours are the best, say around 7:30 of a June or July evening. In other months, start out about an hour before sunset. A night-time ride is a memorable, sometimes magical experience, when the canals are quiet, the palace windows illuminated and the water laps at the centuries-old stones.

Gondolas are wonderfully graceful in the water. If you look closely you'll see that they are lopsided to allow for the weight of the gondolier who stands on one side, maneuvering his single long oar in the *forcola,* or oarlock, which has several indentations and lends itself to scores of movements. Until the 16th century the nobles vied with each other to have the most beautifully decorated gondola in the richest colors, but in 1562 the Republic decreed that all gondolas should be painted black in order to put an end to the wasteful rivalry. The *ferro,* or metal comb on the prow, represents the city's six *sestieri* (districts). You'll hear the gondolier use a distinctive cry to signal his presence as he rounds a corner.

Officially, Venice's 400 licensed gondoliers charge a fixed minimum rate for up to five people: 50,000 lire for 50 minutes, about 25,000 for each successive 25-minute period. Between 8 P.M. and 8 A.M. the rate goes up to 60,000 lire. These are the official rates; in practice, you'll be asked double that for a 30–40 minute ride, and the tab is even higher after 8 P.M. It pays to put your bargaining skills to work; if the gondolier likes you (especially if you're a pretty girl) he may give you a bargain rate. Like taxi drivers the world over, gondoliers are a proud breed unto themselves. To avoid arguments, come to terms with him before you step into the boat.

Gondola stations are strategically located throughout Venice; you can deal with them directly or have your hotel *portiere* make the arrangements. You'll find gondolas at:

Bacino Orseolo	Santa Sofia
Calle Vallaresso	Campo San Moisè
Danieli–Riva degli Schiavoni	Rialto (Riva Carbon)
Santa Maria del Giglio	Railway station
San Marco	Piazzale Roma

By Motoscafo. Watertaxis—*motoscafi*—can be expensive. The fare system is based on distance and is Byzantine in its complexity. The minimum you will pay is about 30,000 lire, but it will cost about three times that for a ride from one end of the Grand Canal to the other. *Always* agree on the fare before starting out. Unless you have a good reason for taking one, and to avoid arguments, overcharging and outright rip-offs, it's generally better to avoid using the *motoscafi* altogether.

If you must, however, there are water taxi stations in front of the railway station; at Piazzale Roma; at Rialto; San Marco, and other locations. Supplements are charged for calls, night service, or baggage. You can call a water taxi on 523.2326 or 522.2303.

By Traghetto. Not many tourists know about the two-man gondolas that ferry people across the Grand Canal at various points. It's the cheapest and shortest gondola ride in Venice and can save an enormous amount of walking. The fare is 300 lire, which you hand to one of the gondoliers as you get on. Every few minutes from early morning until late afternoon (some operate well into the evening) the gondola leaves its little wooden landing stage and makes the brief crossing. The Venetians usually stand up all the way, but you can sit on the narrow side bench if you feel unsteady. Look for "Traghetto" signs. Traghettos cross between:

Santa Maria del Giglio and San Gregorio
San Barnaba and San Samuele
Sant'Angelo and San Tomà
Riva del Carbon and Riva del Vin
Santa Sofia and Pescheria (Market)
San Marcuola and Fondaco dei Turchi

Ferrovia (railway station) and San Simeon Piccolo.

On Foot. Everybody walks in Venice. It's the only way to reach many parts of the city. But, in addition to the general difficulties of finding your way around (see "Orientation" above), there are a couple of practical points to bear in mind. First, wear comfortable shoes. If you want to get away from the main tourist areas, you will find yourself faced with a considerable amount of foot slogging. Plus, many of the smaller streets are uneven and not suitable for any sort of fancy footwear. Second, make sure your map shows all the *vaporetti* and *traghetti* lines. These can provide immensely useful short cuts and save a great deal of wearisome walking. Third, don't worry if you get lost (as you most certainly will). The odds are that the place you want is probably just around the corner anyway, however unattainable it may seem.

CITY TOURS. Group tours are a dreary way to see Venice. Nonetheless, a considerable number are on offer. CIT and American Express both offer tours on foot and by gondola, though the latter are best avoided. From May to October on weekdays the Bassani travel agency (tel. 520.8633) organizes offbeat tours that you can book through your hotel *portiere* or at travel agencies. One is called "A Day in Venice" and shows you some of the hidden corners of the city on foot and by launch; it includes lunch and costs about 65,000 lire. "A Night in Venice" includes dinner, a gondola serenade and a nightspot; it costs about 80,000 lire. During the summer, free guided tours of the Basilica San Marco are offered under the auspices of the Patriarchate of Venice; information is available in the atrium of the basilica.

The AAST Information Office in Piazza San Marco will give you a list of licensed guides and their rates. Alternatively, call the Associazione Guide Turistiche, Calle delle Bande 5267 (tel. 520.9038).

Where to Stay

HOTELS. Most of Venice's hotels are in renovated *palazzi* that lend themselves more or less successfully to the task of keeping you warm in winter, cool in summer and comfortable all year round. The top hotels offer a distinguished ambiance and assiduous service, though some rooms may vary from sumptuous to ordinary. Hotels in the lower categories can be quite cramped and spartan; baths may occupy space subtracted from fair-sized rooms, and showers are often the drain-in-the-floor type that guarantees instant flooding. Airconditioning is essential for survival during the July and August dog-days; in many places you will be charged a hefty supplement per person for its use. Remember that the room rate is posted inside the door of the room or the closet, and that any additional charges for breakfast and airconditioning should be posted as well. Rates may vary in the same hotel according to the room's type or location. You are expected to take breakfast at the hotel, and the cost is usually included in the rate quoted. If the hotel has a restaurant you will have to agree to half-pension terms—to eat at least one meal there every day in addition to breakfast—if you want a room during high season. Very few hotels in the lower categories have restaurants. For a longer stay we highly recommend the charming old pensions in our list. Because of landmark preservation regulations, many smaller hotels cannot install elevators, so you may have to walk up a flight or two to your room.

The high season is from March 15 to November 2 and again from December 20 to January 8 and the two-week Carnival period before Lent, usually in February. Many hotels close for two or three weeks during the winter. Convenient winter packages and promotional offers, together with low off-season rates, can save you money. It's always a good idea to reserve in advance, especially if your heart is set on a particular hotel, but the AVA Hotel Association booths at the rail station, airport and Piazzale Roma municipal garage can almost always find you a room in any category, even in high season. They are open daily from 9 A.M. to 9 P.M. The 20,000 lire deposit they require is rebated on your hotel bill.

Our hotel listings give details of which of the major credit cards are accepted by each hotel we list. These appear as AE for American Express, DC for Diners Card, MC for MasterCard (incorporating Access, Cartasi, and EuroCard), and V for Visa.

Hotel Prices. We have divided all the hotels in our listings into price categories. Two people in a double room in a Venetian hotel can expect to pay, in lire (considerably less in low season):

Superdeluxe	350,000–700,000
Deluxe	275,000–500,000
Expensive	225,000–350,000
Moderate	120,000–180,000
Inexpensive	95,000–120,000
Rock Bottom	40,000–70,000

Superdeluxe

Bauer Grünwald, Campo San Moisè 1459, San Marco (tel. 520.7022). 200 rooms. Rooms all pleasant and attractively furnished, with varying standards of creature comforts; tops is Suite 303 with peacock blue carpet and marble bath, but Twin 316 is lovely too at half the price. On the Grand Canal, near Piazza San Marco, the hotel upholds the European tradition of spaciousness and opulent decor. Relax in its posh salons, the *Blue Bar,* or dine on a terrace on the Grand Canal. AE, DC, MC, V.

Cipriani, Giudecca 10 (tel. 520.7744). 94 rooms. Stunningly decorated rooms and suites, some with garden patios. Superb hotel away from the madding crowd on the Giudecca island, across St. Mark's Basin—the hotel launch whisks you back and forth to St. Mark's at any hour of the day or night. A sybaritic oasis with huge heated pool, tennis courts, extensive gardens, cooking courses and fitness programs, and one of Venice's best restaurants. Closed mid-Nov. to mid-Feb. AE, DC, MC, V.

Danieli, Riva degli Schiavoni 4196, Castello (tel. 522.6480). 240 rooms. A Prestige hotel. Has some palatial suites, but lower-priced rooms can be dowdy. Near St. Mark's, and Venice's largest luxury hotel, long a favorite with English-speaking travelers. The 15th-century Palazzo Dandolo has loads of old Venetian atmosphere, and the modern wing next door has balconies overlooking the lagoon. The rooftop terrace restaurant is justly famous for top-notch cuisine and heavenly view. AE, DC, MC, V.

Gritti Palace, Campo Santa Maria del Giglio 2467, San Marco (tel. 794.611). 90 rooms and suites. A Ciga hotel. Quiet elegance on the Grand Canal, five minutes from St. Mark's; beautifully appointed accommodations with the atmosphere of an aristocratic private home. Dining terrace on the Grand Canal with a head-on view of the church of the Salute. AE, DC, MC, V.

Deluxe

Londra Palace, Riva degli Schiavoni 4171, Castello (tel. 520.0533). 69 rooms. Distinguished ambiance; overlooks St. Mark's Basin, five minutes from Piazza San Marco. Whether in rooftop Suite 502 or in a room with a balcony on the lagoon, you sleep in luxury in a canopied bed. Excellent *Do Leoni* restaurant and elegant little bar. AE, DC, MC, V.

Monaco e Grand Canal, Calle Vallaresso 1325, San Marco (tel. 520.0211). 75 rooms. Rooms are spacious in this hotel known for its understated chic, a few steps from St. Mark's, and some have a view of the Grand Canal. Warm, intimate atmosphere. Garden courtyard and dining terrace on the Grand Canal, at its peak in the evening when the traffic dies down and the view can be best enjoyed. AE, V.

Expensive

Cavalletto e Doge Orseolo, Calle Cavalletto 1107, San Marco (tel. 520.0955). 81 rooms. Nicely furnished rooms in a reliable establishment with a long tradition of comfort, hospitality and good service. Excellent central location on little canal next to Piazza San Marco. AE, V.

Metropole, Riva degli Schiavoni 4149, Castello (tel. 520.5044). 65 rooms. On St. Mark's Basin, five minutes from St. Mark's itself; many rooms have a view of the lagoon, but the quiet, spacious rooms on the garden are inviting, especially 141. Elegant hotel decorated with exquisite taste and run with careful attention to detail. Small and fine *Zodiac* bar and new *Quattro Stagioni* restaurant. AE, DC, MC, V.

Saturnia International, Calle Larga XXII Marzo 2398, San Marco (tel. 520.8377). 99 rooms. Many rooms redecorated; new rooms (80, 82, 84) are delightful; even the smaller rooms are attractive and well organized. Well-run hotel in quiet but central location near San Moisè and St. Mark's; with lots of atmosphere, solid comfort, and cordial staff. Excellent *Caravella* and *Cortile* restaurants and small, pleasant bar. AE, DC, MC, V.

Moderate

Bel Sito, Campo Santa Maria del Giglio 2517, San Marco (tel. 522.3365). 34 rooms. At the Santa Maria del Giglio landing stage on the Grand Canal, five minutes from St. Mark's. Four very nice rooms in new wing; other pleasant rooms on courtyard have new baths, pleasing decor, some have fridge-bar and T.V.; older rooms are short on closet space. No elevator. You can admire the facade of Santa Maria del Giglio while you breakfast outdoors at tiny tables. AE, DC.

Bisanzio, Calle della Pietà 3651, Castello (tel. 520.3100). 39 rooms. Near Riva degli Schiavoni and the San Zaccaria landing stage and Piazza San Marco. Entrance rather elegant, rooms smallish but comfortable and quiet. But it's the location that counts—you are just a few steps away from the main sights and the *vaporetto* landing stages. AE, DC, MC, V.

Bonvecchiati, Calle Goldoni 4488, San Marco (tel. 528.5017). 86 rooms. Between Piazza San Marco and the Rialto landing stage, in the heart of the shopping district. Tides of tourists swirl around this oasis, with its somewhat erratic blend of antique and modern decor. Pleasant. AE, MC.

Carpaccio, Calle Corner 2765, San Polo (tel. 523.5946). 17 rooms. Some rooms have view of the Grand Canal. Small, friendly hotel on a cul-de-sac near the Frari—a quiet location between San Polo and the San Tomà landing stage. For those who want to get off the beaten track but have everything at hand. V.

Do Pozzi, Corte do Pozzi 2373 (Calle Larga XXII Marzo), San Marco (tel. 520.7855). 29 rooms. Rooms rather basic, with fridge-bar and optional airconditioning. Near San Moisè and the St. Mark's landing-stage, in a very quiet location on a tiny courtyard. Friendly young staff. Meals at canalside restaurant next door. AE, MC, V.

La Fenice, Campiello Fenice 1936, San Marco (tel. 523.2333). 68 rooms. Central, in an interesting part of the city, near Teatro La Fenice and Santa Maria del Giglio or St. Mark's landing stages, this is an old favorite for atmosphere and charm, of which rooms in the older wing have plenty. Pretty garden lobby, lounges.

Flora, Calle Bergamaschi 2283 (Calle Larga XXII Marzo), San Marco (tel. 520.5844). 44 rooms. Central but quiet location off a main thoroughfare near San Moisè and the St. Mark's landing stage. Rooms are comfortable and nicely furnished; some are small, as are most bathrooms. Pretty garden and sitting rooms are a big plus. AE, DC, MC, V.

Giorgione, Santi Apostoli 4587, Cannaregio (tel. 522.5810). 56 rooms. Rooms have all the basic comforts. Attractive lobby, but this hotel's most appealing feature is its location—just behind Santi Apostoli, between the railway station and St. Mark's near Ca d'Oro landing stage—in a quiet zone with real Venetian atmosphere, and good trattorias and cafes. AE.

Panada, Calle Specchieri 646, San Marco (tel. 520.9088). 46 rooms. Satisfactory standard of comfort at Piazza San Marco; in the tourist mainstream but manages to keep its cool. AE, DC, MC, V.

Pausania, Fondamenta Gherardini 2824 on Rio San Barnaba, Dorsoduro (tel. 522.2083). 25 rooms. Near the Ca' Rezzonico landing stage. In medieval palazzo with courtyard and garden. Good atmosphere and smart blend of antiques and light pastel fabrics in rooms, all airconditioned, with frigobar and TV. AE, MC, V.

San Cassiano, Calle della Rosa 2232, Santa Croce (tel. 522.3051). 35 rooms. On the Grand Canal, near Rialto markets and San Stae landing stage. Some of the rooms in this attractive old palazzo have views of the Grand Canal, but the rear rooms are quieter. In a fascinating area and near good eating places. AE, DC.

Torino, Calle delle Ostreghe 2356, San Marco (tel. 520.5222). 20 rooms. Near Santa Maria del Giglio landing stage, five minutes from St. Mark's. Don't be put off by the garish lobby. New management is gradually renovating it: most rooms nicely redecorated with new baths, some with fridge-bar and T.V. Rooms are smallish, but there's a pleasant sitting-room. No elevator. Rates include breakfast and airconditioning, very reasonable in low season.

Inexpensive

Accademia, Fondamenta Bollani 1058, Dorsoduro (tel. 521.0188). 26 rooms. Just off the Grand Canal on Rio San Trovaso, near the Accademia landing stage. Plenty of atmosphere and a touch of the romantic in this delightful pension in a 17th-century villa. Rooms are comfortable and nicely furnished, as are the sitting-rooms on the ground floor; many rooms overlook the pretty gardens, where you can sit in warm weather. Breakfast only. Regulars book from year to year for this gem. AE, DC, MC, V.

Agli Alboretti, Rio Terrà Sant'Agnese 882, Dorsoduro (tel. 523.0058). 19 rooms. Near the Accademia landing stage. Basic rooms, good atmosphere and a few antique furnishings in attractive 15th-century building. On an airy street leading to the Zattere, this pension has been a favorite with European travelers for 30 years. Garden courtyard. Closed Nov. 14 to Dec. 15. AE, MC, V.

Casa Frollo, Fondamenta Zitelle 50, Giudecca (tel. 522.2723). 26 rooms. Historic pension in 17th-century palazzo on the island of the Giudecca, a few minutes by Line 5 *vaporetto* from Piazza San Marco. One of Venice's hidden treasures, admired for its romantic garden; kitchen full of antique utensils; fine views and deliciously demode furnishings. Closed Dec. through Mar. Sadly, threatened with eviction and may have to close.

La Calcina, Zattere 780, Dorsoduro (tel. 520.6466). 37 rooms. Near the Zattere landing stage and the Gesuati. It's Venice's oldest pension; John Ruskin stayed here in 1877. Remodeled in part since then, it's old-fashioned and genteel, with good views of the Giudecca canal and the Redentore church across the way. In good weather you breakfast by the canal.

Madonna dell'Orto, Fondamenta Madonna dell'Orto 3499, Cannaregio (tel. 719.955). 39 rooms. Near the Gothic church of the same name, just around the corner from Line 5 landing stage. Beautiful patrician palace in tranquil area behind the Ghetto. Some rooms are enormous and ideal for families; few private baths and no elevator, as no extensive alterations are allowed in historic buildings. Nicely furnished in old-fashioned Venetian style, the hotel has a lovely garden and ample sitting-rooms.

Paganelli, Riva degli Schiavoni 4182, Castello (tel. 522.4324). 15 rooms, plus 7 in annex. A few steps from San Marco, near the San Zaccaria landing stage. Rooms range from the spacious and attractive Twins 9 and 5, with new baths, to older, more basic and very reasonable rooms. Half-pension at the hotel restaurant just around the corner.

La Residenza, Campo Bandiera e Moro 3608, Castello (tel. 528.5315). 14 rooms. Only five minutes from St. Mark's and a step away from Riva degli Schiavoni and the San Zaccaria landing stage. Unusual and charming hotel occupying the main floor of a Gothic palace; comfy salon furnished with antiques and nice older rooms, most with bath, and a handful of newer rooms on lower floor that are very pretty indeed, with new baths and fridge-bars. Air conditioners are available at low extra charge. Closed in winter except for Christmas and Carnival. AE, DC, MC.

San Fantin, Campiello Fenice 1930, San Marco (tel. 523.1401). 14 rooms. A simple little hotel with good central location near Teatro La Fenice and the Santa Maria del Giglio landing stage; adequate rooms and friendly atmosphere. Closed mid-Nov. to Apr. 1.

San Stefano, Campo Santo Stefano 2957, San Marco (tel. 700.166). 14 rooms. On a large and central square, handy to everything and just across the bridge from the Accademia landing stage. Decor is pseudo-18th century but rooms are immaculate and comfortable with nice new baths and fridge-bar. Elevator and tiny breakfast room; airconditioning and T.V. on request. One of Venice's greatest bargains.

Scandinavia, Santa Maria Formosa 5240, Castello (tel. 522.3507). 27 rooms. Just off Campo Santa Maria Formosa, near San Zaccaria landing stage. Efficient, but pleasant, offering reasonable low-season rates for basic satisfactory rooms. You may have to take half-pension terms. AE, MC, V.

Seguso, Zattere 779, Dorsoduro (tel. 522.2340). 36 rooms. Near the Zattere landing stage and the Gesuati. Quiet, well-furnished rooms. Ezra Pound was a regular at this pension, which has been in the same family for 80 years and has all the atmosphere of an old Venetian home. Mandatory half-pension terms are quite reasonable.

Rock Bottom

Alla Salute Da Cici, Fondamenta Ca Balà 222, Dorsoduro (tel. 522.2271). 50 rooms. Just off the Zattere near Punta della Dogana and the Salute landing stage. Rooms are basic, many with bath. Good atmosphere in fairly large 17th-century building with some stucco decorations and a garden.

Antico Capon, Campo Santa Margherita 3004, Dorsoduro (tel. 528.5292). 8 rooms. On one of the city's most interesting squares, near Ca' Rezzonico landing stage. Rooms are spartan and you share the bath; over the restaurant of the same name. Plenty of inexpensive eating places in the area, including the osteria just a few doors down.

Bernardi Semenzato, Santi Apostoli 4366, Cannaregio (tel. 522.7257). 15 rooms. Near Ca' d'Oro landing stage, within walking distance of the station. Modest rooming house run by a friendly couple and popular with American back-packers. Rooms can accommodate several people, and showers and breakfast are included in room rate.

Iris, Calle del Cristo 2910/A (tel. 522.2882). 25 rooms. Near San Tomà landing stage and the Frari church. Neat, pleasantly decorated rooms, cheerful atmosphere. Over popular restaurant with dining in courtyard, hence some aromas and noise during day and evening, but handy for meals.

Dalla Mora, Salizzada San Pantalon 42, Santa Croce (tel. 35.703). 14 rooms. Near San Tomà landing stage, the Frari, and within walking distance of the station. Modest but clean rooms, and a pretty terrace on a canal.

San Samuele, Piscina San Samuele 3358, San Marco (tel. 522.8045). 10 rooms. Near the Church of Santo Stefano and landing stages of San Samuele (Line 2), Sant'Angelo or Accademia (Line 1). At one end of the Salizzada San Samuele, this little inn has a nondescript entrance but pleasant rooms and friendly management.

Sant'Anna, Calle Sant'Anna 269, Castello (tel. 528.6466). 8 rooms. From the Arsenale landing stage take Via Garibaldi and go straight ahead to the end of the canal, then left. Family-run inn with plenty of baths and atmosphere, in a neighborhood where there are few tourists and lots of down-to-earth eating places.

Sturion, Calle del Sturion 679, San Polo (tel. 523.6243). 12 rooms. Just off Fondamenta del Vin, along the Grand Canal near the Rialto Bridge and landing stage. This belongs in a category by itself; rates are low but value is high, in historic inn overlooking Grand Canal. Bright, spacious rooms in Venetian style. Some can accommodate up to four beds; some have private baths. A bargain, and a classy one at that.

Lido Hotels

Deluxe

Excelsior, Lungomare Marconi 41 (tel. 526.0201). 230 rooms. A Ciga hotel. Most rooms are rather stark and modern; grand ones include Suite 37–38 and Twin 32 in Empire style. Odd blend of Moorish and modern, this was the Lido's most fashionable hotel and is still smart, though tourists, vacationers and conventions have taken the place of royalty and stylesetters. However, it regains some of the old glitz during the September movie festival. Closed mid-Oct. to mid-Apr. AE, DC, MC, V.

Expensive

Des Bains, Lungomare Marconi 17 (tel. 765.921). 266 rooms. A Ciga hotel. This beautiful white palace hotel, built in 1900, has the elegance and style of times past, with the added comforts of a Sporting Club and jewel-like pool in a garden setting. Much more atmosphere than the Excelsior. AE, DC, MC, V.

Quattro Fontane, Via Quattro Fontane 16 (tel. 526.0227). 72 rooms. Delightful villa in a pretty park, with the air of an aristocratic country home. Relaxed but refined atmosphere with antique furnishings and modern comforts. Closed Oct. to Apr. AE, MC, V.

Moderate

Biasutti Adria-Urania, Via Dandolo 29 (tel. 526.0120). 73 rooms. A cluster of old villas, nicely decorated and very comfortable, with gardens and a pleasant atmosphere. Closed mid-Oct. to mid-Apr. AE, DC, MC, V.

Religious Institutes

Domus Cavanis, Rio Terrà Foscarini 899, Dorsoduro (tel. 87.374). Near the Accademia landing stage. An institution run by nuns that takes both men and women; midnight curfew. Closed mid-Nov. to mid-Feb.

Istituto San Giuseppe, Calle Tasca 5402, Castello (tel. 25.352). Near Santa Maria Formosa, on a parallel of Calle delle Bande, halfway between Rialto and San Zaccaria landing stages. Six bedded rooms. Good central location and nice garden; both men and women. Send a 16,000 lire deposit to hold your pad.

Youth Hostel

Ostello (I.Y.H.F. Hostel), Fondamenta delle Zitelle 86, Giudecca (tel. 523.8211). Near the Zitelle landing stage of Line 5 or Line 8 waterbus. You have to get there early (3 P.M.) to get a berth at 6 P.M. opening. 11 P.M. curfew. Transportation will increase your expenses as you've got to use a *vaporetto* to go anywhere. Advance reservations required from Mar. 1 to Oct. 31. In summer, additional pads (for sleeping bags) are made available in a few public schools; inquire at AAST tourist office.

Camping. Obviously, there are no campsites in Venice proper, and municipal authorities have cracked down on backpackers who used to unfurl their sleeping bags in the plaza in front of the railway station and under the arcades in Piazza San Marco. It's now a no-no, though the city has promised to provide inexpensive pads, perhaps at the old Sant'Anna military hospital at the far end of the Castello district.

There are campsites at Punta Sabbioni and Cavallino, on the peninsula east of Venice; they are accessible from the Lido and are open from May to September. Those closest to Venice are on the mainland at Mestre and Fusina.

The EPT-AAST Tourist Information Offices will provide a list of current camping sites in the Venice area. These are among the best-equipped:

At **Cavallino**—*Dei Fiori,* Ca' Vio, Via delle Batterie (tel. 966.448); *Joker,* Cavallino, Via Fausta (tel. 968.019); *Ca' Savio,* Via Mare 51 (tel. 966.017).

At **Fusina**—*Fusina,* Malcontenta, Via Moranzani (tel. 969.055).

At **Mestre**—*Alba d'Oro,* at Ca' Noghera (tel. 541.5102).

Eating and Drinking

FOOD AND DRINK. A city built on water, Venice has appropriately based its cuisine on water creatures. Its cooks have natural affinity for seafood, and over the centuries have mastered all the secrets of cooking the infinite varieties of fish, crustaceans and mollusks that are found in the waters of the lagoon and beyond in the salty Adriatic.

Yet possibly oddly for a city that was unrivaled mistress of trade with the Orient, Venetian cooking is not significantly spicy. Rather, you will find seafood treated with respect, never overcooked and only lightly seasoned to allow its delicate natural flavor to reach your palate. A fresh *antipasto di mare,* or seafood antipasto, is an exquisite starter and sets the stage for what is to come. It may consist of mussels, clams and various other shellfish tossed with chopped squid and cuttlefish and a few whole shrimp in a tangy oil and lemon sauce with just a hint of garlic. From the Venetian hinterland comes another antipasto favorite, *prosciutto di San Daniele,* a particularly tasty raw cured-ham from the cool foothills of the eastern Alps. As elsewhere in Italy, it may be served with melon as a cool summer starter, or with salame during the winter.

As a first course the Venetians favor *risotto,* a creamy rice dish that may be cooked with vegetables such as artichokes, asparagus or peas, as in the thick, soupy *risi e bisi,* a traditional Venetian dish rarely found on the menu nowadays, except in neighborhood trattorias. *Frutti di mare,* literally "the fruits of the sea," also make a marvelous shellfish-studded *risotto,* but the tastiest of all, according to the Venetians, is *risotto alle seppie,* in which pearly grains of rice are veiled by the silky black ink of the cuttlefish.

With a few exceptions, pasta is not a forte of Venetian cooking, despite the fact that Marco Polo is said to have brought the art of noodle-making back with him from China. Spaghetti *al pomodoro,* with tomato sauce, is a southern Italian dish, not worth ordering in a Venetian restaurant. But spaghetti *alle vongole,* with clams, or *ai frutti di mare,* with various shellfish, is something else again. Usually any kind of pasta—*spaghetti, tagliolini, linguine*—ordered here with any kind of seafood—*alla marinara* (mixed seafood), *alle vongole* (with clams) or, best of all, *con granseola* (with crab)—is eminently satisfactory. And *pasticcio di pesce* is a delicious casserole of baked pasta with *baccalà* (dried cod). Then, too, there's *pasta e fagioli,* another dish usually associated in tourists' minds with more southerly climes. Yet it is also a Venetian specialty and very good indeed, a thick soup of hearty reddish legumes to which pasta is added. The only pasta that is peculiar to Venice and a few other parts of the Veneto region is *bigoli.* These are thick, dark strands made of whole wheat flour, usually served with a tuna fish or anchovy sauce that tends to be too salty for the uninitiated.

Another pillar of regional cooking is *polenta,* and here white corn meal is used in preference to the yellow meal used in other areas of northern Italy. In Venice *polenta* serves as an accompaniment to *baccalà mantecata,* a creamy mixture of dried cod and butter or oil, or to *fegato alla veneziana,* a sometimes sublime dish that you should try more than once in Venetian restaurants, where the menu is likely to offer the utterly banal translation of the dish as "liver and onions." When properly done, meltingly tender liver is cut into thin strips that are cooked briefly in a smooth sauce of sautéed onions and then served with sticks of grilled polenta.

But seafood predominates as a second course. Indeed many of Venice's good little restaurants serve only fish dishes. If you take a walk one morning through the fish market at the Pescheria in the Rialto district, you will see the myriad varieties from which Venetian cooks choose their day's dinner. Trays of slippery, silvery fishes drip briny water onto the pavement. There is *spigola* (sea bass), *orata* (sea bream), *sogliola* (sole), *rombo* (turbot), pinkish-red *triglie* (mullet), candid fillets of *San Pietro* (John Dory) and monstrous *coda di rospo* (angler fish), all suitable for a *griglia mista,* or mixed grill. Then there are the *seppie* and *seppioline* (cuttlefish), *calamari* (squid) *polipi* (octopus) and *sarde* (sardines), all delicious either sautéed in a sauce or fried in batter. Mounds of *vongole* (clams), shiny black *cozze* (mussels) and red-tongued *cappesante* (scallops) rattle as the vendors scoop up quantities suitable for a seafood antipasto or for a sauce for spaghetti or risotto. Crates of shrimp, crayfish and other leggy creatures are arranged in hierarchical order around trays of majestic *scampi* and regal *granseola* (spider crab). Grayish-green *anguille* (eels) writhe in tubs from which they will be plucked to be roasted in the oven with coarse salt, onion and bay leaf. And at certain times of year, gourmets will crowd around stalls selling *moleche,* the soft-shell crabs that Venetians love.

Across the way, vegetable stands do a brisk business in the makings of salads—greens, fennel and ruby-red *radicchio* from Treviso on the mainland. Sacks of onions are steadily depleted as housewives carry them away to make *fegato alla veneziana* or *sarde in saor,* sardines marinated in vinegar and sliced onions, a choice antipasto that you will often find also on the counters of wineshops.

Throughout Venice, pastry shop windows bear witness to the Austrian influence on Venetian patisserie, an assemblage of delectable tortes and *crostate* (fruit tarts). Amid the sachertortes, *baicoli,* sweet toasted biscuits, are the only truly Venetian specialty. The very popular *tiramesù,* a creamy concoction of *mascarpone* cheese, heavy cream, coffee and chocolate, originated on the mainland, though Venetians have adopted it enthusiastically.

Drink. Not since the days when the Giudecca and Murano were covered with vineyards has any wine been produced in Venice. But the mainland more than compensates. The Friuli region to the north furnishes some excellent wines that are little-known outside Italy but are well worth looking into. The house wine served in Venice's trattorias is usually a dry white Tocai from Friuli, which also produces the pale white, dry Pinot and Merlot and Cabernet, dry reds. More full-bodied reds, Valpollicella and Bardolino, come from the Verona area, where the well-known Soave originates. Venetians often like to have bubbly white *prosecco* with their meals, a naturally fermented sparkling white wine that is a shade less dry that the usual Tocai and Pinot. The best *prosecco* comes from the Valdobbiadene. Cartizze is a wine having much the same qualities, and is considered superior by some. You can sample all of these wines by the glass in one of Venice's many wineshops, where the proprietor will be pleased to serve you what he considers the best of the many wines he keeps, often drawing it from the huge demijohn which he chose personally at the producer's vineyard.

The typical digestif in this area is *grappa,* a very strong acquavit, often bottled with herbs to give it flavor. And there are a variety of types of beer, for here you are not far away from the Alto Adige, or South Tirol.

Venice's water is perfectly safe to drink. In many *campi* and *campielli* drinking fountains splash away, and their pavement basins serve as birdbaths for the pigeons. Otherwise, excellent bottled water is available everywhere.

RESTAURANTS. The general standard of Venetian restaurants has suffered from the onslaught of mass tourism. It is difficult to eat well in Venice, and to do so you must either pay top money in the most expensive restaurants or seek out the special little places that the Venetians like. In any case, reserve your table in advance, or have your hotel *portiere* do it for you, even for the inexpensive places. Dining hours are short; lunch starts at 12:30 or 1 and ends at about 2:30, when the restaurants close until they start serving again at about 8 P.M., closing around 11 or midnight at the latest. All close one day a week and are also likely to close without notice for vacation or renovations. Few have signs on the outside, so when their metal blinds are shut tight you can't tell a closed restaurant from a closed T.V. repair shop. This makes them hard to spot when you are exploring the city.

Obviously, you should shun restaurants decorated with various national flags and those advertising hot dogs, English breakfasts and pizzas that you can see soggily stacked up on the counter. We have included a few of the worthier tourist-oriented establishments in our list, but we suggest you also try the places where the Venetians go. The waiter may not speak English, but you'll probably have a good meal. Generally speaking, the run-of-the-mill restaurants around St. Mark's are poor. Look for those in other parts of the city.

At the AAST Information Office or your hotel, ask for the AEPE (Restaurateur's Association) booklet, *Ristorazione a Venezia,* a handy list of locales offering special menus at low prices, in all categories. It's conveniently arranged by *sestiere* and contains a lot of useful information.

You may not always find a cover charge *(pane e coperto)* but a service charge of 15–20 percent will surely appear on your check. An additional tip is not necessary, but a few hundred lire are appreciated, and more would be in order in expensive and deluxe restaurants, of course. A tip is superfluous in the smaller places where a member of the family waits on you.

Remember that seafood is usually more expensive than other dishes, and that the house wine is usually quite good and is less costly than bottled wine.

Restaurants are required by law to give you a receipt *(ricevuta fiscale),* which you in turn are required to take away with you.

Our restaurant listings give details of which of the major credit cards are accepted by each restaurant we list. These appear as AE for American Express, DC for Diners Club, MC for MasterCard (incorporating Access, Cartasi, and EuroCard), and V for Visa.

Restaurant Prices. We have divided all the restaurants in our listings into price categories. Prices, per person, including wine are, in lire:

Expensive	80,000–150,000
Moderate	45,000–70,000
Inexpensive	30,000–40,000

Some trattorias and osterie may charge a little less than the price range of our Inexpensive category.

Expensive

Antico Martini, Campo San Fantin (tel. 522.4121). In good weather you dine outdoors with a view of Teatro La Fenice, otherwise in an attractive wood-paneled room. Service is discreet and the cuisine is mainly Venetian with a few concessions to international palates. The fixed-price *menu gastronomico,* at about 60,000 lire, is good value. Closed Tues. and Wed. for lunch, and Dec. and Feb. AE, DC, MC, V.

La Caravella, Hotel Saturnia International, Calle Larga XXII Marzo (tel. 708.901). One of the best and most relaxed of Venice's top locales. Tiny and intimate, decorated like the dining saloon of an old Venetian sailing ship. Service is cordial and attentive; choosing from the extensive menu can be a problem but the highly competent *maitre* will advise you well. The *granseola* is marvelous in any of several versions. Closed Wed. from Nov. to Apr. AE, DC, MC, V.

Cipriani, Hotel Cipriani, Giudecca (tel. 520.7744). In the ultra-chic garden setting of Venice's top hotel, either on a terrace overlooking the lagoon or in an elegant dining room, you will enjoy superb cuisine and service. Among the gustatory delights is an exquisite *carpaccio.* Hotel launch from San Marco. Open daily. Closed Dec. through Feb. AE, DC, MC, V.

Il Cortile, Hotel Saturnia International, Calle Larga XXII Marzo (tel. 520.8938). An attractive candlelit patio restaurant that moves indoors in winter; fine dining in a romantic atmosphere. Closed Wed. AE, DC, MC, V.

Danieli Terrace, Hotel Danieli, Riva Degli Schiavoni (tel. 522.6480). Fantastic view and marvelous cuisine. Seafood is the star, of course, with *scampi* taking top honors, but wait till you get to the desserts! There's a minimum charge, excluding beverages. Open daily. AE, DC, MC, V.

Do Forni, Calle Specchieri (tel. 523.2148). Briefly, Orient Express decor in one salon, a stunning display of seafood in another, and moneyed tourists enjoying it all. You can start with *cappesante* (scallops) *Ca' d'Oro* and work your way through a repertory of beautifully prepared fish dishes and vegetables. The service could stand improvement. Closed Thurs. except in summer, and from end Nov. to mid-Dec. AE, DC, MC, V.

Do Leoni, Hotel Londra Palace, Riva degli Schiavoni (tel. 522.5032). In a posh, mirrored dining room on the airy terrace overlooking the lagoon, you are served creative cuisine with great style. Try avocado with scampi or *tagliolini con granchi.* The new brunch menu suits those desiring a light lunch. Closed Tues. and mid-Nov. to mid-Dec. AE, DC, MC, V.

La Fenice, Campiello Fenice (tel. 522.3856). A classic with elegant atmosphere and a large dining terrace for the summer. It serves both international and typically Venetian cuisine. Closed Sun. and Mon. for lunch. AE, DC, MC, V.

Gritti, Hotel Gritti, Campo Santa Maria del Giglio (tel. 794.611). The cuisine matches the exceptional setting on the terrace on the Grand Canal or in an elegant dining room inside. Impeccably executed Italian regional dishes, some classic specialties and what one critic calls "the best scampi in Venice." Open daily. AE, DC, MC, V.

Harry's Bar, Calle Vallaresso (tel. 523.6797). Inconspicuous exterior and plain decor leave the spotlight to the customers and the cuisine. There have been fewer celebrities around lately, but the kitchen keeps up its standards, anyway, winning acclaim for exquisite soups, salads and pastas. Closed Mon. and Jan. 8–21. AE, DC, MC, V.

Moderate

Ai Coristi, Calle della Chiesa (tel. 522.6677). From the steps of La Fenice, go straight ahead to this pleasant, family-run restaurant, with a good atmosphere and reasonable prices. There's an attractive summer terrace just across the *calle,* very nice in the evening when it's lit by candlelight. The menu has some appealing variations such as *pappardelle alla buranea,* with scallops, and really good salads. Closed Wed.

Agli Schiavoni, Calle del Dose (tel. 26.763). Between Riva degli Schiavoni and Campo Bandiera e Moro. Another current favorite of Venetians, it's a small, lively place, very informal, with classic Venetian cooking and exquisite seafood. The house wine is good, too. Closed Wed. and in Jan.

Ai Padovani, Fondamenta Gheradini 2839 (tel. 523.8660). On Rio San Barnaba, with Venice's only floating vegetable market moored in front, this attractively decorated restaurant offers the bounty of the mainland in the tasty dishes of Treviso, and some Venetian specialties, too. Cordial service. Reserve. Closed Sun. in July, Aug. and Sept. AE, DC, V.

Antica Besseta, Calle Salvio, just off Campo San Giacomo dell'Orio (tel. 721.687). A favorite with Venetians for straightforward atmosphere and excellent seafood. Follow host Daniele's (or papa Nereo's) advice in ordering. Closed Tues. and Wed., Jan. and mid-summer.

Conte Pescaor, Piscina San Zulian (tel. 522.1483). Near San Marco. A relaxed atmosphere and typical Venetian specialties, including *zuppa di datteri* and *spaghetti* with scampi or other shellfish. Closed Sun. and Mon. lunch, first half of Aug., mid-Jan. to mid-Feb. AE, DC, MC, V.

Corte Sconta, Calle del Pestrin (tel. 522.7024). Near San Giovanni in Bragora. Its totally unpretentious aspect belies its upmarket clientele. This informal seafood restaurant is hard to find but well known for all that. The combination of celebrities and the hard-to-please Venetians who flock here keep the place lively and the chef on his toes. Closed Sun. and Mon. AE, DC, V.

Da Arturo, Calle dei Assassini (tel. 528.6974). Near Campo Sant'Angelo. A simple place where Venetians go for a change from the usual seafood. The owners are from Treviso and they do meat, vegetables, mushrooms and salads very well indeed. Closed Sun.

Da Fiore, Calle del Scaleter (tel. 721.308). A busy and informal seafood restaurant where you can be sure of getting the finest and the freshest fish from the market. Favored by both Venetians and visitors, it's always crowded. Closed Sun. and Mon., and Aug. 10 to Sept. 3. AE, DC, V.

Da Ignazio, Calle dei Saoneri, San Polo (tel. 523.4852). Good classic cuisine in a pleasant restaurant just off the beaten track. Closed Sat.

Da Ivo, Ramo dei Fuseri (tel. 705.889). Small, intimate and romantic, this upmarket place does interesting variations of the classics, and is at the top of the price range. Closed Sun. AE, DC, MC, V.

Fiaschetteria Toscana, Campo San Giovanni Crisostomo (tel. 528.5281). An attractive place with an upstairs dining room and a terrace on the square for summer dining; a favorite with Venetians for excellent seafood and wines; top quality makes some choices expensive, so order carefully from menu. Courteous service. Closed Tues. and early July. DC, MC, V.

Harry's Dolci, Giudecca at Sant'Eufemia (tel. 522.4844). A smart little place, and a delight in summer with tables under umbrellas right beside the canal. The menu consists of a few select dishes from the chefs of *Harry's Bar,* at one-third the price. It's also a chic tearoom, and the *dolci* (desserts) are heavenly. In all, a pleasant detour. Closed Sun. eve. and Mon.

Locanda Montin, Fondamenta delle Eremite (tel. 522.7151). Between Campo San Barnaba and Ognissanti. Out of the way but worth looking for. A pleasant place with garden, traditional Venetian cooking and lots of tourists who have found the way. Closed Tues. eve. and Wed.

Noemi, Calle dei Fabbri (tel. 522.5238). A central, tourist-oriented restaurant serving good food in a pleasant setting. Closed Sun. AE, DC, MC, V.

Trattorias

Moderate

Poste Vecie, Pescheria (tel. 721.822). At the Rialto fish market. A colorful, bustling seafood trattoria that looks touristy but is not disdained by Venetians. Closed Mon. eve. and Tues., and Nov. 10 to Dec. 20. AE, DC, V.

Inexpensive

Antica Adelaide, Calle Priuli, off Strada Nuova (tel. 520.3451). Look for the barrel in front of the door just before Calle Priuli becomes Calle Racchetta. A well-known osteria, it is blossoming into a fully-fledged trattoria serving *pasticcio alla gorgonzola* and light, crunchy *calamari fritti.* The house wine is good and a bit heady, and there's a nice garden courtyard. Closed Mon.

Antica Mola, Fondamenta degli Ormesini. Behind the Ghetto. Very inconspicuous and open for lunch only. Venetian home-style cooking dispensed with disarming simplicity.

Da Crecola, behind San Giacomo dell'Orio (tel. 89.481). A family-run pizzeria where papa makes very good pizzas and mamma whips up other dishes in the kitchen. This is a place you'll keep coming back to, like the neighborhood regulars, for good food at modest prices. The tables outside in warm weather make it even nicer. Closed Tues.

Ai Cugnai, Calle San Vio (tel. 528.9238). Near the Accademia, a popular neighborhood tavern run by efficient ladies who serve Venetian dishes in a modest dining room and vine-shaded courtyard. Closed Mon. and Jan.

Da Franz, Fondamenta San Isepo, Castello (tel. 27.505). The cooking and the atmosphere are typically Venetian. Get directions before you start out. Closed Mon. AE.

Gazebo, Rio Terrà San Leonardo 1333/A (tel. 716.380). Near the station and Ghetto, a friendly trattoria with courtyard dining and courteous service. Pizza is on the menu, too. Closed Thurs. AE, DC, MC, V.

Zucca, Ponte del Megio, near San Giacomo dell'Orio (tel. 522.0861). Straight ahead from San Stae landing stage. A trendy little place with inventive cooking and good wines. Closed Mon.

Osterie

Despite their erratic closing hours—and, sometimes, days—Venice's osterie offer one of the most enjoyable ways of eating out inexpensively in the city. Don't be intimidated by their plain exteriors or the gang of locals inside. Do as the Venetians do and walk right in.

A few osterie have tables and reasonably full menus, but most simply have snacks—*cicchetti* to the Italians—laid out on the counter. Just ask for anything that takes your fancy, or point if your Italian isn't up to it, and the bartender will serve you. He'll keep track of your order, totaling up the bill as you go along.

Al Mascaron, Calle Lunga Santa Maria Formosa. A wide range of snacks and usually one hot dish. You can order at the counter and carry your food to one of the tables. Closed Sun.

Al Milion, behind San Giovanni Crisostomo. A good choice of tasty tidbits, and one hot dish. There are tables and it's always crowded; get there early and don't expect to linger. Closed Sun.

Altanella, Calle delle Erbe, Giudecca (tel. 522.7780). A family-run osteria that serves traditional Venetian fare, especially some good vegetable dishes. There's a tiny garden on the canal, and it's always crowded. Closed Mon., Tues. and fall to winter, when *acqua alta* floods the place.

Antico Dolo, at the Rialto market. Closed Sun. and Aug.

Ca' d'Oro, straight ahead from the Ca' d'Oro landing stage, across the Strada Nuova. One of the nicest, with charming touches and lots of atmosphere.

Do Mori, at the Rialto market. Where the vendors hang out.

Do Spade, Sottoportego Do Spade, at the Rialto market. Known for good sandwiches.

Vino Vino, Calle delle Veste, Campo San Fantin (tel. 522.4121). An informal wine bar that's an annex of the famous Antico Martini restaurant,

serving a selected buffet from the upscale kitchen next door. Closed Tues.
AE, DC, MC, V.

Fast Food

A plethora of self-service restaurants and snack bars sustains the masses of tourists who flow into Venice with the morning tide and, like the tide, flow out again after a few hours. While many places offer prefabricated pizzas and the ubiquitous hot dog, there are some better cafeterias, where you can eat fairly well at moderate prices.

In addition, most bars have assorted sandwiches *(panini)* and snacks that can see you through the day, and you can always buy the makings of a sandwich in an *alimentari* store. You'll find lots of tempting delicatessen displays in food shops along Calle della Mandola between Campo Sant'Angelo and Campo Manin, in the Rialto market area, and along the Strada Nuova. Supermarkets are scattered throughout Venice; there's a food department in the *Standa* store on Strada Nuova near the Ca' d'Oro landing stage.

Al Mondo Nuovo, San Lio 5409, near Rialto Bridge. Closed Wed.

Al Teatro Goldoni, Calle dei Fabbri 4747, between San Marco and Rialto. Closed Sat.

Al Teatro, Campo San Fantin 1917. Closed Mon.

Le Chat Qui Rit, Frezzerie 1131, near San Marco. Closed Sat.

San Bartolomeo, Calle della Bissa 5423, off Campo San Bartolomeo, near Rialto Bridge.

Self-Service Rialto, at Rialto Bridge 4173. Closed Sun.

CAFES. Venice has some elegant and charming bars and cafes. Of them, the **Caffè Florian** in Piazza San Marco is undoubtedly its most famous. It carries on the tradition of the city's 18th-century coffee houses. A meeting place of Venetian society since 1720, Florian has period decor and great atmosphere. You can linger as long as you like at the tiny tables in its intimate little mirrored salons, or sit outside on Piazza San Marco, listening to the orchestra and watching the passing parade. But in either case, whatever you order will be pricey. Not many people know about the little three-stool bar to the left inside the entrance, where you can enjoy the bartender's excellent cocktails or a creamy cappuccino for much less than you pay at a table. Closed Wed.

Among the hotel bars, those in the **Gritti** and **Danieli** are smart meeting places, especially welcoming in the cooler months. The bar of the hotel **Saturnia,** Calle Larga XXII Marzo, is small and intimate.

Venetians like the **Bar al Theatro,** Campo San Fantin, especially after an evening at La Fenice, next door. And Americans love **Harry's Bar,** Calle Vallaresso, at the San Marco landing stage. A traditional hangout of American tourists and international celebrities, Harry's is the place where the Bellini cocktail (peach juice and *prosecco*) was invented. You pay about 10,000 lire for a dry martini at the bar, 12,000 for a Bellini, or its wintertime equivalent, a Mimosa (with orange juice); you'll pay even more at a table.

There are delightful outdoor cafes in Venice's larger squares, Campo Santo Stefano, Campo Santa Maria Formosa and Campo Santa Margherita, and in some of its smaller byways as well; the **Caffè dei Frari,**

Toppo San Polo, opposite the front of the Frari, has '20s decor. The Venetians like to have their aperitifs before lunch or dinner at the bars around the Rialto, at **Rosa Salva** in Campo San Luca or the wineshops around the market on the other side of the bridge (see "Osterie"). On the Zattere there are several cafes with terraces on the canal; opposite, near Sant'Eufemia on the Giudecca, **La Palanca** serves an interesting variety of cocktails and sandwiches.

Ice Cream and Pastry Shops

You'll find what is reputed to be the best ice cream in Venice at **Paolin** on Campo Santo Stefano; there's not much room indoors but lots of tables on the attractive square. **Nico,** on the Zattere, has a terrace on the canal and is another favorite for such goodies as the *gianduia,* a wedge of creamy chocolate ice cream with whipped cream. You can indulge in the same specialty at the **Gelatone,** a small but extremely popular ice cream shop on Rio Terrà Maddalena, halfway between the station and Santi Apostoli. **Causin** on Campo Santa Margherita is a pleasant place to sit and enjoy your *gelato.* And **Harry's Dolci,** on the Giudecca at Sant'Eufemia, is Venice's latest cure for dessert cravings.

For pastries and cakes to take out, Venetians esteem **Rosa Salva** on Calle Fiubera near Campo San Zulian, at San Marco, and **Colussi** in Calle Lunga San Barnaba, near the Frari, where you can find traditional Venetian cakes. **Marchini** in Calle del Spezier, off Campo Sant'Angelo, is good, and there are a number of fine *pasticcerie* along the Strada Nuova.

Shopping

Although you can find a greater variety of goods at wider price ranges in Rome and Florence, shopping in Venice can be more fun. In curious little shops amid the *calli* and *campi* you'll see droll masks and quaint curios and full-fledged carnival costumes. And there are, surprisingly, bargains to be found in Venice: glass and lace, of course, though you have to be selective; luggage, shoes and other leather goods; hand-crafted paper objects and imaginative masks and jewelry; old prints and unusual souvenirs.

The main shopping areas are the Mercerie, that succession of narrow and crowded streets winding from Piazza San Marco to the Rialto, and the area around Campo San Salvador, Calle del Teatro, Campo Manin and Campo San Fantin. If you can't face the crowds on the Merceria, try the Strada Nuova, where many Venetians shop. However, you'll find some of the most interesting shops hidden away in odd corners of the city. If you plan to return to one, mark its location on your map or you may never find it again.

In Venice prices are fixed and discount rarely conceded. Most shops accept credit cards, but you may find a few artisans who won't. You can change your money or travelers' checks in shops, but always ask what exchange rate they are using.

Glass. For centuries Venetians had a monopoly on glass-making; they were the only craftsmen in the world who knew how to make mirrors, and the glass that they produced was unique for its clarity and delicacy. Then, in the 17th century, Venice's artisans began turning out immensely fragile and largely completely useless objects to suit current tastes. Gradually the industry slipped into a decline that continued until the end of the 19th century, when the furnaces of Murano's factories began to glow again as the industry was revived. Now Murano's craftsmen produce great quantities of glass for the world's markets. Traditional or contemporary, often kitsch, Murano glass remains Venice's number one product. Don't be discouraged by the hideous glass you'll see on display in showrooms in Venice and Murano; sooner or later you will come across the beautiful pieces that Venetian craftsmen copy from antique models or create for contemporary designers.

Should you buy glass in Venice's shops or in Murano? You will probably find that prices are pretty much the same. Showrooms in Venice that are outlets of Murano glassworks sell at the same prices in either place. But because of the competition, shops in Venice that carry glass from various glassworks may charge slightly lower prices. There are some factories on Murano that produce glass for other Italian and foreign markets; since they have no outlets in Venice, you can buy from their Murano showrooms at factory prices. Nonetheless, all the experts recommend that you visit the glass museum on Murano to get an idea of the best Venetian glass *before* you buy.

In Venice, **Venini,** Piazzetta dei Leoncini 314, is known for stunning contemporary creations in decorator colors, and **Pauly,** next door at 316, has more of the same. Another **Pauly,** at Calle dell'Ascensione 72, opposite the Tourist Information Office, offers faithful copies of antique glass and sleek contemporary pieces, too. **Salviati** is a reliable and respected firm; it has showrooms on Piazza San Marco at #s 78 and 110, and another in its palace on the Grand Canal (entrance at San Gregorio 195), where you can watch a demonstration of glassblowing. For top-of-the-line contemporary glassware, Carlo Moretti is an excellent choice. You can see his signature designs at the **Isola** shops on Campo San Moisè and Mercerie 723. **Cenedese,** Piazza San Marco 139, has vast displays of glass in its upstairs showrooms, where you can see everything from gaudy colored goblets to elegant crystal glassware in open stock. All of the reliable shops and factories will ship your purchases; state-of-the-art packaging makes the process much less risky than it used to be. But, take note that some customers have complained that the glass delivered is not what they ordered. *Caveat emptor.*

If you're not dying to buy a huge chandelier or a 72-piece set of glassware, you will surely find some stylish glass jewelry to tuck away in your suitcase as a gift for yourself or friends. **Archimede Seguso,** Piazza San Marco, has gorgeous beads, pins and earrings in stylish colors; red and black or pastels and gold are particularly attractive combinations. The **Vetri d'Arte** shop on Piazza San Marco also has bright colors and contemporary designs and sells pretty necklaces of twisted strands of beads and blown glass pendant earrings at moderate prices.

In a category all his own is **Gianfranco Penzo,** Campo del Ghetto Nuovo 2895. This mild-mannered artisan creates artistic glass objects inspired by his Jewish heritage. He decorates ritual vessels and seder plates and takes orders for special pieces with dedications commemorating bar mitzvahs, weddings and anniversaries. Much of his work is commissioned by customers in the United States. In a picturesque corner of the Ghetto, his shop is well worth a visit.

On Murano, among the numerous showrooms and glassworks, the firms of **Foscarini** and **Barovier and Toso,** both near the Colonna landing stage, are noteworthy for their good-looking contemporary glass. The **Domus** shop on Fondamenta dei Vetrai has a tasteful selection of smaller glass objects and jewelry and some lovely beaded bags. **La Murrina,** Fondamenta Cavour 17, not far from the glass museum, is a factory outlet for lighting fixtures and glass lamps of the kind that you might see in smart decorators' studios in London, New York or Dallas; they will ship your purchase.

Lace. The top name in lace in Venice is **Jesurum,** which has a shop at Piazza San Marco 60 and a much larger establishment at Ponte Canonica, just behind the Basilica of San Marco, where you can see the lacemakers at work. The stuff that dreams are made of, Jesurum lace is fabulous, whether in a handkerchief or a tablecloth, a christening dress or a sexy negligée. Prices, too, are in the realm of fantasy, for this is the real thing. There are a few other reliable shops around Piazza San Marco. **Brocchi,** on Salizzada San Moisè opposite Calla Vallaresso, is a small, old-fashioned place. **Martinuzzi, Fabris** and **Tokatzian** are all on Piazza San Marco. Near San Zaccaria, on Campo San Provolo, **El Stringhesso** is a charming little shop that deals in small pieces such as lace doilies and collars at accessible prices. If you try elsewhere, be very selective and remember that much of the lace and embroidery sold in tourist-oriented shops in Venice and on Burano is made in China or Taiwan. It may be handmade, but it certainly isn't Venetian.

For the same sumptuous brocades, damasks and cut velvets used at La Scala, the White House and royal palaces all over the world, go to **Lorenzo Rubelli,** just off Piazza San Marco at # 3877, or **Luigi Bevilacqua,** San Zandegolà 1320, near San Giacomo dell'Orio. At **Norelene,** Campo San Maurizio 2606, you'll see stunning hand-printed fabrics inspired by the creations of famous designer Fortuny, whose home in a medieval palace not too far away is now a museum.

Jewelry and Masks. Among Venice's prestigious jewelers, **Attilio Codognato,** Piazza San Marco 1295, has a fine reputation for antique Venetian gold jewelry. **Marforio,** Merceria 737, has a good selection of gold earrings, and **Brondino,** Calle della Mandola, offers both contemporary and antique pieces. Costume jewelry can be found everywhere, but for bright colors and showy shapes in inexpensive earrings and necklaces, look for **Al Canale,** Ruga Rialto 973, just beyond Ruga Vecchia San Giovanni near the Rialto market.

Masks are a tradition in Venice. During the 18th century they were worn everywhere; spectators at La Fenice theater and gamblers at the tables of the Ridotto donned masks, helping create that aura of sinister ambiguity that characterized the Venetian Republic in its declining years. Now the revival of the city's extravagant carnival season has made masks fashionable again. You'll find craft shops throughout Venice making and selling masks of all types. One of the most interesting is **Mondonovo,** Rio Terrà Canal, just around the corner from Campo Santa Margherita. The young artisans here create highly inventive and attractive masks that could become unusual decorative accents in your home. Children love the Hansel and Gretel and Pinocchio masks, and you may be tempted to become a beaming sun or a melancholy moon. At the *Ca Macana* shop, Calle delle Botteghe, near San Barnaba, you can watch traditional and innovative masks being made. The feathered follies of **Magica Follia**, Calle dei Saoneri, near the Rialto market, are sure to be a hit at a Halloween party. A few steps away, **Mangiafuoco**, Calle dei Saoneri 2718, makes masks and charming puppets. On the other side of Venice, the artisans of the **Laboratorio Artigiano Maschere** on Barbaria delle Tole in the Castello district have an unusual selection.

Prints and Books. An old print of Venice makes a distinctive gift or souvenir. You'll find an excellent selection at **O. Bohm,** just off Piazza San Marco on Salizzada San Moisè. And if you continue on to the end of Calle Larga XXII Marzo you'll come upon Venice's oldest bookshop, **Cassini,** a treasure house of antique books and prints. **Fantoni,** on Salizzada San Luca, specializes in art books and has some gorgeous coffee-table books, studies of Venice by the world's top photographers. **Filippi,** Calle del Paradiso 5762 at San Lio, carries only books on Venice. On Campo San Tomà, at # 2916, **Manlio Penso** deals in antique prints, rare editions and antiques.

In the realm of art, there's a fascinating and unique shop at Salizzada San Samuele 3147 where artist-artisan **Livio de Marchi** creates his spirited and surreal wooden sculptures, turning everyday objects into works of art.

The **Piazzesi** shop on Campiello della Feltrina, near Santa Maria del Giglio, is known for its extraordinary selection of hand-printed paper and brilliantly colored, paper-covered objects such as boxes, memo pads, address books and even ducks and obelisks. This delightful shop is a place to browse in; you're sure to find the solutions to your gift problems, with the advantage that what you buy is lightweight and easy to tuck into a suitcase. Several other shops in Venice produce similar paper crafts. Look for **Polliero,** Campo dei Frari 2995; **Paolo Olbi,** Calle delle Mandola; and **Ebrù,** Salizzada San Samuele.

Fashions. Italy's star fashion designers are very much a part of the Venetian scene. You'll find a stylish double-header on Salizzada San Moisè, where **Valentino's** boutique is at # 1473 and **Fendi** is next door at # 1474. **Gianfranco Ferre** holds the spotlight at Calle Larga San Marco 287. You can indulge your passion for **Missoni's** distinctive multicolored knits for men and women at their shop on Calle Vallaresso. There's a **Versace** boutique at Frezzeria 1722, and **Armani** has an emporium at Calle dei Fabbri 989. You can't miss **Krizia's** glamorous shop at Calle delle Ostreghe 2359, between San Moisè and Santa Maria del Giglio. Venice's own **Roberta da Camerino** holds forth at Ascensione 1255. For trendy casual wear, **Genny's** on Campo San Salvador is the place, though prices are high. Nearby on Salizzada San Luca, **York Club** features Ken Scott's colorful, wearable designs. **Benetton** has several shops in Venice; the ones you are most likely to run into are on Salizzada San Moisè, Salizzada San Giovanni Crisostomo and Merceria del Capitello. If you want to treat yourself to some lovely lingerie or buy a dress for a special little girl, head for **Mariela,** on Calle Larga XXII Marzo. Elegant Venetian ladies buy their lingerie at **Sorelle Brandes** on Calle dei Fuseri. On Campo

Sant'Angelo, the *Maneki-Neko* shop has a wide selection of pretty blouses, many embroidered. If you're on a budget you can find bargains at the **Standa** stores on Campo San Luca and on Strada Nuova.

Shoes and Leather Goods. Shoes are always a good buy in Italy, and Venice is no exception. Besides, with all the walking you have to do here, you have a good excuse to treat yourself to a new pair. There are a number of good shoe stores in the area around Campo San Bartolomeo, starting with **Casella,** right on the Campo. This large and attractive shop carries a wide range of top-quality shoes for men and women and sells leather jackets and handbags as well. The reliable and slightly less costly **Di Varese** is just across the way. On Salizzada San Giovanni Crisostomo you'll find **Ballin's** classic models.

For leather handbags, wallets and luggage, do a little window shopping at **Marforio,** Campo San Salvador, and **Bona,** Merceria San Salvador, before you make your final choice. A few steps away on Calle del Teatro, **Bussola** carries leather goods by name designers. And if what you really want is an authentic Louis Vuitton, head for the **Vuitton** shop on the corner of Campo San Moisè.

Souvenirs. By far the most unique souvenir of Venice that you could take home with you is a *forcola,* the wooden oar lock used on gondolas. With their flowing lines and polished surfaces, *forcole* look something like Brancusi's sculptures and make interesting conversation pieces. At **La Scialuppa,** Calle dei Saoneri 2695, near the Rialto market, you will find both full-size and scale-model *forcole* mounted on wooden bases. Prices vary according to size. This artisan shop also has other wooden sculptures and models of gondolas and other boats that are sure to delight a collector of any age.

You will find a bewildering array of souvenirs along the Merceria and around Piazza San Marco. Among the trash, gondoliers' hats and striped shirts and pretty necklaces of glass flowers and beads stand out as possible purchases. And for anyone who collects kitsch, a music box in the form of a plastic gondola that lights up and plays a Neapolitan song is a must.

Entertainment

As in all of Italy, much of the entertainment you will find in Venice is impromptu—the pleasure of sitting at Florian or Quadri on Piazza San Marco and watching the world go by as the orchestra plays away, the sheer thrill of gliding in a gondola up the Grand Canal. Still, the Biennale, a cultural institution, organizes a wealth of events throughout the year, and there's always something going on, whether music, theater, the film festival or the big biennial art exhibition held from the end of June to the end of September in even-numbered years. Now that a Fiat foundation has renovated Palazzo Grassi as a cultural center, Venice's already consistent calendar of art shows promises to become even fuller. There's often an interesting show at Palazzo Ducale.

Concerts. A Vivaldi Festival is held in September, and concerts of classical and contemporary music are performed in the city's churches throughout the year. Watch for posters or inquire at the AAST Tourist Information Office at Piazza San Marco. The **Kele e Teo Agency,** San Marco 4930 (tel. 520.8722) handles tickets for many musical events.

Opera and Ballet. La Fenice, on Campo San Fantin, is one of Italy's oldest and most famous opera houses. Although the state-subsidized opera company is continually plagued by threats of bankruptcy and/or strikes, it miraculously manages to come up with a good (sometimes excellent) season from December to May. Concerts, ballets and other musical events are scheduled at La Fenice throughout the year, except in August. For programs and tickets, write to *Biglietteria, Teatro La Fenice,* Campo San Fantin, 30124 Venice, or call 521.0661. The box office is open Mon. to Sat. 9:30–12:30 and 4–6. If there is a performance on Sunday the box office remains open, closing on Monday.

Theater. Aside from the theatrical performances staged as part of the Carnival celebrations in February, a theater season brings Italian companies to the **Teatro Goldoni,** on Calle Goldoni, and the **Ridotto,** on Calle Vallaresso. You need a good command of Italian to enjoy them.

Casino. A gambling casino is operated by the city of Venice in a modern building on the Lido from April through September and in the beautiful Palazzo Vendramin Calergi on the Grand Canal during the other months. The casino is open from 3 P.M. until about 4:30 A.M.; you must show your passport and pay a fee to get in. ACTV runs a Casino Express (Line 28, from the railway station and Piazzale Roma to the casino on the Lido, with a stop at San Zaccaria) during casino opening hours.

Nightlife. In a word, none—or practically none anyway. The **Martini Scala Club,** Calle delle Veste, Campo San Fantin (tel. 522.4121) is an elegant piano bar with late-night restaurant. The bars of the top hotels stay open as long as their customers keep on drinking, and there's an attractive bar, **Al Cherubim,** where young Venetians and tourists in-the-know socialize over drinks. It's on Calle Sant'Antonin, just off Salizzada San Luca.

The disco scene is dismal. Except for their sporadic outbursts of hedonism at Carnival and on the Festa del Redentore, the Venetians are very private people who prefer to stay home in the evening. But on a warm summer night you may see them out walking with children and dogs in Piazza San Marco, stopping to listen to the music at the cafes and eyeing the tourists with a smug air, as if to say, "Sooner or later *you*'ll have to get on a plane or train and leave this extraordinary city, but *we* live here."

Miscellaneous

CHILDREN. Venice enchants children at first with its canals and gondolas and streets without cars. But churches, museums and art tend to wear them out fast, and when you come right down to it, there's not much else for them to do. Aside from such diversions as climbing on Daniele Manin's big bronze lion and ogling the boat models in the Museo Navale at the Arsenale, Venice has few attractions for children.

CLOSING TIMES. Shops are usually open from 8 or 9 to 1, and from 4:30 or 5 to 7:30 or 8 P.M. and are closed on Sunday and Monday morning. However, many tourist-oriented shops are open all day, every day. Food shops are closed on Wednesday afternoon, except in July and August, when they close Saturday afternoon. Bars, restaurants and shops are very erratic about vacation closings; many close for periods during both winter and summer. Hairdressers and barbers close on Sunday and Monday, but top-level salons stay open all week in high season.

CONVENIENT CONVENIENCES. W.C.s in bars and hotels have to make up for the lack of public toilets in Venice; in the less fancy places you may find a modern version of the Turkish toilet. There are public W.C.s near the public gardens between the San Marco landing stage and the Zecca (150 lire), closed at night and during the winter. There are free and pay toilets at the rail station. Public pay toilets under the Accademia end of the bridge of the same name were installed when the bridge was restored a few years ago.

There is an *Albergo Diurno* (day hotel), with toilets, baths, showers, barber and other facilities, off Calle Ascension, just off Piazza San Marco, and another at the railway station. You pay a small fee for use of their facilities.

HOLIDAYS. Aside from the national holidays, Venice celebrates its own throughout the year. In chronological order, they start with Carnival, the two-week period in **February** before Lent, when the city doubles its population as merrymakers in costume throng the *calli* and *campi*. There are theatricals and balls, both indoors and out.

April 25 is the feast of San Marco, and special services are held in the Basilica.

In **May,** on a Sunday that is designated from year to year, the *Vogalonga* (literally "Long Row") takes place. It is a rowing contest open to anyone who wants to attempt the 32-km. (20-mile) course from Venice to Murano and Burano and back. You can see the departure at 9:30 in the morning from the Zattere and Riva degli Schiavoni and watch the boats returning through the Cannaregio Canal and Grand Canal, starting about two hours later and continuing well into the afternoon as the stragglers come in.

The *Festa della Sensa* takes place on the Sunday after Ascension Day, usually in **June.** Crowds flock to San Marco to watch the figures on the clock make a special appearance, and ecclesiastical and municipal authorities sail from the Molo to San Nicolò on the Lido to celebrate the wedding of Venice to the sea by throwing a ring into the lagoon.

On the third Sunday in **July** is the *Festa del Redentore* (Feast of the Redeemer), Venice's favorite holiday. Everyone goes to Il Redentore (the church of the Redeemer) on the Giudecca over a bridge of boats, and many sail their own brightly decorated boats into St. Mark's Basin in the evening to picnic aboard and watch the spectacular fireworks display.

The *Regata Storica,* or Historical Regatta, on the first Sunday in **September,** starts with a procession of beautifully caparisoned boats that reenact Venice's ceremonial welcome to Caterina Cornaro when she returned to Venice as queen of Cyprus to sign her kingdom over to the Republic. The regatta continues with races of various types of gondolas and other boats. The Venetians moor their own boats—everything from speedboats to barges to dinghies—along the Grand Canal early in the morning and settle in to watch the proceedings, picnicking and making merry all day.

The *Festa della Salute* on **November** 21 is marked by a procession and religious celebrations at the church of the Salute, which is reached over a bridge of boats across the Grand Canal.

PHARMACIES. Venetian pharmacies carry a range of international specialties, and those near San Marco usually have bilingual personnel. Opening hours are 9– 12:30 and 4–7:45; Saturday 9–12:45. Pharmacies take turns in providing night and holiday service, posting the locations of those that are open. Among those catering to English-speaking tourists are: **Farmacia Italo-Inglese,** Calle della Cortesia, end of Calle della Mandola, off Campo Manin; **International Pharmacy,** Calle Lunga San Marco.

POST OFFICES. The main post office is at Fondaco dei Tedeschi on Campo San Bartolomeo near the Rialto Bridge. It is open every day but Sunday, 8 A.M.–2 P.M. Letters marked *Ferma Posta* (poste restante) and addressed to you c/o *Palazzo delle Poste,* Campo San Bartolomeo, 30100 Venezia, can be collected by showing your passport and paying a small fee. There are branch post offices throughout the city. The one nearest San Marco is on Calle dell'Ascensione. Remember that you can buy stamps at *Tabacchi* stores, marked with a blue "T" sign.

Telegrams. The telegram office at the main post office at Fondaco dei Tedeschi at the Rialto Bridge is open 24 hours a day.

TELEPHONES. The Venice area code is 041. Telephone numbers in Venice are being changed progressively. You may hear a recorded announcement advising you to add 52 in front of the number you have dialed. The telephone service office *(ASST),* where operators will help you place your call, is at the main post office in Campo San Bartolomeo and is open 24 hours a day. Though a new regulation prohibits hotels from charging more than the normal 200 lire for a local call, they tend to overcharge for long-distance calls. We strongly advise that you use the ASST service office.

READING MATTER. Newsstands carry the English-language newspapers, usually a day late. You'll find English and American pocket books and books on Venice at bookshops around San Marco. The following have a good selection: **Il Libraio,** Fondamenta Gheradini, near San Barnaba; **Serenissima,** San Zulian, near San Marco; **Studium,** Calle Canonica, off Piazzetta dei Leoncini; **Zanco,** Campo San Bartolomeo, near the Rialto Bridge.

RELIGIOUS SERVICES. Services are held in English at the following locations. **Anglican:** St. George's, Campo San Vio 870 (tel. 520.0751); services at 8:30 and 11:30, matins at 10:30. **Lutheran:** Campo Santi Apostoli 443 (tel. 524.2040). **Methodist:** Santa Maria Formosa 5170 (tel. 522.7599): Sunday service at 11. **Roman Catholic:** confessions heard in English on Sunday at 7–10 A.M. in San Marco, Santi Giovanni e Paolo, the Gesuiti, the Scalzi, the Redentore and San Giorgio Maggiore (Sunday masses in Italian until noon and 5:30–7 P.M. High mass at San Marco at 10 A.M. on

Sunday). **Jewish:** Synagogue, Campo del Ghetto Vecchio (tel. 715.012); service on Saturday at 9:30 A.M.

SIGHTSEEING TIPS. Museums. Opening hours vary and may change without notice. You can obtain a list of current hours at the AAST Information Office under the arcade at the far end of Piazza San Marco; hours are also published in the weekly *Un Ospite a Venezia,* available from the information office or from your hotel *portiere.* Many museums are closed on Monday, but there are plenty of Scuole, churches and other places of interest to see instead. Remember that ticket offices close approximately one hour before the official closing time.

Churches. Opening hours are erratic, and many of the minor churches are closed. Churches are usually open from 8 or 9 in the morning to noon, and again in the afternoon from 3 to 7, but these hours can change from day to day, depending on the liturgical calendar and the whims of the sacristan.

SPORTS. The Lido is the best place for sports in Venice. There's the golf course at Alberoni, on the western tip of the Lido; the Sporting Club of the Des Bains hotel, with tennis courts and a beautiful outdoor swimming pool; and municipal tennis courts and a riding club. The exclusive Sea Gull Club of the hotel Cipriani has a swimming pool, tennis and yachting.

The broad sandy beach of the Lido still attracts fashionable Venetians who sun and socialize among its exotic cabanas, but few of them risk bathing in the tepid brew that passes for sea water. The upper Adriatic is, to all effects, out of bounds for swimming. But then Venice is not the place to come for a beach holiday.

Golf. *Golf Club Lido di Venezia,* Via del Forte 1, Alberoni (tel. 731.015). 18 holes. Open all year to members and guests.

Riding. *Circolo Ippico Veneziano,* Ca' Bianca, Lido (tel. 765.162). Open all year.

Swimming. *Sporting Des Bains,* Lungomare Marconi 16 (tel. 765.921). Tennis too. Open all year. *Sporting Excelsior,* Lungomare Marconi 52a (tel. 526.0201). Open May to Sept.

Tennis. *Municipal Tennis Courts,* Lungotevere D'Annunzio (tel. 709.955). Open summer only. *Tennis Club Lido,* Via San Gallo 163 (tel. 760.954). Open all year to members and guests. *Tennis Club Venezia,* Lungomare Marconi 41d (tel. 760.335). Open all year to members and guests.

USEFUL ADDRESSES. Consulates. *American,* the U.S. Consulate is in Trieste, Via Roma 9, P.O. Box 604 (tel. 040.68728); *British,* Campo Santa Maria della Carità 1051, Dorsoduro (tel. 522.7207), at the Accademia landing stage.

Airlines. *Alitalia,* San Moisè 1463 (tel. 521.6222; 521.6333 for reservations); *British Airways,* Riva degli Schiavoni 4158 (tel. 528.5026); *TWA,* San Moisè 1471.

Travel Agents. *American Express,* San Moisè 1471 (tel. 520.0844); *CIT,* Piazza San Marco 48 (tel. 528.5480); *Wagons Lits/Cook,* Piazzetta dei Leoncini 289 (tel. 522.3405).

INDEX

(Page numbers in Italics refer to maps and plans of buildings)

Fodor's Travel Guides

U.S. Guides

Alaska
American Cities
The American South
Arizona
Atlantic City & the
  New Jersey Shore
Boston
California
Cape Cod
Carolinas & the
  Georgia Coast
Chesapeake
Chicago
Colorado
Dallas & Fort Worth
Disney World & the
  Orlando Area

The Far West
Florida
Greater Miami,
  Fort Lauderdale,
  Palm Beach
Hawaii
Hawaii (Great Travel
  Values)
Houston & Galveston
I-10: California to
  Florida
I-55: Chicago to New
  Orleans
I-75: Michigan to
  Florida
I-80: San Francisco to
  New York

I-95: Maine to Miami
Las Vegas
Los Angeles, Orange
  County, Palm Springs
Maui
New England
New Mexico
New Orleans
New Orleans (Pocket
  Guide)
New York City
New York City (Pocket
  Guide)
New York State
Pacific North Coast
Philadelphia
Puerto Rico (Fun in)

Rockies
San Diego
San Francisco
San Francisco (Pocket
  Guide)
Texas
United States of
  America
Virgin Islands
  (U.S. & British)
Virginia
Waikiki
Washington, DC
Williamsburg,
  Jamestown &
  Yorktown

Foreign Guides

Acapulco
Amsterdam
Australia, New Zealand
  & the South Pacific
Austria
The Bahamas
The Bahamas (Pocket
  Guide)
Barbados (Fun in)
Beijing, Guangzhou &
  Shanghai
Belgium & Luxembourg
Bermuda
Brazil
Britain (Great Travel
  Values)
Canada
Canada (Great Travel
  Values)
Canada's Maritime
  Provinces
Cancún, Cozumel,
  Mérida, The
  Yucatán
Caribbean
Caribbean (Great
  Travel Values)

Central America
Copenhagen,
  Stockholm, Oslo,
  Helsinki, Reykjavik
Eastern Europe
Egypt
Europe
Europe (Budget)
Florence & Venice
France
France (Great Travel
  Values)
Germany
Germany (Great Travel
  Values)
Great Britain
Greece
Holland
Hong Kong & Macau
Hungary
India
Ireland
Israel
Italy
Italy (Great Travel
  Values)
Jamaica (Fun in)

Japan
Japan (Great Travel
  Values)
Jordan & the Holy Land
Kenya
Korea
Lisbon
Loire Valley
London
London (Pocket Guide)
London (Great Travel
  Values)
Madrid
Mexico
Mexico (Great Travel
  Values)
Mexico City & Acapulco
Mexico's Baja & Puerto
  Vallarta, Mazatlán,
  Manzanillo, Copper
  Canyon
Montreal
Munich
New Zealand
North Africa
Paris
Paris (Pocket Guide)

People's Republic of
  China
Portugal
Province of Quebec
Rio de Janeiro
The Riviera (Fun on)
Rome
St. Martin/St. Maarten
Scandinavia
Scotland
Singapore
South America
South Pacific
Southeast Asia
Soviet Union
Spain
Spain (Great Travel
  Values)
Sweden
Switzerland
Sydney
Tokyo
Toronto
Turkey
Vienna
Yugoslavia

Special-Interest Guides

Bed & Breakfast
  Guide: North America
1936...On the
  Continent

Royalty Watching
Selected Hotels of
  Europe

Selected Resorts
  and Hotels of the U.S.
Ski Resorts of North
  America

Views to Dine by
  around the World